Transforming Gender and Food Security in the Global South

Drawing on studies from Africa, Asia and South America, this book provides empirical evidence and conceptual explorations of the gendered dimensions of food security. It investigates how food security and gender inequity are conceptualized within interventions, assesses the impacts and outcomes of gender-responsive programs on food security and gender equity, and addresses diverse approaches to gender research and practice that range from descriptive and analytical to strategic and transformative. The chapters draw on diverse theoretical perspectives, including transformative learning, feminist theory, deliberative democracy and technology adoption. As a result, they add important conceptual and empirical material to a growing literature on the challenges of gender equity in food production.

A unique feature of this book is the integration of both analytic and transformative approaches to understanding gender and food security. The analytic material shows how food security interventions enable women and men to meet the long-term nutritional needs of their households, and to enhance their economic position. The transformative chapters also document efforts to build durable and equitable relationships between men and women, addressing underlying social, cultural and economic causes of gender inequality. Taken together, these combined approaches enable women and men to reflect on gendered divisions of labour and resources related to food, and to reshape these divisions in ways which benefit families and communities.

Jemimah Njuki is a senior program officer in the Agriculture and Food Security program at the International Development Research Centre (IDRC), based in Nairobi, Kenya.

John R. Parkins is a professor in the Department of Resource Economics and Environmental Sociology, University of Alberta, Canada.

Amy Kaler is a professor in the Department of Sociology, University of Alberta, Canada.

Routledge Studies in Food, Society and the Environment

For further details please visit the series page on the Routledge website:
www.routledge.com/books/series/RSFSE/

Transforming Gender and Food Security in the Global South

Edited by Jemimah Njuki,
John R. Parkins and Amy Kaler

Routledge
Taylor & Francis Group

LONDON AND NEW YORK

International Development
Research Centre
Ottawa • Cairo • Montevideo
• Nairobi • New Delhi

earthscan
from Routledge

First published 2016 by Routledge

2 Park Square, Milton Park, Abingdon, Oxfordshire OX14 4RN
52 Vanderbilt Avenue, New York, NY 10017

Routledge is an imprint of the Taylor & Francis Group, an informa business

First issued in paperback 2019

Co-published with the
International Development Research Centre
PO Box 8500, Ottawa, ON K1G 3H9, Canada
info@idrc.ca/www.idrc.ca
(IDRC published an ebook edition of this book, ISBN 978-1-55250-590-8)

The research presented in this publication was carried out with the
financial assistance of Canada's International Development Research
Centre. The views expressed herein do not necessarily represent those
of IDRC or its Board of Governors.

British Library Cataloguing-in-Publication Data
A catalogue record for this book is available from the British Library

Library of Congress Cataloging in Publication Data
Names: Njuki, Jemimah, editor. | Parkins, J. (John), 1967– editor. |
Kaler, Amy, editor.
Title: Transforming gender and food security in the Global
South/edited by Jemimah Njuki, John R. Parkins and Amy Kaler.
Description: Abingdon, Oxon; New York, NY: Routledge, 2016. |
Series: Routledge studies in food, society and the environment |
Includes bibliographical references and index.
Identifiers: LCCN 2016006625 | ISBN 9781138680418 (hbk) |
ISBN 9781315564111 (ebk)
Subjects: LCSH: Women in economic development—Developing
countries. | Food security—Developing countries. | Women in
agriculture—Developing countries. | Women—Developing
countries—Social conditions. | Feminism—Developing countries.
Classification: LCC HQ1240.5.D44 T73 2016 |
DDC 305.409172/4—dc23
LC record available at http://lccn.loc.gov/2016006625

ISBN: 978-1-138-68041-8 (hbk)
ISBN: 978-0-367-22767-8 (pbk)

Typeset in Bembo
by Keystroke, Neville Lodge, Tettenhall, Wolverhampton

Dr Paula Kantor, 1969–2015

To Paula, for her dedication to improving rural livelihoods through gender transformative approaches with rigorous science and a deep sense of humanity, ethics, and friendship.

Paula died on 13 May 2015 in the aftermath of a terrorist attack on the hotel where she was staying in Kabul, Afghanistan. She committed her life and work to gender analysis in agricultural systems, enhancing the lives of rural women and men in the Global South. In 2012, Paula joined CGIAR to champion gender transformative approaches in agricultural research for development. Prior to this engagement, Paula worked at the International Center for Research on Women and as director of the gender and livelihoods portfolio in the Afghanistan Research and Evaluation Unit.

Contents

Acronyms and abbreviations

5DE	five domains of empowerment (sub-index of WEAI)
ADB	Asian Development Bank Group
AED/NARC	Agricultural Engineering Division/Nepal Agricultural Research Council
AEZ	agro-ecological zone
APM	"Alleviating poverty and malnutrition in agro-biodiversity hotspots" (IDRC-funded research project, India)
AR4D	Agricultural Research for Development
CAPAC	Cadenas Productivas Agricolas de Calidad (Agricultural Productivity and Quality Brands) (Peru)
CARE [International]	Cooperative for Assistance and Relief Everywhere (international aid organisation)
CFA	currency used in West and Central Africa
CGIAR	Formerly (until 2010) the acronym for the Consultative Group for International Agricultural Research (Penang, Malaysia); now used as a name in itself
CGP	Crop and Goat Project (Tanzania) (full name: "Integrating Dairy Goat and Root Crop Production for Increasing Food, Nutrition, and Income Security of Smallholder Farmers in Tanzania")
CIDA	Canadian International Development Agency
CIFOR	Center for International Forestry Research (Bogor, Indonesia)
CIFSRF	Canadian International Food Security Research Fund
CIPOAP	*Central Indígena de la Pueblos Originarios Amazónicos de Pando* (Indigenous Centre of the Original Amazon Peoples of Pando)

CIRABO	*Central Indígena de la Región Norte Amazónica de Bolivia* (Indigenous Centre of the North Amazon Region of Bolivia)
COGEPAN	Management Consortium of Native Potatoes Producers – Junín and Huancavelica (Peru) (Spanish acronym)
CRP	CGIAR Research Program
CSRC	Community Self-Reliance Center (Nepal)
DFATD	Department of Foreign Affairs, Trade and Development (Canada); now Global Affairs Canada
DFID	Department for International Development (UK)
DOFE	Department of Foreign Employment (Nepal)
EDRI	Ethiopian Development Research Institute
ESSP	Ethiopia Strategy Support Program
EVE	*estudios de viabilidad economico* (economic feasibility analysis [workshops]) (Bolivia)
FAO	Food and Agriculture Organization of the United Nations
FGD	focus group discussion
FOVIDA	Fomento de la Vida (Life Fund) (Peru)
FRT	farmer research team
GDP	gross domestic product
GIAHS	Globally Important Agricultural Heritage System (FAO designation)
GPI	Gender Parity Index (sub-index of WEAI)
GTA	gender transformative approach
HFZ	humid forest zone (Cameroon)
ICRW	International Center for Research on Women
IDRC	International Development Research Centre (Ottawa, Canada)
IDS	Institute of Development Studies (Sussex, UK)
IFAD	International Fund for Agricultural Development
IFPRI	International Food Policy Research Institute
ILRI	International Livestock Research Institute (head office: Nairobi, Kenya)
INEI	Instituto Nacional de Estadística e Informática (National Institute of Statistics and Informatics) (Peru)
INRA [Law]	*Ley del Servicio Nacional de Reforma Agraria*, or National Agrarian Reform Service Law, commonly referred to as *Ley INRA* (Bolivia)
IPU	Inter-Parliamentary Union
KAP	Knowledge, Attitude, and Practices [study]

KARI	Kenya Agricultural Research Institute
LI-BIRD	Local Initiatives for Biodiversity, Research and Development (Nepal)
LKR	Sri Lankan rupee
MFARD	Ministry of Fisheries and Aquatic Resources Development (Sri Lanka)
MFI	microfinance institution
MSSRF	M.S. Swaminathan Research Foundation (India)
NARA	National Aquatic Resources Research and Development Agency (Sri Lanka)
NARC	Nepal Agricultural Research Council
NGO	non-governmental organisation
NLRF	National Land Rights Forum
NTFPs	non-timber forest products
OECD	Organisation for Economic Co-operation and Development
PAR	participatory action research
PLAR	participatory learning and action research
PMCA	Participatory Market Chain Approach
PPATE	primary participatory agricultural technology evaluation
PPV	*Peces para la vida* ("Fish for Life") (research project, Bolivia)
PRA	participatory rapid appraisal (survey method)
PUG	Pond Users' Group (India)
RESMISA	"Revalourising small millets in rain-fed regions of South Asia" (IDRC-funded research project, Nepal)
SACCO	Savings and Credit Cooperative
SAS²	Social Analysis Systems Approach
SAWTEE	South Asia Watch on Trade, Economics and Environment
SFHC	Soils, Food, and Healthy Communities (research project, Ekwendeni, Malawi)
SHG	self-help group
SIG	Supporting Inclusive Growth program (IDRC, Canada)
SPATE	secondary participatory agricultural technology evaluation
TANGO International	Technical Assistance to NGOs International
TCO	*Tierras Comunitarias de Origen* (Original Indigenous Territories) (Bolivia)
TIM	*Territorio Indígena Multiétnico* (Multiethnic Indigenous Territory) (Bolivia)
UN	United Nations

UNFPA	United Nations Population Fund
USAID	United States Agency for International Development
VDC	Village Development Committee (Nepal)
VICOBA	Village and Community Bank
VLW	village level worker (India)
VSLA	Village Savings and Loans Association
WEAI	Women's Empowerment in Agriculture Index
WEI	Women's Empowerment Index
WFP	World Food Programme
WID	women in development [approach]
XAF	currency used in West and Central Africa

Notes on contributors

Lead editor

Jemimah Njuki holds a PhD in development studies and has been involved in gender and agriculture research in Africa and Asia for the past 15 years. She is a senior program officer in the Agriculture and Food Security program at Canada's International Development Research Centre, and the editor in chief of the *Gender, Agriculture and Food Security Journal*. Previously, she led the Women in Agriculture Program at CARE USA, and the Gender, Poverty and Impact program at the International Livestock Research Institute. Her work has been published in multidisciplinary journals, including *Development in Practice*, *European Journal of Development Research*, and *Gender, Technology and Development*, and she has co-edited two books on gender and agriculture.

Contributing editors

Amy Kaler is a professor in the Department of Sociology, University of Alberta. Her research interests include gender transformation, family and community survival in rural Africa in the context of rapid social and environmental change, and the social and cultural contexts of health challenges. She has participated in funded research projects in Zimbabwe, Malawi, Uganda, Ethiopia, and Canada. Her work has been published in multidisciplinary journals, including *Signs: Journal of Women in Culture and Society*, *Social Science and Medicine*, *Qualitative Sociology*, *Population and Development Review*, *Journal of Southern African Studies*, *Demographic Research*, and *Journal of Family History*. She is the author of three books and the editor of one multi-author collection now in its third edition.

John R. Parkins is a professor in the Department of Resource Economics and Environmental Sociology, University of Alberta, Canada. His research and teaching interests include rural community development, community resilience, social impact assessment, and social dimensions of natural resource management. His research has been published in a wide range of scholarly journals and government reports, with recent publications on the topics of culture and food security in South Africa and community-based environmental assessment in Tanzania.

Chapter authors

Sara Ahmed is an independent researcher looking at the intersection between gender equity, poverty, and innovation to address food and water security in India. For the previous six years, she was a senior program specialist with the Agriculture and Food Security program based at the Asia Regional Office of Canada's International Development Research Centre.

Rachel Bezner Kerr is an associate professor in the Department of Development Sociology at Cornell University, New York. Her research focuses on agroecology, food security, nutrition, and social inequalities, particularly in Malawi and Tanzania. For over 15 years she has been research coordinator for the Soils, Food, and Healthy Communities project in Malawi, now expanded to thousands of farmers with the Malawi Farmer-to-Farmer Agroecology project. She has published over 30 articles and book chapters.

Leigh Brownhill teaches sociology at Athabasca University, Alberta, Canada. She holds a PhD from the University of Toronto, Canada, and is an independent scholar, writer, and editor focused on gender, food sovereignty, and environmental justice. While cultivating a global and interdisciplinary perspective, her work has been strongly focused on subsistence agricultural systems in Kenya. She is the author of the 2009 book *Land, Food, Freedom: Struggles for the Gendered Commons in Kenya, 1870–2007.*

Joachim Carolsfeld is the executive director of World Fisheries Trust in Victoria, BC, Canada. He obtained his PhD working with fish pheromones and reproduction, and completed a master's degree in invertebrate neurophysiology and an honours BSc in marine biology. His extensive experience includes working with fisheries, aquaculture, environmental surveys, boat mechanics, and SCUBA instruction. For the last decade, he has devoted his time to blending his diverse technical expertise with social sciences to design and implement multidisciplinary and multistakeholder projects that foster environmental conservation blended with equitable sustainable resource-based livelihoods.

Pashupati Chaudhary is the program development director at Local Initiatives for Biodiversity, Research and Development in Pokhara, Nepal. He is an environmental scientist specialising in biodiversity conservation, integrated conservation and development, climate change, ecosystem services, agriculture and food security, participatory research, and sustainable landscape development. Dr Chaudhary completed his

PhD in environmental science at the University of Massachusetts, Boston, USA. He has written articles for numerous scientific publications, and contributed to the first draft of the Intergovernmental Panel on Climate Change's *Fifth Assessment Report* (2013–14).

Anita Chitaya joined the Soils, Food, and Healthy Communities project in Ekwendeni, Malawi, as a member of the Farmer Research Team, and has played an important part in the project work. She is also involved with the Malawi Farmer-to-Farmer Agroecology project at Ekwendeni Hospital. In 2009 she was hired as a Soils, Food, and Healthy Communities project community promoter. Of all the outcomes of the project's work, she most likes seeing soil fertility improved through crop residue incorporation.

Claudia I. Coca Méndez is a Bolivian researcher and field biologist with over ten years of experience in animal community ecology, specifically mammals. Since 2006, through her work with indigenous and campesino communities, she has contributed to the conservation and management of aquatic resources in the Bolivian Amazon from a socio-environmental perspective, and specialising in strengthening productive organisations, fair-trade bio-commerce, and sustainable value chain development. She is currently a research associate with FAUNAGUA (Institute for Action-Research on Hydrobiological Resources) in Cochabamba, Bolivia.

Laifolo Dakishoni has been working with the Soils, Food, and Healthy Communities project in Ekwendeni, Malawi, since 2001. He has been active in the project's evolution, greatly motivated by farmers' eagerness to learn and try new things. He is currently the acting project coordinator for the Malawi Farmer-to-Farmer Agroecology project at Ekwendeni Hospital. Mr Dakishoni holds a diploma in accounting from Malawi College of Accounting.

Tim Dejager is managing director and co-founder of Divron Bioventures (Pvt.) Ltd., established in May 2015 in Sri Lanka to commercialise sustainable aquaculture with community partnerships. He has been an entrepreneur, researcher, and consultant in Canadian and international aquaculture since 1997, and was co-leader of the International Development Research Centre-funded Canadian International Food Security Research Fund project "Scaling up sustainable aquaculture in Sri Lanka". Dr Dejager holds a PhD in the history and philosophy of science and technology from the University of Toronto, Canada.

Rachana Devkota is a senior manager at Local Initiatives for Biodiversity, Research and Development in Pokhara, Nepal, where she coordinates the social research and policy advocacy unit and serves as a gender focal person. Her training and experience lie in coordinating national and regional level projects on agro-biodiversity conservation, climate change, food security, and gender. Ms Devkota holds an MSc in agricultural economics from Himachal Pradesh Agriculture University in India.

Alessandra Galiè works as a gender scientist at the International Livestock Research Institute in Nairobi, Kenya, where she leads gender research on empowerment and food security related to livestock value chains in East Africa and Southeast Asia. She previously worked for the International Centre for Agricultural Research in the Dry Areas on gender research in seed governance and participatory plant breeding. Dr Galiè holds a PhD from Wageningen University, Netherlands, and an MA from the University of London, UK.

Hom Gartaula is a postdoctoral researcher in the International Development Studies program at Canadian Mennonite University in Winnipeg, Manitoba, Canada. He completed his PhD in social sciences (with an interdisciplinary focus on the sociology and anthropology of development) at Wageningen University in the Netherlands. Dr Gartaula is an experienced researcher, educator, and practitioner in the field of international development, with a particular interest in agrarian change, food security, labour migration, gender, and social well-being.

Tinkani Gondwe joined the Soils, Food, and Healthy Communities project in Ekwendeni, Malawi, in its first year (2000) as a member of the Farmer Research Team. Since then he has been an active project leader as well as a keen experimenter in his own fields. In 2012, thanks to his impressive leadership skills and great commitment to sustainable agriculture in his community, he joined the staff of the Malawi Farmer-to-Farmer Agroecology project as a community promoter.

Helen Hambly Odame holds a PhD from York University, Ontario, Canada, where she is an associate professor in the School of Environmental Design and Rural Development. She has more than 25 years of experience in international research and development programs in Africa, North Africa, and Latin America. Her work involves social analysis of agricultural innovation systems, including such topics as communication for social and environmental change, gender, and participatory development. She previously worked with CGIAR, the International Development Research Centre, and the non-governmental sector in Canada.

Gordon M. Hickey is an associate professor and William Dawson Scholar in the Department of Natural Resource Sciences at McGill University, Montreal, Canada. His international research applies mixed-method techniques to explore the institutional processes affecting sustainable natural resource-related policy and implementation, with a particular focus on integrating scientific knowledge for innovation. Dr Hickey holds a PhD from the University of British Columbia, Canada.

Emily Hillenbrand is senior technical advisor for Gender and Livelihoods at CARE USA, where she leads the women's empowerment and men-engage strategies for CARE's Pathways program, and provides technical guidance to other programs in Africa and South Asia. Her research focus is on integrating gender transformative approaches to food and nutrition security programming. She holds an MA in women, gender, and development from the International Institute of Social Studies in The Hague, Netherlands.

JoAnn Jaffe is a professor in the Department of Sociology and Social Studies at the University of Regina, Saskatchewan, Canada. She has conducted research in Haiti, Canada, East Africa, and Central and Latin America. She is past president of the Rural Sociological Society and was review editor for the Global Volume of the International Assessment of Agricultural Knowledge, Science, and Technology for Development.

Chamila Jayasinghe is a professor and head of the Department of Food Science and Technology, Faculty of Livestock, Fisheries and Nutrition, Wayamba University of Sri Lanka. She worked as a research team member and the gender focal point of the International Development Research Centre-funded Canadian International Food Security Research Fund project "Scaling up sustainable aquaculture in Sri Lanka". Her research interests include empowering rural women through post-harvest technology-related entrepreneurship development. Dr Jayasinghe holds a PhD in food science and technology from Tokyo University of Marine Science and Technology, Japan.

Paula Kantor died on 13 May 2015, in the aftermath of a terrorist attack in Kabul, Afghanistan. At the time of her death, she was working with the International Maize and Wheat Improvement Center, leading an ambitious new project to empower and improve the livelihoods of women, men, and youth in wheat-based systems of Afghanistan, Ethiopia, and Pakistan. Dr Kantor was a great champion for gender equality, and a science leader who was committed, passionate, and hard working.

Swikar Karki holds a BSc in agricultural science with a major in economics, and an MSc in soil sciences from Tribhuvan University, Nepal. In 2013, as a project officer with Local Initiatives for Biodiversity, Research and Development in Pokhara, Nepal, he participated in crop trials and technology testing for the International Development Research Centre-funded interdisciplinary project "Revalourising small millets in rain-fed regions of South Asia".

Kamal Khadka has more than seven years of professional experience in participatory research and development. He started his career as a rice breeder with the Agriculture Innovations for Livelihood Security program of Local Initiatives for Biodiversity, Research and Development in

Pokhara, Nepal, where he also coordinated crop improvement programs on maize, finger millet, and potato. He has key expertise in participatory plant breeding, agronomy, and community biodiversity management. Mr Khadka holds an MSc in plant breeding from Tribhuvan University in Nepal, and is currently completing his PhD in plant breeding at the University of Guelph, Canada.

Esther Kihoro is a researcher with an MA in agricultural and applied economics. Currently she is working at the International Livestock Institute as a survey coordinator in the Livelihoods, Gender and Impact program. She previously worked as a research assistant in the gender stream of the Kenya Agricultural Research Institute/McGill University food security project. She has written on women, youth, agriculture, climate change, rural farming systems, and related markets.

Elizabeth Kruger is an evaluation officer at Margaret A. Cargill Philanthropies. She previously worked as a technical advisor for learning, impact, and communication at CARE, and in evaluation for Land O'Lakes International Development. Her work focuses on developing and implementing evaluation strategies to track and assess program progress and impact, and ensuring that evaluation deliverables improve organisational performance. She holds a master's degree in public health from the University of Minnesota.

Esther Lupafya is the AIDS coordinator and gender coordinator for the Malawi Farmer-to-Farmer Agroecology project and deputy director of the primary health care department, both at Ekwendeni Hospital. She is a trained nurse midwife with a master's degree in social development and health from Queen's University, Edinburgh, UK. For over 25 years, Ms Lupafya has coordinated programs to address maternal and child health, AIDS care and prevention, youth empowerment, and gender inequalities in Malawi.

Alison E. Macnaughton has worked with World Fisheries Trust for over a decade, designing and implementing projects to improve livelihoods, empowerment, and conservation in coastal and inland small-scale fisheries in Brazil and Bolivia. She holds a BA in geography from the University of Victoria, Canada, and an MA in planning from the University of British Columbia, Canada, and is currently working towards her PhD in geography at the University of Victoria.

Rajakishor Mahana completed his PhD in anthropology at the Madras Institute of Development Studies, Chennai, and is currently a lecturer in anthropology at the Kalinga Institute of Social Sciences, KIIT University, India. His research interests include anthropology of development, post-colonial state, indigenous movements and social power, theories in anthropology, anthropology of violence, and social suffering.

Esther Maona joined the Soils, Food, and Healthy Communities project in Ekwendeni, Malawi, in its first year (2000) as a farmer volunteer, and became a farmer promoter in 2009. As part of her involvement with the Malawi Farmer-to-Farmer Agroecology project, she has travelled to Canada to learn more about organic agriculture. She is an active leader in her community, and loves seeing people's food security, soil, and nutrition improved through her work.

Maureen Miruka is a team leader with CARE USA's Pathways Women in Agriculture Program and is based in Nairobi, Kenya. She previously worked as a senior technical advisor for sustainable agriculture at CARE, and principal researcher at the Kenya Agricultural Research Institute. Her research and development focus is on gender and women's empowerment in agriculture-based livelihoods. She holds a PhD in natural resources from the University of Greenwich, London, UK.

Mwapi Mkandawire became a Malawi Farmer-to-Farmer Agroecology project promoter in 2012, after ten years on the Farmer Research Team with the Soils, Food, and Healthy Communities project. The changes she has seen in that time inspired her to do what she's doing now. Ms Mkandawire takes pleasure in seeing farmers growing their fields well as a result of the Soils, Food, and Healthy Communities project work.

Rodgers Msachi joined the Soils, Food, and Healthy Communities project in Ekwendeni, Malawi, in 2000 as a participating farmer and Farmer Research Team member. He became the project's agricultural promoter in 2005; as such, he promotes the farmer-to-farmer model of education for scaling up use of agroecological methods in the Malawi Farmer-to-Farmer Agroecology project.

Lutta Muhammad is an economist at the Kenya Agricultural and Livestock Research Organization. He previously worked in Kenya's Ministry of Agriculture, as senior lecturer/head of economics at the Embu Institute of Agriculture, and as an economist at the Tea Research Foundation. His research interests span analyses of smallholder farming systems, risk and uncertainty in agriculture, agricultural innovation, impact assessment, and science, technology, and innovation policy.

Esther Njuguna is the gender research coordinator in CGIAR's Research Program on Grain Legumes, based at the International Crops Research Institute for the Semi-Arid Tropics, Nairobi, Kenya. She is a graduate of Wageningen University and Research Centre (development economics), Netherlands, and the University of Nairobi (agricultural development and economics). She previously worked for 15 years at the Kenya Agricultural Research Institute, most recently coordinating gender and participatory market research for the project "Innovating for Resilient Farming Systems in Eastern Kenya".

Paul Nkhonjera joined the Soils, Food, and Healthy Communities project in Ekwendeni, Malawi, in 2000 as a participating farmer, and is also involved with the Malawi Farmer-to-Farmer Agroecology project at Ekwendeni Hospital. An enthusiastic farmer himself, he enjoys teaching and demonstrating agroecological methods to improve crops and harvests.

Kirit Patel is an assistant professor at Menno Simons College, a college of Canadian Mennonite University in affiliation with the University of Winnipeg, Canada. He has extensive experience as an academic, development policy analyst, and community development practitioner. His research is focused on food and nutrition security, farm conservation of agrobiodiversity, farmers' innovations, technology and gender, environmental justice, and farmers' rights. As lead principal investigator, Dr Patel coordinated the International Development Research Centre-funded interdisciplinary project "Revalourising small millets in rain-fed regions of South Asia".

Tiffanie K. Rainville has worked with Ecuador's coastal fishing communities, looking at impacts and perceptions of climate change. She is currently the project officer, fisheries and social research at World Fisheries Trust, which she joined in 2011 to work on the *Peces para la vida* project, focused on fisheries, aquaculture, and food security in the Bolivian Amazon region. She has a BScH from Queen's University, Canada, and a master's degree in environmental studies from Dalhousie University, Canada.

Durairaja Ramulu is an assistant professor at Tamil Nadu Fisheries University based at Fisheries College and Research Institute, Ponneri, Tamil Nadu, India, where he obtained his MFSc in fishery resource management. His research experience includes Asian catfish, cage culture of Asian sea bass, mud crab fattening, and community carp fish farming.

Silvia Sarapura Escobar is an adjunct professor at the University of Guelph, Ontario, Canada. She is an interdisciplinary researcher with specialisation in social and gender research, agricultural innovation systems, and capacity development. She has worked in Southeast Asia, sub-Saharan Africa, and Latin America. Dr Sarapura Escobar holds a PhD from the University of Guelph and recently completed a two-year postdoctoral fellowship with WorldFish, CGIAR Malaysia.

Asis Shrestha completed his BSc in agriculture science from the Institute for Agriculture and Animal Sciences in Rampur, Nepal, before joining Local Initiatives for Biodiversity, Research and Development, where he worked from June 2011 to December 2013, developing valuable skills in the field of crop research and socioecomonic studies. He is currently completing a postgraduate degree in agriculture resource management at the University of Bonn, Germany.

Lizzie Shumba has worked for over a decade for the Soils, Food, and Healthy Communities project in Ekwendeni, Malawi, and currently works with the Malawi Farmer-to-Farmer Agroecology project at Ekwendeni Hospital. She has a college diploma in nutrition from Natural Resources College, Malawi, and is pursuing a BSc in agricultural extension and rural development at Lilongwe University for Agriculture and Natural Resources. Ms Shumba is passionate about improving nutrition using agroecological and participatory approaches.

Lauren Q. Sneyd completed her PhD in geography and international development studies in 2015 at the University of Guelph, Ontario, Canada. She is currently an assistant professor of development studies at St. Francis Xavier University, Nova Scotia, Canada. She has published articles in *Food Security*, *Geoforum*, *Journal of Contemporary African Studies*, and *Sustainability*.

Laurie Starr is a senior technical advisor for Technical Assistance to NGOs International. She has participated in numerous studies and program evaluations involving food security and nutrition, resilience, and gender equality. Much of her current research is on bringing a gendered focus to resilience measurement. Her field experience includes Latin America, South Asia, and East and West Africa. She holds an MA in international development practice from Prescott College in Prescott, Arizona.

Graham Thiele leads CGIAR's Research Program on Roots, Tubers and Bananas, which seeks to improve food security and reduce rural poverty through research for development, with improving gender equity as a core commitment. Previously, as leader of the International Potato Center's Social Science group, he guided work on targeting, priority setting, and impact and adoption studies of new agricultural technologies and participatory methods. Dr Thiele holds a PhD in social anthropology from Cambridge University, UK, and an MSc in agricultural economics from the University of London, UK.

Elaine M. Ward holds a law degree from the University of Calgary, Canada, and a master's degree in international law from Lund University, Sweden. She has specialised and published in human rights and the environment, with a focus on gender and racial equality. Ms Ward served as a gender and development specialist with World Fisheries Trust's International Development Research Centre/Canadian International Development Agency-funded project on food security, fisheries, and aquaculture in the Bolivian Amazon, acting as a senior program advisor to assist in gender mainstreaming.

John M. Wojciechowski has worked with World Fisheries Trust since 2006 on value chain development, food safety, occupational health, economic development, and solidarity economy in small coastal and inland fishing communities. His research focuses on state interventions in the development of coastal small-scale fisheries. He holds a degree in urban and regional planning from the University of Waterloo, Canada, and master's degrees in local economic development (University of Waterloo) and territorial planning and management (Federal University of ABC, Santo André, Brazil), and is currently in the process of obtaining a PhD in rural development.

Introduction

Gender, agriculture, and food security: where are we?

Jemimah Njuki, John R. Parkins, Amy Kaler, and Sara Ahmed

Linking gender to food and nutrition security

The 1996 World Food Summit Plan of Action defined food security as existing "when all people, at all times, have access to sufficient, safe, nutritious food to maintain a healthy and active life" (World Food Summit 1996). Food security is built on three pillars:

1 Food availability: sufficient quantities of food available on a consistent basis;
2 Food access: sufficient resources to obtain appropriate foods for a nutritious diet; and
3 Food use: appropriate use based on knowledge of basic nutrition and care, as well as adequate water and sanitation.

While the number of hungry people has been going down, recent estimates by the Food and Agriculture Organization of the United Nations (FAO) indicate that 795 million people are chronically undernourished (FAO et al. 2015), with over one in nine people in the world still suffering from hunger. The highest burden of hunger occurs in Southern Asia, where as many as 281 million people are undernourished. In sub-Saharan Africa, one in every four people, or 23.2 percent of the population, are hungry.

A large body of evidence based on household-level data shows that reducing gender inequality is an important part of the solution to global hunger (Smith et al. 2003; ADB 2013). In 2009, the International Food Policy Research Institute (IFPRI) compared the 2009 Global Hunger Index rankings to the World Economic Forum's 2008 Global Gender Gap Index, which measures the well-being of women relative to men. The results indicated that countries with the most severe hunger problems also had the highest levels of gender inequality.

Similar studies have found a relationship between nutrition, especially children's nutrition, and women's empowerment. An IFPRI study explored the relationship between women's status – defined as women's power relative to men's power in their households and communities – and children's nutrition in 39 countries in three developing regions: South Asia, sub-Saharan Africa, and Latin America and the Caribbean (Smith et al. 2003). The study found that women's status significantly affects child nutrition. Women with higher status have better nutritional status themselves, are better cared for, and provide higher-quality care for their children.

The relationship between gender inequality and food and nutrition insecurity is complex and mediated by several factors.

Access to inputs and technology is decisive in explaining differences in yields between male and female smallholders. A review of literature by IFPRI on use of fertiliser, seed varieties, tools, and pesticide found that 79 percent of the studies concluded that men have higher mean access to these inputs (Peterman et al. 2010). A similar analysis by the World Bank (2014) found that a simple comparison of average male and female productivity shows that productivity gaps range from a low of 13 percent in Uganda to a high of 25 percent in Malawi. This means that in Malawi, for instance, male-managed plots produce on average 25 percent more per hectare than female-managed plots. After controlling for differences in plot size and geographic factors, productivity differences are starker, ranging from 23 percent in Tanzania to 66 percent in Niger. Analysis by FAO concluded that if women had the same access to productive resources as men, they could increase yields on their farms by 20 to 30 percent. This could raise total agricultural output in developing countries by 2.5 to 4 percent, which could in turn reduce the number of hungry people in the world by 12 to 17 percent (FAO 2011). However, the World Bank argues that there is more to this issue than access to technologies: even when women and men have equal access to inputs, that balance is not reflected in their agricultural productivity, mainly because of gender norms, market failures, or institutional constraints that alter the effectiveness of these resources for women (World Bank 2014).

Women produce, process, distribute, and market food as unpaid workers, family farmers, and members of the paid agricultural labour force: the female share of the agricultural labour force ranges from about 20 percent in Latin America to almost 50 percent in Eastern and Southeastern Asia and sub-Saharan Africa (FAO 2011). Rural women play a critical role in attaining each of the pillars of food security – availability, access, and use – from production on the family plot, to food preparation, to distribution within the household. However, that role is generally undervalued and constrained by limitations on women's access to resources, services, and labour market opportunities. Studies show that in most regions of the world, women perform the bulk of unpaid work in both agricultural production and the "care" economy. This includes child care, fetching water and fuel wood, purchasing and preparing food, cleaning, and caring for the sick and elderly (Folbre 2006; Kabeer 2012).

Even where enough food is produced, differential feeding and caregiving practices can favour men over women and boys over girls in food allocation within the household, leading to poorer nutritional outcomes for women and girls. This in turn affects women's ability to adequately fulfil their traditional roles in caregiving and food systems (Behrman 1988; Thomas 1990; Gittelsohn 1991).

For women, the ability to access food depends on power – power to produce, power to purchase, and power to access food in intra-household allocation mechanisms. When women have less power than men, it translates directly into weaker access to food (Patel 2012). Women's control over income from agricultural activities (e.g., intra-household allocation of income between men and women, or the extent of women's ability to make decisions about purchases) can enhance their decision-making and increase their bargaining power, which can in turn give them a voice, both within the household and at the community level. As well, women's bargaining power has been associated with better health and education outcomes for children (Quisumbing and Maluccio 2003).

For researchers and development practitioners, the big question in the second decade of the 21st century is not whether gender equality can reduce food insecurity, but what strategies are successful in reducing gender inequalities. This book provides empirical evidence and conceptual explorations of the gendered dimensions of food security, drawing on studies from Africa, Asia, and South America. The cases investigate how food security and gender inequity are conceptualised within interventions; assess the impacts and outcomes of gender-responsive programs on food security and gender equity; and weigh diverse approaches to gender research and practice, ranging from descriptive and analytical to strategic and transformative. The intent of this collection is to extend the global conversation on gender and food security, engaging scholars, practitioners, and students.

Approaches to gender and food security research

The widespread recognition of the importance of gender in agriculture and food security is reflected in the growing prominence of gender strategies being tested and used by research and development organisations in their programs; the emergence of compelling approaches for gender integration; and the development of indicators and tools for tracking outcomes of research and development interventions that integrate gender. However, despite evidence that gender-responsive approaches are needed to improve food and nutrition security, they are not yet a mainstay of development and agricultural programs. A recent report by the Institute of Development Studies (IDS) on gender and food security (IDS 2014) makes the case for a gender-aware understanding of food security, arguing that partial, apolitical, and gender-blind diagnoses of the problem of food and nutrition insecurity lead to inadequate policies, and, ultimately, the failure of people's entitlement to food.

The past few years have seen several approaches aimed at strengthening the links between gender equality and food and nutrition security by addressing factors such as women's agency in agriculture and food production; markets, policies, and other structural barriers; and underlying gender and social norms and practices.

Women's agency in agriculture and food production

These approaches take an instrumental view of women's roles in food production, and actions that can be taken to optimise these roles. The underlying assumption is that women face gender-based constraints that limit their contribution to agriculture and food security. Researchers working from this perspective argue that women make crucial contributions to agriculture and rural enterprises, as well as to household nutrition, through their food processing and preparation activities. Indeed, studies show that, globally, women provide 43 percent of agricultural labour, and up to 50 percent in some regions such as sub-Saharan Africa (FAO 2011). Women also play a critical role in ensuring household nutrition, especially of children, through their caregiving role. However, their productivity is constrained by lower access to productive resources and services, which has implications for production, food security, economic growth, and the well-being of their families, communities, and countries.

Interventions addressing women's access to resources are driven by the evidence on gender differentials in access to and use of these resources. Peterman et al. (2010) found that there were significant gender differences in the adoption of improved technologies and the use of purchased inputs across regions in developing countries. In Ghana, Doss and Morris (2001) found that only 39 percent of female farmers adopted improved crop varieties (compared with 59 percent of male farmers) because they had less access to land, family labour, and extension services. Similar patterns have been observed for use of agricultural tools, such as motor cultivators used for ploughing and transport (FAO 2011). This leads to drudgery by women, delays in ploughing and planting, low market participation, and lower adoption of other technologies (Quisumbing 1996; Kinkingninhoun-Mêdagbé et al. 2010).

Results of programs addressing inequalities in access to productive resources have shown improvements not only in productivity and food and nutrition security, but also in the status of women, thanks to increased access to assets and resources. Research by the World Bank in six countries in Africa showed that giving women access to resources equal to those of men and addressing barriers to increasing returns from these resources can remove any productivity gaps between male- and female-managed farms (World Bank 2014). Research has also demonstrated that when women have secure property rights, they gain status and have more influence in household decisions, including decisions on food production, nutrition, and use of income (Smith et al. 2003; FAO 2011; World Bank 2011).

Addressing markets, policies, and other structural barriers

The last few years have seen concerted efforts to improve and expand both food security initiatives at the household level, and efforts related to markets, trade and competitiveness, and agricultural policies. Agriculture is an important source of income for participating rural households. The resulting increases in income are important for nutrition, in that they enable people to purchase more non-food items and services such as health care, as well as a more diverse diet, which tends to imply a higher dietary quality. For example, evidence from Guatemala shows higher incomes are positively correlated with uptake of nutrients such as vitamin B-12 and vitamin A (Lannotti et al. 2012).

Participation in agricultural product markets is, however, gendered (Njuki and Sanginga 2013). Gendered value-chain analysis has unmasked previously underdocumented gender patterns in market participation. Overall, women tend to be less integrated in markets than men. Their lack of mobility, demands on their time for household and child care responsibilities, and social norms impede their interaction with participants in the value chain. Their lack of access to formal credit and other financial services restricts their activity primarily to the production and low-return sectors of the chain.

Despite these constraints, women are integral to agricultural value chains. Efforts to improve women's meaningful and beneficial participation in agricultural value chains have largely focussed on three strategies. The first is *improving horizontal coordination* by developing relationships among actors within functional "nodes" (people playing the same function in one part of the chain, such as production, processing, etc.) of the value chains. An example of this would be organising women fish traders into a cooperative, thereby increasing their bargaining power, or improving their access to resources (Coles and Mitchell 2010).

The second strategy is *improving vertical coordination* by developing relationships between smallholder producers – and in many cases women producers – or traders with other actors higher up the chain. Mechanisms such as contract farming, credit provision by microfinance organisations, and organic certification schemes linking smallholder women producers directly to organic traders and consumers can facilitate these relationships.

The third strategy is *product and process upgrading*, which involves transforming the product so that value is added before it moves to the next link in the chain. For example, rather than selling a raw product, producers can increase its value by taking it through primary processing or transformation. Process upgrading could involve changing production practices to provide organic products for niche markets, thereby increasing market value.

The United States Agency for International Development (USAID 2005) provides a summary of donor programs and best practices for addressing women's access to markets. Coles and Mitchell (2010), however, caution that this benefit depends on persistent tensions, such as the intra-household dynamics that govern income control.

A key element of gender research in value-chain development is the implication of value addition and market integration on the roles and positions of women, and on intra-household distribution and management of income. For example, as products become more valuable, they may become the subject of conflict among household members, or shift allocations of labour, leaving some household members more labour burdened than others.

Addressing underlying gender and social norms and practices

A gender transformative approach (GTA) goes beyond improving women's access to resources: it enables communities to understand and challenge the social norms that create inequalities between men and women, and can either help or hinder an individual's capacity to take advantage of available opportunities. Gender norms in particular are often resistant to change, partly because they are widely held and practised in daily life (because they benefit the gender that already holds the balance of social and economic power), and partly because they instil unconscious biases about gender differences that make it easier to conform to long-standing norms than to adopt new ones (Kandiyoti 1988; Butler 2004; England 2010; Alesina et al. 2013). Gender disparities manifest in different ways, including intra-household allocation of time, food, responsibilities, and power.

However, gender and social norms can and do change in response to both internal and external influences. Kandiyoti (1988) suggests such changes are more likely where men and women are motivated by more egalitarian models than by abstract ideas of gender equality, and where people do not fear social disapproval for failing to conform to gender stereotypes. For example, Evans (2014) documents that, in Zambia, women without exposure to men performing care work often expressed resentment, were more resigned to their fate than women who had grown up sharing care work with brothers, and were more optimistic about social change.

Increased agency can allow women to move from complete compliance with constraining and unequal gender norms to questioning such norms and exploring potential opportunities, changing their aspirations as well as their ability to seek and achieve desired outcomes. For example, women's economic participation has the potential to alter traditional definitions of gender roles, duties, and responsibilities, but it can also change the main components of both men's and women's identities. Changes in education, employment, and family formation are areas where women see their agency and decision-making influence expanding.

Changing social norms can provoke backlash, particularly if widespread cultural change occurs simultaneously, leading to marginalisation of particular social groups. The World Bank (2011) documents the role of assets and of technological and legal changes in addressing social norms. Women's asset ownership has been associated with greater decision-making power and challenging social norms on women's role in the household and society, but it can also lead to an increase in some forms of domestic violence or threats of such violence, particularly in the short term. Ensuring that men are active participants in strategies for empowerment of women is essential to the cultural change required for the redistribution of tasks and decision-making within the household.

Some development programs have pioneered household approaches through which men and women can come together and challenge norms or cross boundaries of traditional gender roles or conduct. These approaches comprise a set of participatory methodologies for encouraging equitable intra-household relations and decision-making processes, encouraging all household members to realise that working together is a win-win solution that benefits everyone. For example, CGIAR's Research Program on Aquatic Agricultural Systems uses a GTA aimed at generating evidence and information on how poor men and women access and use resources, who has power and makes decisions, whose priorities are being addressed, and who is impacted by, or benefiting from, different development alternatives. Although some of the household methodologies set achieving gender justice as their goal, others work with the understanding that gender-based constraints severely limit the achievement of wider program goals such as food and nutrition security, and thus seek to identify and tackle them through a transformative process (Kantor 2013; Cole et al. 2015).

About this book

Drawing on diverse theoretical perspectives, including transformative learning, feminist theory, deliberative democracy, and technology adoption, this collection adds important conceptual and empirical material to the growing literature on the challenges of gender equity in agricultural production.

For researchers, the collection offers insights into the complexity of gender relations and pathways to empowerment. For practitioners, it highlights innovative strategic and practical approaches to the transformation of gender relations through project design and implementation. For students, it provides a wide-ranging introduction to the challenges and conundrums of enhancing food security in the Global South.

A unique feature of this collection is the integration of both analytic and transformative approaches to understanding gender and food security. The analytic material shows how food security interventions enable women and men to meet the long-term nutritional needs of their households, and to enhance their economic position. The transformative chapters document efforts to build durable and equitable relationships between men and women, addressing underlying social, cultural, and economic causes of gender inequality. Taken together, these approaches enable women and men to reflect on the gendered allocation of labour and resources related to food, and to reshape these distributions in ways that benefit families and communities.

The book is the result of five years of research on agriculture and food security under the Canadian International Food Security Research Fund (CIFSRF). Launched in 2009, the fund was a five-and-a-half-year, CA$62-million program funded jointly by the Department of Foreign Affairs, Trade and Development (DFATD) and the International Development Research Centre (IDRC). Between 30 October 2009 and 31 March 2015, CIFSRF supported 21 large-scale projects that had a direct impact on smallholder farmers – especially women farmers – and consumers.

The first phase of the research emphasised women farmers and gender-specific needs in the design and implementation of research and the communication of results. To ensure that gender analysis and action were implemented in practice (and not just in proposals), a gender strategy was developed by IDRC staff. Projects were monitored for several criteria: their use of gender analysis tools; the participation of women in research and their involvement in testing new practices and technologies; how the projects affected women's access to resources and income-generating opportunities; their impact on dietary diversity and nutrition for women and children; and their consideration of gender in monitoring and evaluation systems and communication strategies.

In November 2013, the editors worked with other IDRC staff to develop a call for contributions to a volume on gender and food security that would identify key approaches for addressing gender and women's empowerment in food security interventions, and assess lessons learned. This call yielded approximately 35 submissions from researchers around the world, and about half were from projects funded by CIFSRF. From these submissions, a preliminary selection of 14 abstracts was made. The authors were invited to present a draft of their chapter at the International Food Security Dialogue 2014 held in Edmonton, Canada, and then attend a writers' workshop in Banff, Canada, for further revisions. At the end of that process, 11 chapters were selected for inclusion in this collection.

Thematic approaches within this collection

This collection was inspired by current efforts to integrate a gender perspective into international research and development on agriculture and food security. From the concept stage, the editors set out to assemble a group of chapters that focussed on practical and strategic aspects of gender integration. The goal was to document the ways that gender inequity is conceptualised within development interventions, assess the impacts and outcomes of gender-responsive programs on food security and gender equity, and extend the global conversation on gender and food security in the direction of strategic and transformative practices. The work in this collection testifies to the strong mandates for gender integration within international research and development agencies worldwide.

The work transcends the gender continuum, from accommodating to transformative approaches. *Accommodating approaches* are those that give attention to local-level differences in access to resources, and target interventions in ways that recognise differences between men and women, but do not intentionally challenge the status quo. Using empirical categories for comparison, accommodating approaches focus on integrating women into the existing social and economic context, but do not question the barriers put up by that context.

Moving beyond accommodation, *GTAs* aim to address the causes of gender inequality and not just the symptoms (Kantor 2013). Consequently, these interventions are focussed on enhancing women's efficacy, changing social norms, and altering institutional structures. Moreover, the research components of GTAs involve identifying ethically appropriate alternatives for project intervention, and testing the possibilities of such project interventions to effect social change. GTAs are clearly about more than the collection of sex-disaggregated data, and call for a much more radical and intentional stance that seeks to redress gender disparities in resources, markets, and technologies with complementary actions to address underlying social norms and power relations (Kantor 2013; Cole et al. 2015).

This commitment to enhancing women's efficacy, addressing social norms, and altering institutional structures is reflected in parts of this edited collection, but the material also offers a slightly different take on the role of measurement and gender analytics. In some respects, there are tensions between those who value more empirical and less invasive approaches to gender integration, and those who are more focussed on challenging problematic social norms as a matter of course. Some of the hesitancy about directing social transformation through food security interventions comes from the laudable desire to avoid situations where outsiders are dictating or declaring "appropriate" or "inappropriate" behaviour in a way that invokes negative aspects of social engineering.

This tension was very much alive in the development of this collection as well. During our writers' workshop, chapter authors spent four days together providing peer-review comments on draft chapters, and working through key themes in the collection. During these discussions, some chapter authors took the position that gender integration requires a move towards more explicitly transformative gender work. These authors maintain strong convictions that thoughtful and purposeful efforts to redress social inequality must be a component of development projects. To do nothing is to simply perpetuate harm.

Other authors took the opposite stand, arguing that good gender analytic work is required to understand the complexities of a given social setting where project interventions are taking place. These analytics may involve careful collection of primary data, and detailed descriptive and analytical work, including multi-variate analysis that offers critical insights into the causal relationships, critical factors, and opportunities to enhance local livelihoods and redress social inequalities. From the perspective of these chapter authors, this work is clearly an important and constant aspect of integrating gender into agricultural research and development interventions.

The editors of this collection take the view that gender integration will require a wide range of approaches that include gender analysis, gender accommodation, and gender transformation. However, this position comes with a number of caveats.

First, high-quality measurement and empirical analysis of gender relations involves more than simple reporting of descriptive statistics from household surveys. A combination of qualitative and quantitative techniques that account for complexity, local context, and multiple pathways towards equity and livelihood sustainability is required.

Second, given the nature of project funding for agricultural interventions, often within a three- to five-year timeframe, there are certain practical challenges in adopting GTAs. Time and resource constraints may allow for solid analytical work or the development of modest gender accommodating approaches within one phase of a project. These approaches may also lead to insights from research and intervention pathways that can be incorporated into gender transformative work over the longer term.

Third, much of the analytical work done by researchers at agricultural research institutes or universities is carried out far from the villages and households where project interventions are taking place. Specialists with analytical expertise may not have the necessary skills to take up these transformative approaches. The diversity of skills and capacities required for comprehensive gender integration clearly delineates the roles of researchers and staff who are engaged in project interventions.

By attempting to illustrate the continuum of work on gender integration, from analytical to transformative, this collection reflects some of the constraints and opportunities noted above.

The call to confront social inequalities is clearly an important aspect of current program interventions, and several of the chapters in this collection offer exemplary case studies of how this work can be undertaken within an agricultural context. The research perspective, however, recognises the important contribution of careful and insightful measurement and analysis, not simply as a stepping stone for further transformative work, but to demonstrate ongoing insights into important trends, causal relationships, and pathways towards social equity. In the absence of good analytical work, these patterns may not be readily apparent.

Gender analysis, gender transformation, and cross-cutting themes

The contributions to this volume are conceptually and epistemologically diverse. They cover a wide spectrum, from local ethnographies to national surveys, from politically neutral to explicitly feminist, and from agriculture to sociology. As discussed above, the diversity of the contributions to this volume is seen not as a trajectory or a progression from an earlier way of thinking about gender to a more highly developed one, but as a spectrum encompassing both analytic and transformative understandings of what it means to do research on gender. The chapters in this volume highlight "best practices" in gender research, and from this diversity certain cross-cutting themes arise.

The more analytically focussed chapters push readers and scholars to be precise, to specify what the phenomenon of interest is, and to think carefully about how changes in that phenomenon might be measured. Dejager and Jayasinghe use participatory rapid appraisal (PRA) processes to bring to light aspects of gender that might not be easily captured by surveys and cross-sectional or snapshot formats – the underestimation of women's time burden, for example. Similarly, Devkota et al. break down the tasks involved in planting and cultivation very closely, so that readers can see the gender distribution across the component tasks of farming, rather than being satisfied with generalisations about agriculture being primarily a masculinised or feminised job. Sneyd examines the entire web of tasks involved in wild food commodification from an ethnographic perspective, and, like that of Devkota et al., her work provides a detailed picture of food security as a complex weave of gendered tasks and relations.

While these authors focus on micro- and meso-level social structures, others turn their analytic gaze to macro-level strategies for measuring and specifying gender relations. Miruka et al. take on the task of conceptualising empowerment at the national and regional level, using multiple indicators and indices. They seek to operationalise the complex question of women's empowerment, to account for varying ideas about what it means to be empowered across different countries, and to derive pathways for change from data collection and analysis.

Miruka et al. caution researchers who might be too quick to make pronouncements about gender and women's lack of empowerment, and remind us that methods matter: questions about gender and women's empowerment elicit different answers when asked in different ways. In their study, focus groups at the local level reported much more variability in empowerment than national-level survey results suggest.

In addition to decomposing gender, these analytic chapters also lead readers to think more broadly about the dynamics of food security. While most chapters focus on what people grow and how, Dejager and Jayasinghe, as well as Sneyd, draw our attention to food that people *don't* grow – the "capture versus culture" distinction. Careful detailing of the work involved in bringing "captured" fish and bush meat into homes draws attention to the distinctive gendered relations that produce non-cultivated food.

The second group of chapters in this collection has a primarily transformative focus. The distinction between analytic and transformative work is not a bright-line transition from one mode of research to another, but refers to a shift in emphasis. It reflects the balance between providing detailed and complex accounts of existing situations on one hand and seeking out means through which these situations may be changed on the other.

Some transformative chapters are strongly normative, laying out not only what *could* be done but what *ought* to be done. Galiè and Kantor call for transformative research as an alternative to business-as-usual, which produces knowledge that allows gender inequity to persist, albeit perhaps less harshly. This business-as-usual they refer to as a gender accommodating approach. Similarly, Sarapura et al. argue that gender transformation is not only normatively good in itself, but is tied to other major forms of social transformation, including environmental and ecological concerns, through a complex cultural vision of the cosmos. In a similar vein, Macnaughton et al. expand the importance of food security beyond simply putting food on the table, arguing that food provision is not just about getting enough to eat, but is also about the cultural survival of the groups concerned. Miruka et al. go even further, producing a generalisable, standardisable theory of change, through the use of research to identify specific pathways to empowerment.

Consistent with their holistic approach to social transformation, these scholars incorporate multiple dimensions of the local cultural context as they set gender alongside other systems of stratification and inequality. Mahana and Ramulu deal with the intersection of gender and caste in shaping the less-than-ideal outcomes of an intervention involving fish ponds in India, while Bezner Kerr et al. attend to the ways in which age stratification affects women's positions within communities. Jaffe and Kaler are similarly attentive to the importance of cultural ritual and symbolism, as expressed in the Ethiopian coffee ceremony, and examine how these practices can simultaneously constrain and enable women's ability to access the resources they need to provide food for their families. This complex understanding of gender as something more than a two-category system of males and females makes these chapters particularly rich and sophisticated, but also generates ever-increasing levels of complexity, leading to the question: how can these situations be changed for the better?

This question is at the heart of the transformative chapters. Several chapters tell the story of interventions intended simultaneously to improve women's positions and enhance food security in local communities. In all cases, the results are ambiguous, and the authors should be commended for not glossing over the limitations and challenges to gender transformation through food-related interventions. For Njuguna et al., innovations intended to enhance production may have had a negative effect on gender relations, as men were able to capture the benefits of innovations for their own purposes. Similarly, in the aquaculture project studied by Mahana and Ramulu, entrenched caste interests meant that only some women were able to benefit from the new fish ponds, as this transformative project was hijacked by local elites.

Other chapters suggest a slower and more subtle, but perhaps no less powerful, change in gender relations as a result of interventions. The long-view longitudinal perspective of Bezner Kerr et al. enables the writers to reflect on many years of work within the community, and on the slow change in norms influencing what is considered appropriate for a man or for a woman. Similarly, Galiè and Kantor found that men's status as primary food providers shifted when women acquired goats of their own.

Many of the transformative chapters stress the importance of consciousness-raising activities, through which men and women come to reflect critically on their experiences of gender relations. The link between consciousness-raising and social change is usually implied rather than explicit. That said, Bezner Kerr et al. treat deliberative dialogue as an independent variable in its own right, examining whether talking (a lot) about gender can produce measurable change, and concluding that, in a modest way, it can. By contrast, Galiè and Kantor find that talking about gender has its limitations: despite educational sessions on gender sensitisation, gender relations changed only when women gained ownership of valuable resources, such as goats. Macnaughton et al. and Sarapura et al. provide thick descriptions of different types of reflection and discussion activities initiated with the hope of cata-lysing change from within communities, which may bear fruit in the long run, beyond the limited time horizon of most intervention projects.

Whether the chapters fall more to the analytical or the transformative end of the spectrum, certain themes arise repeatedly.

The first such cross-cutting theme is *chain or process approaches*. Many chapters rely on the concept of a chain of some sort, whether it be a market chain, a value chain, an adoption chain, or some other set of sequential steps. Macnaughton et al. describe the "value chain" of the fisheries, for instance, which draws attention to the role of the middlemen. Sarapura et al. draw on the participatory market chain, a value-chain approach adapted to small-scale rural enterprise, while Njuguna et al. develop the concept of an adoption chain, drawing on the phases through which innovations integrate (or fail to integrate) with existing practices and technologies. This attention to process is partly a way of compensating for the cross-sectional nature of much of the data collection. By identifying a chain, researchers can estimate processes of change over time, even if they do not have access to longitudinal data (unlike long-term studies such as the one conducted by Bezner Kerr et al.).

The second cross-cutting theme is an emphasis on *deliberation*. As noted above, many researchers built some form of community dialogue or partici-patory conversation process into their projects. These opportunities for reflection and critique are central to several chapters, but the connection between discussion and social change is, as yet, underspecified. Are these conversations transformative in themselves, and, if so, what can they transform? Can they have measurable impacts within the community? Even if the outcomes of these discussions cannot be precisely tracked with existing methodologies, do they enhance researchers' understanding of communities in ways that can inform future interventions? The incorpora-tion of such discussions into research and interventions appears to be an emergent norm, and by all accounts the opportunity to reflect is welcomed by most community members; however, the impact of these discussions remains opaque.

The third cross-cutting theme is *intersectionality*, the intertwining of gender with other social categories such as class, ethnicity, age, or caste. Gender is never simply a matter of men and women: other identities and categories shape the experience of being male or female under particular historical circumstances. These circumstances may also be considered another form of intersectionality, as gender relations emerge at the crossroads of many historical trajectories, including colonialism, globalisation, environmental change, and economic destabilisation, to name only a few of the paths evident in this collection.

Finally, one theme is notable by its absence. *Men and masculinity* are under-represented in this collection, as though "gender" means only "women", and "disempowered women" at that. Most of the projects represented in this collection had as their explicit aim the alleviation of women's burdens or the increase in women's access to resources and earning power, which makes the focus on women's experiences understandable. However, when men figure mainly as a comparison group for women's status, our understanding of gender as a dynamic relational process, involving the experiences of both men and women, is necessarily truncated. Some chapters, such as Bezner Kerr et al. and Njuguna et al., do explicitly address men as gendered beings, but for most authors, masculinity remains the final frontier of gender.

Structure of this book

The book is divided into four interrelated sections.

Part I: Measuring gender relations and women's empowerment

The first section focusses on the Women's Empowerment in Agriculture Index (WEAI) and its adaptations for different projects and contexts.

Using data from six countries, Miruka et al. (Ch. 1) adapted the index to capture additional individual and social dimensions of empowerment. Their results show relatively low empowerment scores for women, with fewer than 5 percent of women surveyed in Bangladesh, Ghana, Mali, and India considered to be empowered. The adapted index provides a comprehensive tool for measurement of women's empowerment that takes into account women's agency and social relations.

Part II: From measurement to action

The second section of the book focusses on moving from measurement to empowerment. In Sri Lanka, Dejager and Jayasinghe (Ch. 2) document the growth of aquaculture in regions where it is still underdeveloped, to provide an opportunity for women to achieve a more equitable position in the food system value chains than exists in traditional capture fishery systems. Unlike fisheries, which is largely a "capture" system, aquaculture is a "culture" system that requires an increasing degree of control over inputs and stock. A context-specific gender livelihood and food security analysis of communities informed the introduction and adaptation of the aquaculture opportunity of oyster culture to enable women to step into significant new positions and to increase their contributions to household incomes and livelihood improvements.

In Nepal, Devkota et al. (Ch. 3) address the impact of improved small farm tools, machinery, and practices on labour efficiency and gender relations in finger millet production. Labour in rural households has been adversely affected by male labour out-migration. The introduction of a pedal-operated thresher decreased the women's workload and increased men's participation in threshing. The chapter analyses the social and efficiency implications of mechanisation of agriculture, especially in contexts of high male migration from rural to urban areas.

In India, Mahana and Ramulu (Ch. 4) explore the gender issues in natural resource management by examining the changing mechanisms of resource allocation in Odisha. The authors argue that, though women's access to and control over natural resources challenges the patriarchal power dynamics in the short term, local politics and patronage relations contradict the prescribed mechanisms of resource allocation that, in turn, reproduce gender inequality and rural poverty in the long term.

Part III: Placing gender in local institutional contexts

Gender roles and relations exist within a broader social and cultural context, and Part III of the book focusses on how gender interacts with this broad context, and the implications for food security.

Jaffe and Kaler (Ch. 5) examine the household coffee ceremony in two Ethiopian villages undergoing rapid social change. The repeated performance of this ceremony is central to the creation and sustenance of the social relations that enable households to mobilise resources to meet their food security needs. The chapter uses the concepts of household bargaining and moral economies to understand the enduring power of the coffee ceremony, despite the investment of both time and resources it requires. Although the labour burden falls disproportionately on women, they also derive gendered benefits from the ceremony.

In Cameroon, Sneyd (Ch. 6) focusses on the trade in forest food products, which is organised around various types of buyers and sellers. Through engaging with and analysing the wild food sector during a time of crisis and change, various ways of improving and developing appropriate gender responses for the trade and for Cameroonian women are explored.

Sarapura Escobar et al. (Ch. 7) use the Papa Andina Regional Initiative to discuss how traditional and modern technologies and institutions combine to create innovation that enables Andean peasant producers of native potatoes to negotiate socioeconomic and ecological changes in the farming system. Using a theoretical approach informed by a feminist standpoint perspective that privileges women's voice and contextualises gender inequality within a feminocentric Andean worldview, the chapter documents the entrenched gender roles and relations affecting access to, and control over, natural resources, and the micro-, meso-, and macro-level gender issues in agricultural innovation systems.

Part IV: Approaches to transforming gender relations

The final part of the book focusses on approaches to transforming gender relations. The chapter by Galiè and Kantor (Ch. 8) discusses the need to engage with GTAs (approaches to gender research that address both the fundamental causes and consequences of gender inequality) and translate them into agricultural development practice. The authors find that interventions that are effective in increasing the independence, decision-making, and food security of the involved livestock keepers can sometimes be of limited scope in changing gender normative roles. They propose a methodology to incorporate local understandings and processes of empowerment into GTAs.

Macnaughton et al. (Ch. 9) discuss work in the Bolivian Amazon to engage women and men together, and across scales, to discuss social and technical "bottlenecks" in the fisheries value chains. Their efforts have contributed to improved transparency and awareness about current activities, and more equitable distribution of responsibilities and benefits among different actors. The authors document a transformative approach implemented with two pilot groups, making use of a capacities and vulnerabilities analysis, followed by action research interventions with tools based on *diálogo de saberes* (knowledge dialogue).

In Malawi, Bezner Kerr et al. (Ch. 10) discuss the focus of many health and nutrition development programs on women of childbearing age, particularly mothers, with limited attention to the roles of men or older women in childcare and feeding. They draw on the Soils, Food, and Healthy Communities (SFHC) project, a long-term intervention that used participatory research and gender sensitive approaches to improve soil fertility, food security, and child nutrition. Through in-depth surveys and focus group discussions, they highlight the ambiguities, tensions, and complementarities that arise between participatory approaches, while taking gender and other power relations into account.

In the last chapter of this section, Njuguna et al. (Ch. 11) examine the outcomes of a participatory research project implemented in Eastern Kenya, looking at how gendered adoption of practices impacts the advancement of food security goals. They examine decision-making processes at the household level, from choice of technology, to provision of labour for various agronomic steps, to marketing and consumption for four field crops and two fruit tree crops, and provide insight into what drives or blocks adoption by women and men, primarily centred on the priced and non-priced benefits of adoption, women's radius of mobility, and the household gendered division of labour.

The concluding chapter focusses on lessons learned and potential ways forward for gender and transformative research in agriculture and food systems.

References

All website URLs accessed on 7 April 2016.

ADB (Asian Development Bank). 2013. *Gender Equality and Food Security: Women's Empowerment as a Tool against Hunger.* Mandaluyong City, Philippines: ADB. www.fao.org/wairdocs/ar259e/ar259e.pdf.

Alesina, Alberto F., Paola Giuliano, and Nathan Nunn. 2013. "On the Origin of Gender Roles: Women and the Plough." *Quarterly Journal of Economics* 128 (2): 469–530. doi:10.3386/w17098.

Behrman, Jere R. 1988. "Intrahousehold Allocation of Nutrients in Rural India: Are Boys Favored? Do Parents Exhibit Inequality Aversion?" *Oxford Economic Papers* 40 (1): 32–54. www.jstor.org/stable/2663253.

Butler, Judith. 2004. *Undoing Gender.* New York: Psychology Press.

Cole, Steven M., Paula Kantor, Silvia Sarapura, and Surendran Rajaratnam. 2015. *Gender-Transformative Approaches to Address Inequalities in Food, Nutrition and Economic Outcomes in Aquatic Agricultural Systems.* Penang, Malaysia: WorldFish.

Coles, Christopher, and Jonathan Mitchell. 2010. *Gender and Agricultural Value Chains: A Review of Current Knowledge and Practice and Their Policy Implications.* Rome: FAO.

Doss, Cheryl R., and Michael L. Morris. 2001. "How Does Gender Affect the Adoption of Agricultural Innovations? The Case of Improved Maize Technology in Ghana." *Agricultural Economics* 25 (1): 27–39. doi:10.1016/S0169-5150(00)00096-7.

England, Paula. 2010. "The Gender Revolution: Uneven and Stalled." *Gender & Society* 24 (2): 149–66.

Evans, Alice. 2014. "'Women Can Do What Men Can Do': The Causes and Consequences of Growing Flexibility in Gender Divisions of Labour in Kitwe, Zambia." *Journal of Southern African Studies* 40 (5): 981–98.

FAO (Food and Agriculture Organization of the United Nations). 2011. *The State of Food and Agriculture 2010–11: Women in Agriculture: Closing the Gender Gap for Development.* Rome: FAO. www.fao.org/docrep/013/i2050e/i2050e00.htm.

FAO, IFAD (International Fund for Agricultural Development), and WFP (World Food Programme). 2015. *The State of Food Insecurity in the World 2015: Meeting the 2015 International Hunger Targets: Taking Stock of Uneven Progress.* Rome: FAO.

Folbre, Nancy. 2006. "Measuring Care: Gender, Empowerment, and the Care Economy." *Journal of Human Development* 7 (2): 183–99.

Gittelsohn, Joel. 1991. "Opening the Box: Intrahousehold Food Allocation in Rural Nepal." *Social Science & Medicine* 33 (10): 1141–54. doi:10.1016/0277-9536(91)90230-A.

IDS (Institute of Development Studies). 2014. *Gender and Food Security: Towards Gender-Just Food and Nutrition Security.* Sussex, UK: IDS.

Kabeer, Naila. 2012. *Women's Economic Empowerment and Inclusive Growth: Labour Markets and Enterprise Development.* SIG Working Paper 2012/1. London, UK: Department for International Development (DFID) and Ottawa, Canada: International Development Research Centre (IDRC) – Supporting Inclusive Growth (SIG) program.

Kandiyoti, Deniz. 1988. "Bargaining with Patriarchy." *Gender & Society* 2 (3): 274–90.

Kantor, Paula. 2013. *Transforming Gender Relations: Key to Positive Development Outcomes in Aquatic Agricultural Systems.* Brief AAS-2013-12, CGIAR Research Program on Aquatic Agricultural Systems.

Kinkingninhoun-Mêdagbé, Florent M., Aliou Diagne, Franklin Simtowe, Afiavi Agboh-Noameshie, and Patrice Ygué Adegbola. 2010. "Gender Discrimination and its Impact on Income, Productivity and Technical Efficiency: Evidence from Benin." *Agriculture and Human Values* 27 (1): 57–69. doi:10.1007/s10460-008-9170-9.

Lannotti, Lora L., Miguel Robles, Helena Pachón, and Christina Chiarella. 2012. "Food Prices and Poverty Negatively Affect Micronutrient Intakes in Guatemala." *Journal of Nutrition* 142 (8): 1568–76. doi:10.3945/jn.111.157321.

Njuki, Jemimah, and Pascal Sanginga. 2013. *Women, Livestock Ownership and Markets: Bridging the Gender Gap in Eastern and Southern Africa.* London, UK: Routledge and Ottawa, Canada: International Development Research Centre (IDRC).

Patel, Rajeev C. 2012. "Food Sovereignty: Power, Gender, and the Right to Food." *PLOS Med* 9 (6): e1001223. doi:10.1371/journal.pmed.1001223.

Peterman, Amber, Julia Behrman, and Agnes R. Quisumbing. 2010. *A Review of Empirical Evidence on Gender Differences in Nonland Agricultural Inputs, Technology, and Services in Developing Countries.* IFPRI Discussion Paper 975. Washington, DC: International Food Policy Research Institute (IFPRI).

Quisumbing, Agnes R. 1996. "Male-Female Differences in Agricultural Productivity: Methodological Issues and Empirical Evidence." *World Development* 24 (10): 1579–95.

Quisumbing, Agnes R., and John A. Maluccio. 2003. "Resources at Marriage and Intrahousehold Allocation: Evidence from Bangladesh, Ethiopia, Indonesia, and South Africa." *Oxford Bulletin of Economics and Statistics* 65 (3): 283–327. doi:10.1111/1468-0084.t01-1-00052.

Smith, Lisa C., Usha Ramakrishnan, Aida Ndiaye, Lawrence Haddad, and Reynaldo Martorell. 2003. *The Importance of Women's Status for Child Nutrition in Developing Countries.* IFPRI Research Report 131. Washington, DC: International Food Policy Research Institute (IFPRI).

Thomas, Duncan. 1990. "Intra-Household Resource Allocation: An Inferential Approach." *Journal of Human Resources* 25 (4): 635–64. doi:10.2307/145670.

USAID (United States Agency for International Development). 2005. *Enhancing Women's Access to Markets: An Overview of Donor Programs and Best Practices.* Washington, DC: USAID.

World Bank. 2011. *World Development Report: Promoting Gender Equality and Women's Empowerment.* Washington, DC: World Bank Group.

World Bank. 2014. *Levelling the Playing Field: Improving Opportunities for Women Farmers in Africa.* Washington, DC: World Bank Group.

World Food Summit. 1996. *World Food Summit Plan of Action.* Adopted at the World Food Summit, Rome, 13–17 November 1996. Rome: FAO.

Part I

Measuring gender relations and women's empowerment

1 Measuring women's empowerment in agriculture

Addressing the multidimensional nature of gender dynamics in agriculture

Maureen Miruka, Jemimah Njuki,
Laurie Starr, Elizabeth Kruger, and
Emily Hillenbrand

Introduction

Gender inequalities continue to undermine the sustainable and inclusive development of the agriculture sector, causing disparities in development outcomes between women and men. These are largely due to the fact that rural women are often constrained by unequal access to productive resources and services, even though evidence has shown that when women control income, they spend more of it on food, health, clothing, and education for their children than men do (FAO 2011). The limitations women face in turn impose huge social, economic, and environmental costs on society as a whole and on rural development in particular, including lags in agricultural productivity (Hill 2011). The World Economic Forum's *Global Gender Gap Report 2013* (World Economic Forum 2013) shows that productivity on women's farms is significantly lower per hectare compared to men's, ranging from 13 percent in Uganda to 25 percent in Malawi. In a bid to address this gender gap, women's empowerment in agriculture and its measurement has been a focus of many research and development organisations in the recent past, and the development of tools and methods for measuring women's empowerment has therefore been growing.

Women are clearly an important part of the agricultural labour force, but agriculture and agricultural value chains are equally important to women as a source of food and employment. Aggregate data show that women represent about 43 percent of the agricultural labour force globally and in developing countries (FAO 2011). In Africa, estimates of the time contribution of women to agricultural activities are as high as 60 to 80 percent in some countries (FAO 2011). Improvements in the status of women, both within and outside the household, are of vital importance to ensure better nutritional outcomes in general and to reduce child malnutrition in particular

(Meinzen-Dick et al. 2012). Worldwide data further indicate that if women had the same access to productive resources as men, they could increase yields on their farms by 20 to 30 percent (FAO 2011). That fact alone could raise total agricultural output in developing countries by 2.5 to 4 percent and reduce the number of hungry people in the world by 100 to 150 million. This demonstrates the critical need for addressing gender inequalities and women's empowerment in agriculture as a matter of food and nutrition security.

The most recent development in the measurement of women's empowerment is the Women's Empowerment in Agriculture Index (WEAI) developed for the Feed the Future program (Alkire et al. 2012; Alkire et al. 2013). It provides a quantifiable index to measure women's empowerment in agriculture programs. The WEAI measures the empowerment, agency, and inclusion of women in the agriculture sector in an effort to identify ways to overcome obstacles and constraints. This index is a significant innovation in its field and aims to increase understanding of the connections between women's empowerment, food security, and agricultural growth. It allows the identification of women who are disempowered, and informs interventions to increase autonomy and decision-making in key areas. The WEAI measures the roles and extent of women's engagement in the agriculture sector in five domains: (1) decisions about agricultural production, (2) access to and decision-making power over productive resources, (3) control over use of income, (4) leadership in the community, and (5) time use. It also measures women's empowerment relative to that of men within their households.

While the WEAI captures many of the fundamental gender inequalities in the agriculture sector, it does not fully reflect the holistic and strategic approach to empowerment reflected in the Cooperative for Assistance and Relief Everywhere's (CARE) theoretical understanding – particularly the definitions of autonomy, self-confidence, mobility, and gender-equitable attitudes – that reflect the agency and structural levels of empowerment relevant to a market-oriented model for empowerment in agriculture. In 2012, CARE, in collaboration with Technical Assistance to non-governmental organisations (TANGO) International, combined the WEAI and the CARE Women's Empowerment Framework to develop an adapted index (the Women's Empowerment Index, or WEI) that captures these individual and social dimensions of women's empowerment. The CARE Women's Empowerment Framework recognises the role of gender transformative approaches that not only change women's agency, but also influence the relations between men and women and between women and the broader society, and that engage men as agents of change in achieving gender equality.

Theoretical background

Defining and measuring women's empowerment

Kabeer (1999) defines empowerment as the process by which those who have been denied the ability to make strategic life choices acquire that ability. This ability to exercise choice has three interrelated dimensions: (1) *resources*, which are a precondition for people to make choices, (2) *agency*, or the process through which people get the ability to define their goals and act upon them, and (3) *achievements*, or the outcomes of those choices. A major contribution of Kabeer's definition of empowerment that has implications for how women's empowerment is defined and measured is the distinction between "differences" and "inequality" – preferences in choices vs. the denial of choice. Sen (1985) refers to empowerment as capabilities, or the potential that people have for living the lives they want. CARE defines women's empowerment as the sum total of changes needed for a woman to realise her full human rights – the interplay of changes in *agency* (her own aspirations and capabilities), *structure* (the environment that surrounds and conditions her choices), and *relations* (the power relations through which she negotiates her path) (CARE 2006).

The conceptualisation of women's empowerment as not just a social justice issue and an end in itself, but also as an instrumental concept that has policy and development implications, has led to efforts to measure it. This instrumentalisation of empowerment has sparked a proliferation of studies, methods, and approaches to measure empowerment with the aim of facilitating comparisons of empowerment across locations or over time, measuring impacts of different interventions on empowerment, and relating empowerment to broader policy and development outcomes. There are two main ways in which women's empowerment has been measured: using indicators of basic needs achievements such as education, political participation, etc.; and using indices that combine multiple aspects of empowerment (such as the Human Development Index or the Gender Empowerment Index used by the United Nations Development Program).

Pertinent to the results presented in this chapter, Narayan (2005), Kabeer (1999), and Ibrahim and Alkire (2007) point to the complexity of measuring empowerment. Challenges include the multidimensional nature of empowerment; the multiplicity of indicators that can be used as proxies for empowerment, and their validity; balancing the need to adjust for context and the need to standardise; and which definition of empowerment to use (the researcher's or the subject's).

Women's empowerment, agriculture productivity, and food security

There are various pathways to improving food and nutrition security: through increasing agricultural production and productivity that leads to an increase in food availability and a reduction in food prices; increasing incomes and therefore people's purchasing power; and empowering women (World Bank 2014). Women's empowerment has been associated with various development outcomes. A cross-country study of developing countries covering the period 1970–95 found that 43 percent of the reduction of hunger that occurred was attributable to progress in women's education.

This was almost as much as the combined effect of increased food availability (26 percent) and improvements to the health environment (19 percent) during that period. An additional 12 percent of the reduction of hunger was attributable to increased life expectancy of women. Thus, fully 55 percent of the gains against hunger in these countries during those 25 years were due to the improvement of women's situation within society (Smith and Haddad 2000).

Various studies have also shown positive associations between such indicators as women's education and children's health outcomes such as height, weight, or immunisation (Dwyer and Bruce 1988; Hobcraft 1993; Buvinic and Valenzuela 1996; Haddad et al. 1997; Quisumbing and Maluccio 2003; Pitt et al. 2006). Studies by Doss (2005), the Organisation for Economic Co-operation and Development (OECD 2010), and the International Center for Research on Women (ICRW 2006) have shown that women's ownership of property can to lead to improved children's welfare. The OECD's Development Centre noted that countries where women lack the right to own land have, on average, 60 percent more malnourished children compared to countries where women have some or equal access to credit and land. This demonstrates that there is clearly a relationship between women's control of assets, their share in decision-making power within the household, and nutritional outcomes (OECD 2010).

Methodology

The CARE Pathways Program

The goal of CARE's Pathways to Empowerment Program (Pathways) is to increase the productivity and empowerment of poor women smallholder farmers in more equitable agriculture systems at scale. The program works with 50,000 poor women smallholder farmers and others in their households and communities in six countries (Mali, Ghana, Tanzania, Malawi, Bangladesh, and India). It is guided by a unifying theory of change focused on five change levers: increased capacity and skills of women smallholders; expanded access to services, assets, and inputs; increased productivity; greater influence over household decisions; and a more enabling environment for gender equity, both within communities and in extension and market systems.

Adapting the WEAI to CARE Pathways' theory of change

CARE has developed a model of women's empowerment that recognises empowerment as a dynamic function of changes in three dimensions: *agency*, the skills, capacities, and confidence to act in one's own interest and meet one's own aspirations; *relations*, the gender rules that govern the interpersonal relationships (within and without the household) that mediate women's ability to make choices, access resources, and take advantage of opportunities; and *structures*, the institutional rules – including informal social norms as well as formal rules of institutions (such as land laws, lending institutions, or extension systems) – that condition women's choices (CARE 2006). This model of social change retains a political focus on shifting power, not only in supporting the individual's ability to make (autonomous) choices, but in challenging and changing the institutional context that restricts women's opportunities and underpins their social subordination.

To ensure that sectoral programming focuses on a holistic expansion of women's strategic life choices, CARE identified a number of core "areas of inquiry" that reflect critical areas in women's lives where gender rules and norms disfavour and limit their choices, capacities, and rights. As each program is designed, gender analysis is carried out across these core areas of inquiry to conceptualise how programmatic models (affecting agency, structure, and relations) would bring about outcomes in these areas. These core areas then become the indicators by which empowerment outcomes are measured.

The eight core areas defined by CARE are: (1) gendered division of labour, (2) household decision-making, (3) control over productive assets, (4) access to public spaces and services, (5) claiming rights and meaningful participation in public decision-making, (6) control over one's body, (7) violence and restorative justice (gender-based violence), and (8) aspirations for oneself. Drawing from CARE's core areas of inquiry and women's empowerment, the WEI was designed and constructed in collaboration with TANGO International to ensure that it aligns with CARE Pathways' theory of change.

CARE's WEI includes 13 indicators nested within five domains of empowerment: (1) production, (2) resources, (3) income, (4) leadership and community, and (5) autonomy. Each of the five domains contributes to 20 percent of the overall index score, similar to the WEAI's five domains of empowerment (5DE) sub-index. The individual weights of the 13 indicators vary depending on how many indicators fall within a domain. For example, because of the importance of women's control over household income and expenditures, the single indicator within the income domain carries a weight of 10 percent. In contrast, the leadership/community domain contains four indicators, and each contributes 5 percent to the overall WEI score. Table 1.1 displays the weight for each of the 13 indicators. Each indicator has a threshold of achievement. If achieved, the indicator's weighted value is added to an individual's empowerment score. Modelling the WEAI, empowerment is considered achieved if the overall index score is 0.80 or greater.

A second key feature of CARE's WEI is the adjustment of indicator thresholds to country-specific values. Gender roles and relations differ depending on context; thus, indicator thresholds were contextualised by country to reflect these differences. Although there is a trade-off to this modification – direct comparisons of the aggregate index values across countries are not possible without resetting thresholds to common values – CARE believed it was more important to have strong, country-specific values for diagnostic purposes, and to track country-specific improvements over time than it was to have identical metrics for all six countries.

Table 1.1 Women's empowerment indicator weights for the CARE Pathways
Program

Domain	Indicator	Weight (%)
Production (20%)	Decision-making input for household productive decisions	10
	Autonomy in household production	10
Resources (20%)	Sole or joint ownership of household assets[a]	6.67
	Sole or joint control over purchase or sale of household assets[a]	6.67
	Access to and decisions on credit	6.67
Income (20%)	Sole or joint control over household income and expenditures[b]	20
Leadership & community (20%)	Participation in formal and informal groups	5
	Confident speaking about gender and other community issues at the local level	5
	Expressing self-confidence	5
	Demonstrating political participation	5
Autonomy (20%)	Satisfied with the amount of time available for leisure activities	6.67
	Mobility	6.67
	Expressing attitudes that support gender-equitable roles in family life★	6.67
Total		100

a Excluding poultry, small consumer durables, and non-mechanised farm equipment as modelled in the WEAI.
b Excluding minor household expenditures as modelled in the WEAI.
★ This indicator not included for Bangladesh.

Data collection and analysis

Data were collected from the regions or areas in the six countries where the program is implemented (Table 1.2). These regions were generally selected based on their suitability for production of project-selected crops and livestock, presence of other CARE programs, and potential for impact on agriculture-, value chain-, and gender-related interventions. Data were collected between July and November 2012 using a mixed-methods approach comprising both quantitative and qualitative research. The quantitative research offers statistically representative results for household and individual level indicators to allow for a pre–post comparison of project results.

Quantitative surveys: The sample frame for the quantitative survey comprised all households that included a female member of a collective[1] with which Pathways was working. In five of the six countries, the studies used a two-stage selection process to randomly sample households;[2] clusters were first randomly selected from the overall operational area using probability

Table 1.2 Sample sizes for quantitative and qualitative studies in six Pathways Program countries

	Malawi	Tanzania	Ghana	Mali	Bangladesh	India	Total
District/region	Dowa, Kasungu	Masasi, Nachingwea	Garu–Tempane	Mopti, Segou	Nilphamari, Rangpur	Kalahandi, Kandhamal	
# of households sampled	763	849	175	785	454	923	3,949
# of FGDs conducted	36	36	12	36	40	48	208

proportionate to size based on female membership in collectives. In the second stage, female collective members were randomly chosen from each sampled cluster.[3] In each country, the qualitative sample of communities was a subset of the quantitative sample, maximising diversity along relevant criteria and varying by country context.

Qualitative methods: The qualitative research used a diverse combination of participatory methods and tools, including focus group discussions (FGDs) with women and men, key informant/stakeholder interviews, seasonal calendars, 24-hour time allocation analyses, and Venn diagrams. The findings provide complementary information on social and cultural norms that influence women's empowerment and power relationships within the household and society, shaping poor women's ability to actively engage in and have control over household decisions relating to food consumption or health and nutrition issues.

Finally, CARE Pathways elected to analyse gender parity at the indicator level, rather than include an aggregate gender parity index component in the WEI. Data were collected and empowerment scores tabulated for women and men in all dual-adult households where both sexes agreed to take part in the survey. Statistically significant differences between sexes were determined using t-tests, and results were examined for each of the 13 indicators. The WEAI comprises two indices: the 5DE, which contributes 90 percent of the overall index, and the Gender Parity Index (GPI), which contributes 10 percent to the overall index. The WEI uses only the 5DE scores.

The 5DE is calculated using the following formula:

$$5DE = H_e + H_dA_e = (1 - H_dA)$$

where H_e is the percentage of empowered women, H_d is the percentage of disempowered women, and A_e is the average absolute empowerment score among the disempowered.

Results

Characteristics of households

A relatively large number of households in the Pathways countries are headed by females (Table 1.3), with Tanzania (33 percent), Malawi (25 percent), and India (23 percent) showing higher figures than Mali, Bangladesh, and Ghana. Although these figures are not statistically significant, in Tanzania, a comparatively higher number of females reported being single (7 percent), and the divorce rate reported by Village Savings and Loans Association (VSLA) members (16 percent) is almost double that of Malawi (7 percent), while divorce in India, Ghana, and Mali is almost non-existent.

Households appear to be largest in Mali (11 members on average), a country that also reports the greatest number of females in a household

Table 1.3 Household characteristics in six Pathways Program countries

	Malawi	Tanzania	Ghana	Mali	Bangladesh	India
%						
Female-headed households	24.8	33.0	16.8	9.8	11.7	22.6
N	189	265	29	74	53	209
Mean						
Number of household members	5.1★	4.1	6.4★	10.7★	4.1★	4.5★
Number of females in household	2.6	2.3	3.1	5.8	2.1	2.3
Number of females engaged in agricultural activities	1.5	1.3	1.1	3.0	0.1	1.2
Age of head of household	43.0	49.3	49.5	53.6	37.9	46.1
Educational achievement by household	79.3	82.8★	0.0ᵃ	40.0	11.0	53.7★
N	763	803	173	779	454	925

★ Significantly different between male- and female-headed households within individual countries at p < 0.10.
a The Ghana data set contained no data points for male household heads for the variable "literacy", thus reported data are only for the very small sample of female household heads.

(almost six), two to three more than any other country in the Pathways portfolio; the smallest households are in Bangladesh (four members on average). This could be due to the high prevalence of polygamy, as Mali data also show the greatest number of females within each household who are engaged in agricultural activities, also likely related to the 48 percent of Malian female respondents who reported they are in polygamous marriages. Bangladeshi households report fewer than one female household member who is engaged in agricultural activities.

Literacy levels are highest in Tanzania, at 82.8 percent, followed by Malawi at 79.3 percent, India at 53.7 percent, Mali at 40 percent, Bangladesh at 11 percent, and Ghana at 0 percent. This is likely because Tanzania and Malawi have the highest numbers of primary (elementary) school level educated households, while Mali, for instance, has the highest number of people that have adult education. The Ghana data set contains no data points for male household heads for the variable "literacy"; thus, reported data are only for the very small sample of female household heads, with 71.5 percent having no education at all. Data disaggregated by sex show statistical differences in literacy levels between male- and female-headed households in

Tanzania (84.8 percent male and 78.5 percent female at p < 0.05), Mali (43.6 percent male and 8.6 percent female at p < 0.001), and India (with 61.1 percent male and 28.2 percent female at p < 0.05) with male-headed households reporting higher literacy levels.

Women's empowerment scores across countries

The WEI score for women's empowerment ranges from lows of 0.29 in Bangladesh and 0.32 in Mali to a high of 0.62 in Malawi (Table 1.4). According to this index, fewer than 1 percent of all women surveyed in Bangladesh and fewer than 5 percent of women surveyed in Ghana, Mali, and India are considered to be empowered. Even in Malawi, the country with the highest score, only 23 percent of women surveyed are considered to be empowered.

Women in different countries have different concepts of what empowerment means for them. In Tanzania, women consider their empowerment as an improvement of their living standards through access to loans and agricultural inputs (for example, fertilisers, tractors), and improved knowledge in agriculture, livestock, and business. In India, women in FGDs defined empowerment as education on the status of women, their ability to work together (unity) (for example, through self-help groups), a greater capacity to speak out on issues of concern to them, a more suitable atmosphere for females in households, and a variety of infrastructural needs relating to latrines, transportation, clean water, and electricity.

Table 1.4 Women's five domains of empowerment (5DE) scores in six Pathways Program countries

	Baseline value					
	Malawi	Tanzania	Ghana	Mali	Bangladesh	India
5DE score	0.66	0.58	0.47	0.32	0.29	—
	Female respondents					
% of women achieving empowerment = or > 0.80	23.2★	13.1★	1.7★	2.2★	0.0	4.4★
Mean empowerment score for all women	0.62★	0.57★	0.47★	0.32★	0.29	0.45
N	763	819	173	776	454	924
Mean empowerment score for disempowered women	0.53★	0.50	0.46★	0.31★	0.29	0.43★
N	586	712	170	759	453	924

★ Significantly different between women in male- and female-headed households within individual countries at p < 0.10.

Combining data on women living in male- and female-headed house-holds can give a skewed picture and mask the intrahousehold dynamics that influence their empowerment. A country-by-country analysis revealed that, with the exception of Bangladesh, women living in female-headed households had significantly higher empowerment scores than women in male-headed households. For example, in Tanzania and Malawi, only 4 percent and 11 percent, respectively, of women in male-headed house-holds are considered to be empowered, compared to 33 percent and 60 percent, respectively, of women residing in female-headed households (p < 0.001); while in India, 0.01 percent of women living in male-headed households are considered to be empowered compared to 17 percent of women in female-headed households (p < 0.05). Country-by-country results are shown in Table 1.5.

Qualitative data from FGDs held with women reveal that there are imbalances in empowerment at the household level, with men being the main decision-makers in all important areas. For example, the women felt that they are "underneath" men (Tanzania) and that men have "supreme power" over decision-making (India). In Ghana and Mali, men decide on such critical points as family size, obtaining and use of loans, major asset control, and land preparation and cropping decisions. In Malawi and Bangladesh, women are paid far less than men for the same kind of work.

Assessing achievements across domains

The production domain

The production domain consists of two main indicators: decision-making inputs in household productive decisions, and autonomy in household pro-duction. CARE defines women's "control" as women's authority to make sole or joint decisions. The *input in productive decisions* indicator therefore means sole or joint decision-making over food and cash crop farming, livestock, and fisheries, while *autonomy in production* (for example, what inputs to buy, what crops to grow, what livestock to raise, and so on) reflects the extent to which the respondent's motivation for decision-making reflects his or her values rather than a desire to please others or avoid harm (Alkire et al. 2012). As shown in Figure 1.1, Bangladesh had the highest percentage of women (77.3 percent) with decision-making input for at least 20 percent of all household production decisions, while Mali had the lowest at 36.6 percent. However, it is interesting to note that at 13.8 percent, Bangladesh has the lowest percentage of women with autonomy in one or more production domains, while Malawi has the highest at 40.4 percent, and a relatively high score for input decision-making (after Bangladesh). These results may mean that for Bangladesh and India, for instance, most decisions are jointly, rather than individually, made by women. Data support these findings and show that the number of women with decision-making roles on type of crop and live-stock production is highest in Malawi (74 percent), followed by Tanzania

Table 1.5 Empowerment and disempowerment scores by country for women in male- and female-headed households

	Malawi		Tanzania		Ghana		Mali		Bangladesh		India	
	MHH[a]	FHH[b]	MHH	FHH	MHH	FHH	MHH	FHH	MHH	FHH	MHH	FHH
% of women achieving empowerment = or > 0.80	11.2**	59.8**	3.6**	32.8**	1.4	17.2	0.7**	14.8	0.0	1.9	0.01*	16.75
Mean empowerment score for all women	0.56**	0.79**	0.50**	0.74**	0.42	0.64	0.29**	0.58	0.28	0.36	0.41*	0.60
N	574	189	553	266	144	29	695	81	401	53	715	209
Mean empowerment score for disempowered women	0.52**	0.61**	0.45	0.68	0.41	0.59	0.29**	0.53	0.28	0.35	0.41*	0.54
N	510	76	534	178	142	24	690	69	401	52	715	209

a MHH: male-headed household.
b FHH: female-headed household.
* Significantly different at p < 0.05.
** Means/percentages are significantly different at p < 0.001.

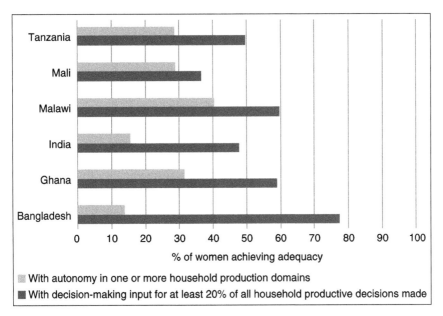

Figure 1.1 Proportion of women achieving adequacy in the production domain in six Pathways Program countries

(66.3 percent), then Ghana and India (45 percent each), and is lowest in Mali (26.8 percent).

At 62 percent, Tanzania has the largest proportion of women who achieved the country-specific threshold set for sole or joint control over agricultural income and expenditures; Mali has the smallest proportion (13 percent). Data also suggest that women in Malawi, Ghana, Mali, and India have fairly restricted control over agricultural assets (Table 1.6), while control over these assets appears to be more equitable in Tanzania and Bangladesh. Included in the decision-making domain of *agricultural assets* are agricultural land, small and large livestock, and mechanised and non-mechanised farm and fishing equipment.

The series of questions for most WEI instances is framed to include not just women who make sole decisions, but those involved in joint decisions as well. Therefore, there is likely wide variation among individual women as to how much of their input might be considered a joint decision. Indeed, qualitative findings suggest that the disparity is far greater than quantitative data indicate. For example, in Malawi, FGD participants relate that there is a general distrust (among both men and women) of women's ability to make the right decisions with regard to cash management, market negotiations, or choosing the right products. In Tanzania, according to FGDs, men control cash crops, sale of food crops, and livestock. Women typically control land only if they are widowed, otherwise their husbands hold the

Table 1.6 Women's control over agricultural income and expenditures in six
Pathways Program countries

	Malawi	Tanzania	Ghana	Mali	Bangladesh	India
	%					
Women with sole or joint control over agricultural income and expenditures	55.5★	62.1★	18.5[a]	13.4★	59.9	49.3★
N	760	816	173	761	167	890

★ Significantly different between women living in male- and female-headed households (MHH and FHH) within individual countries at p < 0.001.
a Sample of female-headed households too small to conduct statistical tests between MHH and FHH.

rights to land and feel entitled to sell the women's produce. FGD input from Bangladesh shows that although a few women may have some say in live-stock decisions, men control the purchasing, selling, and feeding decisions related to livestock. The prevalence of decision-making questions means that female-only households are likely to be identified as empowered (although there may be others, such as parents, in-laws, or children, with whom such women also need to negotiate) (Alkire et al. 2013). To address this potential challenge, the autonomy indicator, unlike decision-making indicators, captures the situation of women living in female-only households, who may indeed be empowered as sole decision-makers but whose autonomy may still be severely constrained by social norms or force of circumstance (Alkire et al. 2013). It also reflects the situation in joint households, where a joint decision may be more or less autonomous, depending on circumstances.

These findings are consistent with a recent report by the World Economic Forum (2013) conducted in six sub-Saharan African countries, which found that even though women make up a large proportion of Africa's farmers, they tend to be locked out of land ownership; access to credit and productive farm inputs like fertilisers, pesticides, and farming tools; support from extension services; and access to markets and other factors essential to their productivity. The report also found that equal access to resources such as fertiliser, farm labour, and training does not always translate into equal returns for women farmers.

Malapit and Quisumbing (2014) find that, in Ghana, a higher score in the production domain of the WEAI is associated with improvements in infants' and young children's diet.

Resources

The resources domain uses three indicators: women with sole or joint ownership of household assets, sole or joint control over purchase or sale of

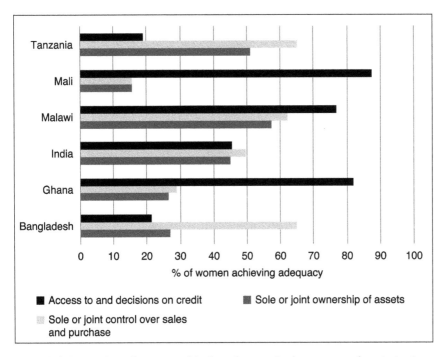

Figure 1.2 Proportion of women achieving adequacy in the resources domain in six
Pathways Program countries

household assets, and access to and decisions on credit. As with the other
indicators, a different threshold is used for each country. In Tanzania and
Bangladesh, the largest contribution to achievement in this domain is the
sole or joint control over sales and purchases, while in Mali, Malawi, and
Ghana, the countries where VSLAs are most entrenched, the largest contribution is from access to and decisions on credit. In India, the contribution
from the three indicators was almost equal (Figure 1.2).

While the quantitative data show medium to high ownership of resources
and decision-making on sale and purchase across countries, the qualitative data suggest that women's control over household assets depends on
whether a woman resides in a male- or female-headed household: women in
female-headed households have more control over assets than do women
in male-headed households. FGD findings suggest that while many assets
may be referred to as jointly owned by husband and wife, control of these
assets is asymmetrically connected to gender identities. Participants in Mali
reported that large assets such as land and livestock, as well as smaller items
such as bicycles and radios, are the exclusive domain of men, who keep
full control of any income that may derive from them – or, in the case of
land, what to grow on it. Small consumer items, such as the tools and utensils
used to prepare food, were often categorised as belonging to women.

The highest access to and control over loans is reported in Mali, Malawi, and Ghana, countries that have a long history of VSLAs. In India, women's access to credit through self-help groups (SHGs) is broadly understood by both men and women as supporting income-generating activities and reacting to emergencies, including medical needs. The majority of women indicate using their own savings as well as credit from VSLAs or SHGs to support agricultural activities in the 12 months prior to the study. Qualitative results suggest that vast gender disparity exists for women who wish to obtain agricultural loans, and also imply that lending terms preclude most women from obtaining loans. In Malawi, FGD participants mentioned that local microfinance institutions (MFIs) focus on well-to-do businesspersons; furthermore, a woman seeking a loan must have her husband's consent even if she owns the collateral.

Control over loans is defined as having sole determination regarding how the borrowed capital is used. In India, men have significantly greater control than do women over access to and use of loans, and two out of three men used loans for income-generating purposes. For women, about 70 percent of the women made sole or joint decisions on whether to take out a loan, while about 80 percent made sole or joint decisions on the use of the loan.

While women made some autonomous decisions on the use of their loans, there were indicators across countries that in many cases, women did not have control of these loans. In Malawi, women indicated investing in small businesses but also giving up a large part of the loan to their husbands. A study in Bangladesh showed that while women retained full or significant control of loan use in 37 percent of cases, in 43 percent of cases they had limited or no control of loan use. More worrying was that in 22 percent of cases, women borrowers could not provide details of loan use, or were unaware of how their husbands or other male household members had used the loans (Goetz and Sen Gupta 1996). Another study in Andhra Pradesh, India, found that 67 percent of women's loans were invested in assets or businesses controlled by their husbands. In 82 to 88 percent of those cases, women had to engage in wage labour to make repayments (Garikipati 2008).

Generally, while credit can be an empowering resource for women, it can end up being less empowering if women do not have control over its use, even as the household's situation improves through diversification of livelihoods – a result Garikipati (2008, 2010) refers to as "impact paradox".

The ownership of resources, particularly assets, has been associated with multiple development outcomes, including child nutrition. Malapit and Quisumbing (2014) find that, in Ghana, the resource domain of the WEAI has an impact on per-adult equivalent calorie availability and household dietary diversity. Regression results from an earlier study using data from a Bangladesh household survey showed that women's decision-making on credit and their ownership of assets are positively associated with calorie availability and household dietary diversity (Sraboni et al. 2014). More recent studies show that though women's access to resources is critical for agriculture, even more important is increasing the returns to these assets (O'Sullivan et al. 2014).

Income

The income domain is constituted with only one indicator, the sole or joint control of household income and expenditures. Women's control over income is critical for household well-being. The data (Figure 1.3) show that the highest percentage of women reporting control over household income and expenditures occurs in Bangladesh (63.4 percent), closely followed by Malawi (58 percent), while the lowest percentage occurs in Mali (18 percent). For Malawi, Tanzania, Mali, and India, there are significant differences in the proportion of women with control over household income and expenditures between women living in male-headed households and women living in female-headed households. For example, in Tanzania, the vast majority (91 percent) of women from female-headed households report having sole or joint control over 60 percent of relevant household decision-making domains. In contrast, only 34 percent of women residing in male-headed households report similar control of household resources.

Across countries, qualitative findings suggest that the disparity in control over household resources is far greater than what quantitative data indicate. In some countries, there are anecdotes about men being better decision-makers than women. However, focus group participants acknowledged that where a woman is the main source of household income, she tends to have

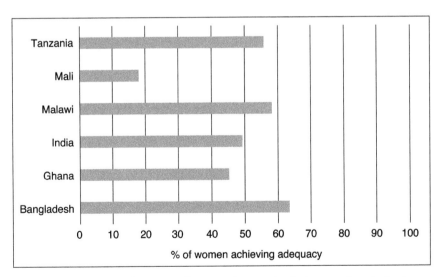

Figure 1.3 Proportion of women achieving adequacy in the income domain in six Pathways Program countries

control over all decisions and resources. Among women, the general perception is that women tend to make decisions that benefit the entire household, whereas men tend to make decisions that are more self-serving. In India, cash crop production is the domain in which women have the least control. This correlates with women's discussion groups indicating that women have little bargaining power, a function in part of their lower access to markets and lack of experience and knowledge in this regard. In Mali, the only areas where at least 50 percent of women had sole or joint decision-making power were in spending income that they had earned themselves or purchasing their own clothes.

Outside VSLA savings and income earned from their vegetable gardens and petty commerce, women have no access to cash. The division of responsibilities in management of livestock is linked to the capacity of each type of animal to generate cash: oxen are rented for transportation or ploughing fields, goats and sheep are sold for meat. Chickens are cared for by women and are mostly used for household consumption; however, women must obtain their husbands' permission to sell a chicken, further emphasising the males' control of cash. For the majority of households, when the husband takes the harvest to the market, the wife will seldom know the amount of sales even though she largely participated in cultivating the crops. The reinforcement of men's role in decision-making has even led women to doubt their decision-making capabilities. An FGD participant in Tanzania put it this way: "Important decisions are made by men. This is because the men are culturally the head of the households and also because women are not capable of making good decisions."

Other studies have shown that women spend over 90 percent of their discretionary income on their families, including food, education, and general well-being. In contrast, only about 40 percent of men's discretionary income is spent on family well-being. A study in Kenya and Malawi showed that not only is household food security influenced by total household income, but the proportion of income controlled by women has a positive and significant influence on household caloric intake (Kennedy and Peters 1992). Haddad and Hoddinott (1994) found similar results in Côte d'Ivoire, where increases in the proportion of cash income accruing to women increased boys' height-for-age relative to that of girls.

Leadership and community

The leadership and community domain is constituted with five indicators: participation in formal and informal groups, women's leadership within these groups, confidence speaking about gender and other community issues at the local level, expressing self-confidence, and demonstrating political participation.

Across the six countries studied, the vast majority of women report participating in at least one formal or informal group in their community

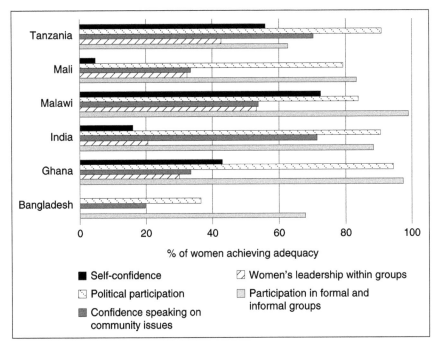

Figure 1.4 Proportion of women achieving adequacy in the leadership and community
domain in six Pathways Program countries

(Figure 1.4). This is not surprising, considering that the criteria for participation in the Pathways Program include membership in a collective. Of women belonging to a group, the percentage holding a leadership position (likely to include those with a designated title and/or defined role or responsibility) is relatively high in Malawi (53 percent) and Tanzania (43 percent). In contrast, just under one-third of surveyed women in Ghana and Mali, and one-fifth of surveyed women in India, state they hold a leadership position. Group membership is deliberately not restricted to formal agriculture-related groups because other types of civic or social groups provide important sources of networks and social capital that are empowering in themselves and may also be an important source of agricultural information or inputs (Alkire et al. 2013; Meinzen-Dick et al. 2014). A 2014 World Bank report reinforces the role of collective action in enhancing women's voice and agency and reducing gender disparities (World Bank 2014). Participation in groups and community processes can enhance women's voice in seeking to change discriminatory social norms. The extent to which women are able to participate in public and community decision-making and make their voices heard is, however, shaped by social norms, the legal framework, and formal and informal institutions.

Women's confidence in speaking about gender and community issues is measured by investigating women's comfort level in speaking about three topics: making decisions on infrastructure, gender issues, and reporting misbehaviour of authorities or elected officials. Women are asked whether they have expressed an opinion in a public meeting in the 12 months prior to the study. Respondents who respond positively to three of the four questions are considered confident in speaking about gender and other community issues at the local level. Close to 70 percent of women in Tanzania and India meet the indicator threshold; slightly more than half do so in Malawi. Approximately one-third of surveyed women are considered confident expressing their opinions in public in Ghana (34 percent) and Mali (33 percent), and fewer than one-fifth (19 percent) are considered so in Bangladesh. Of note is that while the majority of women in India state that they are comfortable speaking up about infrastructure decisions, gender issues, and misbehaviour of authorities or elected officials, only a minority state that they have actually expressed an opinion in a public meeting in the last 12 months. Fewer than 5 percent of surveyed women in Mali and Bangladesh report expressing an opinion in a public meeting in the last 12 months. Alkire et al. (2013) state that although it does not cover the entire range of possibilities for public engagement, this variable provides some indication of the respondent's agency in exerting voice and engaging in collective action.

Focus group findings offer other facets to understanding women's participation in community affairs. For example, in Ghana, although quantitative findings show that a minority of women speak out on the issues asked about in the survey, qualitative information indicates that Ghanaian women feel comfortable publicly addressing topics such as education, health facilities, and water. In India, female FGD participants stated that when issues are discussed at the local level, women sometimes believe they are "rubber stamping" men's opinions. It was observed that in mixed-sex FGDs, women were much less expressive than men and were deferential to men's input; however, in female-only FGDs women robustly expressed their opinions.

Women's self-confidence (their convictions about their skills and capabilities) is measured using a set of questions to which mostly or strongly agreeing with a set number of statements is considered adequate in that indicator. Women's self-confidence appears to be most challenged in Mali and India, and greatest in Malawi and Tanzania. Notably, the Mali baseline had the lowest threshold for achievement of this indicator (agreeing with three of the seven statements). Most of the women from Malawi expressed confidence related to all the statements. Women in Ghana, Mali, and Tanzania indicated being least confident in the topics related to agricultural production (skills, information, resources, and services). It is less common for women to flatly disagree with the statements than to agree; although, with the exception of Malawi, women would frequently respond "no difference", indicating they neither agreed nor disagreed with the statements.

Political participation is measured by examining women's participation in the last parliamentary elections, whether women stand for elected posts, and their participation in local government committees. Political participation was highest in Ghana, Tanzania, and India, and lowest in Bangladesh. While the percentage of women voting in parliamentary elections was very high (the lowest was in Mali at 79.9 percent), women's involvement in local government committees and the proportion of women running for political office was very low (the highest figures were 17.6 percent in Malawi and 9 percent in Tanzania). This is despite evidence showing that the presence of women in parliament can lead to prioritisation of social issues. A study of members of parliament across 110 countries showed that compared to their male counterparts, female parliamentarians were more likely to prioritise social issues such as child care, equal pay, reproductive rights, and development matters such as poverty reduction and service delivery (IPU 2008). In India, Mansuri and Rao (2013) found that women's participation in leadership has positively affected social norms and increased investments in public services. Some of the causes of women's low political participation include discriminatory social norms, weak networks, limited access to campaign financing, lower levels of education, greater family responsibilities, and fewer opportunities for acquiring political experience (World Bank 2014).

Autonomy

Three indicators constitute the autonomy domain: women's satisfaction with the time available for leisure activities, mobility, and expressing attitudes that support gender-equitable roles in family life.

Women in the six countries have approximately two to three hours available each day for leisure activities, such as visiting neighbours, listening to the radio, or playing sports or games. A large majority (79 to 90 percent) of surveyed women in India, Malawi, and Mali report they are satisfied with the amount of leisure time available. While still a majority, fewer women in Tanzania report such satisfaction (69 percent). Surveyed women in Ghana appear least satisfied with the amount of leisure time available.

Alkire et al. (2013) posit that the satisfaction with leisure question is subjective and may reflect adaptive preferences – that is, women may be more satisfied with their leisure than are men because their expectations have adapted to what is possible in their circumstances. Findings from FGDs agree that men have much more time for leisure activities, as well as more opportunities to use their cash to participate in these activities. In India, women reported having no "personal time", while men do have it and tend to go to bed an hour earlier than women. In Malawi, similar findings indicate that men have on average three hours of leisure time a day, compared to women's 2.6 hours. In Tanzania, it emerged that men are perceived to have more time and opportunity for leisure activities than women, and had specified time allocated to "leisure activities" on their daily calendars, while women did not.

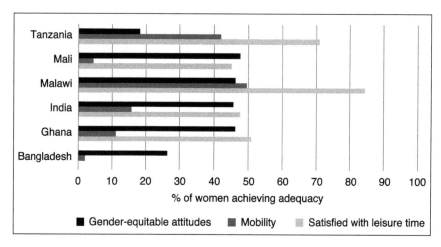

Figure 1.5 Proportion of women achieving adequacy in the autonomy domain in six
        Pathways Program countries

Mobility was measured by asking women if they had to ask permission
from their spouse or another family member to go to ten different locations.
As shown in Figure 1.5, just about half the female respondents in Malawi
and Tanzania are considered to be mobile (49.6 and 42 percent, respectively),
while fewer than one in six meet this threshold in the other Pathways
countries. Among the countries where very few women report mobility, the
percentages range from a high of 16 percent in India to a low of 2 percent
in Bangladesh.

Across all six countries, mobility is significantly greater for women who
reside in a female-headed household than for those who reside in a male-
headed household. In Tanzania, both sexes unanimously indicated that
their communities believe women should ask permission from their partners
to leave the home. In Mali, which had the second lowest mobility score
(after Bangladesh), FGDs show that women's mobility is limited not only
by a lack of personal autonomy but also by a number of other factors,
including care duties, negative attitudes, and lack of travel means and skills.
In India, men say they are generally suspicious of women who leave the
household outside of their regular patterns; one man asserted, "This leaves
a bad impression".

To measure attitudes towards gender-equitable roles in family life,
respondents were asked whether they agreed or disagreed with four statements
that reflect men's and women's roles in family life:

1   Most household decisions should be made by the man.
2   There is men's work and women's work, and the one shouldn't ever do
    the work of the other.

3   If a woman works outside the home, her husband should help with child care and household chores.
4   A husband should spend his free time with his wife and children.

Those who respond towards a more equitable position on all four statements are considered to have attitudes that support gender-equitable roles in family life.

The results show that patriarchal attitudes are somewhat ingrained in women's opinions of their role in family life. Fewer than half of all surveyed women express attitudes supporting gender-equitable roles as defined by this indicator. The highest percentages of women expressing gender-equitable attitudes occur in Ghana, India, Malawi, and Mali (between 46 and 47.5 percent in each country), achieving a score of four. Approximately one-third of women in Tanzania and India achieved a score of four, and only a quarter of Bangladeshi women did so. Only 18 percent of women in Mali voice attitudes supporting gender-equitable roles within the household.

Across all countries, the difference in overall attitudes regarding gender equity stems primarily from women's perceptions regarding who should make household decisions and division of household labour, with women often agreeing with statements 1 and 2 above. In contrast, the majority of surveyed women in all Pathways countries agreed with statements related to men's helping with child care and household chores when a woman works outside the home, and spending time with the family (statements 3 and 4 above). Although these data provide insight on *attitudes* related to gender-equitable roles, they may or may not reflect actual *practice*.

Conclusions

Applied as a baseline, CARE's WEI serves as a diagnostic tool and pointer to specific areas of intervention for Pathways and similar programs seeking to empower women in agricultural programs. The Pathways Program seeks to raise the bar on women's empowerment over a five-year period, and the index will be used to measure performance by indicator at the endline study and therefore contribute to knowledge on its effectiveness and on the adaptability of the WEAI as a benchmarking tool.

The integration and combination of quantitative and qualitative methods helps to optimise the strengths of each method and provides an opportunity to integrate real-life contextual understandings and cultural influences. It gives insights into women's own views and measures of empowerment and how these relate to the index. In most cultures, gender roles are shaped early in life, sometimes on the basis of different levels of physical strength and agility. These and other beliefs around gender roles need to be taken into account when interpreting findings from this and similar studies. The contradiction between qualitative and quantitative data in this study serves to emphasise the importance of combining qualitative and quantitative methods, rather than keeping them separate.

Women's empowerment is a complex and context-specific concept. The role of the WEAI in identifying aspects of empowerment that are important to women in agriculture comes to the fore in this work; but more important is its adaptability to specific country contexts and other dimensions, such as the CARE Women's Empowerment Framework. The resulting WEI used in this study aids the comprehensive measurement of women's empowerment that looks at women's agency as well as social relations, and provides a tool for research and development programs to prioritise interventions to increase women's empowerment for food and nutrition security.

Notes

1 For example, Village Savings and Loans Associations (VSLAs), farming/livestock collectives, or empowerment groups.
2 The Ghana study executed by CARE, rather than TANGO International, used a simple random sample design.
3 Budgetary limitations precluded a stratified sample design that would allow for cross-country comparison; thus, although indicator results from each country baseline are presented in common tables, the reader is cautioned against making such comparisons. No statistical tests were carried out to compare the results between the six countries.

References

All website URLs accessed on 6 April 2016.

Alkire, Sabina, Ruth Meinzen-Dick, Amber Peterman, Agnes R. Quisumbing, Greg Seymour, and Ana Vaz. 2012. *The Women's Empowerment in Agriculture Index.* IFPRI Discussion Paper 1240. Washington, DC: International Food Policy Research Institute (IFPRI).

Alkire, Sabina, Hazel Malapit, Ruth Meinzen-Dick, Amber Peterman, Agnes R. Quisumbing, Greg Seymour, and Ana Vaz. 2013. *Instructional Guide on the Women's Empowerment in Agriculture Index.* www.ifpri.org/sites/default/files/weai_instructionalguide.pdf.

Buvinic, M., and Valenzuela, J.P. 1996. *Investing in Women.* ICRW Policy Series 1992. Washington, DC: International Center for Research on Women (ICRW).

CARE International. 2006. *The Courage to Change: Confronting the Limits and Unleashing the Potential of CARE's Programming for Women.* Synthesis Report: Phase 2. CARE International Strategic Impact Inquiry on Women's Empowerment.

Doss, Cheryl R. 2005. "The Effects of Intrahousehold Property Ownership on Expenditure Patterns in Ghana." *Journal of African Economies* 15 (1): 149–80. doi: 10.1093/jae/eji025.

Dwyer, Daisy, and Judith Bruce, eds. 1988. *A Home Divided: Women and Income in the Third World.* Redwood City, CA: Stanford University Press.

FAO (Food and Agriculture Organization of the United Nations). 2011. *The State of Food and Agriculture 2010–11: Women in Agriculture: Closing the Gender Gap for Development.* Rome: FAO.

Garikipati, Supriya. 2008. "The Impact of Lending to Women on Household Vulnerability and Women's Empowerment: Evidence from India." *World Development* 36 (12): 2620–42.

Garikipati, Supriya. 2010. "Microcredit and Women's Empowerment: Understanding the 'Impact Paradox' with Particular Reference to South India." In S. Chant, ed., *The International Handbook of Gender and Poverty: Concepts, Research, Policy.* Cheltenham, UK: Edward Elgar, 599–605.

Goetz, Anne Marie, and Rina Sen Gupta. 1996. "Who Takes the Credit? Gender, Power, and Control over Loan Use in Rural Credit Programs in Bangladesh." *World Development* 24 (1): 45–63.

Haddad, Lawrence, and John Hoddinott. 1994. "Women's Income and Boy–Girl Anthropometric Status in the Côte d'Ivoire." *World Development* 22 (4): 543–53.

Haddad, Lawrence, John Hoddinott, and Harold Alderman. 1997. *Intrahousehold Resource Allocation: Policy Issues and Research Methods.* Baltimore, MD: Johns Hopkins University Press for the International Food Policy Research Institute (IFPRI).

Hill, Catherine. 2011. *Enabling Rural Women's Economic Empowerment: Institutions, Opportunities and Participation.* Background paper for Expert Group Meeting, Commission on the Status of Women, United Nations Entity for Gender Equality and the Empowerment of Women (UN Women), Accra, Ghana, 20–23 September.

Hobcraft, John. 1993. "Women's Education, Child Welfare and Child Survival: A Review of the Evidence." *Health Transition Review* 3 (2): 159–75.

Ibrahim, Solava, and Sabina Alkire. 2007. *Agency and Empowerment: A Proposal for Internationally Comparable Indicators.* Oxford: Oxford Poverty and Human Development Initiative.

ICRW (International Center for Research on Women). 2006. *Property Ownership and Inheritance Rights of Women for Social Protection: The South Asia Experience Synthesis.* Washington, DC: ICRW.

IPU (Inter-Parliamentary Union). 2008. *Equality in Politics: A Survey of Men and Women in Parliaments.* Geneva: IPU.

Kabeer, Naila. 1999. "Resources, Agency, Achievements: Reflections on the Measurement of Women's Empowerment." *Development and Change* 30: 435–64. doi:10.1111/1467-7660.00125.

Kennedy, Eileen, and Pauline Peters. 1992. "Household Food Security and Child Nutrition: The Interaction of Income and Gender of Household Head." *World Development* 20 (8): 1077–85.

Malapit, Hazel, and Agnes R. Quisumbing. 2014. *What Dimensions of Women's Empowerment in Agriculture Matter for Nutrition-Related Practices and Outcomes in Ghana?* IFPRI Discussion Paper 01367. Washington, DC: International Food Policy Research Institute (IFPRI).

Mansuri, Ghazala, and Vijayendra Rao. 2013. *Localizing Development: Does Participation Work?* World Bank Policy Research Report. Washington, DC: World Bank. doi:10.1596/978-0-8213-8256-1. License: Creative Commons Attribution CC BY 3.0.

Meinzen-Dick, Ruth, Julia A. Behrman, Purnima Menon, and Agnes R. Quisumbing. 2012. "Gender: A Key Dimension Linking Agricultural Programs to Improved Nutrition and Health." In Shenggen Fan and Rajul Pandya-Lorch, eds, *Reshaping Agriculture for Nutrition and Health.* Washington, DC: International Food Policy Research Institute (IFPRI), 135–44.

Meinzen-Dick, Ruth, Julia A. Behrman, Lauren Pandolfelli, Amber Peterman, and Agnes R. Quisumbing. 2014. "Gender and Social Capital for Agricultural Development." In Agnes R. Quisumbing, Ruth Meinzen-Dick, Terri Raney,

André Croppenstedt, Julia A. Behrman, and Amber Peterman, eds, *Gender in Agriculture: Closing the Knowledge Gap.* Dordrecht, The Netherlands/Rome: Springer/Food and Agriculture Organization of the United Nations (FAO), 235–66.

Narayan, Deepa. 2005, *Measuring Empowerment: Cross-Disciplinary Perspectives.* Washington, DC: World Bank.

OECD (Organisation for Economic Co-operation and Development). Development Centre. 2010. *Gender Inequality and the MDGs: What are the Missing Dimensions?* Paris: OECD. www.oecd.org/dev/development-gender/45987065.pdf.

O'Sullivan, Michael, Arathi Rao, Raka Banerjee, Kajal Gulati, and Margaux Vinez. 2014. *Levelling the Field: Improving Opportunities for Women Farmers in Africa.* Washington, DC: World Bank Group and ONE. http://documents.worldbank. org/curated/en/2014/01/19243625/levelling-field-improving-opportunities-women-farmers-africa.

Pitt, Mark, Shahidur Khandker, and Jennifer Cartwright. 2006. "Empowering Women with Micro Finance: Evidence from Bangladesh." *Economic Development and Cultural Change* 54 (4): 791–831. doi:10.1086/503580.

Quisumbing, Agnes R., and John Maluccio. 2003. "Resources at Marriage and Intrahousehold Allocation: Evidence from Bangladesh, Ethiopia, Indonesia, and South Africa." *Oxford Bulletin of Economics and Statistics* 65 (3): 283–328.

Sen, Amartya K. 1985. "Wellbeing, Agency and Freedom." The Dewey Lectures 1984. *Journal of Philosophy* 82 (4): 169–224.

Smith, L.C., and Lawrence Haddad. 2000. *Explaining Child Malnutrition in Developing Countries: A Cross-Country Analysis.* IFPRI Research Report 111. Washington, DC: International Food Policy Research Institute (IFPRI).

Sraboni, Esha, Hazel Malapit, Agnes R. Quisumbing, and Ahmed Akhter. 2014. "Women's Empowerment in Agriculture: What Role for Food Security in Bangladesh?" *World Development* 61 (C): 11–52.

World Bank. 2014. *Voice and Agency: Empowering Women and Girls for Shared Prosperity.* Washington, DC: The World Bank Group.

World Economic Forum. 2013. *The Global Gender Gap Report 2013.* Geneva: World Economic Forum.

Part II

From measurement to action

2 From capture to culture

Space for mainstreaming women in coastal aquaculture development in Sri Lanka

Tim Dejager and Chamila Jayasinghe

Introduction

Aquaculture is growing at a global average annual rate of almost 6 percent, producing 66.6 million tonnes of food fish in 2012, while food fish from capture fisheries remains stagnant at around 90 million tonnes. Thanks largely to aquaculture's contribution to the food fish supply, global per capita fish consumption has doubled since the 1960s. Fish now represent 16.7 percent of the world's total animal protein supply: they provide 2.9 billion people with 20 percent of their animal protein intake, and 4.3 billion people with 15 percent of their animal protein intake. Aquaculture contributes to the livelihoods of nearly 19 million people globally, 84 percent of whom are in Asia (FAO 2014). With all of this growth, little has been done to understand the position of women in these emerging value chains and channel the development of the chains in a gender-equitable manner. In a country like Sri Lanka, where aquaculture has major potential yet remains significantly underdeveloped, there may be a greater opportunity to mainstream gender.

An estimated 650,000 people in Sri Lanka's coastal zones and rural areas depend for their livelihoods on fish production. Of those, approximately 262,500 are directly engaged in marine and inland fishing and aquaculture. According to Ministry of Fisheries and Aquatic Resources Development (MFARD) statistics, in 2012, the fisheries sector contributed 1.8 percent of the country's gross domestic product and generated 31,792,000 Sri Lankan rupees (LKR) (US$246,000)[1] in export earnings, nearly 2.5 percent of the country's total. However, aquaculture contributed only a tiny share of the nearly half a million tonnes of fish Sri Lanka brought to domestic and export markets in 2012 (10,720 out of 486,170 tonnes, a mere 2 percent). Marine capture fisheries, on the other hand, contributed 417,220 tonnes (86 percent), while inland capture fisheries from the country's extensive reservoir system contributed 58,680 tonnes (12 percent). Other countries in the region, such as Bangladesh, have developed aquaculture to such an extent that it now provides half of their total fish production (Belton et al. 2011).

Fish are also vital to food and nutritional security in Sri Lanka. Per capita consumption of fish is high, 10.8 kg per year (2011), providing more than 50 percent of individuals' dietary animal protein as well as essential minor nutrients. MFARD aims to increase this to an annual per capita consumption of 22 kg by 2016. In order to achieve this goal, the ministry has committed to increasing total fish production to 980,400 tonnes by 2016, to which the contribution of inland fisheries and aquaculture is expected to double to 127,300 tonnes (MFARD 2013). This is an ambitious goal given the historical growth of aquaculture in Sri Lanka. While annual growth in inland aquaculture averaged around 20 percent between 2009 and 2012, coastal aquaculture, including shrimp farming, has experienced uneven production, resulting in no growth over the same period. To reach the target of 6,060 tonnes for coastal aquaculture by 2016, an annual growth rate of 20 percent will be necessary.

But aquaculture remains significantly underdeveloped in Sri Lanka, particularly in coastal areas of the Eastern and Northern Provinces and the northern region of the North Western Province. This is largely because of the 30-year civil conflict that the country endured. Hence, the government of Sri Lanka is increasingly emphasising aquaculture as a key means of promoting economic development in coastal areas, increasing food and nutrition security, reducing poverty, and enhancing household income.

Two key considerations arise with respect to gender equity for aquaculture in Sri Lanka: (1) How can these targets, specifically with respect to coastal aquaculture, be reached in a gender-equitable and inclusive manner? (2) Since these opportunities are to be developed largely in the context of fishery communities, will the conditions, roles, and positions of women in the fisheries sector be replicated in aquaculture development, or will they follow a different, more equitable path?

Our approach to addressing these questions was based on gender research conducted in the context of rural and agricultural development, with a particular emphasis on gender analysis of fisheries and aquaculture. We applied what we learned in a case study involving two fishery communities in the Puttalam Lagoon area of Sri Lanka's North Western Province, where our research for development project, under the Canadian International Food Security Research Fund (CIFSRF), initiated pilot-scale coastal oyster farming. In both communities, the opportunity for oyster farming was presented to both women and men interested in participating, and, in the two communities, women were prepared to be engaged in developing the opportunity. The initiative was supported by a private-sector partner, which purchased oysters from the communities and developed the market, and by a government partner, the National Aquatic Resources Research and Development Agency (NARA), which provided research capacity and allocation of lagoon areas for developing oyster aquaculture.

In the analysis and development of these pilot oyster farms, we incorporated three dimensions of gender in aquaculture that we considered critical.

First, the contribution of women to existing fishery value chains and the conditions and contexts in which they support livelihoods and income generation had to be revealed and understood (Woolcock 2000; S.B. Williams et al. 2005; M.J. Williams, Agbayani et al. 2012; M.J. Williams, Porter et al. 2012). In addition to the gender division of labour in the fishery, we wanted to know what technology was available to women, how they accessed and utilised fishery and related resources to support their household – for example, gleaning small near-shore fish or clams – and what decisions they made and how much control they had over income and assets. This would enable us to leverage and enhance their knowledge and social capital towards undertaking aquaculture activities.

Second, it was important to recognise that aquaculture is distinct from fisheries as a food production system. Fisheries is a "capture" system that relies primarily on natural resources such as fish stocks and assets such as boats and nets, while aquaculture is a "culture" system that requires a greater degree of control over inputs and stock (Anderson 2002; Muir 2013). Further, unlike capture fisheries, which have largely stagnated over the past decade or more, aquaculture is undergoing significant growth, especially in developing countries, and in Asia in particular. Hence, the types of activities undertaken, the inputs, knowledge, and skills required, and the development of the value chain and markets could be significantly different from the customary position most women occupy in fishery value chains.

Third, different aquaculture sectors require distinct strategies and approaches to gender mainstreaming, which will also vary depending on the degree of development in the sector. For example, more mature sub-sectors such as shrimp farming require access to resources, capital, and ownership of land, factors that often pose a barrier to women's ownership and management positions. Consequently, the position of women in many shrimp farming value chains is marginalised, and often invisible and undervalued. Women provide unpaid labour on family farms and undervalued labour at the "lower end" of the supply chain, for example in processing factories and collection of shrimp fry for production (Islam 2008). Strategies to improve the condition and position of women in such value chains require a focus on addressing equitable access to land and capital for farming, and more equitable payment for labour provided in the supply chain. Sectors that are new or emerging, such as bivalve aquaculture in coastal Sri Lanka, can provide more space to develop in a gender-equitable manner without having to deconstruct the institutions and relationships built over time in which women have been marginalised or under-represented.

Theoretical perspective

Gender analysis of fisheries and aquaculture lags behind that of agriculture, and, although much has been done since 2000, data on the participation, position, and contribution of women are still relatively scanty (M.J. Williams

2008; Weeratunge et al. 2010). The FAO's 2014 report, *The State of World Fisheries and Aquaculture*, notes,

> The information provided to FAO still lacks sufficient detail to allow full analyses by gender. However, based on the data available, it is estimated that, overall, women accounted for more than 15 percent of all people directly engaged in the fisheries primary sector in 2012. The proportion of women exceeded 20 percent in inland water fishing and is considered far more important, as high as 90 percent, in secondary activities, such as processing.
>
> (FAO 2014: 6)

The same statement appears in the 2012 report, which also includes a special section on mainstreaming gender in fisheries and aquaculture (FAO 2012).

Since the focus of our case studies is on developing aquaculture opportunities in the context of fishery communities, it is important as a first step to understand the role and position of women in capture fishery value chains. Second, we review literature that advocates applying a richer perspective on understanding the contribution of women not just to the value chain but to livelihoods. Third, we consider literature that attempts to distinguish aquaculture from fisheries. Fourth, we look at case studies and analyses specific to aquaculture. Finally, we consider the space for gender mainstreaming for aquaculture development in capture fishery communities and regions.

The role and position of women in capture fishery value chains

Traditionally, capture fisheries have been associated with fish stocks, boats, and fishing gear, and all of these generally associated with men (S.B. Williams et al. 2005; Choo et al. 2006; M.J. Williams 2008). However, in recent years, more attention has been paid to the large number of women involved in a much wider range of activities in fishery value chains (Bennett 2005; Weeratunge et al. 2010; De Silva 2011; Zhao et al. 2013; FAO 2014). What becomes clear from these analyses is that women perform many tasks that are often unpaid, unacknowledged, or undervalued, rendering their contribution and position in the "deck to dish" or "fish to fork" process largely invisible to traditional analysis of capture fisheries. In pre-harvest, women are involved in maintaining fishing gear (for example, cleaning and mending nets) and harvesting non-commercial small fish, shellfish, and aquatic plants in near-shore areas, often with primitive gear and non-motorised boats. In post-harvest, women are involved in marketing and trading, value adding and preserving of fish catches, and extensively in fish processing (Medard et al. 2002; S.B. Williams et al. 2005; M.J. Williams 2008; Veliu et al. 2009; Matthews et al. 2012; M.J. Williams, Agbayani et al. 2012; Kabeer et al. 2013; Zhao et al. 2013).

Data obtained by FAO (2012) confirm the significant level of women's contribution to fisheries: for example, women comprise at least 50 percent of the workforce in inland fisheries, and in Asia and West Africa as much as 60 percent of seafood is marketed by women. FAO estimates women may constitute 30 percent of the employed workforce in fisheries, including primary and secondary activities. However, even this estimate is probably much lower than the real contribution. Defining employment strictly as remuneration for work performed may itself significantly underestimate women's contribution to fishery value chains. Weeratunge et al. (2010: 32) consider employment as

> any activity, occupation, work, business or service performed by force or for remuneration, profit, social or family gain, in cash or kind, including a contract of hire, written or oral, expressed or implied, regardless of whether the activity is performed on a self-directed, part-time, full-time or casual basis.

In this light, "fisheries employment itself begins to look like a female sphere if you account for the roles of gleaning, trading, processing and fish farming."

This is also reflected in the lack of recognition of women as workers in or contributors to fisheries management and policy. Traditional beliefs, social norms, and values, along with inequitable laws and regulations, hinder women fish workers' ability to self-organise, gain access to resources and assets, control resources, and negotiate with different actors in the sector. Therefore, women's participation tends to be confined to the lower end of the supply chain and the informal sector (Weeratunge et al. 2010), and their access to institutional and state support, financing, and capacity-building interventions has been limited. Sri Lanka is no exception to this (De Silva and Yamao 2006; Lokuge 2014). As well, women in the fisheries sector have limited opportunity to influence the decisions that affect their lives, and consequently those decisions are less likely to represent women's interests. Although still rarely implemented, there is a growing recognition of the importance of taking a gendered view of natural resource management in the fisheries sector (Tietze 1995; Diamond et al. 2003).

Women's contribution to livelihoods

In order to bring women's real contribution to light, it is important to understand and reveal the livelihoods interwoven into the social, economic, and environmental contexts within which women work in fisheries value chains (Weeratunge et al. 2010). Simply considering gender division of labour in the value chain is insufficient. This may reveal the extent of women's participation as post-harvest value chain actors, but it ignores other dimensions of women's contribution to fisheries livelihoods. What technology is available to women? How do they utilise fishery resources in the context of maintaining household food security? What decisions do they make in fishery households? What species do they have access to, and what resources do they use to maximise value from what they have access to? Such a "systems" approach is central to revealing and understanding gender in fisheries and opening up pathways for gender equity in its development (M.J. Williams, Porter et al. 2012). The importance of gleaning, for example, is often neglected in gender analysis of fisheries. Women harvesting clams from a lagoon as a source of family food is as important a contribution to sustaining livelihoods as is the capture of fish by nets at sea. The invisibility and exclusion of women in planning and decision-making processes, outcomes, and interventions is "hindering development" (FAO 2012). Furthermore, making the contribution of women visible in such "systems" highlights the social capital available for inclusive development, including that of aquaculture.

Aquaculture as distinct from fisheries

Aquaculture is a very different form of activity from fisheries and draws attention to a distinct set of issues for gender mainstreaming. M.J. Williams, Porter et al. (2012: 5) note that

> compared to fisheries, gender and aquaculture needs a totally different framework of analysis. The issues for gender and aquaculture are more similar to issues in gender and agriculture or gender and enterprise development. Hence, basic gender analysis concepts such as gender division of labour and access/control over resources provide us considerable insights into the gender issues in gender and aquaculture.

While this concept is not fully explored in this chapter, it provides a point of departure for our approach to developing gender-equitable aquaculture opportunities in fishery communities. For that we need to understand gender roles in both fishery and aquaculture value chains. Aquaculture is developed in rural areas and in communities where, for the most part, farming or fishing is the predominant economic activity, with historical and often entrenched gender positions. Unless gender inequities are first fully revealed in these specific contexts, and second directly addressed in shaping and adapting the aquaculture opportunity to make it accessible to women and enhance their position, there is a risk that aquaculture development will replicate the inequities of the existing food production system, be it farming or fishing. This has even more significance in regions where aquaculture is underdeveloped and where there is a push to develop it – Sri Lanka, for example, which wants to double fish production in five years (2011–16).

Aquaculture is a farming activity rather than a capture activity, requiring specific resources, investments, skills, knowledge, and tasks. Seed is produced in hatcheries or collected from natural sources, cultured in nursery and grow-out systems oriented to market demands, harvested and prepared for delivery to buyers, processed in various forms (live, fresh, frozen, smoked, etc.), and shipped to distributors or direct to restaurants or retailers. The opportunity for fishery communities in this value chain involves using their social capital (what they know and do and their capabilities), their opportunity costs (in relation to other forms of income-earning opportunities), and various forms of financing and support provided by value chain actors, government agencies, and local credit sources. To enable women to take on leading roles in aquaculture therefore requires an understanding of their condition in the full context of their livelihoods, as M.J. Williams, Porter et al. (2012) suggest.

Case studies and analyses specific to aquaculture

To date, only a handful of gender analyses have looked specifically at aquaculture *development*, i.e., how gender is embedded in these emerging food production systems. Since, in this case study, the communities in Sri Lanka in which aquaculture is developing are fishing rather than farming communities, the gender analysis is done in the context of the capture fisheries sector. It is also important to distinguish in what ways specific forms of aquaculture to be developed differ from existing fisheries practices in these communities, in order to understand what "spaces" exist in fisheries communities for women to take on and sustain a strong position in what may become a distinct value chain.

Clearly aquaculture can grow, and in many cases has grown, without explicit consideration of gender equity, and with a number of consequences, intended or not, that may offer some opportunity for women, but at a cost of increased vulnerability and low pay. The introduction of new high-value species, the requirements of technology, and intensive production systems can favour the participation of men over women, as shown in case studies from the development of inland aquaculture in Vietnam (Kibria and Mowla 2006) and northeastern Thailand (Kusakabe 2003). More intensive production systems usually require higher levels of inputs and have higher capital requirements. In such scenarios, women may be assigned little or no authority in the value chain. Furthermore, social expectations and norms regarding women's roles and responsibilities may limit what they can gain through aquaculture (Kusakabe 2003). Globalisation of particular commodity chains in aquaculture, such as shrimp, has also resulted in large numbers of women being hired in processing facilities (usually with male-dominated management, and greater security and higher pay for male workers) but, as is often the case in other agri-food and fisheries value chains, under unsatisfactory employment conditions, such as part time, low pay, irregular hours and seasonality, that make women particularly vulnerable (Islam 2008). As Weeratunge et al. (2010: 409) note, "The overall trend appears to be that increased value from the fish trade, both nationally and globally, as well as productivity increases in aquaculture do not necessarily accrue to women."

At the same time, aquaculture as an emerging high-growth sector can also provide significant opportunity for women to achieve more equitable positions, provided that gender-disaggregated data are obtained for communities and value chains, and targeted measures and interventions are put in place. In a comparative analysis of gender in two aquaculture value chains, one in northern Vietnam (shrimp farms) and the other in Nigeria (catfish aquaculture), a World Bank report notes that "success in achieving development objectives through aquaculture depends on contextual realities, mechanisms, and structures in place to ensure equity and environmental sustainability" (Veliu et al. 2009: x).

For example, the position of women as actors in the marketing end of the value chain differs significantly between Nigeria and Vietnam. In the latter, women's ability to negotiate and bargain is socially respected, opening opportunities for women to become traders and sellers. In Nigeria, however, though women have organised themselves into the market position in some cases, they are not respected by many men, and in fact farmers often find ways to block women traders' access to markets. Other interventions identified in the report to enhance the position of women in these value chains include developing "community technological platforms" to address infrastructure and technology constraints (for example, water supply, electricity), and supporting "meso-level" organisations in the value chain that explicitly assist women by, for example, providing access to credit, training, and knowledge (Veliu et al. 2009).

A study of women participating in a three-year aquaculture project in Bangladesh, where underutilised ponds and rice fields were enhanced with aquaculture, concluded that such participation had a significant impact on women's empowerment, as measured by five factors: a woman's decision-making ability within the family, spending ability, cosmopolitism (general orientation outside her immediate social circle), social participation, and access to assets and resources (for example, having her own bank account; access to institutional credit; ability to contact public services such as health, nutrition, and farming; access to family income and resources; access to valuable instruments and machinery; access to farm management and budgeting; and access to inherited properties) (Rahman and Naoroze 2007). However, the authors also noted that women's level of participation was far below what was hoped for. In an analysis of a case from Thailand, many women were participating in the production as well as the management of cage culture of tilapia, which led to empowerment of these women at the household level. However, this rarely translated into greater empowerment at the community level (Lebel et al. 2009).

A final case to consider, and one that is perhaps most closely related to our case in Sri Lanka, is the development of mussel culture in the coastal areas of the state of Kerala, India. This was promoted beginning the mid-1990s as a means of poverty reduction and livelihood enhancement in several districts of Kerala. This area produced over 10,000 metric tonnes with a value of approximately US$2 million in 2008. The industry continues to grow, and there are now approximately 900 operating farms of three different ownership types: individual, family (group of families), and self-help groups (SHGs) (Kripa and Mohamed 2008).

Two-thirds of the farms are in Kasaragod district (the SHG ownership model is found only in this district), and of these nearly 90 percent are owned and operated by women, with approximately 2,000 women involved. Still, about 30 percent of individual and family farms in this district are also owned and operated by women.

In neighbouring Malappuram district, the majority of both individual and family farms are owned and operated by women. The predominance of women-owned farms in these two districts, and the SHGs in Kasaragod, is largely due to vehicles for financial support that are targeted to women entrepreneurs (Kripa and Mohamed 2008). Evidence also indicates that the functional effectiveness of the group is positively correlated with higher cost-benefit ratios.

Gender mainstreaming for aquaculture development in capture fishery communities and regions

A few common themes emerge in the gender analysis of aquaculture where women are involved in the production segment of the value chain. (1) Women are attracted to aquaculture by the need to earn supplementary income, but their aquaculture activities are in addition to or integrated with existing household and community responsibilities; this constraint requires flexibility and dictates the level of their involvement (Kibria and Mowla 2006; Veliu et al. 2009). As Lebel et al. (2009: 215) note, "Again and again, we heard how a challenging portfolio of income-generating activities was interwoven with a life as mother and wife rather than challenging the norms of family." (2) The domestic or reproductive burden limits women's ability to participate in aquaculture, and specifically in traditionally delivered training activities such as workshops, field schools, and demonstrations, where being away from home is required (Kibria and Mowla 2006). (3) Access to productive resources such as land (where land is required for aquaculture activities such as pond or tank construction), machinery, and equipment can significantly constrain women's participation as enterprise owners or managers. (4) Women often are less mobile than men, and distance from home is an important consideration for women engaging in aquaculture (Brugère et al. 2001; Kripa and Mohamed 2008). (5) Women are often marginalised from traditional mechanisms for knowledge acquisition and training, and these must be adapted to women's situations and context (Veliu et al. 2009). These are not dissimilar to those in agriculture, confirming the distinction made by M.J. Williams, Porter et al. (2012).

A precautionary approach is also warranted as gender equity strategies are put into play. For example, formalisation of rights and tenure can threaten food and nutrition security, particularly if gleaning practices have been subsequently limited and women are not provided with control (Matthews et al. 2012). It is also important to avoid falling into essentialism, both when developing aquaculture opportunities for women and when analysing roles and participation in existing value chains: for example, identifying the kinds of tasks to which women are most "suited", such as those involving meticulous attention and care and greater reliability (for example, fish hatcheries and nurseries, feeding, health treatment, etc.) (Lebel et al. 2009).

We must also understand how the opportunity of aquaculture for women in poverty is embedded in household and social norms, relationships, and practices that restrict their access to and control of resources and income. Poverty is not just about lack of income and financial resources, but inequalities in access to and control over material and non-material resources (Arenas and Lentisco 2011). In this respect, we must understand what constraints women face, what decisions they make, and whether those decisions are based on choice or constraint. New opportunities may be more easily introduced in areas where women already have some degree of decision-making authority or control. For example, gathering clams or small fish from a lagoon often plays an important role in household food security, and this may be more easily transitioned into women undertaking culture of shellfish or fish in these lagoons than, for example, taking over fishing activities normally done by men. While this may be initiated in a way that does not directly challenge social norms and practices, it can also be transformative as women take on new responsibilities and new decision-making, negotiating, and leadership roles.

This case study, then, proposes a localised and context-specific approach to understanding what can be done, and how, in developing an opportunity such as aquaculture.

Methods

Areas in the Puttalam Lagoon area of North Western Province and the Trincomalee area of Eastern Province were assessed between June 2011 and May 2012 for suitability to develop and test oyster aquaculture. Selection of communities for participation in the oyster culture trials was based on six criteria: (1) close proximity of available natural stocks of oysters (*Crassostrea madrasensis* or *Crassostrea belcheri*), (2) some previous history of harvesting and selling oysters from natural stocks, (3) a relationship to an oyster buyer/marketer willing to participate in the project, (4) suitable locations for culture and seed collection of oysters that were in close proximity to community homes and could be accessed without motorised boats, (5) low household income, such that the community would benefit from an alternative livelihood and income opportunity, and (6) a location accessible to regular monitoring by NARA. Two communities in Sri Lanka's Puttalam Lagoon area, Gangewadiya and Kandakuliya, were selected (see Figure 2.1). In both communities, capture fishing was the dominant livelihood activity.

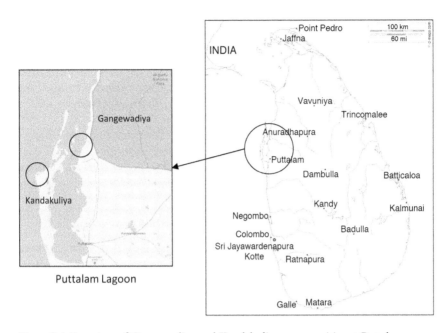

Figure 2.1 Location of Gangewadiya and Kandakuliya communities at Puttalam
Lagoon, North Western Province, Sri Lanka

Source: d-maps.com/openstreetmap.org.

The project research team carried out an initial period of testing at several
sites close to each of the two communities to ensure that oyster seed was
available with a reasonable degree of predictability, and that growth of
oysters in culture systems could yield product that could meet market criteria
for size and quality for single oysters sold in the shell (fresh or frozen).
Monitoring and laboratory analysis of oysters as well as water quality at
culture sites were conducted to determine whether a risk for consumer
health existed. The presence and level of contaminants such as heavy metals
(for example, cadmium, lead, and arsenic) and of bacteria (total coliform,
faecal coliform, and *Vibrio parahaemolyticus*), and the occurrence of harmful
algal blooms that could result in phytotoxins in oysters were analysed by
NARA. Preliminary results indicated risks could be managed by a monitoring
program and purification (depuration) of oysters.

The community engagement process started with an awareness meeting
in each community. An open invitation was extended to community members, both women and men. In both communities, most of the attendees
were women. Techniques for seed collection, culturing oysters in trays
and pouches suspended from racks, grading oysters to meet market
criteria, and handling at harvest were demonstrated. The project team,
NARA, and the private-sector buyer collaborated and combined resources

to provide materials, and worked with the community members to construct the seed collection and culture apparatus and stock the trays and pouches with seed oysters. Systems were designed to support and promote the participation of women in aquaculture enterprises. For example, boats were constructed with platforms built upon two "pontoons" created from small fibreglass fishing canoes. The boats could be manoeuvred with paddles and poles in the shallow lagoons, and the decks provided a place where oysters could be sorted and cleaned without having to return to shore.

As the community oyster farms were operationalised, an assessment of community livelihoods and the situation and position of women in each community was undertaken. Participatory rapid appraisal (PRA) methods were applied to obtain a snapshot of the condition, context, and perspective of community members involved in the aquaculture interventions of the project. Areas of appraisal were identified based on project goals of achieving outcomes in livelihoods, income, food security, the status and position of women, productivity, risks related to production, knowledge of practices, connectivity to knowledge resources, issues of governance, and management of common resources. Next, a questionnaire was sent to women in the community to survey their perceptions of the socioeconomic status of their households, level of food security, activities and opportunities available to them to enhance their livelihood, and their awareness of and connectivity to knowledge sources.

PRA participants were selected through an open process in which people involved or interested in oyster farming were invited to attend two meetings held in December 2013. In Gangewadiya, 8 men and 12 women participated; in Kandakuliya, 6 men and 12 women participated. Following an initial orientation, introductions, and discussion, the participants were divided into focus groups, with men and women in separate groups. The focus group participants then engaged in various exercises designed to solicit their active input on various themes and questions. Questions were answered by group consensus using a variety of visualisation tools such as seasonal calendars, Venn diagrams, wagon wheel diagrams, and activity clocks. Income status and vulnerabilities were addressed with questions about the local economy, sources and seasonality of household income, contribution of women and men to household income, and household expenses. Activities and decision-making questions were explored by men and women to understand household gender dynamics. Food security was explored using questions and visualisation of food types and sources in the household diet, sources of food from markets or own production (gardens, fishery, etc.), and utilisation of food within the household. Awareness of and connectivity to knowledge sources and governance were explored through questions and linkage diagrams relating to education and accessibility of agencies and organisations providing technical or resource management assistance in fisheries, aquaculture, or other resource uses. Gender-disaggregated results were summarised graphically and descriptively to characterise communities.

This first phase was followed, in March 2013, by a questionnaire for women in these communities to obtain data on their perceptions of demographic and socioeconomic factors, knowledge and connectivity, governance, and food security. Sixteen women in Gangewadiya and 20 women in Kandakuliya participated in the survey. The respondents were selected based on their active participation in the aquaculture activities undertaken and, where possible, their involvement in the earlier participatory process. Each interview lasted approximately 45 minutes. The data were tabulated in a spreadsheet, and descriptive analytical techniques were used to generate results relevant to understanding gender dimensions of activities, incomes, food security, and related dimensions of livelihoods.

Results and discussion

This chapter addresses two key questions: (1) Can pathways can be charted for gender-inclusive aquaculture development in communities dependent primarily on capture fisheries for livelihoods and income? (2) Can an emerging sector such as bivalve mollusc cultivation provide the spaces for women to stand in strong and equitable positions as producers in the value chain, or will it simply replicate the conditions, roles, and positions of women in the existing capture fisheries sector?

The results indicated that the former is a real possibility. The researchers attempted to understand the context, conditions, and positions of women in fishing and livelihood support as well as their role in households, communities, and income-earning activities. This highlighted constraints that women faced, activities that could be channelled to open spaces for aquaculture opportunities, and the women's interest and motivation to supplement their income through aquaculture.

Kandakuliya lies in the northern part of a narrow arm of land bordering the western side of Puttalam Lagoon. A segment of the community living in close proximity to a largely enclosed lagoon was selected for aquaculture development (Table 2.1). The lagoon has a narrow, shallow channel that provides shelter for small fishing boats and access to the open sea to the west. Fishing is generally conducted in near-shore areas of the open sea in small day boats. The monsoon season (April to November) brings prevailing southwesterly winds and strong waves, significantly limiting the boats' ability to venture into open waters. While fishing remains the area's main economic activity, vegetable farming supported by irrigation has recently emerged in areas to the south of the community. This has provided some opportunity for residents of the region to earn income, including many women. Tourism, particularly adventure tourism, is also a growing sector, and new hotels, both small and large, are being built on the far northern tip of the peninsula. The lagoon of Kandakuliya had a rich bed of oysters, many of which were removed in 2009 and following years as small-scale tourism operators used the lagoon for water sports such as kite surfing. Some commercial harvesting of wild oysters was also done.

Table 2.1 Socioeconomic characteristics of women interview respondents and sample households

Socioeconomic characteristic	Both villages *n* = 36	Gangewadiya *n* = 16	Kandakuliya *n* = 20
Average age of respondent (years)	35.2	33.8	36.6
	Respondents (%)		
Educational attainment			
No schooling	9	13	5
Grade 1–10	78	75	80
General Certificate of Education (GCE), Ordinary Level (O/L)	12	7	16
General Certificate of Education (GCE), Advanced Level (A/L)	3	6	0
Tertiary education	0	0	0
Average household size (*N*)	3.9	3.8	4
Annual household income (in LRK)			
>300,000	0	0	0
200,001–300,000	6	13	0
100,001–200,000	9	19	0
50,000–100,000	25	25	26
<50,000	60	44	74
Woman is the main income earner of the family	13	6	20
Household income from fishing			
100%	36	56	15
50–99%	35	25	45
1–49%	19	19	20
No contribution (0%)	10	0	20
Average years of fishing (*n*)	8.9	10.7	7.2

Gangewadiya is situated on the estuary of the Kala Oya River on the eastern (mainland) side of Puttalam Lagoon (Figure 2.1). It is significantly more isolated from other communities than Kandakuliya, and is highly dependent on fisheries as an income-generating activity. Fishing here is also done in small day boats, but access to the extensive estuary and mangrove areas as well as the main body of Puttalam Lagoon means that fishing is less restricted seasonally than at Kandakuliya, and access to the resources, particularly the mangrove estuary, is less competitive. A large firm involved in mineral mining and cement preparation, located a few kilometres from the village, provides some infrastructure and community support, as well as limited employment.

Fishing is the primary income-generating activity in both communities: over two-thirds (71 percent) of the respondents reported that they derived at least half of their total annual income from fishing alone. However, because of the lack of alternative income sources and the greater access to fisheries resources in Gangewadiya, fishing income plays a greater role in that community's livelihoods and income. Over half the women interviewed there (56 percent) indicated that their households depended exclusively on income from fishing. In Kandakuliya, only 15 percent of the women interviewed indicated exclusive dependence on the capture fishery for household income (Table 2.1).

The data obtained through both the PRA process and the interviews indicate that poverty levels are high in both communities. In the interviews, the women reported an average household size of four persons. These are generally younger families: the average female respondent age was 35.3 years, and 77 percent of the respondents were under 40.

When women were asked to report level of household income within given ranges, 60 percent of respondents in the two communities reported that their total annual household income was less than LKR 50,000 (US$382), which means they earn less than the global lowest poverty line indicator of US$1.25 per day and are among the approximately 800,000 people in this situation in Sri Lanka (World Bank 2010). A further 25 percent earn between LKR 50,000 and 100,000 (US$382–764). None of the households interviewed in Kandakuliya earned over LKR 100,000, while 31 percent of households in Gangewadiya earned between LKR 100,000 and 300,000 (US$764–2,292) (Table 2.1). Two-thirds of the respondents indicated that they were unable to save any money at all during the year, with only 32 percent able to save some money in higher-income months.

The poverty line in Puttalam District for August 2014 was LKR 3,920, defined as minimum expenditure per person per month to fulfil the basic needs (Department of Census and Statistics, Sri Lanka 2014). For a household of four, this represents LKR 15,680 per month and LKR 188,160 per year. All of the women interviewed in Kandakuliya and 88 percent of the women in Gangewadiya reported household incomes below the national poverty line. National surveys conducted in Sri Lanka show that level of education attainment by adults has a significant effect on household food security, income, and assets. However, there is a significant gendered dimension to poverty in Sri Lanka, where female-headed households tend to do worse across a range of livelihood outcome indicators such as assets and level of food insecurity (Mayadunne et al. 2014). Despite the fact that 78 percent of the women in the two communities had completed education through grade 10, they clearly had been unable to transform this attainment into household income and a larger asset base.

In addition to levels of income below the national poverty line for most households, the seasonality of fishing and other income opportunities, such as vegetable harvesting, increases household and community vulnerability.

Because of the monsoonal conditions that prevail in this area from April to November, fishing is often not possible, severely impacting household income and necessitating at least temporary indebtedness for many households. Annual income distributed over 12 months was portrayed during the PRA by means of a bar graph drawn on the floor in chalk, with women and men grouped separately and each group drawing their own perception. The two groups drew similar graphs (Figure 2.2).

Widespread poverty among fisheries communities in Southeast Asia is almost always linked to food insecurity (FAO 2011). The role and economic status of women have long been identified as key determinants of the food security and nutritional status of households (Quisumbing et al. 1995; Smith et al. 2003). The percentage of total household income spent on food is a

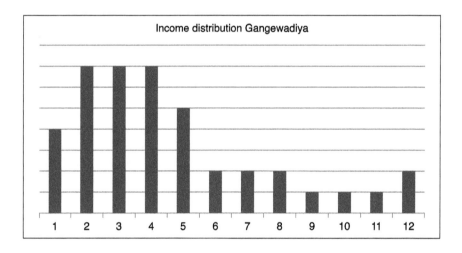

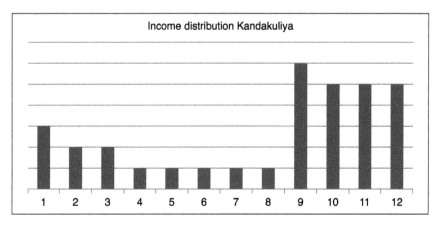

Figure 2.2 Income distribution over 12 months in Gangewadiya and Kandakuliya as perceived by women participating in the PRA process

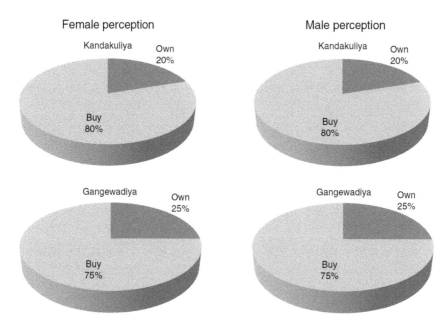

Figure 2.3 Perceptions of food security using percentage of food purchased in markets (cash transaction) as an indicator in the PRA process

key indicator of food security, in particular as a measure of food afford-ability (Banerjee and Duflo 2006; EIU 2014). Food can be obtained from a variety of sources: it can be harvested from home gardens or locally avail-able food resources such as fish stocks, or purchased for cash at food markets. During the PRA process, both communities registered similar perceptions on the percentage of food they obtained from market purchases: 80 percent in Kandakuliya and 75 percent in Gangewadiya (Figure 2.3). The percentage of income spent on food relative to other household expense categories was assessed at 50 percent by women in both communities, 60 percent by men in Kandakuliya, and 50 percent by men in Gangewadiya (Figure 2.4).

However, during the questionnaire survey of women in the two commun-ities, they reported lower values, with an average of 39 percent of income spent on food. No one reported spending more than 50 percent of income on food. Since food security is often episodic and fluctuates in response to a variety of factors, perceptions are likely to be influenced by the immediate situation. Despite this variation, there is still sufficient evidence to conclude that food security is a concern in these communities. This was reinforced through the response to a related question concerning the need to borrow money to purchase food: 87 percent responded that they had borrowed money to meet household food expenses at some time during the year.

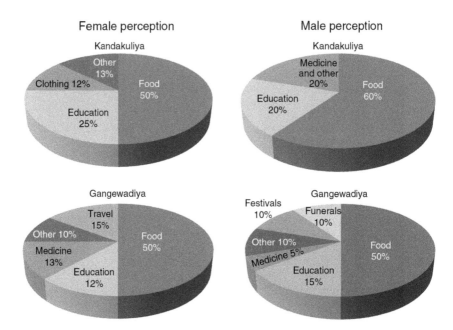

Figure 2.4 Perceptions of food security using proportion of income spent on food relative to other categories of household expenditure as an indicator in the PRA process

We also attempted to get a picture of dietary diversity in households, an indicator that is increasingly considered to be one of the most useful (Headey and Ecker 2013). In both locations, the majority of women felt that, in certain months of the year, their household members did not receive enough of important food groups such as meat/poultry/fish/eggs (68 percent), dairy/ beans and lentils (85 percent), grains/rice (86 percent), fruits (89 percent), and vegetables (83 percent) (Table 2.2).

Without appropriate recognition of women's role as regular and stable food providers, household food and nutritional security may be threatened. Improvement of dietary intakes, especially consumption of non-staple food, is usually positively correlated with increased women's income (Nielsen et al. 2003; Hawkes and Ruel 2006; World Bank 2007; Iannotti et al. 2009).

Building up capital in housing is a primary condition for enabling house-holds to invest in further physical and social capital assets such as education, income generation, entrepreneurial opportunities, and ownership of land and homes (Moser 2006). The PRA process revealed that poor housing was an issue for some community members. Three key factors were identified: some housing materials are unable to withstand severe weather such as mon-soon storms; both communities are vulnerable to flooding during monsoon periods; and there is a high level of housing insecurity related to ownership

Table 2.2 Women's perceptions of household food security and dietary diversity

Response	Respondents (%)		
	Both villages	Gangewadiya	Kandakuliya
All household members had at least one serving of meat/poultry/fish/eggs every day	59	38	78
Felt that household members did not get enough meat/poultry/fish/eggs in certain months	68	53	82
All household members had at least one serving of dairy/beans every day	56	36	74
Felt that household members did not get enough dairy/beans in certain months	85	80	89
All household members had at least one serving of grain/rice every day	61	47	74
Felt that household members did not get enough grain/rice in certain months	86	92	80
All household members had at least one serving of vegetables every day	41	31	50
Felt that household members did not get enough vegetables in certain months	83	69	95
All household members had at least one serving of fruit every day	46	31	60
Felt that household members did not get enough fruit in certain months	89	77	100

of land or fear of loss of housing. Many houses are constructed of cadjan (palm leaf), and one-third of the women interviewed in Kandakuliya live in such homes. Homes are crowded, with most (70 percent) having only two rooms. A majority of homes (72 percent) have electricity, but this underscores the impact on households with no electricity. Women respondents also cited insufficient access to clean water and inadequate sanitation facilities as challenges in maintaining households.

Poor income earning in fisheries with little prospect of growth, limited permanent or seasonal employment opportunities (especially for women) outside of fisheries, and seasonal income vulnerabilities from fishing provide the initial space into which aquaculture can be introduced as an opportunity for both women and men to gain interest and motivation in the community.

Are women in a position in their communities and households to earn income through aquaculture? Do their responsibilities and obligations in fishing activity and in household and reproductive tasks allow them to engage their social capital to work in and manage aquaculture enterprises? Is the opportunity cost of aquaculture adequate for them to substitute other possible income-earning activities? Women's contribution to the income earning of capture fisheries, to the household economy through activities that save on direct expenses such as harvesting of plant or fish resources (gleaning), and to household income through activities such as vegetable harvesting at area farms must also be made visible as a means to understand their position and capacity to undertake activities in an emerging aquaculture value chain such as oyster farming.

The women in these fishing communities are involved in many of the activities associated with small-scale fishing, on which they spend a considerable amount of time, often over seven hours per day during fishing periods. In Gangewadiya, where fishing generates a higher percentage of total household income, women contribute more to fishing activities than do women in Kandakuliya. For example, in Gangewadiya, 87 percent of women clean fishing nets and 56 percent do fish drying, while in Kandakuliya the figures are 30 and 15 percent, respectively. Selling of fish, however, is done by more than half (56 percent) of the women in both communities. None of the women interviewed in either community set nets or caught fish using fishing boats.

These activities are not often factored into women's contribution to household income, and indeed, both their direct and indirect contributions are undervalued. In the PRA process, with women and men reporting in separate groups, men tended to under-report women's contribution to household income. Participants were asked to shade the proportion of women's contribution to monthly household income in a 12-month bar graph. In Kandakuliya, the men did not perceive that the women contributed to household income, while women perceived their contribution to be about 20 percent. In Gangewadiya, women's contribution was relatively evenly recognised as 10 percent by both men and women. The activity profile of women in the communities clearly shows that women's contribution to income is undervalued by both men and women.

In addition to their direct involvement in fisheries activities, women also have various indirect inputs, generating income from other sources – either directly, by earning income, or indirectly, by supplementing food sources through such activities as harvesting clams, maintaining the household by cleaning and cooking, obtaining drinking water, and serving as main care-givers to children. In the PRA process, groups of participants represented their daily activities by means of an activity clock. Generally, women reported starting their day at 5 a.m. and spending six to seven hours a day preparing meals and cleaning. Women are also responsible for caring for pre-school-age children, as well as for escorting or transporting children to and from school and assisting them with homework.

Accounting for women's daily responsibilities is a critical consideration in assessing their capacity and willingness to engage in other income-earning opportunities. They will likely need to make trade-offs and possibly forgo other income-earning opportunities, such as working in fish post-harvest activities and farming labour. Women in both villages reported that during the fishing season they would be able to allocate two to four hours per day to oyster-farming activities, and three to six hours per day in the off-season. Their reproductive and household burden, however, is not likely to be lighter. Considering this, when developing an aquaculture opportunity, it is important to ensure that women's participation can be accomplished in ways that accommodate their household and reproductive responsibilities: for example, by choosing culture locations close to their home village and developing methods of culture that do not require travel by boat or involve tasks of which they would not feel capable.

Since oyster aquaculture is an emerging value chain in Sri Lanka, there is greater opportunity to adapt the relationships and structures to the condition of women in villages. Once the natural resources have been identified as suitable for culturing the required species, additional criteria can be applied to facilitate women's participation. For example, linking the cultivation of oysters with activities over which women already have some degree of decision-making authority or control, such as gathering clams or small fish from local lagoons, may significantly strengthen women's position in the emerging value chain. Rather than being seen as women taking over fishing activities normally done by men, or seeking employment and status in more mature value chains, such strategies actually open up new spaces for women and may more readily be initiated in a way that does not directly challenge social norms and practices. Consequently, this new opportunity becomes transformative as women take on new responsibilities and new decision-making, negotiating, and leadership roles.

Limited access to knowledge and training opportunities for women is repeatedly cited as a barrier to strengthening women's position in food production system value chains, be they fisheries, agriculture, or aquaculture (Kibria and Mowla 2006; Veliu et al. 2009). Social capital is often considered in terms of several components: groups and networks, trust, collective action, social inclusion, and information and communication (World Bank 2011). Our use of the framework of knowledge mobilisation captures all of these elements but focuses them on the sharing, adaptation, and implementation of knowledge involving people, technology, data, and information as well as institutions. It involves both the "what you know" and the "whom you know" (Woolcock 2000).

While educational capacity among women is relatively high in Sri Lanka, even in these relatively remote communities, compared to other countries in the region, women's capacity to advance their livelihoods through knowledge acquisition is limited. They are weakly connected to programs and sources of information that are key to their economic development. In developing the aquaculture opportunity for women in these two communities, the project has worked directly to enhance knowledge connectivity along the value chain and strengthen support from government agencies, particularly NARA, to provide training and resources to women. The private-sector buyer and market developer of the oysters communicates directly with the oyster growers to guide them in producing and selecting oysters that meet market criteria for meat quality and shape. The firm also provides some of the equipment and on-site training. Training resources such as manuals and on-site demonstrations have been developed in collaboration with NARA and the private sector. Further, NARA supports the communities through ongoing water quality analysis and monitoring of oyster growth, condition, and timing for collection of seed. An important consideration for market access is to ensure that the oysters are free of water-borne contaminants, which may enter from land sources such as agriculture or from poor sanitation in coastal communities. The private sector has constructed a facility for a purification process known as depuration, through which oysters are treated in sterilised seawater to remove any bacterial contamination; the system is part of the research conducted by the project and NARA to ensure the effectiveness of such treatment. Communities are educated about possible sources of contamination and other risk factors to culture, such as low salinity levels.

Oyster culture activities were first initiated through the project activities in Gangewadiya in 2011. Unfortunately, in the first year severe flooding killed much of the stock. However, a few stakeholders worked with the project and the private-sector partner to help rebuild this first effort. After an initial wild stock harvest in Kandakuliya, the women became very interested in undertaking culture of oysters, and this activity was started there in early 2013.

Based on this experience, 92 percent of women believed that oyster farming would help improve their household income. Moreover, 86 percent considered oyster farming an enterprise that women can do on their own, and 89 percent felt they had enough time to dedicate to oyster farming. If oyster farming were started, 88 percent thought they would have to dedicate less time to other activities such as cooking and caring for children. In addition, 65 percent of women indicated that they would make the primary financial decisions on commercial oyster culture, while 97 percent believed oyster farming would help them assume stronger leadership positions in the community. The women in Kandakuliya village have formed an Oyster Culturing Society to carry out the aquaculture enterprise.

Conclusion

As coastal aquaculture of oysters (as well as other molluscs, invertebrates such as sea cucumber, and finfish) develops in Sri Lanka, the opportunity will increase for the participation of communities that are presently largely dependent on capture fisheries. Because of declining stocks, increasing costs, and seasonality, the capture fishery in near-shore waters in Sri Lanka affords little opportunity for growth, and it is increasingly difficult for fishery communities and households to depend on it exclusively or even for a significant part of household income. Women have helped make this activity feasible by contributing to immediate inputs, such as mending nets and post-harvest handling, or value extension by drying or other methods of preservation. However, this too will soon reach a limit; hence, there is an eagerness and willingness to undertake new initiatives such as aquaculture.

Participatory approaches and strategies to increase opportunities in emerging sectors can open up new spaces that are more equitable and empowering for women. In many cases, this can be advanced without having to deconstruct long-standing institutions and relationships in which women have been marginalised or under-represented. In more mature sub-sectors, such as shrimp farming or traditional fishing, women's limited access to resources, capital, ownership of land, and similar factors perpetuates their marginal position in those value chains.

The participatory processes and interviews conducted during the project revealed the conditions and contexts in which the women in these communities support livelihoods. This process encouraged self-recognition and self-revelation, thereby providing a foundation for value and a platform for the emergence of stronger leadership among women. Identification of weak or non-existent links between the community – women in particular – and governing and knowledge-providing people and institutions was a significant revelation, and allowed strategies to be directly targeted to supporting women's entry into oyster aquaculture. Continuous monitoring and knowledge sharing through observation and discussion were maintained via mobile phones, site visits, and training materials. Market linkages were developed through participation of a key private-sector buyer and marketer, who guided the participants in the techniques required to produce the high-quality products demanded by the market. The culture systems for seed collection and growing of mature oysters were adapted to make it easy for women to engage in the activity – for example, by locating culture racks close to homes, and utilising a specially designed small boat, thereby enabling women to assume full responsibility for and ownership of the operation, an outcome especially evident in Kandakuliya. The proof of the concept is now evident, with delivery of increasing volumes of oysters to markets in Sri Lanka and beyond. New space has been made for more equitable participation of women in the development of emerging aquaculture sectors in Sri Lanka.

Acknowledgements

This project was undertaken with the financial support of the International Development Research Centre (IDRC), www.idrc.ca, and the Government of Canada through the Department of Foreign Affairs, Trade and Development (Canada) (DFATD), www.international.gc.ca.

The authors would like to thank the community members of Kandakuliya and Gangewadiya, particularly Mrs Shamila Perera of Kandakuliya and Mr Lindamulage Ajith Kumara of Gangewadiya, Hasantha Gunaweera, Shan Meemanage, Dr Palitha Kithsiri, and the researchers and field staff of the National Aquatic Resources Research and Development Agency (Sri Lanka), Prof. W.M.T.B. Wanninayake, D. Sam Daniel, Prof. D.S. Jayakody, Bea Vanderlinden, Sara Ahmed, the project teams of Wayamba University of Sri Lanka, the Ministry of Agriculture and Fisheries North Western Province (Sri Lanka), and the British Columbia Aquatic Food Resources Society (Canada).

Note

1 Exchange rate at 7 April 2016: 100 LKR = US$0.68.

References

All website URLs accessed on 7 April 2016.

Anderson, James L. 2002. "Aquaculture and the Future: Why Fisheries Economists Should Care." *Marine Resource Economics* 17 (2): 133–51.
Arenas, M.C., and A. Lentisco. 2011. *Mainstreaming Gender into Project Cycle Management in the Fisheries Sector.* Bangkok: FAO. www.fao.org/docrep/014/ba0004e/ba0004e00.pdf.
Banerjee, Abhijit, and Esther Duflo. 2006. "The Economic Lives of the Poor." *Journal of Economic Perspectives* 21 (1): 141–68. doi:10.1257/jep.21.1.141.
Belton, Ben, Manjurul Karim, Shakuntala Thilsted, Khondker Murshed E-Jahan, William Collis, and Michael Phillips. 2011. "Review of Aquaculture and Fish Consumption in Bangladesh." *Studies and Reviews 2011–53*. Penang, Malaysia: WorldFish Center.
Bennett, Elizabeth. 2005. "Gender, Fisheries and Development." *Marine Policy* 29 (5): 451–9.
Brugère, Cécile, Kenneth Mcandrew, and Paul Bulcock. 2001. "Does Cage Aquaculture Address Gender Goals in Development? Results of a Case Study in Bangladesh." *Aquaculture Economics & Management* 5 (3–4): 179–89. doi:10.1080/13657300109380286.
Choo, Poh Sze, Stephen J. Hall, and Meryl J. Williams, eds. 2006. *Global Symposium on Gender and Fisheries: Seventh Asian Fisheries Forum, 1–2 December 2004, Penang, Malaysia.* Penang, Malaysia: WorldFish Center.
Department of Census and Statistics, Sri Lanka. 2014. *District Official Poverty Lines.* www.statistics.gov.lk/poverty/monthly_poverty/index.htm.
De Silva, D.A.M. 2011. *Faces of Women in Global Fishery Value Chains: Female Involvement, Impact and Importance in the Fisheries of Developed and Developing Countries.* NORAD/FAO Value Chain Project.
De Silva, D.A.M., and M. Yamao. 2006. "The Involvement of Female Labor in Seafood Processing in Sri Lanka: Impact of Organizational Fairness and Supervisor Evaluation on Employee Commitment." In Poh Sze Choo, Stephen J. Hall, and Meryl J. Williams, eds, *Global Symposium on Gender and Fisheries: Seventh Asian*

Fisheries Forum, 1–2 December 2004, Penang, Malaysia. Penang, Malaysia: WorldFish Center, 103–14.

Diamond, Nancy K., Lesley Squillante, and Lynne Z. Hale. 2003. "Cross Currents: Navigating Gender and Population Linkages for Integrated Coastal Management." *Marine Policy* 27 (4): 325–31.

EIU (Economist Intelligence Unit). 2014. *Global Food Security Index 2014: An Annual Measure of the State of Global Food Security*. http://foodsecurityindex.eiu.com.

FAO (Food and Agriculture Organization of the United Nations). 2011. *Gender Analysis: Negombo and Puttalam Districts, Sri Lanka*. FAO Regional Fisheries Livelihoods Programme for South and Southeast Asia. Rome: FAO. www.fao. org/3/a-ar299e.pdf.

FAO. 2012. *The State of World Fisheries and Aquaculture 2012*. Rome: FAO.

FAO. 2014. *The State of World Fisheries and Aquaculture: Opportunities and Challenges*. Rome: FAO.

Hawkes, Corinna, and Marie Ruel. 2006. "The Links between Agriculture and Health: An Intersectoral Opportunity to Improve the Health and Livelihoods of the Poor." *Bulletin of the World Health Organization* 84 (12): 984.

Headey, Derek, and Olivier Ecker. 2013. "Rethinking the Measurement of Food Security: From First Principles to Best Practice." *Food Security* 5 (3): 327–43.

Iannotti, Lora, Kenda Cunningham, and Marie Ruel. 2009. *Improving Diet Quality and Micronutrient Nutrition: Homestead Food Production in Bangladesh*. IFPRI Discussion Paper 00928. Washington, DC: International Food Policy Research Institute (IFPRI).

Islam, Md. Saidul. 2008. "From Sea to Shrimp Processing Factories in Bangladesh: Gender and Employment at the Bottom of a Global Commodity Chain." *Journal of South Asian Development* 3 (2): 211–36. doi:10.1177/097317410800300202.

Kabeer, Naila, Kirsty Milward, and Ratna Sudarshan. 2013. "Organizing Women Workers in the Informal Economy." *Gender & Development* 21 (2): 249–63. doi: 10.1080/13552074.2013.802145.

Kibria, Md. Ghulam, and Runia Mowla. 2006. "Sustainable Aquaculture Development: Impacts on the Social Livelihood of Ethnic Minorities in Northern Vietnam with Emphasis on Gender." In Poh Sze Choo, Stephen J. Hall, and Meryl J. Williams, eds, *Global Symposium on Gender and Fisheries: Seventh Asian Fisheries Forum, 1–2 December 2004, Penang, Malaysia*. Penang, Malaysia: WorldFish Center, 21–8.

Kripa, Vasanth, and Kolliyil Sunilkumar Mohamed. 2008. "Green Mussel (*Pernavirides*) Farming in India: Technology Diffusion Process and Socioeconomic Impacts." *Journal of the World Aquaculture Society* 39 (5): 612–24. doi: 10.1111/j.1749-7345. 2008.00191.x.

Kusakabe, Kyoko. 2003. "Women's Involvement in Small-Scale Aquaculture in Northeast Thailand." *Development in Practice* 13 (4): 333–45. doi:10.1080/09614 52032000112392.

Lebel, Phimphakan, Prachaub Chaibu, and Louis Lebel. 2009. "Women Farm Fish: Gender and Commercial Fish Cage Culture on the Upper Ping River, Northern Thailand." *Gender, Technology and Development* 13 (2): 199–224.

Lokuge, Gayathri. 2014. "'Outside the Net': Women's Participation in Fishing Activities in Trincomalee District of Sri Lanka" [Weblog entry]. London, UK: Secure Livelihooods Research Consortium, 19 March. www.securelivelihoods. org/blogs_entry.aspx?id=56.

Matthews, Elizabeth, Jamie Bechtel, Easkey Britton, Karl Morrison, and Caleb McClennen. 2012. *A Gender Perspective on Securing Livelihoods and Nutrition in Fish-Dependent Coastal Communities.* Report to the Rockefeller Foundation from Wildlife Conservation Society, Bronx, New York.

Mayadunne, Geetha, Richard Mallett, and Jessica Hagen-Zanker. 2014. *Surveying Livelihoods, Service Delivery and Governance: Baseline Evidence from Sri Lanka.* SLRC Working Paper 20. London, UK: Secure Livelihoods Research Consortium.

Medard, M., F. Sobo, T. Ngatunga, and S. Chirwa. 2002. *Women and Gender Participation in the Fisheries Sector in Lake Victoria.* WorldFish Center Working Paper No. 36255. Penang, Malaysia: WorldFish Center. www.worldfishcenter.org/Pubs/Wif/wifglobal/wifg_africa_victoria.pdf.

MFARD (Sri Lanka Ministry of Fisheries and Aquatic Resources Development). 2013. *Fisheries Statistics Report 2013.* Colombo, Sri Lanka: MFARD. www.fisheries.gov.lk/content.php?cnid=stst.

Moser, Caroline O.N. 2006. *Asset-based Approaches to Poverty Reduction in a Globalized Context: An Introduction to Asset Accumulation Policy and Summary of Workshop Findings.* Brookings Institution Global Development and Economy Working Paper No. 1. Washington, DC: The Brookings Institution. www.brookings.edu/~/media/research/files/papers/2006/11/sustainabledevelopment%20moser/200611 moser.pdf.

Muir, James F. 2013. "Fish, Feeds and Food Security." *Animal Frontiers* 3 (1): 28–34. doi:10.2527/af.2013-0005.

Nielsen, Hanne, Nanna Roos, and Shakuntala H. Thilsted. 2003. "The Impact of Semi-Scavenging Poultry Production on the Consumption of Animal Source Foods by Women and Girls in Bangladesh." *Journal of Nutrition* 133 (11): 4027S–4030S.

Quisumbing, Agnes, Lawrence Haddad, and Christine Peña. 1995. *Gender and Poverty: New Evidence from 10 Developing Countries.* FCND Discussion Paper No. 9. Washington, DC: International Food Policy Research Institute (IFPRI), Food Consumption and Nutrition Division (FCND). www.ifpri.org/sites/default/files/publications/dp09.pdf.

Rahman, M. Hammadur, and Kazi Naoroze. 2007. "Women Empowerment Through Participation in Aquaculture: Experience of a Large-Scale Technology Demonstration Project in Bangladesh." *Journal of Social Sciences* 3 (4): 164–71. doi:10.3844/jssp.2007.164.171.

Smith, Lisa C., Usha Ramakrishnan, Aida Ndiaye, Lawrence Haddad, and Reynaldo Martorell. 2003. *The Importance of Women's Status for Child Nutrition in Developing Countries.* IFPRI Research Report 131. Washington, DC: International Food Policy Research Institute (IFPRI).

Tietze, Uwe. 1995. *FAO's Role and Experiences with Improving the Social and Economic Status of Women in Fishing Communities in Asia and the Pacific.* Rome: FAO.

Veliu, Atdhe, Nebiyeluel Gessese, Catherine Ragasa, and Christine Okali. 2009. *Gender Analysis of Aquaculture Value Chain in Northeast Vietnam and Nigeria.* Agriculture and Rural Development Discussion Paper 44. Washington, DC: World Bank. http://siteresources.worldbank.org/INTARD/Resources/Gender_Aquaculture_web.pdf.

Weeratunge, Nireka, Katherine Snyder, and Poh Sze Choo. 2010. "Gleaner, Fisher, Trader, Processor: Understanding Gendered Employment in Fisheries and Aquaculture." *Fish and Fisheries* 11 (4): 405–20.

Williams, Meryl J. 2008. "Why Look at Fisheries Through a Gender Lens?" *Development* 51: 180–5. doi:10.1057/dev.2008.2.

Williams, Meryl J., Marilyn Porter, Poh Sze Choo, Kyoko Kusakabe, Veikila Vuki, Nikita Gopal, and Melba Bondad-Reantaso. 2012. "Gender in Aquaculture and Fisheries: Moving the Agenda Forward." *Asian Fisheries Science* Special Issue 25: 1–13.

Williams, Meryl J., R. Agbayani, Ram C. Bhujel, Melba G. Bondad-Reantaso, Cécile Brugère, Poh Sze Choo, Jean Dhont, Angel Galmiche-Tejeda, K. Ghulam, Kyoko Kusakabe, David Little, Mudnakudu C. Nandeesha, Patrick Sorgeloos, Nireka Weeratunge, S. Williams, and P. Xu. 2012. "Sustaining Aquaculture by Developing Human Capacity and Enhancing Opportunities for Women." In R.P. Subasinghe, J.R. Arthur, D.M. Bartley, S.S. De Silva, M. Halwart, N. Hishamunda, C.V. Mohan, and P. Sorgeloos, eds, *Farming the Waters for People and Food: Proceedings of the Global Conference on Aquaculture 2010, Phuket, Thailand, 22–25 September 2010*. Rome: FAO, and Bangkok: Network of Aquaculture Centres in Asia-Pacific, 785–874.

Williams, Stella B., Anne-Marie Hochet-Kibongui, and Cornelia E. Nauen, eds. 2005. *Gender, Fisheries and Aquaculture: Social Capital and Knowledge for the Transition towards Sustainable Use of Aquatic Ecosystems*. ACP-EU Fisheries Research Report 16. Brussels, Belgium: European Commission.

Woolcock, Michael. 2000. *The Place of Social Capital in Understanding Social and Economic Outcomes*. Paris: Organisation for Economic Co-operation and Development (OECD). www.oecd.org/innovation/research/1824913.pdf.

World Bank. 2007. *From Agriculture to Nutrition: Pathways, Synergies and Outcomes*. Washington, DC: World Bank.

World Bank. 2010. *Sri Lanka Data 2010*. http://data.worldbank.org/country/sri-lanka.

World Bank. 2011. *Social Capital*. http://go.worldbank.org/K4LUMW43B0.

Zhao, Minghua, Marilyn Tyzack, Rodney Anderson, and Estera Onoakpovike. 2013. "Women as Visible and Invisible Workers in Fisheries: A Case Study of Northern England." *Marine Policy* 37 (11): 69–76. doi:10.1016/j.marpol.2012.04.013.

3 Gender and labour efficiency in finger millet production in Nepal

Rachana Devkota, Kamal Khadka,
Hom Gartaula, Asis Shrestha,
Swikar Karki, Kirit Patel, and
Pashupati Chaudhary

Introduction

Finger millet is one of the major crops grown under the maize-millet crop-ping system in the hills of Nepal. It is an important crop for Nepal's upland farmers because it is a climate-smart crop that withstands environmental adversities and can be cultivated in rain-fed marginal lands with minimum or low external inputs (Joshi et al. 2002; Adhikari 2012). It is a rich and inexpensive source of dietary fibre, iron, calcium, and zinc (NARC 2005; Dida and Devos 2006; Mal et al. 2010). The role of finger millet as a cheap source of valuable nutrients becomes more prominent in a country like Nepal, where 25 percent of the population makes less than US$1.25 per day and where the indicators of human development and food security – such as life expectancy (69 years), child mortality (50 children U5/1,000 live births), underweight child (38.6 percent), maternal mortality (170 women/ 100,000 live births), and adult literacy (60 percent) – are dismal at regional as well as global levels. However, farmers are progressively losing interest in finger millet cultivation because of its tedious and labour-intensive agro-nomic practices and post-harvest operations. Moreover, it is neglected in the national research and extension system and generally perceived as a low-status food crop in Nepal.

As in many other countries, women do most of the agricultural work in Nepal. In the case of finger millet cultivation, they assume over 90 percent of the workload (Adhikari 2012; RESMISA 2012). Finger millet is a labour-intensive crop, and women perform most of the tedious and time-consuming manual activities (Shirahatti et al. 2007; Singh et al. 2007). There are no specific men's or women's crops, but because of their closer association with certain crops and the gender-neutral policy environment, women and associated crops are less favoured in the policymaking process (Doss 2002). The situation is exacerbated because of the increased migration of male house-hold members into non-agricultural jobs within and outside the country, which has resulted in the feminisation of agriculture (Gartaula et al. 2010), making women the de facto heads of the households and the key decision-makers. This changing household organisation has made women's triple role in productive, reproductive, and community managing activities (Moser 1993) more significant in the changing gender relations. However, because "machines" and "technologies" are traditionally considered men's domain, women are less involved in technology development. It has, however, been realised that proper measures to address gender gaps would contribute significantly to agricultural and societal development (World Bank 2009; FAO 2011).

In this context, this chapter analyses the impact of gender-related interventions in labour efficiency and gender relations in the context of male labour migration in Nepal. Specifically, the chapter analyses the impact of small farm tools and machinery (thresher and weeder), cultivation practices (line transplanting), and women's participation in technology development. The interventions were piloted in the study areas during 2012 and 2013 through a multidisciplinary action research project (details in *Methodology* section below). Women's overall participation in agriculture is well documented in the research, but there is limited literature available on issues such as drudgery and women's workload, and their empowerment through participation in technology development, testing, and dissemination. In addition, there is limited research on the impact of new technologies on agriculture, specifically those used in the cultivation of neglected crops like finger millet.

This chapter attempts to address these gaps and analyse the effectiveness of new technologies in reducing women's workload. Using a mixed research design combining the collection of quantitative and qualitative data and field experimentation, the chapter illustrates that the introduction of small farm machinery, improved agricultural practices, and women's participation in the process not only reduces women's drudgery, time commitment, and workload, but also improves their status in the community through changes in gender relations, capacity building, and empowerment.

Conceptual framework

Informed by Giddens' concept of *structure-agency dualism*, the men and women in this study are considered *social actors* who have the knowledge and capacity to understand what they do while they do it, which is determined by their day-to-day conduct in the context of social activities (Giddens 1986). According to Long (2001), social actors are not passive observers of the situation, but active participants who can analyse information and strategise their conduct in the process of interaction and negotiation with other actors and the wider social structure. They should be treated not as passive recipients of the development interventions, but as active and powerful agents of change. The social actors are influenced by the structure, but in the process of interaction they also influence the structure, which is in fact the driver of social change. In this context, the chapter adopts an actor-oriented approach that recognises social heterogeneity and the conscious actions of actors for social change, which is an outcome of the interplay and cumulative effect of internal and external factors (Long and Long 1992).

With this theoretical orientation, the conceptual framing of this chapter stems from the premise that the construction of gender relations is the product of conscious interactions between men and women, which are influenced by social, cultural, and economic factors of Nepalese society. More important, the situation of men and women is determined not only by broad societal structures, but also by their day-to-day life experience, interaction, and negotiation, which give rise to new forms of social organisation that ultimately effect changes in gender relations. The level and scale of influence may differ depending on the social position of a particular actor, but it is the interaction between actors and structures that causes change, in a dynamic and cyclical process in time and space (Elder-Vass 2007). In this context, it can be assumed that women's participation in the intervention process increases their access to information and the outside world, thereby increasing their self-confidence and influence in household decision-making. The following paragraphs outline a contextual background for the chapter.

Women, agriculture, and technology adoption

Women form 50 percent of Nepal's total population, and their literacy rate is 25 percent, less than half the rate for men (54.5 percent). About 81 percent of the economically active population is engaged in agriculture and allied industries. Even though the proportion of the persons engaged in this sector is substantially higher among women (91 percent) than men (75 percent), access to land and other production resources is biased towards men: for example, data show only about 20 percent of land registered under women's names (NLRF and CSRC 2013). Besides being a status symbol, land is one of the secured entitlements required to access both formal and informal credit. Women's lesser involvement in economic activities (or outside activities) thus impedes their empowerment and gender equality.

Bennett (2006) points out that despite various efforts made, especially after the political change of the 1990s, progress towards gender equality in Nepal is slow. Women are under-represented in public and political spheres, and this imbalance remains a major constraint to the mainstreaming of policies and programs that focus on women and other excluded groups. Thapa (2008) found differences in the farm productivity of male- versus female-headed households. The United Nations Population Fund (UNFPA 2009) also advocates for gender-responsive approaches to promote gender equality. Women are traditionally responsible for tedious and time-consuming activities such as weeding and harvesting, home gardening, livestock and poultry rearing, and fuel and water collection, which are not considered economic activities and hence are excluded from government censuses and surveys. Contrary to this, men are involved in ploughing, farm management, marketing, storing, and transporting, which demand more decision-making (Upadhyay 2005) and are associated with economic incentive. This situation not only undervalues women's work, but also excludes them from the technology development and policymaking process.

In this context, men and women experience different levels of drudgery and constraint. Studies show that women ranked harvesting, weeding, and threshing as drudgery-prone jobs, while men reported marketing, tillage operation, manuring, and fertilising as difficult jobs (Mrunalini and Snehalatha 2010; Thakur et al. 2001). Though not solely responsible, studies suggest that gender is a significant factor affecting the adoption rate of technology (Quisumbing and Pandolfelli 2010). Moreover, studies have shown that if women used the same level of resources as men on the land they farm, they would produce more, and overall agricultural production would increase (Saxena 2012). Thus, it is important to see how men and women perceive the interventions piloted in the research areas.

Labour out-migration in Nepal

In recent years, Nepal has become a labour-exporting country: 25 percent of its households send their members out to work. Official statistics show that over two million Nepalese (3.2 percent of the country's total population) live outside the country (World Bank 2011). In the 2010–11 fiscal year, about 335,000 people officially left the country in search of employment abroad; of these, 97 percent were male. About 22 percent of the national gross domestic product (GDP) is supplied through remittances (Nepal: DOFE 2011). Because of Nepal's open border policy with India, it is believed that about an equal number leave the country unofficially to and through India.

On the one hand, many male members of remittance-receiving households, having less incentive to work, have reduced their labour supply, exacerbating labour shortages (Lokshin and Glinskaya 2009; Gartaula and Niehof 2013). On the other hand, the increased male out-migration leaves women behind as the main custodians of agriculture. In this changing situation, investing in women and empowering them with new techniques yields better incomes and improved quality of life for their families.

Farm mechanisation in Nepal

Nepal is an agriculture-based economy, with about 81 percent of the population dependent on agriculture and 80 percent of the population working as agriculture labourers (Nepal: Central Bureau of Statistics 2011). Lack of labour in the peak agricultural season, out-migration of rural youth, and poor investment capacity of farmers has resulted in more barren agricultural land in rural areas. Despite strenuous efforts, rural farmers are not able to improve their quality of living.

Farm mechanisation can play a significant role in addressing migration and labour shortage issues in Nepalese agriculture. Currently, animal power is the main source of draft power in Nepalese agriculture: animal and human power represent 40 and 36 percent, respectively, of total farm power available in the country (Shrestha 2012). Most of the country's mechanical power (92 percent) is concentrated in the terai (southern plains) (Full Bright Consultancy 2006).

Because of the lack of infrastructure (particularly roads and electricity) and the narrow bench terraced cultivation systems, agriculture depends primarily upon human and animal power. The traditional wooden plough, sickle, spade, and hoe are the major agricultural tools used throughout the country; the Nepalese government does not yet have an agriculture mechanisation policy (Shrestha 2012). The advances that have been made in farm machinery have targeted major crops like rice, maize, and wheat rather than neglected crops like small millets. Though threshers and milling machines are common in Nepal, they are used mainly for rice, maize, and wheat. The promotion of farm machinery for intercultural operations, especially for minor crops like finger millet, is almost nonexistent. Thus, these interventions are intended not only to address women's drudgery and workload, but also to promote these largely neglected crops.

Methodology

Research locations

The study was conducted in Dhikurpokhari and Kaskikot Village Development Committees (VDCs) of Kaski district, and Jogimara VDC of Dhading district of Nepal. The Dhikurpokhari and Kaskikot VDCs are located in the western hills about 25 kilometres west of the city of Pokhara, while Jogimara VDC is in the central region, about 80 kilometres southwest of Kathmandu (Figure 3.1). All three VDCs are characterised by rain-fed farming with no permanent irrigation facilities; a maize-millet cropping system dominates the higher elevations and a rice-based system the lower elevations, especially along riverbanks. Dhikurpokhari (population 8,081) is located at an altitude of 841 to 2,074 metres above sea level; Kaskikot (population 6,540) at 700 to 1,788 metres above sea level; and Jogimara (population 6,982) at 292 to 1,770 metres above sea level.

Research design, data collection, and analysis

The research that informs this chapter is part of a larger project named "Revalourising small millets in rain-fed regions of South Asia" (RESMISA), implemented by, among other Canadian and South Asian partners, Local Initiatives for Biodiversity, Research and Development (LI-BIRD), Nepal, with financial support from Canada's International Development Research Centre (IDRC) and Department of Foreign Affairs, Trade and Development

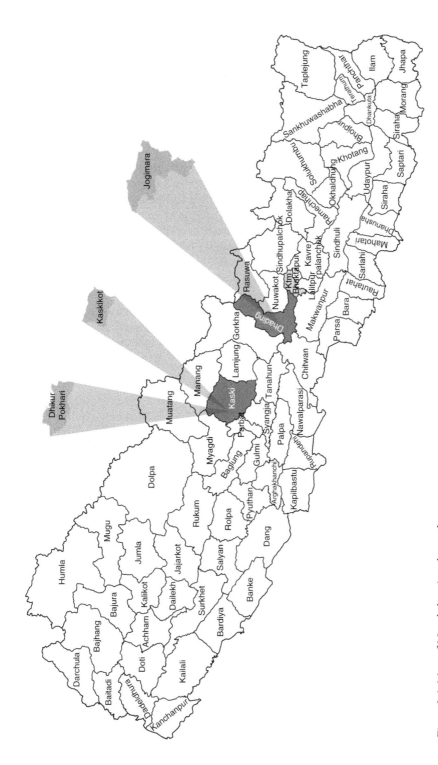

Figure 3.1 Map of Nepal showing the study areas

Source: Mahesh Shrestha, LI-BIRD, Nepal.

(DFATD) under the Canadian International Food Security Research Fund (CIFSRF). This is an action research project that aims to improve the food and nutrition security of women and children in South Asia. It emphasises the generation and dissemination of gender-based participatory knowledge and technology to address the issues of women in finger millet cultivation and post-harvest operations in millet-growing areas of South Asia. The project addresses both the pre- and post-harvest constraints associated with finger millet cultivation by testing small farm tools and machinery, creating varietal options, and implementing various sustainable agricultural practices to address practical gender needs, while strategic gender needs are addressed by engaging women farmers as key players in participatory technology development.

The research embraces a mixed design as part of an action-based approach consisting of three stages of data collection and process documentation: (1) identifying needs or problems through a baseline survey, (2) conducting interventions by piloting improved small farm equipment and agricultural practices, and (3) collecting feedback for scaling up. At the time of data collection, the RESMISA project was still at the pilot stage; however, indications and conditions for scaling up were observed, and are presented in the *Results* section below. The present subsection describes the procedures followed for intervention, which were part of the process of data collection.

Problem identification: baseline survey

A baseline survey was conducted in 2011 that covered 357 randomly selected households: 137 from Dhikurpokhari, 113 from Kaskikot, and 107 from Jogimara. The purpose of the survey was to increase the understanding of cultivation- and production-related constraints for finger millet in Nepal. The baseline results indicated that labour constraints were one of the main reasons for the farmers' declining interest in finger millet cultivation. About 22 percent of respondents perceived finger millet as highly labour intensive, and 30 percent reported that threshing finger millet was a difficult operation. Another study performed as part of RESMISA revealed that 100 percent of farmers in the research area threshed finger millet either by beating the heads with sticks or trampling them with their feet; women did 56 percent of the threshing work (RESMISA 2012). The baseline results also identified lack of labour (24 percent) and difficulty in weeding (12 percent) as the key production constraints of finger millet. Another survey conducted by the project indicated that 56 percent of weeding was done by women (RESMISA 2012). It was also reported that weeding could eliminate up to 50 percent of the production loss in finger millet.

Interventions: piloting small farm equipment and agricultural practices

In order to address the problems associated with finger millet cultivation, three interventions arose in consultation with men and women farmers at the project sites: a pedal thresher, a weeder, and line transplanting.

Pedal thresher: we explored the availability of threshing machines for finger millet. After consulting with the Agricultural Engineering Division of the Nepal Agricultural Research Council (AED/NARC), we arranged to test a pedal thresher they had recently developed. In 2012, three threshers were tested at the project sites by groups from Dhikurpokhari VDC, Kaskikot VDC from Kaski, and Jogimara VDC from Dhading. All three groups were keen to test the new thresher. The group members were shown how to operate the thresher, and the participation of women farmers was encouraged (all our test groups had a significant number of women members). The groups were also oriented on the management of threshers so that more farmers would have an opportunity to use the machine.

After each group had tested the thresher, the farmers' feedback on the equipment was collected and reported to the manufacturer. The Jogimara group gave the machine's performance a positive rating, and requested more threshers; accordingly, they were provided with two more threshers on a 15 percent cost-sharing basis. Similarly, one farmer group in Kaskikot also requested and received a thresher.

Weeder: the availability of weeding tools across Nepal and India was explored, including contact with RESMISA partners and other organisations working in the field. However, no tools appropriate for hilly conditions were found. In discussing this issue with men and women farmers, the idea of developing these tools locally with the help of local blacksmiths was suggested. Nine fork weeders were developed locally, and tested by three groups of farmers (i.e., three weeders were given to farmers' groups in each of the three project VDCs). Since farmers transplant finger millet randomly in between maize rows, the weeders were tested in experimental plots only, as the tool requires line sowing or transplanting. Since the experiments were conducted in one of their plots, the farmers were involved throughout the process. In addition, the farmers tested the weeders on finger millet and other crops in their fields. The pedal thresher and the fork weeder are described in Box 3.1.

Line transplanting: in addition to promoting the use of improved farm tools like the fork weeder, other agronomic interventions to reduce labour requirements for weeding were tested. In the 2012 season, line sowing of finger millet was experimented with in hope of reducing the labour required to raise nursery plants and transplant them, and to see if weeding was easier between the rows. These line sowing experiments did not show promise for the maize-millet cropping system. In the 2013 season, armed with the information gathered from the experiments conducted in 2012, the experiment was redesigned by making a slight change to the farmers' transplanting method. Finger millet transplanting was not a new technology to farmers, but, for the purposes of our experiment, a joint decision was made to adopt the nationally recommended spacing for line transplanting: rows were spaced 15 centimetres apart, and plants 10 centimetres. The experiments were conducted by 27 farmers (10 male and 17 female) from

Box 3.1   Description of pedal thresher and fork weeder

Pedal thresher: the Agricultural Engineering Division of the Nepal Agricultural Research Council (AED/NARC) designed, fabricated, and tested a pedal-operated millet thresher cum pearler. The main purpose of this machine was to reduce drudgery for women farmers in millet threshing and pearling. The machine can thresh and pearl 40 to 50 kilograms of millet per hour, with a threshing efficiency of 97 percent and pearling efficiency of 98 percent. The unit weighs about 50 kilograms. The machine was first released for commercial fabrication in 2007.

Fork weeder: the fork weeder is a locally made hand tool designed to remove weeds from crop fields. It has a handle about a metre long (adjustable for the user's convenience) and four iron spikes, like a fork. The weeder head is 14 centimetres wide; each spike in the fork is two centimetres wide, and the gap between adjacent spikes is also two centimetres. These measurements can be adjusted in the field to match the spacing used between rows of finger millet seedlings. The weeder weighs less than one kilogram if a wooden handle is used, and about one kilogram if a metal handle is used.

six groups in the three project VDCs. The farmers were asked to minutely evaluate any differences they found between the new practice and their traditional practice.

Feedback, evaluation, and scaling up

In the third and final stage, in early 2014, the interventions of the finger millet thresher, the fork weeder, and line transplanting were assessed via a purposive survey of 106 respondents from all three VDCs. The distribution of candidates involved in testing these machines and technologies is presented in Table 3.1. The main purpose of the survey was to determine whether the piloted interventions were working well in the field and helping to reduce

Table 3.1 Respondents' detail for the purposive survey conducted in early 2014

Intervention	Distribution of respondents		
	Men	Women	Total
Thresher	19	22	41
Fork weeder	16	22	38
Line transplanting	10	17	27
Total	45	61	106

drudgery for women, and also to evaluate how the situation of the women involved changed over time. The survey consisted of a semi-structured questionnaire administered in a direct interview with each respondent.

In addition, focus group discussions and in-depth interviews were conducted throughout the process at all three sites to improve the understanding of the underlying causes and issues behind the tested machinery and practices. Quantitative data were analysed using SPSS and Excel software, while qualitative data were analysed manually.

Results and discussion

The cultivation of finger millet is tedious and time-consuming, and women do most of it. The gender interventions made by the project have helped reduce drudgery for women, reduce time spent in intercultural operations, and increase the efficiency of men and women, resulting in increased production and productivity of finger millet. Likewise, the extensive participation of women and men farmers at every stage – from need identification to collection of feedback for scaling up of small farm machinery and practices through farmer groups – helped increase the women's self-confidence, self-esteem, and social status, and improved their empowerment and gender equality. The following section elaborates on the positive impacts of the interventions in the research areas.

Tools to reduce drudgery, time, effort, and safety hazards

Harvesting and threshing of finger millet is done mainly in October–November, which is also the festival season in Nepal. This puts huge time pressure on farmers, especially women, as they have to prepare for the festival while taking care of the crops that are ready for harvesting. When the millet is ready to harvest, the mature ear heads (panicles) are picked using iron sickles, and the plant stalks are left in the field. The manual threshing is a long procedure: the harvested panicles are collected in containers (usually bamboo baskets) and/or are heaped at a convenient place. The heaps of panicles are left for a period of a week to a month, as farmers believe that the heat generated in the heap helps in easy separation of grains while threshing. Traditionally, the grains are separated from the ear heads in three ways: (1) sun-drying the heaped ear heads for a couple of days, then beating the panicles with sticks on a threshing floor (generally a levelled mud floor, or more commonly a home courtyard smeared with cow dung slurry), (2) trampling the ear heads (in this case the ear heads are not sun-dried, as dried panicles are hard on the feet), or (3) if there is a large quantity of ear heads, the heads are sun-dried, then threshed by the trampling of bullocks; this practice is less commonly used. Smaller quantities of grain or partially threshed panicles are usually pounded (threshed) by hand. Farmers who use the trampling method of threshing have to keep the ear heads in the heap longer, but no longer than 15 days lest the grains deteriorate in quality.

Weeding of finger millet fields is also done manually. Especially in the context of male out-migration, women farmers often have trouble finding labour for weeding. Even though weeding is exclusively a women's job, men's absence from home has increased women's workload.

The results show that introduction of these improved small farm tools has reduced the drudgery for women, notably by reducing the time required for manual threshing and weeding by 30 percent. Eighty-three percent of respondents (94.7 percent of them women) found pedal threshers to be an important alternative to manual threshing, while 85 percent (82.4 percent of them women) found the fork weeders helpful.

Table 3.2 summarises the advantages the respondents reported when using each tool in their agricultural activities. Farmers found the pedal thresher effective for grain separation, grain cleaning, and husk removal, and reported that the grain was free of dust and other inert materials. They also noted that the pedal thresher required less effort to operate, completed the task more quickly, and, more importantly, prevented injury to their feet and reduced back pain compared to manual threshing (though a few farmers complained of leg pain while operating the thresher). They used the saved time for social work, household activities, and rest. One respondent described her experience:

> [The] thresher is easier and quicker than using a stick and feet. It reduces our workload since men are supporting us to operate this machine. The machine also improves post-harvest quality of the grains, as fermented and tempered grains do not have good cooking quality.
>
> (BMG (F), 34, Jogimara, 7 February 2014)

The responses regarding the fork weeder were similar in terms of drudgery reduction and time saving. The respondents reported that using the fork weeder required less effort and less time than manual weeding, reduced bending and back pain, and protected them from insect and snake bites and other injuries, as they did not have to weed with their bare hands (Table 3.2).

One of the important aspects of the piloted pedal thresher is that it requires two people to operate, one to run the pedal and the other to feed the panicles and collect the grains. The trial resulted in increased involvement of men in threshing (from 15 to 32 percent), a change that helped reduce women's workload from 85 to 65 percent. In the case of the fork weeder, the labour required for weeding was reduced by 17 percent and the involvement of men in weeding increased from 8 to 15 percent. In contrast to their usual reluctance to participate in weeding, the men showed interest in testing the weeding tools, and their involvement not only reduced women's workload, but helped complete the job faster and promoted labour sharing between men and women. This has important implications for gender roles in the Nepalese sociocultural context.

Table 3.2 Experiences of men and women farmers in the use of improved small farm machinery

Intervention	Advantages	Response (%)		
		Men	Women	Total
Pedal thresher	Grain separation	94.7	77.3	85.4
	Cleaning	84.2	72.7	78.0
	Husk removal	84.2	77.3	80.5
	Less effort	73.7	59.1	65.9
	Less time	78.9	50.0	63.4
	Less dust	63.2	72.7	68.3
	Less injury	94.7	95.5	95.1
	Less back pain	84.2	72.7	78.0
	Total	100.0	100.0	100.0
Fork weeder	Less effort	80.0	82.4	81.5
	Less time	70.0	70.6	70.4
	Less labour	50.0	64.7	59.3
	Easy weeding	80.0	82.4	81.5
	Saves from snake and insect bites	90.0	94.1	92.6
	Less back pain	70.0	88.2	81.5
	Less injury	90.0	94.1	92.6
	Total	100.0	100.0	100.0

Source: Purposive survey, 2014.

In Nepal, machinery is generally considered men's domain, which suggests that there is potential for increased participation by males in the threshing of finger millet. For example, operating the pedal of the threshing machine requires a lot of physical power, but since it is a "machine" men will not mind doing the job. Men's entry into the threshing process provides some relief to women from the heavy work they have been doing, which can play an important role in reducing women's drudgery. As well, men traditionally perform outdoor tasks, while women remain at home doing household chores. Since machines are community assets, men would enjoy the outdoor activity of threshing. As an added benefit, women participating in threshing are venturing out of their traditional (indoor) territory and entering the men's space, changing gender ideology.

The respondents reported that the fork weeder had significant advantages over manual weeding. According to the farmers, the snake and insect infestation is high, especially in Kaski. Snakes and insects can easily hide among weeds and may bite women as they do the weeding. However, respondents soon discovered that the fork weeder could be used to chase snakes and insects away before they started weeding. Singh et al. (2007) reported that weeding is a strenuous job, and that the odd posture adopted by women while weeding may significantly increase their heart rate, leading to irreparable damage to the body. They found that the weeders proved efficient from an ergonomic perspective, and reduced users' average working heart rate and energy expenditure as compared to traditional methods.

A labour-saving practice

In Jogimara VDC, cowpea, blackgram, horsegram, and soybean are grown as a mixed crop with finger millet, while in the other two VDCs finger millet is rotated, as a sole crop, with maize. Hence, the problems associated with finger millet cultivation cannot be viewed in isolation. Therefore, the proposed agronomic practices were implemented by taking into account the maize-millet farming system, and tested in the field in 2012, 2013, and 2014. Among the various practices tested, line transplanting of seedlings was found to have the highest potential in terms of reducing the labour required for finger millet cultivation.

The majority of farmers (85 percent of women and 92 percent of men) reported that maize sown in line makes intercultural operations, including the transplanting and weeding of finger millet, easier. Thus, this practice can reduce labour and drudgery to some extent. When using traditional sowing methods, the plant number per unit area is very high, since seeds are either broadcast or sown behind the plough; consequently, about 83 percent of women reported that they always had difficulty thinning the plants when using the traditional method. With the new intervention, they realised that thinning is much easier if crops are line transplanted. Moreover, 63 percent of women felt that this method also made it easier to apply fertiliser, do the weeding, and harvest maize cobs. Similarly, 59 percent of women and 46 percent of men reported that with line sowing, there were more maize plants in the field, with thicker stems and bigger cobs than maize grown using traditional methods. Fifty-three percent of respondents (46 percent of them women) found the line sowing method useful, and indicated their interest in continuing it in the next cropping season.

Participation, empowerment, and gender equality

The RESMISA project has adopted a group approach to test interventions, with a primary focus on women. The project has supported more than 2,500 farmers (about 77 percent of them women) who participated in several research and awareness related activities (RESMISA 2013). This has contributed significantly to women's empowerment and gender equality, as illustrated by the cases of SUG (Box 3.2) and TNP (Box 3.3).

These cases indicate two things: (1) the way women articulate their needs and requirements for scaling up machines and technologies to improve agricultural practices definitely go beyond the traditional view of women's subordination to men; and (2) the changes illustrated by SUG and

Box 3.2   Transformative changes in SUG's life.

SUG (age 50) lives in Paudurkot village of Dhikurpokhari VDC with one son and two daughters. She has up to high school education and is active in women's education in the village. Her husband has been working abroad since the time they got married some 30 years ago, and she bears all the responsibilities for her children, her in-laws, and the household management. She actively participated in field experiments and other projects in the village. She is one of the farmers who tested the finger millet thresher and fork weeder, and participated in a field trial for line transplanting in 2013.

SUG believes education and public awareness are the key factors in women's empowerment and gender equality. On that basis, she became involved in providing informal education to village women. Since women are busy during the day, she teaches at night. She has helped many women learn to write their names, clean their homes, and build toilets on their home premises. Through various projects and activities of governmental and non-governmental organisations, she has built her capacity to speak and interact, and developed her confidence: "Earlier, I felt so difficult to pronounce my name and introduce myself in small group meetings, but now I can fight for our rights." She expresses gratitude to all the government and non-government programs that provided her with the opportunity to develop her skills to speak up and interact with others.

She now works in key positions for several groups at the local and even national level, and she feels that she gets respect from the community members. In the absence of her husband, she is the head of her household, and by being involved in group activities and other social initiatives she has become a role model for many villagers. She says, "Earlier nobody believed me, but now village members put my name in any kind of group or social works without asking me." She adds, "Education, opportunity, and interest are the three key things to bring transformative change in women's life." She sees these as positive changes in her life, and says,

> Managing [the] house without [my] husband was not easy. I had to do both household chores and agricultural works. Now, [my] children are grown up and they give big hands. If my husband was not gone out, I doubt if I could be involved in these activities this closely. I would be working in the kitchen and my husband would be taking charge of everything, which now I have been doing. I would never come out of the house, like many women in the village.

She also acknowledged the efforts made in her village by organisations like LI-BIRD, and how they get villagers involved in different project activities. She chairs her VDC's steering committee for RESMISA implementation. She added that being involved in the project gave her a chance to interact with visitors from Canada and India, and to learn new finger millet recipes. She commented,

> If you had not approached us, we would not have known how these new technologies work. Now, we know how to select good varieties. We are doing these things for years, but you taught us how to do it systematically and thanks to the idea that seeks farmers' involvement in their work.
>
> (Interview, Dhikurpokhari, 5 February 2014)

Box 3.3 A women's group in Kaski

TNP (age 34) lives with her husband, one son, and two daughters in Dhikurpokhari VDC of Kaski. She has been chairing a women's group formed by the project for the past three years. Being from the Dalit community, she sees a huge change in her life brought about by her engagement in several project activities. She has a small goat farm and also produces vegetables for home consumption and the local market. According to TNP, local women were initially reluctant to join the group, and some members left shortly after joining. But now the group has 32 members.

TNP reported that thanks to the group, she has learned many things. She can now play an important role in household decision-making, and can speak up in public. The progressive development led her from being a general member of the group to the leadership role. She feels that she is now respected to some extent in society, even if she is from the Dalit community. She proudly says that her husband is known by her name, not the other way round, and in Nepal, that matters. She says, "Knowledge and opportunity are the two wheels for women's empowerment."

(Interview, Dhikurpokhari, 9 February 2014)

TNP's cases demonstrate how education and other opportunities to participate in local initiatives help build women's self-confidence and self-esteem, and raise their social status in a hierarchical society.

It is thus important to understand the complexity and diversity of "actors" as agents of change and development. It is increasingly recognised that there has always been a gap between researchers and farmers in the understanding of technology. By identifying persistent gaps and involving the end users in the process of technology development, the adoption of new technologies can be promoted and contributions are made to the empowerment of the communities we work for.

Scaling up: conditions and motivations

For about 85 percent of male and 97 percent of female respondents, the finger millet thresher introduced as part of this research project was the first one they had ever seen. Eighty-five percent of the men and 80 percent of the women were interested in using the machine in future, as they found it saved them time and effort in threshing. It was not a flawless intervention, however. The thresher requires physical effort to operate its pedal, and farmers were curious about whether they would get electric ones. Indeed, electric threshers have the potential to reduce drudgery further while addressing the issue of labour scarcity because of male out-migration.

Another issue flagged by the farmers was the difficulty of transporting the machine from one household to another due to the uneven terrain and scattered settlement. No single household could afford to buy a machine, yet carrying the machine from one house to another proved difficult. Therefore the farmers, especially the women, requested lightweight machines with wheels, if available.

About 90 percent of the women and 84 percent of the men found the fork weeder useful for removing trailing type weeds, but not as effective on weeds with an upright growth habit, especially in Kaski. Clearly the fork weeder needs modification to increase its efficiency in weeding. The farmers found the fork weeders more effective on other crops, especially vegetables such as cauliflower and cabbage, which are grown in line and with wider spacing. The farmers appreciated the usefulness of the fork weeder and wanted to keep this tool for future use; as well, they were curious as to whether there were any weeding tools applicable to a variety of weeds and agronomic practices.

It was observed that the line transplanting method of finger millet cultivation, along with line sowing of maize, will very likely be adopted in the future, since these practices make many intercultural and other operations easier. Forty-six percent of the women and 62 percent of the men showed interest in trying line transplanting of finger millet in the following year in at least one of their terraces. As well, 89 percent of the women and 93 percent of the men suggested that spacing between rows and plants be reduced by more than half, thus reducing weed infestation and increasing crop yield. These points clearly indicate that line transplanting, with optimal spacing, of finger millet could lead to adoption of this practice without any loss in yield. However, most of the farmers (96 percent of the women and 89 percent of the men) shared that line sowing of maize is difficult without a sowing machine suitable for the hill terraces; thus, 43 percent of the women and 75 percent of the men requested a machine for sowing maize in line. The project recently provided 12 auto-seeders, and farmers have started using this tool. Shirahatti et al. (2007) reported that arduous operations like sowing and transplanting can be made more comfortable by the use of direct seeders; Sreelata and Antony (2012), on the other hand, were not optimistic that technology would reduce drudgery for women farm workers. However, and interestingly, women in our study sample showed more interest than men in these new practices and tools.

Of the 77 respondents interested in continuing to use these improved farm tools and practices, 55 percent were women. This figure contradicts previous studies that indicated women are less likely than men to adopt improved agricultural technologies (Thapa 2008; Akudugu et al. 2012; Ragasa et al. 2012). This study confirmed that if women are given access to technology development by including them right from the beginning and addressing their needs, they are attracted to technology and engaged in the process. As stated earlier, because of the absence of their husbands and the women's increased involvement in the management role, these women have increased their decision-making capacity, which has also been demonstrated through the high participation of women in technology testing and their stated interest in applying these innovations in future. It is important to note that this study focused on the response of men and women farmers on newly piloted technology like the thresher and weeder – efficient tools and machinery designed to reduce women's workload and minimise the gender gap. It was not an adoption study, which would be conducted after a few years of scaling up and would furnish a better idea of gender differences in technology adoption. Nevertheless, the present study showed that since the adoption of new technologies depends on who makes decisions on productive resources such as land, labour, and capital, women are entering into the sphere of household decision-making, altering traditional notions of gender roles in Nepal.

Conclusion

Whether or not the suggested farm machinery and agricultural practices are feasible for long-term agricultural development, their contribution to increasing women's self-confidence and self-esteem is a key factor in women's empowerment and gender equality. The positive outcomes brought about by these interventions addressed the major gender issues and primary concerns of the project as a whole. They still had to go through a number of trials and errors to get final approval from the field and scaling up of a particular piece of farm equipment or agricultural practice. Even so, the qualitative changes observed in women's lives indicated a path towards gender equality. Moreover, the study proved that if women are given an opportunity to participate in technology development, they can be equally involved in long-term agricultural development.

It should also be noted that these changes are not solely the result of the interventions mentioned, but are a cumulative effect of the diverse activities conducted by many organisations, including LI-BIRD. Some of the changes are quantifiable, visible, and traceable – for instance, the gender equality implied by men's acceptance of the threshing machine. Before the machine was introduced, the men would never have considered helping the women with threshing. Moreover, thanks to the time saved by using the machinery, women have more time to spend on social activities or rest, and men have more time to support women's health and well-being. Other changes cannot be quantified, but they clearly have a positive impact on quality of life: for example, the men's entry into the traditional women's domain changes the idea of gender roles.

This research study of improved farm machinery and agricultural practices in Nepal illustrates that, when it comes to agriculture, men and women have different and gender-specific interests, motivation, and attitudes to technology. Farmers cannot be considered a single, homogenous group, because men and women farmers have different and gender-specific needs. It is important to understand the complexity and diversity of these social actors as agents of development.

Acknowledgements

The authors acknowledge the support of the Canadian International Food Security Research Fund (CIFSRF), a program of Canada's International Development Research Centre (IDRC) undertaken with the financial support of the Government of Canada through the Department of Foreign Affairs, Trade and Development (DFATD).

References

All website URLs accessed on 7 April 2016.

Adhikari, Raj K. 2012. "Economics of Finger Millet (*Elecusine coracana* G.) Production and Marketing in Peri Urban Area of Pokhara Valley of Nepal." *Journal of Development and Agricultural Economics* 4 (6): 151–7.

Akudugu, Mamudu Abunga, Emelia Guo, and Samuel Kwezi Ndzebah Dadzie. 2012. "Adoption of Modern Agricultural Production Technologies by Farm Households in Ghana: What Factors Influence their Decisions?" *Journal of Biology, Agriculture and Healthcare* 2 (3): 1–14.

Bennett, Lynn. 2006. *Unequal Citizens: Gender, Caste and Ethnic Exclusions in Nepal.* Kathmandu: Department for International Development, UK (DFID) and World Bank.

Dida, Mathews M., and Katrien M. Devos. 2006. "Finger Millet." In Chittaranjan Kole, ed., *Cereals and Millets. Genome Mapping and Molecular Breeding in Plants* series, Vol. 1. Berlin: Springer-Verlag, 333–43.

Doss, Cheryl R. (2002). "Men's Crops? Women's Crops? The Gender Patterns of Cropping in Ghana." *World Development* 30 (11): 1987–2000.

Elder-Vass, Dave. 2007. "Reconciling Archer and Bourdieu in an Emergentist Theory of Action." *Sociological Theory* 25 (4): 325–46.

FAO (Food and Agriculture Organization of the United Nations). 2011. *The State of Food and Agriculture 2010–11*. Rome: FAO.

Full Bright Consultancy. 2006. *Feasibility Study on Agriculture Mechanization in Terai Region of Nepal*. Report submitted to Agricultural Engineering Directorate, Department of Agriculture, Government of Nepal.

Gartaula, Hom Nath, and Anke Niehof. 2013. "Migration To and From the Nepal Terai: Shifting Movements and Motives." *South Asianist* 2 (2): 28–50.

Gartaula, Hom Nath, Anke Niehof, and Leontine Visser. 2010. "Feminisation of Agriculture as an Effect of Male Out-Migration: Unexpected Outcomes from Jhapa District, Eastern Nepal." *International Journal of Interdisciplinary Social Sciences* 5 (2): 565–78.

Giddens, Anthony. 1986. *The Constitution of Society: Outline of the Theory of Structuration*. Berkeley: University of California Press.

Joshi, V., P.L. Gautam, Bhag Mal, G.D. Sharma, and S. Kochhar. 2002. "Conservation and Use of Underutilized Crops: An Indian Perspective." In J.M.M. Engels, V.R. Rao, A.H.D. Brown, and M.T. Jackson, eds, *Managing Plant Genetic Diversity*. Rome: International Plant Genetic Resource Institute, 61–73.

Lokshin, Michael, and Elena Glinskaya. 2009. "The Effect of Male Migration on Employment Patterns of Women in Nepal." *World Bank Economic Review* 23 (3): 481–507.

Long, Norman. 2001. *Development Sociology: Actor Perspective*. London and New York: Routledge.

Long, Norman, and Ann Long. 1992. "From Paradigm Lost to Paradigm Regained? The Case for an Actor-Oriented Sociology of Development." In Norman Long and Ann Long, eds, *Battlefields of Knowledge: The Interlocking of Theory and Practice in Social Research and Development*. London and New York: Routledge, 16–46.

Mal, Bhag, S. Padulosi, and S. Bala Ravi, eds. 2010. *Minor Millets in South Asia: Learnings from IFAD-NUS Project in India and Nepal*. Rome: Bioversity International and M.S. Swaminathan Research Foundation.

Moser, Caroline O.N. 1993. *Gender Planning and Development: Theory, Practice and Training*. London and New York: Routledge.

Mrunalini, A., and Ch. Snehalatha. 2010. "Drudgery Experiences of Gender in Crop Production Activities." *Journal of Agricultural Sciences* 1 (1): 49–51.

NARC (Nepal Agricultural Research Council). 2005. *NARC Newsletter* 12 (1): 5.

Nepal: Central Bureau of Statistics. 2011. *National Sample Census of Agriculture, Nepal 2011*. Kathmandu: Central Bureau of Statistics.

Nepal: DOFE (Department of Foreign Employment). 2011. *Annual Report 2067–68 (2010–11)*. Kathmandu: DOFE, Ministry of Labour and Transport Management.

NLRF (National Land Rights Forum) and CSRC (Community Self-Reliance Center). 2013. *Women's Land Ownership and Identity: Livelihood and Self-Dignity*. Summary report, Second National Conference of Women Farmer, Kathmandu.

Quisumbing, Agnes R., and Lauren Pandolfelli. 2010. "Promising Approaches to Address the Needs of Poor Female Farmers: Resources, Constraints, and Interventions." *World Development* 38 (4): 581–92.

Ragasa, Catherine, Guush Berhane, Fanaye Tadesse, and Alemayehu Seyoum Taffesse. 2012. *Gender Differences in Access to Extension Services and Agricultural Productivity*. ESSP Working Paper 49. Washington, DC: Ethiopia Strategy Support

Program II (ESSP), Ethiopian Development Research Institute (EDRI), and International Food Policy Research Institute (IFPRI).

RESMISA ("Revalourising small millets in rain-fed regions of South Asia") [research project]. 2012. *Baseline Survey in Project Sites: A Report.* Tamil Nadu, India, and Winnipeg, Canada: Development of Humane Action Foundation and Canadian Mennonite University.

RESMISA. 2013. *Third Interim Report, March 2013.* Tamil Nadu, India, and Winnipeg, Canada: Development of Humane Action Foundation and Canadian Mennonite University.

Saxena, Lopamudra Patnaik. 2012. *Gender Dimension of Climate Change and Food Security.* SAWTEE Briefing Paper No. 13. Kathmandu, Nepal: South Asia Watch on Trade, Economics and Environment (SAWTEE).

Shirahatti, S.S., M.S. Badiger, and K.V. Prakash. 2007. *Agricultural Engineering Interventions to Increase the Productivity of Women in Agriculture: Some Studies from India.* www.fao.org/fileadmin/user_upload/fsn/docs/Gender_and_Ag_Engineering.pdf.

Shrestha, Shreemat. 2012. *Status of Agricultural Mechanization in Nepal.* Presentation prepared for the United Nations Economic and Social Commission for Asia and the Pacific Centre for Sustainable Agricultural Mechanization. www.unapcaem.org/Activities%20Files/A1112Rt/np_ppt.pdf.

Singh, Suman, Puja Mathur, and Madhu Rathore. 2007. "Weeders for Drudgery Reduction of Women Farm Workers in India." *Journal of Agricultural Engineering* 44 (3): 33–8.

Sreelata, M., and Naomi Antony. 2012. "Can Technology Rescue Women Farm Workers from Drudgery?" [Weblog entry]. SciDev.Net, 4 December. www.scidev.net/global/r-d/feature/can-technology-rescue-women-farm-workers-from-drudgery—1.html.

Thakur, Sonika, Shashi Kanta Varma, and Patricia A. Goldey. 2001. "Perceptions of Drudgery in Agricultural and Animal Husbandry Operations: A Gender Analysis from Haryana State, India." *Journal of International Development* 13 (8): 1165–78.

Thapa, Sridhar. 2008. *Gender Differentials in Agricultural Productivity: Evidence from Nepalese Household Data.* Munich, Germany: Munich Archive.

UNFPA (United Nations Population Fund). 2009. *Gender Equality and Empowerment of Women in Nepal.* Kathmandu: UNFPA.

Upadhyay, Bhawana. 2005. "Women and Natural Resource Management: Illustrations from India and Nepal." *Natural Resources Forum* 29 (3): 224–32.

World Bank. 2009. *Gender in Agriculture Sourcebook.* Washington, DC: World Bank.

World Bank. 2011. *Migration and Remittances Factbook 2011* (2nd ed.). Washington, DC: International Bank for Reconstruction and Development/World Bank. http://siteresources.worldbank.org/INTLAC/Resources/Factbook2011-Ebook.pdf.

4   Teach a woman to fish

Encountering empowerment in community fish farming in Eastern India

Rajakishor Mahana and Durairaja Ramulu

Introduction

Traditionally, fish farming in Asia has been a male-dominated activity, with women making large-scale contributions to feeding and taking care of fish (Barman 2001; Kelkar 2001; Kusakabe 2003; Sullivan 2004; Sriputinibondh et al. 2005). Thus, ownership of the natural resources associated with fish farming, such as rivers, ponds, etc., remains in the hands of the men. Access to and control over natural resources, as a form of capital, reinforce men's authority over women. Neo-liberal approaches to poverty alleviation often emphasise entrepreneurial and market-based strategies intended to contribute to empowerment through enhanced access to resources by poor and marginalised people. Building on a poverty alleviation project in the Kundra block in the Koraput district of southern Odisha (India), the chapter investigates gender issues in natural resource management (particularly ponds) by examining the changing mechanisms of resource allocation. Aiming at understanding agency and the process of empowerment, this study investigates how women expand their access to and control over the natural and social resources that enable them to participate in decision-making, local accountability, and performance evaluation, which in turn brings them social and economic freedom and empowerment (Agarwal 1997; Kabeer 2005).

In other words, this research was designed to answer the following question: Do access to and control over natural resources make women socially and economically empowered? As part of the interventions of a project funded by the International Development Research Centre (IDRC), "Alleviating poverty and malnutrition in agro-biodiversity hotspots" (APM), the M.S. Swaminathan Research Foundation (MSSRF) promoted fish farming among the farmers in 32 tribal-dominated settlements of the Kundra block in the Koraput district of Odisha. Most of the community ponds were leased by the men of their respective villages. Interestingly, however, we found that a group of Bhumia tribal women farmers had leased two community ponds – successfully bidding against the local dominant Dom (Scheduled Caste) male group – and had farmed fish there from 2006 to 2011. The women's success at fish farming (not to mention their ownership of the ponds) gave an initial impression that they had challenged the male-dominated society by mobilising resource allocation mechanisms in their favour. In recognition of their effort, MSSRF provided support to the women's group, among others, for fish farming in 2012. However, the impression of women's empowerment and gender equality quickly faded when the dominant Dom male group reappropriated the community pond through local politics and social and economic capital. The study therefore also investigates how village culture, local politics, and male patriarchy do not conform to the development ideology of resource allocation (to women) for ensuring gender equity and women's empowerment, and how, in turn, gender inequality and rural poverty are perpetuated.

Revisiting Bourdieu's "relational thinking" of field, capital, and habitus

Poverty alleviation has been a topic of intense debate among scholars of various disciplines, from economists to anthropologists and biotechnologists to botanists. Drawing on modernisation theory and its allied neo-liberal economic agenda, scholars have argued that improved access to productive assets is vital for enhancing "capabilities" and empowering the poor (Sen 1999; Bhagwati and Panagariya 2013). A handful of authors have also investigated how politics and power influence resource allocation mechanisms in organisations (Covaleski and Dirsmith 1983, 1986; Macintosh and Quattrone 1994; Kurunmäki 1999a, 1999b; Everett 2003; Neu et al. 2003). But little attention has been paid to how village culture and politics influence organisational budgeting and resource allocation mechanisms (Wickramasinghe and Hopper 2005; Jayasinghe and Wickramasinghe 2006; Alawattage et al. 2007; Alawattage and Wickramasinghe 2009; Hopper et al. 2009; Jayasinghe and Thomas 2009). A study on development accounting by Kalum Jayasinghe and Danture Wikramasinghe examines how "discursive domination, material relations, patronage politics and resultant everyday practices" (2011: 397) influence resource allocation mechanisms in a Sri Lankan fishing village.

However, these theoretical postulations and frameworks do little to explain the role of village culture and local politics in influencing village level resource allocation mechanisms, particularly those related to women. A primary analysis shows that, in spite of progress in development accounting and women's empowerment, poverty continues to prevail because of the village politics and cultural practices embedded in the social structure. Here, Bourdieu's theoretical concepts of *field*, *capital*, and *habitus* help us to capture thick descriptions of how resource allocation mechanisms in tribal villages of Koraput are governed and controlled by a particular structural logic, and how poverty is perpetuated by the same mechanisms. The following paragraphs provide a brief description of Bourdieu's ethnographic approach and its relevance to the present work.

Why Bourdieu? One of the authors finds parallels between his own ethnographic encounters and Bourdieu's notable ethnographic experiences in the villages of Kabylia and Bearn (Bourdieu 1962). Drawing on earlier experiences elsewhere in Odisha and two years of engagement in a poverty alleviation project in Koraput, Odisha, the author confirmed that, despite many international donor agency-led poverty alleviation programs along with benevolent delivery mechanisms of the welfare state and, importantly, 20 years of committed services from a reputed non-governmental organisation (NGO), the prevailing dynamics of power relations in villages have maintained poverty and underdevelopment (Mahana 2011, 2016). Bourdieu found that village politics (a legacy of French colonisation, in the case of Kabylia village) was central to the status quo, and this research in the tribal villages of Koraput led to the same conclusion: village politics, linked with people's conventional beliefs, values, and practices, determine the life experience of the villagers. According to Bourdieu, poverty alleviation is a *field*, a social space,[1] where actors are involved in a game towards accumulating *capital* (economic or other) based on their acting, feeling, and being – what Bourdieu calls *habitus*. As well, the whole social system is embedded in the structural logic of what Bourdieu calls *symbolic violence*, often propagated by village politics, state welfarism, market capitalism, and NGO professionalism.

Field is external in nature, and simply means a social space (Bourdieu 1993, 2005). Bourdieu defines field as "a network, or a configuration, of objective relations between positions" (Bourdieu and Wacquant 1992: 97). The key of the concept is that field consists of social relations rather than individuals or social structures. Using a game analogy, Bourdieu explains that the field represents the game itself, and the players are engaged in maintaining a set of relations as they anticipate and react to the moves of the other players occupying various positions. He further explains that the social relations are competitive (Vandenberghe 1999) where social actors therein vie for accumulation of what Bourdieu calls *capital* (economic and symbolic capital). (For details of different forms of capital, see Bourdieu 2006.) The role of capital influences the operation of the field. Bourdieu (1985) observes that the relative weight (volume) and structure (composition) of the capital determines the distribution of agents into a particular field and their positional power in social relations with other agents. In social space, the social agents compete with each other to channel these forms of capital into their ventures and to accumulate economic capital, while often misrecognising, though not violating, the rights of "low capital owners", i.e., the poor – what Bourdieu calls *symbolic violence*. However, the poor do not perceive it as violence, so firmly is the social system embedded in their lives and expectations.

Central to this observation is what Bourdieu calls *habitus*, which he defines as "a system of lasting and transposable dispositions which, integrating past experiences, functions at every moment as a matrix of perceptions, appreciations, and actions and makes possible the achievement of infinitely diversified tasks" (1977: 214) – in other words, an internalised structural logic that is expressed through an agent's actions. (For details, see Bourdieu 1990, 2004.) Thus, habitus is internal in nature, and comprises the taken-for-granted, shared meanings and behaviours utilised by the individuals within the social space. In contrast to rational choice theory, which believes that social action is determined by conscious, objective, and rational decisions for achieving a particular goal, habitus assumes a practical logic that may be vague and fuzzy. Again using sport analogy, Bourdieu equates habitus with the "feel or sense of the game" that guides a player's performance. A player's actions in the field are guided by his or her perceptions and general feel for the game more than by a conscious, rational decision-making process.

Though habitus is central to the works of Bourdieu, it cannot be treated as a stand-alone concept. Rather, it is important to consider habitus in relation to field and capital. Transcending the traditional theoretical frameworks that either focus on social actors and their immediate actions, values, and perceptions or take a more macro approach and focus on social structures, the relational thinking approach addresses the relationship between objective and subjective without diverting attention from the role of the social actors. Building on these theoretical concepts, the following section reflects on governance and control and the process of resource allocation mechanisms from the perspective of habitus that links to capital, in the field of poverty alleviation in general and fish farming in particular.

Methodology

This study benefited from a detailed ethnography (based on interviews, focus group discussions, observation, and case studies) enriched with rich oral cultures and participatory observations gathered in two years of project implementation. The data were substantiated with two detailed quantitative household surveys (one carried out in 2011 among 2,004 households in 32 tribal-dominated settlements in the Kundra block of Koraput district in southern Odisha, and the other, which included a nutrition survey, conducted in 2013 among 500 households); quantitative fish farming data collected regularly in 9 community ponds during 2012–13 and 16 community ponds during 2013–14; and finally, reiterated analyses.

The area and people

The study was conducted in the tribal-dominated Kundra block of the Koraput district of southern Odisha, India. Geographically, the study area is located in hilly terrain comprising plateaus where people have settled and carved out lands for farming. Upland cultivation, including shifting cultivation, is also practised. As one of the KBK (Koraput, Bolangir, and Kalahandi) districts known as hunger hotspots of India, Koraput has received significant state funding and support from national and international development agencies. Though it was recognised in 2012 as one of the Food and Agriculture Organization of the United Nations' (FAO) Globally Important Agricultural Heritage Systems (GIAHSs) for its biodiversity, traditional knowledge system, and importance as a centre of origin for rice, Koraput also has the dubious distinction of being known for its poverty, hunger, and backwardness, thus presenting a paradoxical picture of resource prosperity and economic poverty. What follows is a brief summary of the findings of the two quantitative surveys of the area and its people.

Of a total population of 8,547 belonging to 2,004 households in 32 settlements, 40 percent belong to Scheduled Tribe, 28 percent to Scheduled Caste, 24 percent to Backward Caste, and the remaining 8 percent to the General category. Of the 2,004 households, 37 are landless, and 56 percent are marginal (less than one hectare) and small farmers (one to two hectares). The average size of landholding per household is 1.07 hectare, of which about 0.4 hectare is lowland and the rest upland. The main crop grown in the lowland is paddy. The primary occupation of household heads is crop farming (57 percent), followed by wage labour (30 percent). From 11 percent of households, at least one person migrated in 2012; the average duration of migration was four months, and average income earned was 14,754 rupees (Rs.). Average household income was Rs. 43,379, derived primarily (54 percent) from the sale of market surplus agricultural produce. Average household expenditure was Rs. 31,336, almost half of which (48 percent) was spent on food. The major source of supply of staple food was farming (49 percent), followed by the Public Distribution System (43 percent). Fifty-three percent of households reported that they were worried about food security all the time, and 38 percent were worried most of the time.

Natural resource management and community fish farming in Koraput

As mentioned earlier, the main occupations of the people in the Kundra block of the Koraput district are crop farming followed by wage earning. Our baseline survey showed that there were 68 private ponds and 32 community ponds, but only a few were used for fish farming. Freshwater aquaculture was initiated in the community in 2012 as part of MSSRF's research project APM. Ponds were selected in consultation with the villagers. For each community pond, a Pond Users' Group (PUG) was formed, consisting of all household heads of the village; from within their number they selected the executive committee members (president, secretary, etc.) who would be responsible for the overall management of the pond. As required, PUGs leased the ponds from the *Panchayat* (the local government body) in order to use them for fish farming. MSSRF provided fish fingerlings on the following terms:

1 Fish fingerlings and technical support (including training programs) would be provided to the community and private pond owners at no cost.
2 As a participatory initiative, the community would be responsible for the overall management of the pond, including cleaning the pond, feeding the fish, etc.

3   All or most of the fish harvested would be consumed by the villagers. Any surplus fish would be sold in the same or neighbouring villages at a subsidised price.

The fish fingerlings were released with help from community members in 9 community ponds and 16 private ponds in 2012. MSSRF also hired training personnel to educate community members on fresh water aquaculture.

In total, 717 households benefited from fish farming, and each household received an average of 2.647 kg of fish for consumption within a harvest period of two months (see Table 4.1). We observed that though the contribution of community fish farming in Kundra to the household consumption of fish was insignificant, the fish farming initiative did have four important results: (1) using underutilised water bodies for fish farming, (2) promoting collective action, (3) providing households with additional fish for consumption, and (4) learning and adopting fish farming technology (by the community) that enabled the community to continue fish farming even after the conclusion of the project. The number of ponds brought under freshwater aquaculture increased to 54 (including 16 community ponds) in 2013–14.

Table 4.1 Details of fish farming production and consumption, 2012–2013

Category of consumers	No. of ponds	No. of households	Production (kg)	Consumption (kg) (% prod.)	Consumption per household (kg/2 months)
Community pond members	9	584	1,068	822 (77%)	1.407
Private pond owners	16	15	830	232 (28%)	15.467
Non-members	0	118	0	844	7.152
Total	25	717	1,898	1,898 (100%)	2.647

Encountering empowerment: a case study of community fish farming by women

One of the intervention villages of the APM project is Pujariguda village, in the Banuaguda Gram *Panchayat* of the Kundra block. The revenue village (administrative region) of Pujariguda consists of two hamlets: Pujariguda, whose residents are predominantly Dom (Scheduled Caste), and Raniguda, which is predominantly Bhumia (Scheduled Tribe) (see Figure 4.1).

A little background about these two communities: the name Domb or Domba – the preferred self-designation is Dom – is said to be derived from

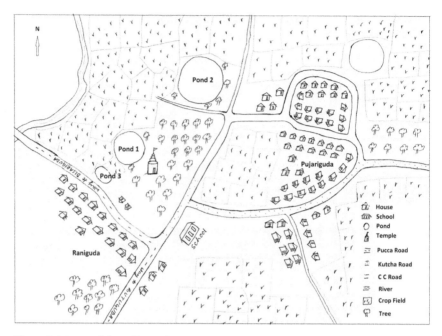

Figure 4.1 Map of the village of Pujariguda

the word *dumba*, meaning "devil", in reference to the thieving propensities of the caste (Senapati and Sahu 1966). The Dom is a Dravidian caste, originally from the hill tracts of Visakhapatnam (Andhra Pradesh); gradually they migrated to different parts of Odisha, and are now found (under various names) all over India. Traditionally, the Dom are a caste of weavers; they also work as menial labourers, scavengers, and basket weavers. They are known for their musical ability: a medieval history describes the Dom as a caste that makes its living from music. They are also well known as petty traders and landlords, and as skilled middlemen between the tribal and non-tribal people.

Bhumia, on the other hand, means "man having *bhumi* (land)" or "landed people". Thus, agriculture is the mainstay of the tribe.

As for the social status of these two communities, Doms occupy the lowest social status in the Hindu caste system – they are considered "untouchable". Though Doms are economically better off than Bhumias, the latter are considered to be socially superior.

Most of the lands and land-based resources (including ponds) in the area are owned by the tribals, but in Pujariguda, where Doms outnumber Bhumias, there has been a tendency for the Doms to take control of community resources (ponds, forests, land, etc.). Though the two communities live together in harmony, the Doms are petty traders, landlords, and

Table 4.2 Social demographic profile of the hamlets of Pujariguda and Raniguda

	No. of households	Dom	Bhumia	Christian	Other
Pujariguda	97	71	21	2	1
Raniguda	26	2	15	–	9
Total	123	73	36	2	10

middlemen who often exploit the Bhumias. Table 4.2 illustrates the social demographic profile of the two hamlets of the village.

Until 2010, there were two ponds in the village: Pond 1, known as the *Deulabandha* ("temple") pond (because of the temple nearby), where people used to take baths, wash their clothing, clean utensils, and bathe cattle; and Pond 2, *Ladibanda* ("the pond with a lot of mud"), which was choked with water hyacinths, making the pond unsuitable for even daily household activities, much less fish farming. (See timeline of fish farming in Pujariguda village in Box 4.1.)

Box 4.1 Timeline of fish farming in Pujariguda village

Date   **Events**

Until 2006   There were two ponds in the village (Pond 1 and Pond 2).

2006   Sixteen Bhumia tribal women from Raniguda formed a self-help group (SHG) and dug a new pond (Pond 3), using a government loan of Rs. 300,000 (with 50 percent subsidy).

Mar. 2007   The SHG leased one of the village's existing ponds (Pond 1) for three years, and farmed fish in Pond 1 and the newly constructed Pond 3.

2008   The SHG leased 0.8 hectare of land for three years from the village landlord in order to cultivate sugarcane. After two years, the landlord sold the land to a third party, but did not refund the SHG's money for the remaining year of their lease.

Mar. 2010   During the harvest of fish from Pond 1, residents of Pujariguda demanded a share of the harvested fish (claiming Pond 1 was a community pond) but were denied.

Mar. 2010   The SHG members repaid the entire government loan.

Apr. 2010	The Dom of Pujariguda contested the auction of Pond 1 by the SHG members of Raniguda, who had leased the pond for two years.
Jul. 2010	The SHG members stocked fish in two of the ponds (Ponds 1 and 3).
Mar. 2011	The SHG members harvested the fish from both ponds without opposition from the residents of Pujariguda.
2011	No fingerlings were released in any pond.
Mar. 2012	In conversation with villagers, MSSRF staff members learned that the SHG members had leased Pond 1.
Jul. 2012	The SHG members released fingerlings provided free of charge by MSSRF in Ponds 1 and 3. Pond 2 remained unused, as it was choked with water hyacinths and unsuitable for fish farming.
Feb. 2013	The residents of Pujariguda started a dialogue with the SHG members to obtain a share of the fish harvested from Pond 1; their request was denied.
Mar. 2013	During harvest, Pujariguda residents claimed a share of the fish from Pond 1, but the conflict was resolved with the help of MSSRF staff members, and the Raniguda SHG members were allowed to harvest the fish without sharing with the Pujariguda residents.
Mar. 2013	Neither the Raniguda SHG members nor the Pujariguda villagers leased the disputed community pond (Pond 1).
May 2013	The villagers of Pujariguda cleaned the water hyacinth pond (Pond 2) with financial support from the government.
Jul. 2013	MSSRF provided fingerlings to stock Ponds 2 and 3, but not the disputed Pond 1, as none of the groups had leased it.
Apr. 2014	The villagers of Pujariguda harvested fish from Ponds 1 and 2, and the villagers of Raniguda harvested fish from Pond 3.

As endorsed by government agencies, a group of Bhumia tribal women from Raniguda formed an SHG to implement various entrepreneurial activities that would contribute both to their empowerment and to their family income. As one of the oldest SHGs in the area, in 2006 they were given a loan of Rs. 300,000 to purchase land and dig a pond for fish farming. As per government regulations, they were eligible for a 50 percent subsidy. The village level worker (VLW), the government official who facilitated the loan process, also acted as a contractor for digging the pond, and managed to get the money for digging the pond up front. The entire amount was spent and a new pond (Pond 3) was dug on 0.2 hectares of land. The VLW was transferred to another village and, in spite of several requests and reminders, never provided an account of the SHG members' investment. As one of the SHG members sighed,

> Our bookkeeper, our own blood (as the bookkeeper happens to be the granddaughter of the secretary of the SHG), cheated us. She used to collect our money, including monthly contributions for the SHG, and deposit [it] in the bank. We got the loan with the help of that excret-aeater, the VLW of Kundra. Every time we withdrew money from the bank, he would be waiting outside the bank to say that we should give the money to him to carry [in] his *venitimuna* (vanity bag), as people may snatch [it] away from us on the way. And we used to give him all the money we withdrew. We trusted him, as our granddaughter was always there with him. But, you know, one fine morning our granddaughter flew away with him with all our money. Though we asked many times, they did not bother to give us an account of the money they took from us – our loan money as well as the money we saved.
>
> (Interview, Kundra, India, 12 December 2013)

The above quote shows how the tribal women were cheated. Nevertheless, the onus remained on them to repay half of the total loan amount. Along with the newly constructed pond (Pond 3), they also leased Pond 1 from the government and started fish farming. As well, they leased 0.8 hectare of land from the village landlord for Rs. 60,000 for three years. They cultivated sugarcane for two years; then the landlord sold the land to a third party but did not refund the SHG's money for the remaining year of their lease (Rs. 20,000). Additionally, the SHG members cultivated millets and pulses on the bunds (embankments) of the ponds.

By 2010, the group had managed to repay almost half of the loan amount by selling two years' worth of harvested fish, sugarcane, millets, and pulses, along with cash contributions from SHG members. However, it is important to note that during the 2010 fish harvest, the Dom community of Pujariguda claimed a share of the fish catch (as it was the community pond), a demand the SHG successfully opposed.

The SHG was left with only two ponds (Ponds 1 and 3) for cultivating fish and reaping the benefit (Pond 2 was choked with water hyacinths and therefore unsuitable for fish farming). In the meantime, the residents of Pujariguda realised that significant resources, both fish and money, could be generated by doing fish farming in the community pond. Unfortunately, the Pujariguda group was also in a vengeful mood against the Raniguda people, who had earlier denied them a share of the fish harvest from Pond 1. So in 2010, the Dom of Pujariguda contested the auction of the pond by the

Raniguda SHG members, who had leased the pond from the *Panchayat* for two years. The SHG members stocked the fish in both ponds. It has been reported that Pujariguda villagers occasionally stole fish from these ponds. However, this did not create any major conflict, and the SHG members harvested fish from both the ponds in 2011 with a sense of pride and victory. The president of the SHG reported,

> You know, *agyan* [roughly translated as *sir*], the Doms outnumber us [the Bhumias]. Though legally they have no right on the fish, they very often force us to give a share to them. But we have learnt how to challenge them. In fact, we have taken the pond on lease from the government by paying money. So we have the right over that pond. Why should we pay them a share? When they behave rough, we take the help of police and government authorities to teach them a lesson. And, you see, we have paid the *panidabu* (water tax) and got the "slip" [referring to the slip they got for paying money towards leasing the pond] from the *Panchayat*. We cultivated and harvested the fish. They could not take a single fish from us, though they ate our excreta by stealing some.
>
> (Interview, Kundra, India, 2 January 2013)

In early 2012, MSSRF's APM project launched a fish farming initiative in all its intervention villages. In recognition of the SHG's efforts, MSSRF provided fish fingerlings for both the ponds free of cost, and provided training for the women in the SHG about the scientific practices of fish farming. In the meantime, the Dom people of Pujariguda became extremely jealous, as everything (fish fingerlings and training) was provided to the SHG members free of charge; as well, they sensed that both the ponds would yield a very good catch. Eager to obtain a share of the fish catch from the community pond (Pond 1), the Pujariguda people initiated a dialogue with the Raniguda SHG members.

When, in our capacity as MSSRF staff members, we inquired about the dispute, one of the Pujariguda village leaders protested, "Sir, why should we do that? They are our brothers and sisters. We won't fight among ourselves. But, you know, some of our villagers feel that Raniguda people should share the fish with our villagers as it is a community pond" (interview, Kundra, India, 3 January 2013). We intervened to convince them that the Raniguda SHG members had taken the pond on lease and were therefore the lawful owners. "Yes, sir, we know that. We also told them that we would contribute towards the auction money and they should share the fish with us. But they did not agree," an aggrieved person responded (interview, Kundra, India, 2 January 2013).

Eventually the Pujariguda people assured us that they would neither start any further fight with the Raniguda people nor claim any share of the fish catch. In turn, we assured the villagers of Pujariguda that if they cleaned the water hyacinth pond (Pond 2), we would be happy to provide fingerlings and training at no cost. The Pujariguda people secured government funding (under the Mahatma Gandhi National Rural Employment Guarantee Act program) and renovated the pond. The point to be noted here is that the villagers of Pujariguda did not contribute the labour to clean the water hyacinths from the pond until they received the government funding, even though we had earlier offered to provide a feast for the whole village if they would clean the pond. When the government money arrived, the villagers were motivated to work on the renovation of the pond, partly because they would earn wages, and partly because they would have a pond for fish farming.

When the time came to harvest the fish, the Raniguda people attempted to harvest the fish from both ponds, but once again the Pujariguda people demanded a share of the catch from the community pond. Finally, with the help of police and MSSRF staff members, the conflict was resolved, and the Raniguda SHG members harvested the fish from both ponds without opposition from the Pujariguda people.

In 2013, neither the Raniguda SHG members nor the villagers of Pujariguda took the disputed community pond (Pond 1) on lease; nor did MSSRF stock fish in that pond, though MSSRF did provide fish fingerlings for the pond constructed and owned by the SHG (Pond 3) and the newly renovated pond (Pond 2) leased by the Pujariguda people. Both groups harvested fish from their respective ponds. In late 2013, the Pujariguda people took out a lease on the temple pond (Pond 1). In a focus group discussion, when we asked the SHG members why they had not taken the temple pond on lease, they replied,

> You know, sir, they are the Doms, the rowdy people. They outnumber us. Physically they are more powerful. And we are a small group of women and it is difficult for us to win over them always. As we are poor, we cannot always fight against but to live with them, though not to depend on them.
>
> (Interview, Kundra, India, 2 January 2013)

Discussion and analysis

As the preceding sections demonstrate, investigating Bourdieu's theoretical ethnographic concepts of field, capital, and habitus helped us to understand the dynamics of power structures and resource allocation mechanisms (in the field of poverty alleviation in general and fish farming in particular) in a rural setting in Pujariguda village. The social agents involved in fish farming in the village were expected to follow democratic principles in resource allocation mechanisms; however, in practice, the villagers of both Pujariguda and Raniguda vied for capital accumulation to enhance their social status. This showed that the field of fish farming was a complex network involving many actors, whose influence on fish farming was correlated with their economic wealth (see Figure 4.2).

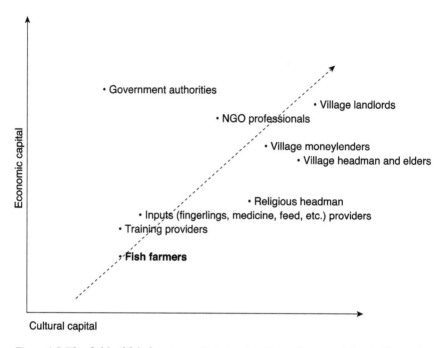

Figure 4.2 The field of fish farming in Pujariguda village. The dotted line indicates the
       probable orientation of the fish farmers towards gaining more cultural and
       economic capital

Until 2012, the social space constructed by the women SHG members of
Raniguda and the social capital they earned helped them secure the ponds,
and the resource allocation mechanisms (for example, the government's
sanctioning a loan for digging and leasing fish ponds) worked in their favour.
As one of the oldest SHGs formed and monitored by government authorities (under the Mission Shakti Program of Tribal Welfare Department,
Government of Odisha), the SHG was given the loan (for digging the pond)
partly to fulfil the program's mandate to provide loans to tribal women's
SHGs and partly because the program representative, who was a woman,
was sympathetic to the welfare of the tribal women. As well, Sibani, the
granddaughter of the SHG secretary and herself an SHG member, worked
as a volunteer for the Mission Shakti Program in tandem with the local
VLW. As such, Sibani was the best person to manage the SHG's finances.
However, the VLW who took the responsibility (as well as the money!) for
digging the new pond happened to fall in love with Sibani, who in turn
helped him manipulate the financial records and appropriate the money. As
long as Sibani and the VLW worked with the group, the SHG members got
the ponds on lease, sometimes for five years at a stretch. However, after
Sibani and the VLW got married, they did not provide an account of the
money to the SHG members.

After Sibani left the village with the VLW, the SHG members continued fish farming in both ponds. The *social capital* that gave the SHG members an edge over the Dom people of Pujariguda was the presence of the Raniguda village landlord, from whom the SHG members leased 0.8 hectare of land for three years for Rs. 60,000. As the lessor, he had an obligation to safeguard the interests of his client, the SHG, and the Pujariguda people did not dare to antagonise the village landlord, on whom they often depended.

The *cultural capital* that privileged the women SHG members over the Dom community in enjoying the community pond (Pond 1) was the fact that the priest of the village temple that stood on the banks of the pond was from Raniguda, and was the son of the SHG secretary. The villagers of Pujariguda feared that fighting with the village priest might provoke the village deity to inflict unforeseen miseries on their village and its people. Their reluctance to antagonise the priest benefited the women of the Raniguda SHG. This shows that the women's access to and control over the community pond and fish farming challenged the patriarchal power dynamics of the dominant Dom male community.

Given these facts, how were the Doms of Pujariguda able to mobilise the resource allocation mechanisms in their favour in 2013? Going against the rational choice theory (mentioned earlier) and development ideals, the actions of the Doms were guided more by practical logic (habitus) than by a rational decision-making process to compete for the community resources for their own betterment (capital). In the meantime, the social agents who favoured the SHG were no longer in place: the district collector was transferred to another district, the VLW left the village with Sibani, and the village landlord died in 2012.

Thus, by 2013, as the dominant group in the village, the Doms took advantage of local political representatives (who needed the Doms' votes) to establish their social network with the local government authorities, bank officials, and other social agents involved in fish farming. The social space and network constructed by the Dom community helped them to take over the temple pond (Pond 1) from the SHG members in 2013.

Being a small group, the women of the SHG did not want to fight the dominant Dom community. As well, the villagers of Raniguda depend on the Pujariguda villagers for earning part of their livelihoods by working in the fields of the rich Doms, and some of the lands owned by Raniguda villagers are within the Pujariguda village limits. The location of the village temple (in Pujariguda village) is another factor: antagonising the villagers of Pujariguda would compromise the Raniguda people's access to the temple. Another important cultural factor that deters the Raniguda people from antagonising the Pujariguda people is the celebration of *Chaita Parab*, the annual hunting festival. Formerly, Pujariguda was a revenue village comprising seven neighbouring hamlets, including Raniguda. Though many of the hamlets were later recognised as independent revenue villages, the original seven hamlets continue to celebrate *Chaita Parab* together in Pujariguda. Last but not least, recently a Dom man from Pujariguda was elected as a ward member, giving the Pujariguda villagers a political advantage over the Raniguda villagers. As one of the SHG members pointed out, the habitus of the SHG is "We are poor, we cannot always fight against but to live with them". All of these factors illustrate how cultural politics and patronage contradict the prescribed mechanisms of resource allocation, and how, in turn, gender inequality and rural poverty are perpetuated.

Conclusion

The aim of this theoretical construction was to understand the dynamics of resource allocation mechanisms in Pujariguda village, and how they either mitigated or exacerbated the poverty and disempowerment of the resource poor, particularly marginalised tribal women. The foregoing analysis confirms the fact that access to and control over natural resources contribute to the empowerment of women in challenging male domination (on the *social* front) and ensuring economic benefit (on the *economic* front) to their households.

Bourdieu's theoretical framework, however, helped us to emphasise the fact that the villagers' everyday practices reflect a certain set of cultural and political assumptions. The dominant male group's habitus prompted them to channel the resource allocation mechanisms in their favour by denying, though not violating, the rights of the subordinate female group. The members of the women's SHG, on the other hand, were led to believe that the community ponds were common resources available to the entire village community. Thus, the subordinate female group's habitus emphasised the fact that, being marginalised and resource poor, they should not (could not) fight against the men, but must find a way to live with them.

This research highlights how these competing logics are constituted and how, in turn, inequality and poverty are perpetuated despite the introduction of development ideals based on gender equity and human rights. This reaffirms the notion that without a clear understanding of the overall dynamics of a social system, its actors, and the prevailing logic behind their everyday practices, development interventions may fail to produce the desired results.

As mentioned earlier, in late 2013 the villagers of Pujariguda took control of Pond 1 by taking the pond on lease. Neither group stocked fish in the pond that year, but the people of Pujariguda harvested fish (symbolically) in early 2014. The tension between the two hamlets over the ownership of Pond 1 steadily increased, and in early 2014, MSSRF staff members intervened and solved the problem by coordinating a formal agreement between the two hamlets that the fish harvest would be equally shared among all the households of both hamlets. Again, MSSRF provided fingerlings for the contested pond at no cost.

In a just and equitable society, women must have equal access to and control over natural resources and resource allocation mechanisms. As things now stand, and regrettably, gender equity and women's empowerment in Koraput remain a distant dream.

Acknowledgements

We are very grateful to the farmers of the village of Kundra block, Odisha, for their kind cooperation and active participation in our research project. We gratefully acknowledge the financial support of the Department of Foreign Affairs, Trade and Development (DFATD), Canada, and the International Development Research Centre (IDRC), Canada, and the project coordination and support provided by the M.S. Swaminathan Research Foundation (MSSRF), India. We are grateful to John Parkins, Amy Kaler, and Jemimah Njuki for their critical review of the manuscript, and for raising many insightful questions that have helped immensely in clarifying and rethinking some of our positions. We would like to thank V.A. Nambi, Amit Mitra, JoAnn Jaffe, Lauren Sneyd, and the participants of the "Gender Group" in Banff, Canada, for their valuable comments and suggestions. Finally, our thanks are due to Diana Tyndale for her meticulous editing of the manuscript.

Note

1 Social space is broadly a structured group of individuals having common interests, principles, and behaviours based in a long-evolving set of values, norms, and habits (Durkheim 1926). The concept of *field* is similar to social networks, as both concepts emphasise social relations; however, social network analysis does not address the relationship between agency and structure that Bourdieu does in the case of field.

References

All website URLs accessed on 7 April 2016.

Agarwal, Bina. 1997. "'Bargaining' and Gender Relations: Within and Beyond the Household." *Feminist Economics* 3 (1): 1–51.

Alawattage, Chandana, and Danture Wickramasinghe. 2009. "Weapons of the Weak: Subalterns' Emancipatory Accounting in Ceylon Tea." *Accounting, Auditing & Accountability Journal* 22 (3): 379–404.

Alawattage, Chandana, Trevor Hopper, and Danture Wickramasinghe. 2007. "Introduction to Management Accounting in Less Developed Countries." *Journal of Accounting & Organizational Change* 3 (3): 183–91.

Barman, Benoy Kumar. 2001. "Women in Small-Scale Aquaculture in North-West Bangladesh." *Gender, Technology and Development* 5 (2): 267–87.

Bhagwati, Jadish, and Arvind Panagariya. 2013. *Why Growth Matters: How Economic Growth in India Reduced Poverty and the Lessons for Other Developing Countries.* New York: PublicAffairs.

Bourdieu, Pierre. 1962. *The Algerians.* Boston: Beacon Press.

Bourdieu, Pierre. 1977. *Outline of a Theory of Practice.* Cambridge: Cambridge University Press.

Bourdieu, Pierre. 1985. "Social Space and the Genesis of Groups." *Theory and Society* 14 (6): 723–44.

Bourdieu, Pierre. 1990. *In Other Words: Essays towards a Reflexive Sociology*. Stanford: Stanford University Press.

Bourdieu, Pierre. 1993. *Sociology in Question*. London: Sage Publications.

Bourdieu, Pierre. 2004. *Science of Science and Reflexivity*. Cambridge: Cambridge University Press.

Bourdieu, Pierre. 2005. *The Social Structures of Economy*. Cambridge: Cambridge University Press.

Bourdieu, Pierre. 2006. "The Forms of Capital." In Hugh Lauder, Phillip Brown, Jo-Anne Dillabough, and A.H. Halsey, eds, *Education, Globalization and Social Change*. Oxford: Oxford University Press, 105–18. Originally published 1986.

Bourdieu, Pierre, and Loïc J.D. Wacquant. 1992. *An Invitation to Reflexive Sociology*. Chicago: University of Chicago Press.

Covaleski, Mark A., and Mark W. Dirsmith. 1983. "Budgeting as a Means for Control and Loose Coupling." *Accounting, Organizations and Society* 8 (4): 323–40.

Covaleski, Mark A., and Mark W. Dirsmith. 1986. "The Budgetary Process of Power and Politics." *Accounting, Organizations and Society* 11 (3): 193–214.

Durkheim, Émile. 1926. *The Elementary Forms of the Religious Life*. New York: Macmillan.

Everett, Jeff. 2003. "The Politics of Comprehensive Auditing in Fields of High Outcome and Cause Uncertainty." *Critical Perspectives on Accounting* 14 (1–2): 77–104.

Hopper, Trevor, Mathew Tsamenyi, Shahzad Uddin, and Danture Wickramasinghe. 2009. "Management Accounting in Less Developed Countries: What is Known and Needs Knowing." *Accounting, Auditing & Accountability Journal* 22 (3): 469–514.

Jayasinghe, Kelum, and Dennis Thomas. 2009. "Preservation of Indigenous Accounting Systems in a Subaltern Community." *Accounting, Auditing & Accountability Journal* 22 (3): 351–78.

Jayasinghe, Kelum, and Danture Wickramasinghe. 2006. "Can NGOs Deliver Accountability? Realities, Predictions and Difficulties: The Case of Sri Lanka." In Harsh Bhargava and Deepak Kumar, eds, *NGOs: Role and Accountability: An Introduction*. Hyderabad, India: ICFAI University Press, 296–327.

Jayasinghe, Kelum, and Danture Wickramasinghe. 2011. "Power Over Empowerment: Encountering Development Accounting in a Sri Lankan Fishing Village." *Critical Perspectives on Accounting* 22: 396–414.

Kabeer, Naila. 2005. "Gender Equality and Women's Empowerment." *Gender and Development* 13 (1): 13–24.

Kelkar, Govind. 2001. "Gender Concerns in Aquaculture: Women's Roles and Capabilities." In Kyoko Kusakabe and Govind Kelkar, eds, *Gender Concerns in Aquaculture in Southeast Asia*. Bangkok: Gender and Development Studies, Asian Institute of Technology, 1–10.

Kurunmäki, Liisa. 1999a. "Making an Accounting Entity: The Case of the Hospital in Finnish Health Care Reforms." *European Accounting Review* 8 (2): 219–37.

Kurunmäki, Liisa. 1999b. "Professional vs. Financial Capital in the Field of Health Care – Struggles for the Redistribution of Power and Control." *Accounting, Organizations and Society* 24 (2): 95–124.

Kusakabe, Kyoko. 2003. "Women's Involvement in Small-Scale Aquaculture in Northeast Thailand." *Development in Practice* 13 (4): 333–45.

Macintosh, Norman B., and Paolo Quattrone. 1994. *Management Accounting and Control Systems: An Organizational and Behavioural Approach.* Chichester: Wiley.

Mahana, Rajakishor. 2011. "Producing Underdevelopment: The Politics of Hunger Deaths in Kashipur, India." FSC Brief No. 16. Stuttgart: Food Security Center (FSC), University of Hohenheim. https://ew.uni-hohenheim.de/fileadmin/einrichtungen/fsc/FSC_Brief_No.16.pdf.

Mahana, Rajakishor. 2016. "The Politics of Hunger Deaths in Odisha (India)." In Einar Braathen, Julian May, Marianne S. Ulriksen, and Gemma Wright, eds, *Poverty and Inequality in Middle Income Countries: Policy Achievements, Political Obstacles.* London: Zed Books, 221–42.

Neu, Dean, Elizabeth Ocampo Gomez, Cameron Graham, and Monica Heincke. 2003. "'Informing' Technologies and the World Bank." *Accounting, Organizations and Society* 31 (7): 635–62.

Sen, Amartya K. 1999. *Development as Freedom.* Oxford: Oxford University Press.

Senapati, Nilamani, and Nabin Sahu. 1966. *Orissa District Gazetteers: Koraput.* Cuttack: Orissa Government Press.

Sriputinibondh, Napaporn, Malasri Khumsri, and W.D. Hartmann. 2005. *Gender in Fisheries Management in the Lower Songkhram River Basin in the Northeast of Thailand.* Seventh Technical Symposium on Mekong Fisheries, Ubon Ratchathani, Thailand, 1–10. www.thaimrcfisheries.org/WEBSITE/June_FMG_report/Gender%20in%20fisheries%20management%20in%20the%20Lower%20Songkhra%20River%20Basin.pdf.

Sullivan, Leah. 2004. "The Impacts of Aquaculture Development in Relation to Gender in Northeastern Thailand." In WorldFish Center, ed., *Global Symposium on Gender and Fisheries.* Penang, Malaysia: WorldFish Center, 29–42. http://pubs.iclarm.net/Pubs/Gender&FisheriesDec04/5_GD.pdf.

Vandenberghe, Frédéric. 1999. "'The Real is Relational': An Epistemological Analysis of Pierre Bourdieu." *Sociological Theory* 7 (1): 26–63.

Wickramasinghe, Danture, and Trevor Hopper. 2005. "Cultural Political Economy of Management Accounting Controls: A Case Study of a Textile Mill in a Traditional Sinhalese Village." *Critical Perspectives on Accounting* 16 (4): 473–503.

Part III
Placing gender in local institutional contexts

5 Coffee ceremonies, gender, and food security in two Ethiopian villages

JoAnn Jaffe and Amy Kaler

Introduction

Figure 5.1 depicts two chickpea fields just past the optimum moment of harvest. The field on the left is owned and managed by a man, who was able to plant his crops in a timely fashion and to mobilise enough labour to ensure that the fields were weeded and harvested well, while the one on the right belongs to a woman whose other responsibilities meant that she planted late, after the rains had already fallen, and who was not able to call on the labour

Figure 5.1 Chickpea fields, Community 2, Ethiopia

Source: Photo courtesy of JoAnn Jaffe.

of neighbours and relatives to plough, plant, or cultivate the crop in a timely fashion. These juxtaposed fields tell a story of gendered discrepancies and of women's disempowerment relative to men.

The story that these fields of chickpeas tell, however, is not only about the categorical differences between men and women. The chickpeas are also an entrée to the Ethiopian coffee ceremony, in which they are featured as snacks to accompany coffee. The research team's involvement with the coffee ceremony began with chickpeas, which were the focus of a food security intervention with which we were associated as research team members, but we soon found that the coffee ceremony in two villages in Ethiopia told a complex story about how inter- and intra-household relations are created, sustained, and sometimes transformed, and how these relations in turn affect the conditions of food security. The coffee ceremony is neither entirely symbolic nor entirely instrumental. It represents the social relations that shape food security, but, through its repeated enactment, it also creates these relations.

In this chapter, the discussion of coffee ceremonies is framed within the anthropological literature on household bargaining and the economy of affection. Then the communities and ceremonies involved in this study are described along with the data collection methods. The findings elaborate three themes: the importance of the coffee ceremony for establishing reputation and reciprocal obligation within the community; the connection between ceremonies and the ability to mobilise labour for food production; and the complexly gendered nature of the ceremony.

The coffee ceremony has both symbolic and material significance. In symbolic terms, proper performance of the ceremony displays important local virtues of generosity and hospitality, as well as feminised aspects of grace, skill, and hard work. The ceremony also enables the hosting household to display their prowess and success at farming, generating admiration and prestige within the community. In material terms, the ceremony is a nexus for the organisation of the social relations that shape a household's ability to assemble the required labour and other resources to secure its food supply. The demands of the coffee ceremony also shape the everyday allocation of labour in these households, especially for women.

These relations also include the dynamics between households in the same community – relations which are reciprocal in some ways, but which are becoming increasingly stratified and asymmetrical in nature. The frequency of coffee ceremonies, the quality of the coffee and food on offer, and the protocol of who is invited to share the ceremony bind households together in ties of mutual obligation. These ties can be activated to mobilise human labour and draft animals in a timely fashion during bottlenecks in agricultural production cycles, or to access direct assistance in times of crisis, in the form of loans, labour, or outright gifts of food or money.

At the same time, in addition to these asymmetric relations in which one party commands resources needed by another, coffee ceremonies serve an important function in "horizontalising" social relations, by bringing together individuals who occupy different levels in social hierarchies. Men, women, well-off community members, and those who are struggling can occupy the same time and space, which serves to smooth tensions that arise in an increasingly competitive environment.

The gender dimension of coffee ceremonies deserves particular mention. These are complexly gendered rituals, in which women provide almost all the labour for a practice where the benefits accrue primarily, though not exclusively, to the men in their households. At the same time, the ceremonies are a site for women's own strategic projects to enhance their status within households, build ties to women in other households, and increase marital harmony. Thus, the gendered nature of the ceremonies should not be understood as being entirely oppressive or disempowering.

Theoretical framing

This work draws on ideas and perspectives that have been developed through both mainstream development thought and feminist theory. The research team believes that the relationships between households in a community, and between individuals in a shared household, are always contested, emergent, and unstable. Rural households – and the individuals within them – are autonomous in some respects and interdependent in others. These relations are a complex mix of reciprocity, asymmetry, competition, and cooperation. Part of the work of social life is to constantly reproduce and transform these relations, as can be seen in the practice of the coffee ceremony.

Individuals constantly seek to solidify and, perhaps, improve their position and status, both individually and as members of collectives. They do so by offering their own labour, time, or social standing as resources that others may draw on in exchange for benefits, whether in the immediate moment or in the long term. There is a long tradition in development studies of characterising these strategic moves as "bargaining" (Kandiyoti 1988; Agarwal 1997), which draws attention both to the unequal distribution of power and influence and to the deliberate awareness of the actors who work within these unequal distributions. The concept of bargaining also helps to clarify why individuals may undertake actions that appear to put them at a disadvantage – wives who devote hours of their day to carrying out the coffee ceremonies, for instance. These actions may enable the individuals to reap benefits by adhering to normative expectations, or put them in a position to make normative claims on others. While remaining individuals, wives may also see their own interests being fulfilled when they work as their husbands' proxies and shield them from the problems, disappointments, or rancour of children, such as when they coordinate and manage household labour and consumption expectations from the short through the long term (Keating 1996; Jaffe 2003).

Such "bargains" are most effective when all actors involved are operating with a shared understanding of the *moral economy* or *economy of affection*

(Scott 1977; Hyden 1980; Thompson 1993). These terms refer to collective understandings of who owes what to whom, and which people have the responsibility of promoting the well-being of others. These economies are profoundly gendered and statused, in that social position and relations reflect the expectations, performances, practices, and knowledge attached to participants. Such economies are deeply rooted in local values and ethics, and personalised through the recognised social relations that connect one individual to another, such as husband to wife or neighbour to neighbour (Warner et al. 1997).

It is common to read of the erosion of these economies in rural Africa, as more and more relationships are mediated through the market – one person paying another for his or her labour, or using money to achieve ends that were previously achieved through moral suasion, such as assistance with agricultural work or the provision of sustenance in times of crisis. Certainly, in the villages in this study, wealthier households were in the process of withdrawing from the moral economy represented by *debo*, the institution of cooperative labour, as money has replaced normative commitments.

However, the substitution of a cash economy for an economy of affection is by no means a straightforward replacement (Waters 1992; Jaffe 1997; Kaler 2006). Even in fully commoditised economies, the importance of reputation, social networks, amiability, and status remains high in helping to determine who gets access to scarce resources, such as good jobs, elite education, low-interest loans, and so on. The power of the coffee ceremony remains because it can secure resources such as reputation, respect, and admiration, which money cannot buy. Indeed, even within a monetising economy, the coffee ceremony remains salient as a vehicle for establishing and maintaining working relationships and for clientelism, the personalised and individualised reciprocity that connects people of unequal status. Through coffee ceremonies, whether as hosts or guests, households can demonstrate themselves to be good farming partners and either worthy patrons or honourable clients.

By treating the coffee ceremony as the site of strategic bargaining between and within households, and locating it within a local moral economy, this study has adopted a practice perspective on the ceremony (Schatzki 2001; Jarzabkowski et al. 2007). A practice perspective requires examining not only *what* is accomplished through a particular action, such as preparing and hosting a coffee ceremony, but also *how* it is accomplished, in real life, rather than in idealised models of how such things should happen. Practice is a middle ground between voluntary action or completely free agency, in which individuals have unlimited decision-making power, and structural determinism, in which social norms or forms of coercion dictate or determine what any individual may do at any time. Practices like the coffee ceremony contain values, express relations, and provide patterns for action. At the same time, they provide the context and form in which certain actions become intelligible, and through which actors may claim symbolic resources and meanings that are used in the struggle for status, solidarity, and identity.

Methodology

The first author spent one month in early 2014 in the communities referred to as C1 and C2. This fieldwork focussed on how gender and access to resources shape food security outcomes. This research was carried out as part of the gender component of a project funded by Canada's International Development Research Centre (IDRC) through the Canadian International Food Security Research Fund (CIFSRF), which situated gender equity concerns as central to food security. The project's goal was to increase food security and enhance local agro-ecologies through improved sustainable agricultural practices and human nutrition, which would be accomplished through research oriented to expanding inclusion of pulse crops in farming systems and diets in southern Ethiopia.

Using an extensive research instrument developed by the authors and pretested by the first author and graduate students in May 2012, the research team interviewed 20 households in each community. These households represent cases (and components of cases) and were chosen using a purposive, stratified sampling strategy that prescribed specific criteria with the intention of maximising differences in order to allow for the exploration of the range of diversity, as well as typicality, in each wealth and gender stratum. The selection was accomplished with the help of the agricultural extension agents in each community, based upon household data they had been collecting as part of their work.

Towards the end of the research process, the team held eight focus groups (two male and two female in each community) that asked participants to analyse three scenarios written by the authors. The scenarios presented issues of interest that had arisen during the interviews and that the researchers felt could be profitably illuminated through group discussion. The focus groups were made up of household heads or household heads' wives, stratified by wealth and gender. These focus groups provided most of the qualitative data for this research.

Other research activities included visits to local markets to talk to vendors about changes in the market in pulses and other staples, key informant interviews of the agricultural extension agents in both communities and of several area people who opportunistically wanted to offer their perspectives on the research, and brief visits to the local health posts to discuss issues around health and food security.

Description of sites

This research involves two very different communities in southern Ethiopia. In particular, land ownership in these communities follows very different patterns. Community 1 (C1) is highly stratified, with distinct "wealthy", "medium", and "poor" strata. Community 2 (C2) is much less stratified, with a tiny "wealthy" group, and most households being smallholders (see

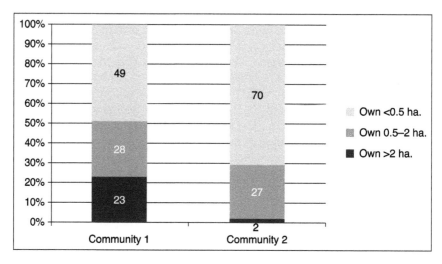

Figure 5.2 Household land ownership in Communities 1 and 2: percentage
      of households exercising effective control over hectares of arable land

Note: Figures do not total 100 due to rounding.

Figure 5.2). Reflecting these stratification patterns, the maximum land ownership in C1 is 11 hectares, while in C2, maximum land ownership is only 4
hectares. C1 is predominantly Muslim and C2 predominantly Christian; in
C1 roughly one-tenth of households are made up of men with multiple
wives, and in both communities over a quarter of the households are
female-headed. Many of the households in C1 are dependent upon the
production of grains (teff, sorghum, millet, and corn), especially for sale, and
haricot bean. C2's production patterns are somewhat different: they grow
corn, *enset* (false banana), root crops (*godere* [cocoyam], sweet potato, potato)
– especially for home consumption, and chickpea or haricot bean.

Both communities have some apiculture and produce chilli pepper for
market. Livestock is important in both communities: as animal traction, as a
liquid asset to be sold in times of need, as a source of food security, and as
status and symbolic capital. Wealth is based on access to multiple factors of
production, of which land is arguably the most important. People may be
too poor, however, to work the land they have, or they may have trouble
getting access to labour to work it or to work it in a timely fashion. In both
communities, survival for many is based upon positive social relations –
being able to obtain loans, food, animals, credit, labour, space for grazing,
seeds, plants, firewood, and so on, when times demand it.

These communities are caught up in ongoing and rapid transformations,
which, according to informants, have been increasing (particularly since
2008), largely as an effect of the world food crisis. Rising food prices have
created opportunities for some and liabilities for others, as richer farmers and

merchants strategise how best to use their asset advantages. Agricultural extension agents and public health workers are active in both communities, as are non-governmental organisations (NGOs) in the area of economic services, such as microcredit.

Recently, some home-grown credit self-help groups have arisen in response to rising crop prices, high local interest rates, scarce money, and the increasing need for cash, particularly in C2, but also somewhat in C1. In C1, some large and medium farmers have begun to form marketing groups to pool crops to take advantage of high prices. Large merchants have also moved into the area for the same reason. Lately, day labour has become increasingly important in both communities. In C1, men may work as day labourers on others' land or in the nearby town; in C2, men work others' land, but may also travel to work away from home in the distant cotton fields of Oromia or the recently established greenhouses near Addis Ababa. In those relatively few families, the women left behind appear to take on the job of managing the day-to-day aspects of their joint home-making and agricultural enterprise, as indicated in our interviews and focus groups. Both communities experience severe food shortages.

Land is owned by the state and distributed by the administration of the local *kebele* (Ethiopia's smallest administrative unit, similar to a ward or neighbourhood). Although there were reportedly a few land purchases in C1 by richer farmers during the previous five years, there is officially no land market in Ethiopia. Overall, the trend in land size in both communities is downward, as household land is divided patrilocally among its male members when they marry and establish their own households. Thus, women often have no independent access to the most important productive resource.

The primary route to accessing more land for well-off households is through relationships with poorer households to work the land that the latter are unable to work themselves, because they lack labour, cash, or oxen. Better-off farmers often use the land of poorer farmers in a relation called "collaboration", in which the richer farmers provide oxen for cultivation and pay for inputs (seed, fertiliser, pesticides) up front. The land-owning household does the weeding and harvesting. The harvest is split 50–50, but the richer farmer will also calculate how much extra they spent on inputs and reduce what the other farmer gets by the amount of inputs applied. Wealthy farmers can also access land through "contract", in which they pay cash or crop for land for a specified period. Farmers also give or take oxen and cows to raise through collaboration or contract, and some farmers will share them, as well. Accessing land and labour through collaboration and contract has become much more common since 2008. At the same time, cooperative labour, in which farmers are able to access the labour power of others by offering an equivalent amount of their own, is becoming less so.

Access to land and labour is highly gendered in these communities; thus, social differentiation happens along lines of gender as well as wealth. Men and women have different accumulation cycles based on different gendered responsibilities for crops and labour, as well as differential valuations placed on those responsibilities. Despite varying levels of inter-household inequality, in both communities intra-household inequality remains high, with women having little formal authority over agriculture.

The focus groups provided details of somewhat different patterns of authority in the two communities based upon the socioeconomic status of the household. In C1, the more stratified of the two communities, poorer wives appear to have very little authority, in some cases even suggesting that their husband would beat them if they defied his word or that in the husband's absence, they should defer to their sons. In contrast, rich wives appear to have more autonomy: they might need to consult with their husbands on important decisions such as selling crops, but they could do so after the fact, by informing him of the action and the reasons for it. In C2, it appears that the rich and medium-wealth wives have little independence of action and need permission to carry out important acts. Poor wives, however, have greater freedom: husbands speak of decisions as being more of a joint activity, with the wife able to act in the husband's absence, while some wives speak of the need for husbands to also consult as they make decisions together. This suggests that in C1, more wealth gives women greater bargaining power, whereas in C2, less wealth puts women on a more equal footing.

In both communities, women's contribution to the production, distribution, and consumption of food (crops and livestock) is considerable, but largely unrecognised. Gardening, for example, is largely unnoticed, but women repeatedly mention it when asked to discuss their and their households' strengths. Women's gardens typically use few extra-household resources and are hand dug, rather than worked using oxen, as is the case with field crops. As in many parts of the world, women's gardens constitute a considerable resource, providing dietary diversity, vitamins, and minerals not accessible in the rest of the diet, medicinal and cooking herbs, and sometimes a source of cash. In C2, they are a considerable source of food security due to the presence of enset (*Ensete ventricosum*, or "false banana", the local starchy staple). Enset is highly labour intensive to process and also provides the focus for the most common form of women's cooperative group, in which several women will come together during harvest time to cut and process some quantity of their enset together. Despite the role of women's crops in alleviating food shortages that strike both communities, they are not considered to be the result of "true" agriculture in the way that men's production for market is regarded, either by community members or by expert advisers such as agricultural extension officers or the architects of intervention projects.

Coffee ceremonies

The coffee ceremony has been chosen as the centrepiece of this chapter as it incorporates both the socioeconomic and the cultural facets of gendered food practices. Through household coffee ceremonies, women in both communities demonstrate whether they are *baalamuya*, or masters of skill. Informants refer to coffee ceremonies as *habesha* (meaning native or authentically Ethiopian). The ubiquity of the coffee ceremony across ethnicities, class, geography, and rural-urban settings indicates how important it is, as a ritual that all Ethiopians can share despite their differences (Mjaaland 2004). Coffee ceremonies follow a series of ritualised and specific steps; these vary across Ethiopia, but the basic concept is the same.

Many households in the communities studied perform coffee ceremonies two to three times per day, and a few hold as many as four or more. C2 has seen the number of coffee ceremonies reduced to only those marking special occasions in many poor or medium-wealth households, while wealthy households in C1 may do up to four or five in a day. The ceremonies are time- and resource-intensive. In both communities, women – wives and older daughters – perform the main tasks for these ceremonies, although men may help with some associated chores if the women are tired and this is the third or fourth ceremony of the day. Coffee ceremonies may include family members, neighbours, fellow members of cooperative work, savings, or self-help groups, or whoever is being shown hospitality.

Homes have a special area where the coffee ceremony takes place. It is often marked by the presence of a *rekbot*, a box or shelf from which the coffee ceremony is staged, topped by *sini*, small, handleless coffee cups. Some households have dedicated coffee braziers on which to place the coffee roasting pan and *jebena* (a ceramic coffee pot with a narrow neck and lip and a spherical body).

First, the woman holding the coffee ceremony must light a fire. If this is a special ceremony, she may put on a traditional dress and shawl. She may spread grass to define the space for the ceremony and to provide fragrance and the presence of nature. Frankincense may be lit and burned in a special burner. The woman blows or fans the flame to keep the fire burning. When the coals are hot enough and the green coffee has been washed, she places the pan of coffee beans on the fire to roast. She pays careful attention and repeatedly shakes and tosses the beans so that they roast evenly. She will re-wash the beans and re-roast them, if necessary. If spices, such as cardamom, are being used, they are added after the beans begin to darken.

Once the beans are uniformly black, shiny, oily, and smoking, they are taken off the coals and passed around so that those present can smell them and their smoke. The beans are then pounded in a *mukecha* and *zenazena* (mortar and pestle). The grounds may be mixed with herbs, such as *besobela* (Ethiopian holy basil) and *tena adam* (rue – literally "the health of Adam"). The common source for these herbs is the woman's own home garden, as may be the coffee, which she also likely will have picked and processed for home use (men often pick the green coffee beans that are destined for market). Water is boiled in the *jebena*; the grounds are added and the mixture is cooled, then brought back to a boil. The coffee may have been made with herbs, salt, garlic, or butter, depending on the tradition of the area and the woman making the coffee. The cups, although already clean, are rinsed with water. The coffee is poured slowly from 20–30 cm above the cups without spilling or splashing, and each cup is filled to the top.

Buna kurs (coffee ceremony snacks) – generally food such as popcorn, *kita* (unleavened corn bread), roasted corn, chickpeas, and *kolo* (barley) – should be prepared and served during the coffee ceremony. These foods commonly come from the household production of the family and are considered important to grow, in part because of their use in ceremonies. A few of the households in C2 have reduced the frequency of coffee ceremonies to holidays and special occasions; with their herbed, buttered, and salted coffee, they serve a more elaborate meal of meat and *teff injera* (fermented flatbread with the spongy consistency of a pancake, cooked on a skillet or griddle) to the neighbours and those with whom they work cooperatively.

Before the guests begin to eat and drink, the woman or her child will bring water to each person so that they can wash their hands. The eldest or most honoured guest is served first. Young and old drink together, although (some) women may stay near the fire or *rekbot* and drink only after others have been served. Coffee may be served up to two more times, as water is added to the grounds and brought to a boil. It is said that drinking a third cup, called the *beraka*, brings the full blessings of the coffee ceremony to the participants.

The woman must show the proper demeanour and bodily discipline when serving, including knowing how far to extend her arm and which hand to use for serving. Local proverbs reflect the importance of performing the coffee ceremony for gendered personhood, such as "better a man should marry a woman who is *baalamuya* (a skilled and gracious woman) than beautiful". A woman who is beautiful without being *baalamuya* is called a "horse", beautiful but useless.

Results/discussion

In this section, we argue that coffee ceremonies are both a window on the social arrangements by which households and communities secure their food needs, and a means of setting these social relations in motion. In doing so, individuals are envisioned as bargaining, strategising actors, who use the means available to them to increase their individual and collective power within asymmetric relations that govern access to resources.

First, we ask why households invest so much effort in these ceremonies, and, in answering this question, connections are drawn between coffee ceremonies, household prestige, and the appearance of wealth, as households compete for reputation and status as successful and well-connected farmers. We postulate that the coffee ceremonies are connected to the ability to mobilise labour for collective work groups, although our cross-sectional data do not allow confirmation of this hypothesis. Finally, the connections between coffee ceremonies and gendered strategies for individual and household success are considered.

Coffee ceremonies are clearly a central part of daily life. Of the 40 households surveyed, 36 respondents said that they performed at least one ceremony per day (and respondents for three of the four that did not perform one ceremony per day said that they performed ceremonies either on Sundays or festival days, which were much more elaborate than the daily ceremonies). The modal number of ceremonies per day was two. The mean number of guests per ceremony was 10.43, ranging from 5 to 20 guests (the average number of guests in C2 was 12, compared to 8.9 in the more deeply stratified community of C1, a distinction that will be discussed later). These ceremonies thus represent a significant investment of labour, time, and money for the food and snacks.

Why do members of these households, many of them struggling for subsistence, invest so much in highly ritualised displays of hospitality? To understand this, a scenario was posed to focus groups in both communities: imagine a household in which the wife wants to reduce the number of coffee ceremonies per day because they demand too much of her time. What should the husband and wife do?

The focus groups all agreed that the coffee ceremonies could not be stopped. Simply not wanting to carry them out is not a reason to reduce the number. In the men's focus group, a few men allowed that if the wife was sick or if she had pressing work in the fields, she might be permitted to reduce the number of ceremonies from three per day to two, but no fewer. A few men also conceded that they or the children might assist with preparations for the third ceremony of the day if the wife was tired, but the ceremonies must go on if at all possible.

> It is a must to make [coffee]; it is a duty, even if it means stopping other jobs. Coffee must be given priority. Two coffee ceremonies are common for our household. . . . For the third, if guests come, I'll help her with the fire and washing the cups, so she can prepare coffee with me.
>
> (Interview with rich and medium-wealth men in C2,
> 24 January 2014)

> If we need to, we can stop coffee at lunchtime by agreement [not hold a late-afternoon ceremony], but if she wants to reduce [the number] more, I will make her continue.
>
> (Interview with poor men in C1, 25 January 2014)

> When I'm harvesting enset, [if] he comes and orders me to prepare coffee, I stop my activity and go to prepare coffee . . . To do otherwise is to bring conflict. I like the coffee ceremony, even if it is extra work. In the morning I prepare coffee, at lunch I prepare coffee.
>
> (Interview with female heads of households in C2,
> 24 January 2014)

Why does the ceremony hold so much power? Focus group participants were unanimous: coffee ceremonies both signify the household's prestige and status to the community at large, and also build that prosperity and status through generating bonds of goodwill and obligation among neighbours. A family that reduced the number of ceremonies or decreased the quality of the food and coffee served was effectively advertising to the world that they were inhospitable or, perhaps worse, were experiencing a decline in their fortunes.

> I have the coffee ceremony three times a day. If I stop doing it three times a day, the neighbours think I am poor.
>> (Interview with wives of male heads of households in C2, 24 January 2014)

W1: If she doesn't prepare [coffee], she [appears to have] a scarcity of crops. Her neighbours won't respect her.

W2: Before, she prepares many [ceremonies] when she was young, but now she has become old, neighbours say.

W3: They'll say to me that I'm weak and also that I have no crops [if I reduce the number of ceremonies].
>> (Interview with female heads of households in C2, 24 January 2014)

> We can't decrease the coffee ceremony . . . Neighbours will increase the amount of gossip, the neighbours will think badly of us, and they may not do coffee with us [invite us to their coffee ceremonies].
>> (Interview with rich and medium-wealth men in C2, 24 January 2014)

Participants spoke of the fear that neighbours would think they were poor in relation to farm and agriculture, tying the ceremonies to the ability of households to meet their own food security needs. A household that reduced the number of ceremonies or attempted to substitute inferior snacks and coffee was a household whose crops were failing. Women in one focus group described the dilemma they faced, as the demands of the coffee ceremony took them away from agricultural labour and drew down their stores of food; but if the ceremonies were not held, they were at risk of being regarded as poor farmers:

W1: Based on our economy, if we have the coffee ceremony three times a day the crops will run out. It [the ceremony] takes much time without working in the field. [But] if there is no more [ceremonies], the neighbours talk, they say "she has no crops in the house, she is poor".

W2: I have the coffee ceremony three times a day. If I stop doing it, neighbours think I am poor.

W3: If I have no more coffee ceremony, neighbours think, "She has no crops for her coffee ceremony." But if I prepare nice coffee, people say, "You are skilled, like *baalamuya* [a skilled and gracious woman]." If I don't prepare nice coffee, I'm not a skilled woman.

(Focus group of wives of male heads of households in C2, 24 January 2014)

Even if households really are getting poorer, the coffee ceremony provides a way to mask the downturn in their circumstances. In the focus group of poor men in C2, participants vividly described the way they would simulate coffee ceremonies when they could not afford to hold real ones, in order to remain within the circuits of normative hospitality:

M1: If we reduce the coffee ceremonies, others will gossip that we're getting poorer.

M2: If we increase the number, it's okay, but if we reduce the number that's a sign of poverty.

M1: During Haile Selassie['s reign] . . . and nowadays more commonly, if they have to reduce the number of coffee ceremonies, they'll make a sound as if they were preparing coffee [using a mukecha and zenazena].

M3: [That behaviour is] purely a sign of poorness. We would make this sound in order to be free of gossip, even if we were crushing non-coffee things [in the mukecha].

M4: Gossip about this may happen by richer neighbours, but even so, the neighbours will call the poor [household] to participate in another coffee ceremony.

(Focus group of poor men, 24 January 2014)

One man laid out succinctly the relationship between the frequency and quality of the coffee ceremony and the reputation of the household:

My neighbour is poor. I am rich. In my house, coffee is prepared with chickpea kolo, but in my neighbour's house, weak coffee with corn kolo . . . My neighbour creates a gap, because I give him good coffee and chickpea kolo and he gives me weak coffee and corn. Neighbours may think badly about me if I reduce the number of coffee ceremonies.

(Interview with rich and medium-wealth men in C2, 24 January 2014)

Who are these "neighbours" whose good opinion is sought through the ceremonies, and why does this opinion matter? The 40 households reported a wide range of guests for the coffee ceremonies, ranging from households (usually poor ones) who invited only resident members of the family, through households who invited their extended family and lateral kin, to households who entertained up to 15 or 20 members of the community on a daily basis.

The strategic value of coffee ceremonies in creating these bonds is suggested by the only focus group participant who did not hold coffee ceremonies, a female household head in C2, who had moved to a new community within the past week. However, she intended to begin holding the ceremonies again once she had met and become acquainted with her new neighbours as a way to integrate herself into her new community.

The people who attended the coffee ceremonies were usually the same people who worked with household members in the informal cooperative work groups. The connection between coffee ceremonies and the assistance provided through cooperative work was not direct and linear, but indirect and allusive, as participants talked about the role of coffee ceremonies in creating feelings of goodwill and making neighbours more inclined to cooperate with each other. Some participants were clear that the coffee ceremony enabled them to "get more work from neighbours" (rich and medium-wealth men, C2), or that coffee and snacks provided the energy needed for agricultural labour. Two men in the C1 focus group of poor men spoke with a mixture of approval and disapproval of households that used coffee ceremonies to gain access to favour or resources from rich neighbours:

> Some women who make good coffee especially when rich people are attending are blamed and called "*bilt*" ["wise" in the local language of the community, with overtones of "crafty" or "clever"]. It's said to mean that they're making good coffee to get benefit from rich people.
> (Focus group of poor men in C1, 25 January 2014)

Others spoke of a less instrumental outcome of the ceremony, namely, building solidarity among people of different levels in the social hierarchy. Coffee ceremonies fostered cohesion among the participants. As one participant put it:

> One [person] is rich, one [person] is poor. Drinking coffee ceremony together helps [to] not bring problems.
> (Interview with poor men in C2, 24 January 2014)

Coffee ceremonies had the same effect on intra-household relations, as they might be the only time when all members, from senior men to children, gathered together and shared food and drink. Informants also talked about the importance of the coffee ceremony for children returning from school to welcome them home, show approval for study, and give them energy to work when they got home.

The connection between coffee ceremonies and the moral economy of mutual assistance is also suggested by the correlation between holding coffee ceremonies for neighbours and participating in cooperative work groups. Of the 40 households, 11 participants, or 28 percent, reported that they held

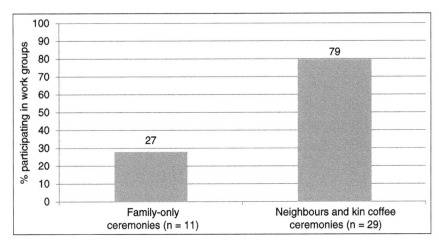

Figure 5.3 Relationship of household to attendees of coffee ceremonies, by number and percentage

small coffee ceremonies for members of their households only (that is, their neighbours and extended kin did not attend their daily ceremonies) (see Figure 5.3). Of these 11 households, a small minority said they took part in neighbourhood-based collective work groups in which neighbours took turns working in each other's gardens. Thus, while a minority of households held family-only ceremonies, these households were less likely to take part in collective work groups than the households that held larger, broader, and more visible ceremonies.

By contrast, among the 29 households that reported holding larger ceremonies for neighbours and community members, 79 percent took part in collective work groups. Holding coffee ceremonies thus appears to be correlated with participation in collective work groups, although it is impossible to determine whether coffee ceremonies lead to work group participation or the other way around.

Because the data are cross-sectional, it is not possible to say whether people held larger ceremonies in order to maintain their position in collaborative work groups, or whether involvement in collective work groups produces an obligation to invite more guests. However, the connection between the composition of the ceremonies and involvement in collaborative work suggests that these ceremonies are linked to the ability to mobilise labour beyond the family.

Another way to look at the relationship between coffee ceremonies and the moral economy of mutual assistance is to examine resource sharing in the form of direct transfers between households. This was measured by asking respondents whether their household *receives resources* (most commonly food and draft power) from other households; and whether they *give resources*

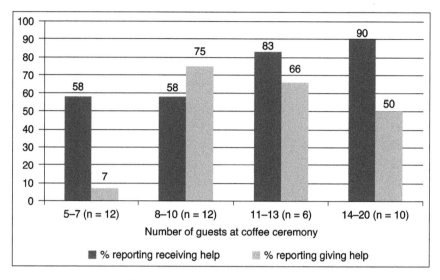

Figure 5.4 Percentage of households that reported giving or receiving farming help or participating in collective work groups, by coffee ceremony size

to other households. The sample was stratified by the number of guests reported at the coffee ceremonies. Four strata were created: 5–7 guests, 8–10 guests, 11–13 guests, and 14–20 guests.

Figure 5.4 shows that households holding larger coffee ceremonies were more likely to *receive* resources than households that held smaller ones. However, they were not more likely to *give* resources than the households with smaller ceremonies. This finding is slightly counter-intuitive, as one might expect the households wealthy enough to have upward of 15 guests daily at a coffee ceremony would also be wealthy enough to have food and draft power to share. However, it is consistent with the finding in Figure 5.2 concerning participation in collective work groups. Having many people at coffee ceremonies is linked to the inflow of resources to the household, and less tightly linked to the outflow of such resources. Bringing people together through coffee ceremonies appears to be a good survival strategy for households in this moral economy.

The differences between the two communities in terms of coffee ceremonies and labour mobilisation must also be stressed. Seventy-three percent of the households that invited only family to their ceremonies were located in C1, the more highly stratified of the two communities. It may be that in C1, where there are more rich people with money to hire labour and more poor people who must sell their labour to make ends meet, labour no longer needs to be mobilised through the moral economy represented by the coffee ceremony.

It is also plausible that holding many large ceremonies with high-quality coffee and snacks communicates that the household is successful and skilled in farming, and may thus be a good partner for other households in reciprocal labour-sharing. A household of poor farmers who cannot manage to grow enough crops for the ceremonies might be less desirable as a partner in other agricultural work. People choose whom they will participate with in ventures such as co-raising animals based on whether they think that person is a good farmer; to appear to be a bad farmer is to risk gossip by neighbours and the loss of potential opportunities.

It is clear that the coffee ceremony is tied to the flow of resources between households. Can a similar line be drawn between coffee ceremonies and direct measures of food security? From the household interviews, indices were constructed to measure the extent to which participants believed their households had enough food (food quantity), and the extent to which they had access to the kinds of food they desired (food quality). On both measures, households in C1 reported substantially better quantity and quality of food than those in C2. These differences between the communities are greater than the differences between the strata of households according to the size of their coffee ceremonies (calculations not shown). In other words, the differences in reported food security between the two communities outweighed the differences between households with large ceremonies and households with smaller ones. This may be simply because C1, the more stratified community, was also wealthier overall than C2, so that even the poorer and more isolated members of C1 were better off than poor and isolated households in C2. The data do not allow the mapping of coffee ceremonies directly on to perceptions of food security, but there is good reason to believe that coffee ceremonies are tied to the achievement of food security, through their connections to status and resource mobilisation.

The coffee ceremony is connected to relations among households through its power to signify who is rich or poor and whose agricultural fortunes are rising or declining, and through its apparent connection to collective work group participation. It also shapes intra-household relations through the gendered division of labour. Focus group participants were unanimous that coffee ceremonies are primarily women's work, although men are often responsible for making sure that necessary components, such as salt or firewood, are purchased or collected. Given how much work this involves, the ceremony might appear to be a fairly simple instance of men's appropriation of women's labour for their own benefit as heads of households.

However, women's discussion of the ceremony suggested it is more complexly gendered, and that their labour for the coffee ceremony provided gender-specific benefits, as well as taking up time that might have been spent on other projects (and indeed, the tension between the time needed for the ceremony and the other things women might be doing with that time ran through the focus groups and interviews).

Women reaped benefits from the ceremonies in two ways. First, their performance of the rituals involved secured their own status within and across households as *baalamuya*, or "masters of skill". A woman who could gracefully and efficiently prepare the coffee and serve her guests was an honoured woman, who could command prestige and respect within her husband's family and within the community. A woman who could not prepare coffee well, on the other hand, reflected badly on her household and even on her mother, who had evidently not trained her daughter well.

Men also used the ceremonies as a marker of women's proper gender performance, as they are woven into social reproduction. Men in C1 talked about deciding whether to marry the woman their father had chosen for them based upon the way the woman conducted her coffee ceremony, including properly keeping her eyes downcast, while visiting the women during the annual community festival. Men in C2 also used the ceremony to identify women who would be good wives, but in this village the men (not their fathers) chose the women and dropped in on them unannounced throughout the year, accompanied by friends who would help them evaluate the women.

A second gendered benefit of the ceremonies lies in the production of solidarity and connection among women. Even as women complained of the effort required for the ceremonies, several said that they did not want to reduce the number of ceremonies because they would lose their social network with other women.

> [If my husband wanted me to reduce the number of ceremonies] I'd be disappointed, because I like it so much. The coffee ceremony is one of my favourite things. It is my major means of relaxation. If he asks me to stop I might get headaches. I like to talk with my neighbours.
> (Interview with wives of male household heads in
> C2, 24 January 2014)

Women also referred to a female-only variation of the coffee ceremony, called *dado*. These ceremonies gave women space to talk about domestic issues in an all-female group, including issues that could not be discussed with husbands:

> We discuss about sex during the coffee, cleaning things, and sanitation, we talk freely if there's no husband there. If the husband is in the house, we talk quietly.
> (Interview with female household heads in C2, 24
> January 2014)

Holding *dado* ceremonies appeared to be a contentious issue in some households, as women reported pressure to discontinue these "idle" ceremonies: one woman reported that "[my] husband tells me that *dado* is killing time" (interview with wives of household heads in C1, 24 January 2014). Another woman in the same group concurred, stating that in her community,

> There's more time [for other work] now that we've stopped doing *dado*, but still no advantage for us [it has not made life better for us].

Implications for food security

At first glance, the relationship between coffee ceremonies and food seems remote. Although coffee is technically a food, it is not a significant source of nutrition; and although *buna kurs* are served in conjunction with coffee, they too do not constitute a major contribution to diet, though granted they may constitute a major portion of poor people's daily caloric intake.

The coffee ceremony is important, however, because it marks the importance of "the social" in mobilising the resources and inputs that households must have in order to survive or thrive. In the two communities studied in Ethiopia, the coffee ceremony offers lessons about how to think about food security. In the broadest definition of food security, such rituals are crucial, as they generate status, reputation, and prestige. These qualities can then be leveraged to grant households access to the inputs needed for production, particularly labour. The time and effort that go into the ceremony compete with the needs of household food production, particularly for women, but also generate possibilities for meeting those needs.

Although coffee ceremonies are tied to the conditions of possibility for food security in both of these communities, they are not monolithic. The size and frequency of the ceremonies varies across the two communities, and the meaning and significance of the ceremonies varies by gender within the communities. The cross-sectional data collected suggest that the number of people invited to coffee ceremonies is connected to household participation in collective work groups, tying this daily ritual to the nuts and bolts of agricultural production. The data also suggest that as communities become more economically stratified and marketised – as is happening in C1, where the rich are richer and the poor are poorer than in C2 – the economy of affection represented by the coffee ceremony may be losing ground to other ways of mobilising resources, such as simple cash transfers.

However, coffee ceremonies and other such rituals are not simply substitutes for a cash nexus. The weight that people in both communities place on the ceremonies testifies to the importance of reputation, status, and prestige in the fabric of social life.

Conclusion

The coffee ceremony demonstrates the embeddedness of food security practices within complex social relations. The same performances and interpersonal relations that allow for the mobilisation of labour also create and maintain hierarchies within and between households. These ceremonies do not simply create superior and inferior social statuses: they also serve to "horizontalise" these relations, opening social spaces in which the more powerful and less powerful come together, and they offer women in particular the opportunity to refine and display their own gendered arts.

Even though the labour demands of the coffee ceremonies weigh most heavily on women, the positive outcomes of the ceremonies appear to outweigh the burdens. Such gendered practices are important not only for women but for the household as a whole, as the performance of gender through the coffee ceremonies becomes a means through which household food security is assured, both symbolically and materially.

Acknowledgements

This work was supported by the project "Improving nutrition in Ethiopia through plant breeding and soil management" (project 106927), supported by Canada's International Development Research Centre (IDRC) through the Canadian International Food Security Research Fund (CIFSRF). The authors are grateful to Demmelash Mulualem, Eshetu Lukas, and Afewok Kebebu for their outstanding assistance during the field research phase of this study. The authors would also like to thank peer reviewers at the gender writing workshop of the Global Food Security Dialog (Edmonton, Alberta, May 2014) for their comments.

References

All website URLs accessed on 7 April 2016.

Agarwal, Bina. 1997. "'Bargaining' and Gender Relations: Within and Beyond the Household." *Feminist Economics* 3 (1): 1–51.

Hyden, Goran. 1980. *Beyond Ujamaa in Tanzania*. Berkeley: University of California Press.

Jaffe, JoAnn. 1997. "Underdevelopment by Design: How Agricultural Development Programs Increase Poverty and Inequality in Poor Countries – The Case of Haiti." *Canadian Journal of Latin American and Caribbean Studies* 21 (42): 5–19.

Jaffe, JoAnn. 2003. "Family Labour Processes, Land, and the Farm Crisis." In Harry P. Diaz, JoAnn Jaffe, and Robert Stirling, eds, *Farm Communities at the Crossroads: Challenge and Resistance*. Regina, SK: CPRC Press, 137–48.

Jarzabkowski, Paula, Julia Balogun, and David Seidl. 2007. "Strategizing: The Challenges of a Practice Perspective." *Human Relations* 60 (1): 5–27.

Kaler, Amy. 2006. "'When They See Money, They Think It's Life': Money, Modernity and Morality in Two Sites in Rural Malawi." *Journal of Southern African Studies* 32 (2): 335–49.

Kandiyoti, Deniz. 1988. "Bargaining with Patriarchy." *Gender & Society* 2 (3): 274–90.

Keating, Norah C. 1996. "Legacy, Aging, and Succession in Farm Families." *Generations* 20 (3): 61–5.

Mjaaland, Thera. 2004. "Beyond the Coffee Ceremony: Women's Agency in Western Tigray, Northern Ethiopia." *Betwixt and Between: Sosialantropologstudentenes Årbok* 14: 71–7.

Schatzki, Theodore R. 2001. "Introduction: Practice Theory." In Theodore R. Schatzki, Karin Knorr Cetina, and Eike von Savigny, eds, *The Practice Turn in Contemporary Theory*. London: Routledge, 1–14.

Scott, James C. 1977. *The Moral Economy of the Peasant: Rebellion and Subsistence in Southeast Asia*. New Haven, CT: Yale University Press.

Thompson, E.P. 1993. *Customs in Common: Studies in Traditional Popular Culture*. London: The New Press.

Warner, Michael W., Ramatu N. Al-Hassan, and Jonathon G. Kydd. 1997. "Beyond Gender Roles? Conceptualizing the Social and Economic Lives of Rural Peoples in Sub-Saharan Africa." *Development and Change* 28 (1): 143–68.

Waters, Tony. 1992. "A Cultural Analysis of the Economy of Affection and the Uncaptured Peasantry in Tanzania." *Journal of Modern African Studies* 30 (1): 163–75.

6 A missed opportunity for research and development interventions

Gender and the forest food trade in urban Cameroon

Lauren Q. Sneyd

> When people argue with my prices I really do not like it because they do not have an idea how much I struggle to get the product.
>
> (Interview, Muea market, Buea, July 2012)

Introduction

Urbanisation rates in Africa are twice the global average, and "cities are fast becoming epicentres of the food security challenge in Africa" (Crush et al. 2012: 287). Despite development-focused policies and action, "poverty remains persistent" across most of Africa (Ingram et al. 2014: 68). In this context, there has also been "limited job creation amongst the poor", and the gender implications of these trends are worth probing.

African women's role in agricultural production and farming has been widely studied, more so than women's participation in food marketing (Fonchingong 1999; Freidberg 2001a, 2001b; Carney 2004; Fonjong and Athanasia 2007). However, urban traders of forest food are often overlooked in this body of research.[1] Congo Basin forests are the world's second largest block of rainforests, after the Amazon. The combination of extensive forest cover and poverty means that the surrounding forests sustain urban livelihoods and contribute to urban food security and diets (Sunderlin et al. 2008; Sneyd 2013). The extent of the forest food trade in Cameroon is often masked by the informality of the sector, and this has gendered implications (Sneyd 2015). The informal trade in food products in Cameroon is organised around various types of buyers and sellers (or *buyam-sellam* in pidgin). While Ngoumou (2010) found that the informal system of feeding Cameroonian cities is effective, the informal food sector is highly gendered and presents considerable challenges to those who seek to reap socioeconomic advancement from wild foods.

Most people involved in the urban food markets in Cameroon are women:

> Women dominate retailing in most chains. Women indicated that this activity is attractive as it can be combined with family activities, often

with young children present whilst retailing, it is not physically demanding, often does not involve long distances and difficult journeys from home as women are urban based, and it is culturally acceptable.

(Ingram et al. 2014: 78)

The trade in forest food products presents a similar profile. The foods in question are not agricultural products; rather, they are gathered from the surrounding environment and represent a consequential portion of the regional food system and local diet (Sneyd 2013). Since the food price crisis of 2007–8, many of the local and forest foods have been priced out of the reach of many households: the April 2014 issue of the UN news and analysis publication *Africa Renewal* reported that Cameroon is still experiencing high food prices, similar to those reported in 2008 and 2010 (Rao 2014).

From the 1990s, the international development research community in Cameroon – including the United Nations Food and Agriculture Organization (FAO), the Center for International Forestry Research (CIFOR), and the World Agroforestry Centre – approached Cameroon's forest food economy using the concept of non-timber forest products (NTFPs). This perspective has driven a quantitative analysis of the rural gathering of these products, and promoted them for forest conservation and as a means of improving rural livelihoods (Belcher 2003; Wiersum et al. 2014). As a result, the top-down intervention in Cameroon's forest economy has done a lot of good in terms of forest conservation and livelihoods from forest products. However, it has missed the mark when it comes to an analysis of forest foods and their implications for improved food security outcomes, particularly in urban areas.

More Africans are living in cities across the continent, and more people need access to cash in these places to buy their food (Cohen and Garrett 2010; Tacoli et al. 2013). So, while the voluminous research material these organisations have produced is of high quality, the focus on rural livelihoods misses: (1) the perceptions and needs (demand) of the people in local cities; (2) perspectives from the local urban traders; and (3) the contributions wild foods make to local food security outcomes.

Most important to this discussion is that the bulk of this research was done before the food price crises of 2007–8 and 2010–11 (Ruiz Pérez et al. 2002). In contrast, the present study was conducted after the food price crisis. It is also significant that the voices of food traders and their perspectives and experiences are silent in the literature. Future pathways to gender equity and to improvements to local food security can be found in the promotion and transformation of forested foods for sustainable local consumption.

The intention of this chapter is to qualitatively document a sector of the urban food economy informed by a broad survey conducted in 2012–13. The study engages primarily with women traders and their experience procuring, storing, and selling their goods. It also considers the improvements that are necessary – for example, improved processing, transformation, and storage of these foods before sale – in the marketing of forest foods that contribute to food security outcomes in urban areas.

This chapter asks: (1) What are the challenges and opportunities facing a *buyam-sellam* of wild foods in urban Cameroon? and (2) According to the *buyam-sellams*, how can the wild food sector be improved? The study considers how these recommendations might improve food security outcomes in cities in Cameroon, and identifies future pathways for development interventions that target the foods that many Cameroonians eat.

The next section reviews concepts from the literature on women's and men's work in the food sector in Africa, and Cameroon in particular. A description of the methodology and data analysis from in-country fieldwork follows. Results from the study are presented to answer the research questions above. The chapter concludes by identifying recommendations for future research and development interventions for the wild food sector in Cameroon.

Ways of understanding gendered work roles and the food trade in Africa

The functioning of African food markets has been studied by researchers from a range of academic disciplines (Watts 1983; Guyer 1987; Flynn 2005; Pinstrup-Andersen 2010). The ways in which gender and work are studied and described in the literature on African food systems assist us in thinking about the *buyam-sellams* of wild food in Cameroon and the food security implications of their work. The sections that follow emphasise the literature on the informal food trade, and on gender and work in that trade. The relationship between food systems and markets is explored to understand the dynamic interactions of these concepts in the African context.

Empirical studies note not only the gender relations that mark the trading of foodstuffs on the one hand, but also the informality of the sector and the urban nature of the exchange on the other (Roitman 1990; Freidberg 2001a, 2001b). Niger-Thomas notes that Cameroon's economic crisis of the 1980s, the subsequent Structural Adjustment Programmes, and the devaluation of the CFA franc (XAF, the currency used in Central Africa) in the 1990s made "informality a way of life for Cameroonians" (2001: 44).

In the early 1970s, anthropologist Keith Hart (1973), after several years of field research in Ghana, coined the phrase "informal economy" to describe the various activities that occur outside the formal framework of a liberal economy. Hart stressed the fact that the informal economy involves self-employed actors who use the market in order to gain supplementary income from a formal activity. In a subsequent study, Hart (1982) highlighted that a real opportunity for exchange existed between the rural sector and fast-growing urban areas. Following a similar thread, Ngoumou highlights that Guyer (1987) noted in the 1980s that, historically, the burgeoning African cities were fed by numerous "craft operators engaged alongside the official system of provisioning cities with food from the rural hinterland, and that public authorities were not able to control this economy" (Ngoumou 2010: 193). In Cameroon, the *buyam-sellams* of various products in this system tend to still be politically controversial and operate according to their own norms, sometimes engaging in what has been termed "fiscal disobedience" (Roitman 2005).[2]

Overall, the marketing of foods in urban markets is geared towards Marx's M–C–M (money–commodities–money) arrangement (Marx 1977). Trading in these systems is the main mechanism of extraction of surplus in many African countries (Bates 1982; Wolf 1982; Gibbon 1997). Traders engage with this arrangement with the hope of a return on investment: "monetary gain is the primary objective" (Ngoumou 2010: 198). In this case, the commodity is a food product, but it is also associated with the labour involved in the procurement and exchange of the product (Gardiner Barber 2004). These traders are involved in the sorting, grading, and (to some degree) processing of agricultural products and wild foods before sale. Women are key players in African food systems, "accounting for 70 percent of farm labour and performing 80 percent of food processing" (Pinstrup-Andersen 2010: 12). Traditionally, women are found to represent a disproportionate percentage of urban traders, and their numbers are greater still in food marketing (Clark 1994; Babb 1998; Seligmann 2001).

Generally, the research approach to explaining the role of women as the main food producers and marketers on the African continent has been to characterise men's and women's work roles (Freidberg 2001a, 2001b; Carney 2004; Hovorka 2006), thereby drawing attention to changing roles in both "visible" work outside the home and "invisible" work inside the home (Waring 1988). Freidberg (2001b) notes that the complexity of gender construction is found not only in place-based local histories but often in the interaction of places. Hovorka (2006) established that everyday notions of gender are important in understanding rural-to-urban linkages around food. For example, during the colonial period, African men were encouraged to produce cash crops for export, and later Boserup (1965) identified the association of men's responsibility with cash crops, whereas women were responsible for food production. Bryceson (1989) found in the 1980s that the sexual demarcation of cash cropping continued, sometimes with the effect of eroding women's claims to cultivable land. Her finding is similar to Carney's (2004) in Gambia and Freidberg's (2001a, 2001b) in Burkina Faso. Hart (1982) associated this trend with men's historically having greater access to both capital and labour, especially in commercial agriculture, which was encouraged for economic growth. While these insights span across Africa, in general, men have a higher social status than women in Central Africa (Ingram et al. 2014).

The stereotype that associates African men with cash crop production and women with food production has its parallel in the forest sector. Here, it dictates that men are involved in the lumber industry and hunting, while women gather a variety of NTFPs. A more refined analysis put forward by Ruiz Pérez et al. (2002) shows that both genders engage in a large number of forest-related activities, and specialisation is less pronounced than in the above dichotomy. Women may be involved in tree nurseries and planting, hunting and fishing, the use of traps and other tools and techniques, and the production of fuel wood for the market; men also collect a number of NTFPs, for both consumption and sale; and both genders are usually engaged in gathering medicinal plants for various uses. The trade in NTFPs makes up a large proportion of the livelihood portfolio in this region, and the wild food trade hinges on gender relations that define this work (Ingram et al. 2014). Two findings from Ruiz Pérez et al. (2002) suggest that (1) most *buyam-sellams* in Cameroon's humid forest zone (HFZ) are women, and they may specialise in selling one NTFP or deal with a combination of NTFPs and agricultural products; and (2) when women are engaged in the retail trade of NTFPs in Cameroon, men tend to dominate the wholesale market, high-value products, and, particularly, the export sector (Ingram et al. 2014). This pattern is typical of NTFPs and food markets in most West and Central African countries.

The buying and selling of food is an intrinsic component of women's social relations in urban environments. Through her urban study, Hovorka (2006) found that African women become involved in the food sector for economic and social advancement. While this trade presents many challenges, the opportunities to earn some cash from an activity in a domain in which women have the greatest control are considerable. For example, a study of women street food vendors who sold cooked food along the streets of Limbe, Cameroon, demonstrated on the one hand the burden of this activity on women, and, on the other hand, the greater economic independence and positive impacts on living conditions in the household (Fonchingong 2005). Fonchingong asks how these cooked food vendors might be guaranteeing an improvement to their livelihoods by staving off poverty while exploring the challenges faced by small-scale entrepreneurs. For these women, taking on additional income-earning roles has not always translated into economic empowerment, and in most cases the women were barely earning enough. Likewise, rents, high taxes, and household management costs eat up the meagre profits earned by food vending. Further, slack periods marked by low sales and limited capital and opportunities for expansion constrain work possibilities in the sector. Without a doubt, these vendors play a crucial role in the urban economy of Cameroon by meeting a growing demand for cheap, prepared food for the working urban population.

Overall, these studies highlight how men and women define and redefine their experience of constraints and opportunities by linking particular gender roles to the production and trade of food. By understanding the different definitions of what is considered "men's work" and "women's work", this body of scholarship seeks to understand women's changing work roles and the challenges they face in earning a living.

Fieldwork and methodology

The data sources for this study included relevant non-governmental organisation (NGO) reports and publications, news stories related to the topic, scholarly materials in this area, and market and household surveys. Fieldwork was conducted in urban food markets in southern Cameroon during five research trips between 2010 and 2013. The research focused on 25 markets in southern Cameroon's humid forest zone (HFZ) in the Congo Basin. The markets included in the study are located in two regions of the country: Yaoundé, the country's French-speaking capital, and the English-speaking peri-urban Southwest region (see Figures 6.1 and 6.2).

Each of the markets varies in size in terms of the number of *buyam-sellams* and the quantity of products sold. The author frequented markets to observe the buying and selling patterns of wild foods and to learn about this trade from *buyam-sellams* themselves (Clark 1994). Wild food vendors were identified based on the products they sold, word of mouth from other traders who knew where the forest products were coming from, and wholesalers

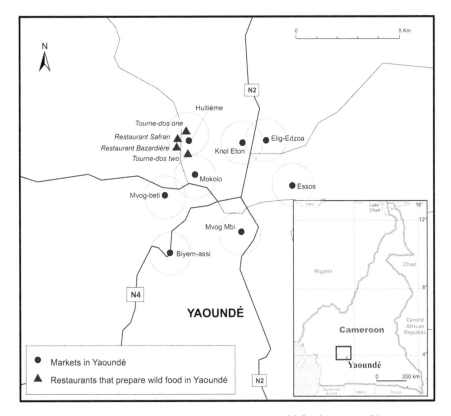

Figure 6.1 Map of markets and restaurants preparing wild food in Yaoundé

Source: Sneyd (2013).

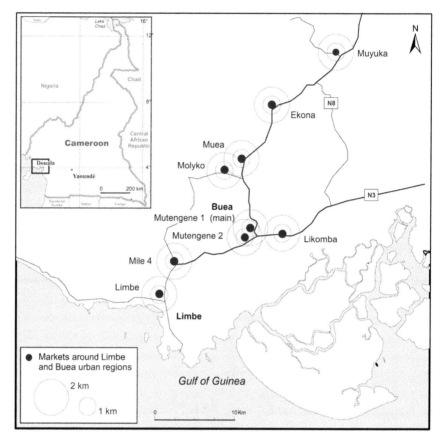

Figure 6.2 Map of markets in the Southwest region

Source: Sneyd (2013).

who were connected to the smaller traders. Research assistants were hired to facilitate the survey, which was field tested in each city for reliability. During the field tests the survey became participatory as questions were added or omitted based on preliminary responses and input from participants. Questions deemed most sensitive were related directly to the amount of income earned; consequently, questions about income were adjusted to focus specifically on estimated quantities of products sold and prices of those products. This information was not quantified, as it would give a false sense of its representativeness: it was learned that the *buyam-sellams* would often misrepresent these quantities.

The survey adapted applied ethnobotany surveys to draw out links between food security and somewhat unconventional food sources. The survey also drew on survey work conducted with market women in Ghana to capture common buying and selling practices and urban African market trends (Clark 1994). The qualitative survey included mostly open-ended questions to give the women an opportunity to reflect on and describe their business, and to talk about possible ways to improve it (Seligmann 2001; Edwards et al. 2005; Miller and Deutsch 2009). Questions that guided the study included: What does the *buyam-sellam* of forest food sell and why? How are its scarcity, perishability, and competition for products managed? How do you make money and how do you lose money? What control do you have over your business?

In total, 410 individuals participated in market interviews ($N = 171$), in-depth interviews ($N = 38$), and household interviews ($N = 201$). Informed consent was obtained from the participants.

Of the 171 traders surveyed, 38 were male and 133 were female. For the in-depth interviews, 8 traders were male and 30 were female. The traders surveyed and interviewed represented all of the forested regions in Cameroon (Central, South, Littoral, Southwest, and West). The average age of the *buyam-sellams* in this study was 40 years; the youngest was 16 and the oldest 67. Many of the sellers had been in the business for at least 10 years, and some for more than 20.

The household surveys mostly involved women, as women are the main food preparers in the household. The interviews were conducted in the wet and dry seasons to appreciate the impact of seasonality on wild food market patterns. The author recognises the limitations of this preliminary study: while many wild food traders and their customers were included in the study, the producers or gatherers of wild food were not, resulting in a primarily urban study of the wild food trade.

Qualitative content analysis of open-ended interview questions was coded based on categories and themes (similarities and differences) deemed relevant during the course of data collection and subsequent analysis. The quotes presented below were selected to illustrate the themes, experiences, and trends that emerged from the data analysis, and are representative of the theme under discussion. The names of the sellers are not included; the city or market names are used instead.

The rich ethnographic data (Robben and Sluka 2007) obtained from the surveys and interviews document the experience of being a *buyam-sellam* of wild food in Cameroon's urban, forested zone.

Gender and the wild food trade in Cameroon

Organisation of the forest food markets

Urban food markets in Cameroon carry a diversity of products displayed mostly in an open-air setting. Though there are rules and norms that govern this space, it operates largely within the informal economy (Roitman 1990, 2005). The selling of forest food makes up a particular livelihood strategy that hinges on the seasonal fluctuations of the harvest calendar, access to forests for harvesting and buying sites across Cameroon's HFZ, and the possibility of getting "a good price" in a highly competitive market. The majority of retailers operating in Cameroon are women: some studies have shown that 94 percent of traders are women (Awono et al. 2010). Men are involved to a lesser degree and tend to specialise in higher-value products and trade on a larger scale. Data collection for this study was greatly impacted by this reality – there were simply more women in the market, and more women than men participated in the study (of the 171 traders surveyed, 133 were female and 38 were male). Notwithstanding this evidence, recent research shows that

> traders are strongly gender differentiated according to their business size, product specialisation and market strategy, with men tending to be engaged in trading more profitable commodities, have larger-sized businesses, with more potential to accumulate wealth, and have displaced women from their traditional trading activities when attractive incomes are possible.
>
> (Ingram et al. 2014: 69)

The informal selling of wild foods is flexible and offers greater options for women, who often have household and child-rearing responsibilities. The markets, formally ruled through local government regulations, are in fact organised and managed, mostly by women, through traditional, group-accepted institutions. The *buyam-sellams* play a key role in assembling and distributing food and forest products, and also in managing the marketplace. In Cameroon, the data show that collectively, women are not only traders of food in urban areas, they are also farmers in rural areas, urban gardeners, and gatherers of wild food from the forest.

The *buyams* were taught how to sell things by their parents, mothers and aunties, siblings, and friends; a few sellers were taught the trade by their husband's family. Men in Yaoundé stated that they learned how to sell in food markets from their grandmothers, mothers, and wives. The men in the study who sold shrimp and crayfish (high-value items) or diversified meat learned how to sell from their grandfathers or uncles.

The traders attend the market every day it is open, often arriving at 6 a.m. and staying until 5 or 6 p.m., when the sun goes down, at which time the women return home to cook for their families. In the smaller cities, where the markets are open only a few days a week, the *buyam-sellams* sell in more than one market to move their stock and to earn enough money throughout the week. In larger cities such as Yaoundé, where the markets are open nearly every day, the *buyam-sellams* attend the market every day. The *buyam-sellams* in both regions buy their stock from wholesalers, who in this business are mostly men (Ruiz Pérez et al. 2002).

The wild food products identified in the survey ranged from forest snails, wild mushrooms, termites, caterpillars (*Rhynchophorus phoenicis*), honey, and bushmeat to vegetables such as eru (*Gnetum africanum*), country onions (*Afrostyrax kamerunensis/Afrostyrax lepidophyllus*), and peppers (*Aframomum melegueta*); spices such as *njangsa* (*Ricinodendron heudelotii*) and *rondelle* (*Scorodophloeus zenkeri Olom*); various tree barks; fruits, including bush plums or *safou* (*Dacryodes edulis*) and bush mangoes (*Irvingia* spp.); and nuts, such as kola (*Cola acuminata*; *Cola pachycarpa K. Schum*; *Cola nitida*). Wild foods are typically sold throughout the market, and are often sold next to their accompaniments by women who share recipes for their preparation. Men in both regions are more likely to sell high-value items such as bushmeat, beef, and fresh fish from the coast.

There was greater specialisation of forest foods in the Southwest region, where 31 of 65 traders sold only one product, whereas in Yaoundé, the *buyams* were more diversified and sold more than one product. In this city, 13 of the 107 interview respondents were specialised. These *buyams* sold eru or snails, both products that require more work in terms of transformation (for example, washing and slicing the eru, and washing and keeping the snails alive) and managing perishability.

Quantity and seasonality

Eighty percent of *buyam-sellams* in the Southwest region noticed an increase in their sales of wild foods during the wet season. Many thought this was linked to greater awareness of their products, more people eating these foods, and, generally, more demand. The sellers who sold less attributed this to a change in the quantity of foods available for harvest, and more competition from other sellers in the business. These trends are closely linked to seasonality, as sellers noted a decrease in sales during the dry season. Demand fluctuates both seasonally and in response to product availability.

In the wet season in Yaoundé, 94 percent of vendors reported that they were selling more now than in the past. All of the *buyam-sellams* interviewed mentioned that they had noticed an increase in the population, resulting in more clients, larger neighbourhoods, more foreigners (from Nigeria, Gabon, and Equatorial Guinea), and a general increase in demand for wild foods. Those who noticed a scarcity of products attributed it to the decline in quantities leaving the forest, because of Forest and Fauna officers' stopping or arresting the *buyams* on the road or confiscating products crossing the border into Nigeria, Gabon, and Equatorial Guinea, where they command higher prices.

Constraints and opportunities

While the wild food trade provides considerable opportunities to earn some cash from an activity in a domain in which women have some control, it also presents many challenges. Indeed, according to the data, the challenges outweigh the opportunities. The high incidence of bribery and corruption in public institutions has consistently impeded the development of the small-business sector in Cameroon, and created an environment in which it is difficult to operate a business. Research from the 25 markets indicated that the vendors in this trade experienced similar challenges. However, the opportunities gained from these activities are sufficient to keep women selling and keep the sector growing.

Infrastructure, taxes, and regulation

The markets in both regions are muddy in the rainy season and dusty in the dry season. The marketplace is pitted with open sewers crossed by makeshift bridges of dusty boards, and large dumpster bins collect the rotting and unsold vegetables and fruits. The women and men surveyed described a situation whereby they pay taxes to sit in a dirty, muddy, un-serviced market space. Each seller is required to pay 100 CFA francs (equivalent to 0.15€) each day to obtain a ticket to sell in that market. This fee can change based on quantity of goods sold and through negotiation. In this context, the women feel undermined by the local authorities, who are usually men.

It has been established that evidence of power in the marketplace is demonstrated through storage capability, as traders can control supply levels and prices (Clark 1994). However, many of the market stalls in both regions are temporary and have no storage capacity. The physical layout of the 25 markets restricts traders' ability to store goods in their stalls, and the associated benefits cannot be realised. Typically, in the Southwest region, because of the lack of infrastructure, women have to sell in more than one market, often carrying goods to each market and back home as they cannot store goods on site.

> If I had a shed for myself, then that would really help me because I will not suffer to [sic] carry this big umbrella every market day and instead carry a bit more kola.
>
> (Interview, Likomba, November 2012)

> Having a permanent stall to store items than moving from market to market [would help my business].
>
> (Interview, Muea, July 2012)

> We don't have enough space to stock our products. We pay stocking fees but the products often stay outside and go to waste.
>
> (Interview, Mokolo, July 2012)

Access to storage allows vendors to increase their stock and potentially their earnings. Men are mostly the wholesalers (in Yaoundé) and are more likely to have more stock and permanent market space. With greater earnings, many of the female *buyam-sellams* said they wanted to invest profits back into their business.

Many *buyam-sellams* are unaware of regulations governing the products they sell:

> [I am] anxious to know the right document needed to trade in eru, they [local officers] are willing to process and acquire the document.
> (Interview, Buea, July 2012)

And many others simply say they do not know about "matters of the state [but] they [administrators] should also realise the economic and social context of the vendors" (interview, Yaoundé, November 2012). This lack of awareness means that "to conform to the regulations, we have to foresee what to bribe them [the officers] with" (interview, Yaoundé, November 2012). Many *buyams* mention these bribes as a drain on their savings, investments, and income.

Perishability and transformation

The perishability of forest foods is absolutely a concern for all traders and sellers, regardless of gender. In markets in the Southwest, perishability is managed through a variety of strategies. The most common is smoking the product over a fire: products preserved this way include prepared snails, mushrooms, bushmeat, and bush mango pits. Wild foods such as eru are kept cool and dry. This is a difficult task during the wet season when green leafy vegetables are harvested and sold in large quantities; access to cold storage is not always reliable, affordable, or possible.

> On the subject of foods in Yaoundé there is a problem of conservation and conditioning. Most of the foods from rural areas are exposed to the elements and poorly conserved [sic]. In periods of abundance, we can see the leaves of vegetables, condiments, tomato, et cetera, in decomposition because they simply have not been sold in time. This leads to a lack of return for the vendor, leading to social and economic losses. A good policy of conservation and transportation of the food products could resolve this problem.
> (Interview, Yaoundé, November 2013)

Without access to the facilities and infrastructure required to manage food perishability and transformation, many traders experience losses and wastage of the foods they procure. This has implications on the income they earn.

Credit and capital

Access to more capital was overwhelmingly identified by the women in the survey as a way to improve the wild food sector (mentioned 100 times), although women's access to credit is severely limited in this context – men have been more successful in obtaining credit and capital to build their business (Ingram et al. 2014). With greater capital, the women plan to increase stock and invest in the business: "If I can stop eating my capital [I can] use it for other things" (interview, Mile 4, November 2012). While this trend of "eating the business", that is, eating unsold foods at home, improves household food security, over time this strategy decreases savings, as the only return on labour is food itself.

Many traders belong to a *tontine* or *njangi*, a small micro-credit institution that helps to organise the women and some men, but many view this organisation as a way "to help us out financially in case of economic problems" (interview, Yaoundé, November 2012). Through established organisations and associations, some women are able to pool their money and purchase in bulk from rural village buying sites. Overall, the lack of access to more formalised credit (mentioned only 13 times) means that many small traders (mostly women) go into debt to wholesalers (mostly men), while at the same time customers go into debt with the *buyam-sellams*. This cycle creates much frustration, especially when the *buyams*, individually and collectively, have to constantly negotiate the setting of prices:

> The eternal problem of coming to a consensus on the price of products [impacts my business]. Sometimes some vendors sell for more or less expensive, there is no standard price.
>
> (Interview, Mokolo, July 2012)

After the food price crisis in Cameroon, the "prices rise every day. Customers complain a lot and the business is slow" (interview, Limbe, November 2012).

Implications for household food security

In Cameroon, many edible wild plants and other food products are culturally meaningful and are regularly included in local food baskets. Household data show that 25 percent of food budgets in Cameroonian cities are spent on wild foods. These foods are important components of traditional recipes that are part of the daily diet, and help to maintain local understandings of what it means to be food secure. The ingredients for these dishes are sold in local markets by traders who themselves use wild foods in their household. Often the traders, both men and women, bring unsold foods home to prepare and consume for the family. For example, the household data from Yaoundé indicated that 20 percent of households interviewed reported eating caterpillars as a type of wild food bought and prepared in their home (among many other wild foods, including termites and large forest snails). A few families even reported that seasonal caterpillars were their children's favourite meal.

THE FOREST FOOD TRADE IN URBAN CAMEROON

Results from the survey show that one forest food in particular, eru or okok prepared with waterleaf, red palm oil, cow skin, and crayfish with *fufu* (a mash of yams or other starches served as an accompaniment to meat or vegetable stews), was overwhelmingly named as the households' favourite dish, mentioned 914 times in the survey of 371 individuals. Those who mentioned this dish indicated that it was their absolute favourite and one that children especially loved to eat. Many studies have documented the chemical composition and nutritional value of eru leaves: they provide important dietary fibre, protein, and numerous vitamins and minerals (Ali et al. 2011). Food price shocks increase the risk of micronutrient deficiencies, so improved access to these local and healthy options has important health benefits.

The greatest barrier to food security in cities comes down to the price of food, especially since the food price crisis. Many urban poor people have little room to manoeuvre as coping mechanisms decrease their food security. Data show that when food prices rise, households buy less food, buy lower quality food, reduce portion sizes, reduce meal frequency, and buy less of a variety of food. In this context, after the Cameroon food riots of 2007–8, Cameroonians increased their consumption of government-subsidised imported rice (Sneyd 2013). A dietary transition most often occurs in cities, where "cheap" foods are readily available and where high food prices exclude the poor from accessing healthier food options or traditional foods.

Implications for the economic empowerment of women

The empowerment opportunities from the food trade are found mostly in improved access to foods and income for households. The reality that these opportunities do not extend to the business is a hard one. The survey found that many participants, especially women, were willing to find ways to improve their business. When asked what might make their business better, many traders identified a variety of strategies based on the product they specialised in:

> Doing a lot [with my] snail products (dry snails, snail soya, snail meat) especially if I have capital. Having a cage to keep live snails to move freely and sell the next market day if not bought.
> (Interview, Limbe, July 2012)

> Get a preservation facility like a fridge to store remains and re-sell. Buy quality vegetables and sell at better prices.
> (Interview, Limbe, July 2012)

> Better means of preserving the meat; high capital to purchase variety; reduce conflict between forest guard and business person.
> (Interview, Mutengene, July 2012)

One *buyam-sellam* said that her (and others') strategy to earn a profit from the unsold vegetables she invested in was to sell her products to vendors who make and sell prepared dishes on non-market days.

Discussion

Ensuring reliable access to forest foods has helped to slow Cameroon's nutrition transition towards a diet of highly processed and refined foods; however, global and even local price spikes have impacted access to the highly nutritious forest foods presented in the study (Sharma et al. 2007; Sneyd 2013; Steyn and Mchiza 2014). When considering food security implications, Crush and Frayne argue that

> to fully understand the complexity of urban food insecurity we need to know much more about urban food supply and distribution systems, both formal and informal (and the ways they interact). According to these researchers, the informal economy is a key determinant of food access for the urban poor and needs to be better supported.
>
> (Crush and Frayne 2011: 540)

Recommendations from the literature for improving the forest food trade

Certain wild foods that are in high demand are undergoing domestication, which is the process of bringing wild species under cultivation through selection and adoption of desirable characteristics (Tchoundjeu et al. 2006). The domestication initiatives underway in Cameroon for *Gnetum*, bitter leaf, *njangsa*, and cane rat and snails help to ensure these foods are available in times of scarcity and inconvenience, by sustainably managing the wild population to avoid overexploitation of the forest. While a few initiatives are underway, there is still great potential for their expansion in urban areas.

A study on CIFOR's training and capacity building programs in the NTFP sector in Cameroon from 2000 to 2006 showed that there are areas to target to improve traders' income and promote local gender empowerment. Improvements that help to "reduce the constraints generally faced by women traders by providing marketing information, accounting tools and helping them to develop processing and storage technology" were strongly encouraged (Awono et al. 2010: 161). Improved training in these areas and greater access to food processing and storage have a positive impact on women's lives, as these same improvements also contribute to higher incomes and greater food security. These findings were similar to a review of gender and agroforestry across Africa: women contribute to this sector as actively as men, but their contributions are constrained by cultural norms and a lack of access to resources (Kiptot et al. 2014). Recommendations for interventions in the food sector include "capacity building in business skills, group dynamics and assessing market trends, product specialisation, process-ing, collective action, [and] provision of improved storage methods" (Kiptot et al. 2014: 106).

Focussing on particular food sources such as honey, bushmeat, snails, and mushrooms, researchers have identified many small-scale improvements (Hardouin et al. 2003). Best practices and lessons learned from these studies can translate to improvements in related forest food sectors. Support for entrepreneurs in apiary and honey harvests has greatly enhanced forest-based beekeeping in Northern Cameroon (Ingram and Njikeu 2011). A study on the bushmeat trade in Yaoundé found that the railway was the most impor-tant carrier of the meat into the city. Most fresh bushmeat ends up in eating places in the city, whereas smoked meat is most often found in the markets (Edderai and Dame 2006). Knowing this transport and value chain is impor-tant for the control and regulation of protected species (something that goes hand in hand with improving biodiversity for agriculture). While this might seem to contradict an argument for identifying ways to improve the wild food trade, in fact "a decline in one wild resource tends to drive up unsustainable exploitation of the other" (Nasi et al. 2011: 360). Therefore, achieving a sustainable harvest of bushmeat by "banning and strictly enforcing the sale of endangered or at risk species in urban markets" is a good recom-mendation (Nasi et al. 2011: 363). These authors also call for improvements to alternative sources of protein. This is especially important in places where food cultures are welcoming of "unconventional" food sources (FAO 2013).

Ngenwi et al. (2010) found that climate change and the use of agrochemi-cals are negatively impacting backyard rearing and wild collection of snails. In the West region of Cameroon, a woman known as the "snail mama" is a local success story for the rearing and transformation of snails. Her snails and their shells are converted into "healing foods": they are crushed into a powder that can be added to fortify baby foods and foods for sick patients. This non-conventional form of heliciculture creates a reliable source of protein and minerals, something that is difficult to access consistently in forested food systems. Because of this simple transformation, she has won awards and was able to diversify her business into rearing hedgehogs, por-cupines, cane rats, and quail (Fomo 2013). Insights from her evolving business are useful for similarly inspired entrepreneurs in this sector.

Mushrooms have similar potential, as they are used locally as a substitute for meat or fish. The cultural valuations of mushrooms are a gendered activ-ity, as women and their daughters are most involved in the harvest and sale. While social stigma ("mushrooms are the meat of the poor") might inhibit widespread cultivation of mushrooms, the potential for raising mushrooms on a small scale is great (van Dijk et al. 2003).

Overall, these recommendations aim to enhance the sustainability of the forest food sector while raising incomes, awareness and education, and access to these culturally significant foods (Vinceti et al. 2013). With improved access to training, services, transformation, credit, and storage, greater

Table 6.1 Ways to improve forest food business and trade

Wild food	Challenge	Recommendation
Eru/Okok (*Gnetum africanum*)	Decreasing stock; limited access to forest for gathering	Increase domestication initiatives; improve training
Snail (*Archachatina archachatina* and *Archachatina marginata* species)	Lack of infrastructure for heliciculture; changing climate	Create industry for cages and snail rearing; improve training
Njangsa (*Ricinodendron heudelotii*)	Drying and storage	Drying, transformation and storage
Caterpillar (*Rhynchophorus phoenicis*)	Decreasing stock; high prices	Drying and transformation
Wild mango (*Irvingia gabonensis*)	Drying and storage	Drying and transformation
Honey	Less available to harvest	Promote apiculture
Bushmeat	Over harvest	Conservation, sustainable harvest practices, and stronger regulations also promote small animal husbandry (cane rat, porcupine, and quail)

food security outcomes in the city can be realised. The recommended improvements outlined in Table 6.1 are also a positive for consumers in the city, as the recommendations improve the availability of and access to nutrient-dense foods.

Conclusion

The deterioration of infrastructure and the failure of the government to deliver services are an ongoing concern for Cameroonians. The present case demonstrates that research and development interventions should target sectors of the local food system that have the potential to make positive impacts on meeting nutritional needs (Pinstrup-Andersen 2010; Vinceti et al. 2013). While the city's food system can support urban growth, the state's abandonment of this sector has raised many barriers (and a few opportunities) for those pursuing work in the urban food trade. This is especially troubling in the context of high food prices.

This chapter aimed to chart the various challenges and opportunities facing women and men involved in the wild food trade. It also described various strategies for greater gender empowerment in this sector. The main conclusions from this chapter are forward looking. Greater gender empowerment can come from creating linkages to organisations that enable and encourage improved transformation of forest food products and access to credit. In this study, collective organisations have been shown to have the potential to improve not only the urban trade in food, but also food security outcomes throughout the city.

Through engaging with and analysing the wild food sector during a time of crisis and change, various ways of improving and developing appropriate gender responses for the trade and for Cameroonian women were explored (see Table 6.1). These initiatives include targeting women's enterprises, including local institutions and credit institutions, involved in the food trade; domesticating products experiencing high demand; bolstering initiatives for small animal rearing (for example, cane rat and forest snails); and improving training and resources for drying, preserving, and transforming forest products for safe consumption.

In light of these insights, research and development interventions should not overlook the various non-agricultural contributions to food security. These should also be considered in the contexts of deforestation (caused by increased commercial logging activities both locally and for export) and ecological and seasonal change.

Notes

1 Wild foods or foods from the forest are not traded on international markets and are separate from traditional staple foods found in Africa. It should be added that the staple foods for African countries – such as cassava, plantain, yams, millet, and sorghum in west and central Africa, and white maize in southern and east Africa – are not internationally traded or traded very much outside the region (Chang 2009). Transportation costs are high in many of these countries, and demand outside the sub-region is relatively low. What this means is that many African countries do not rely on international trade for their traditional staple foods (except wheat or rice) as much as they might. Thus, for countries with low levels of economic development, whose staple foods have limited tradability and whose transportation infrastructure is poor (Chang 2009; Cooksey 2011), focussing on the local trade of wild and traditional foods is not a misguided concept. (For a conceptualisation of wild foods in Cameroon, see Sneyd 2013.)

2 Roitman's (2005) book *Fiscal Disobedience: An Anthropology of Economic Regulation in Central Africa* documents the civil disobedience movement in Cameroon during the 1990s. The movement rose to counter the state's fiscal authority after a failed coup attempt in 1984 kept President Paul Biya in power. As he tightened his grip on the country, practices and norms associated with fiscally undermining the state became the new political and economic reality as citizens and the state struggled for power, money, and authority. These trends continue today: *buyam-sellams* often talked about harassment from market officials and police, and at times were reluctant to answer questions for fear the information would be used to foster higher taxes and fuel corruption.

References

All website URLs accessed on 7 April 2016.

Ali, Fadi, Mafu Akier Assanta, and Carole Robert. 2011. "*Gnetum africanum*: A Wild Food Plant from the African Forest with Many Nutritional and Medicinal Properties." *Journal of Medicinal Food* 14 (11): 1289–97. doi:10.1089/jmf.2010.0327.

Awono, Abdon, Ousseynou Ndoye, and Luke Preece. 2010. "Empowering Women's Capacity for Improved Livelihoods in Non-Timber Forest Product Trade in Cameroon." *International Journal of Social Forestry* 3 (2): 151–63.

Babb, Florence E. (1998). *Between Field and Cooking Pot: The Political Economy of Marketwomen in Peru* (revised edition). Austin: University of Texas Press.

Bates, Robert H. (1982). *Markets and States in Tropical Africa*. Berkeley: University of California Press.

Belcher, B.M. (2003). "What Isn't an NTFP ?" *International Forestry Review* 5 (2): 161–8.

Boserup, Ester. 1965. *The Conditions of Agricultural Growth: The Economics of Agrarian Change under Population Pressure*. Chicago, IL: Aldine.

Bryceson, Deborah Fahy. 1989. "Nutrition and Commoditization of Food in Sub-Saharan Africa." *Social Science & Medicine* 28 (5): 425–40. doi:10.1016/0277-9536 (89)90098-1.

Carney, Judith A. 2004. "Gender Conflict in Gambian Wetlands." In R. Peet and M. Watts, eds, *Liberation Ecologies: Environment, Development, Social Movements*. London: Routledge, 316–35.

Chang, Ha-Joon. 2009. "Rethinking Public Policy in Agriculture: Lessons from History, Distant and Recent." *Journal of Peasant Studies* 36 (3): 477–515. doi:10.1080/03066150903142741.

Clark, Gracia. 1994. *Onions are my Husband: Survival and Accumulation by West African Market Women*. Chicago: University of Chicago Press.

Cohen, Marc J., and James L. Garrett. 2010. "The Food Price Crisis and Urban Food (In)security." *Environment and Urbanization* 22 (2): 467–82. doi:10.1177/09562478 10380375.

Cooksey, Brian. 2011. "Marketing Reform? The Rise and Fall of Agricultural Liberalisation in Tanzania." *Development Policy Review* 29 (S1): S57–S81.

Crush, Jonathan, and Bruce Frayne. 2011. "Urban Food Insecurity and the New International Food Security Agenda." *Development Southern Africa* 28 (4): 527–44. doi:10.1080/0376835X.2011.605571.

Crush, Jonathan, Bruce Frayne, and Wade Pendleton. 2012. "The Crisis of Food Insecurity in African Cities." *Journal of Hunger & Environmental Nutrition* 7 (2–3): 271–92. doi:10.1080/19320248.2012.702448.

Edderai, David, and Mireille Dame. 2006. "A Census of the Commercial Bushmeat Market in Yaoundé, Cameroon." *Oryx* 40 (04): 472–5. doi:10.1017/S00306 05306001256.

Edwards, Sarah, Sabine Nebel, and Michael Heinrich. 2005. "Questionnaire Surveys: Methodological and Epistemological Problems for Field-Based Ethnopharmacologists." *Journal of Ethnopharmacology* 100 (1–2): 30–6. doi:10.1016/j. jep.2005.05.026.

FAO (Food and Agriculture Organization of the United Nations). 2013. *Edible Insects: Future Prospects for Food and Feed Security*. Rome: FAO.

Flynn, Karen Coen. 2005. *Food, Culture, and Survival in an African City*. Basingstoke, UK: Palgrave Macmillan.

Fomo, E.V. 2013. "La mère des escargots." *Cameroon Tribune* (Yaoundé, Cameroon), 27 November, p. 18.

Fonchingong, Charles C. 1999. "Structural Adjustment, Women, and Agriculture in Cameroon." *Gender and Development* 7 (3): 73–9.

Fonchingong, Charles C. 2005. "Negotiating Livelihoods Beyond Beijing: The Burden of Women Food Vendors in the Informal Economy of Limbe, Cameroon."

International Social Science Journal 57 (184): 243–53. doi:10.1111/j.1468-2451. 2005.00548.x.

Fonjong, Lotsmart N., and Mbah Fongkimeh Athanasia. 2007. "The Fortunes and Misfortunes of Women Rice Producers in Ndop, Cameroon and the Implications for Gender Roles." *Journal of International Women's Studies* 8 (4): 133–47.

Freidberg, Susanne. 2001a. "Gardening on the Edge: The Social Conditions of Unsustainability on an African Urban Periphery." *Annals of the Association of American Geographers* 91 (2): 349–69.

Freidberg, Susanne. 2001b. "To Garden, to Market: Gendered Meanings of Work on an African Urban Periphery." *Gender, Place & Culture* 8 (1): 5–24.

Gardiner Barber, Pauline. 2004. "Contradictions of Class Consumption when the Commodity is Labour." *Anthropologica* 46 (2): 203–18.

Gibbon, Peter. 1997. "Prawns and Piranhas: The Political Economy of a Tanzanian Private Sector Marketing Chain." *Journal of Peasant Studies* 24 (4): 1–86. doi:10.1080/03066159708438658.

Guyer, Jane I., ed. 1987. *Feeding African Cities: Studies in Regional Social History.* Indianapolis: Indiana University Press.

Hardouin, J., É. Thys, V. Joiris, and D. Fielding. 2003. "Mini-Livestock Breeding with Indigenous Species in the Tropics." *Livestock Research for Rural Development* 15 (4). www.lrrd.org/lrrd15/4/hard154.htm.

Hart, Keith. 1973. "Informal Income Opportunities and Urban Employment in Ghana." *Journal of Modern African Studies* 11 (1): 61–89. doi:10.1017/S00222 78X00008089.

Hart, Keith. 1982. *The Political Economy of West African Agriculture.* Cambridge: Cambridge University Press.

Hovorka, Alice J. 2006. "The No. 1 Ladies' Poultry Farm: A Feminist Political Ecology of Urban Agriculture in Botswana." *Gender, Place and Culture: A Journal of Feminist Geography* 13 (3): 207–25. doi:10.1080/09663690600700956.

Ingram, Verina, and Justin Njikeu. 2011. "Sweet, Sticky, and Sustainable Social Business." *Ecology and Society* 16 (1): 37.

Ingram, Verina, Jolien Schure, Julius Chupezi Tieguhong, Ousseynou Ndoye, Abdon Awono, and Donald Midoko Iponga. 2014. "Gender Implications of Forest Product Value Chains in the Congo Basin." *Forests, Trees and Livelihoods* 23 (1–2): 67–86. doi:10.1080/14728028.2014.887610.

Kiptot, Evelyne, Steven Franzel, and Ann Degrande. 2014. "Gender, Agroforestry and Food Security in Africa." *Current Opinion in Environmental Sustainability* 6 (Feb.): 104–9. doi:10.1016/j.cosust.2013.10.019.

Marx, Karl. 1977 [original work published 1867]. *Capital: A Critique of Political Economy*, vol. 1 (*Das Kapital, Kritik der politischen Ökonomie*). Translated by Ben Fowkes. New York: Vintage Books.

Miller, Jeff, and Jonathan Deutsch. 2009. *Food Studies: An Introduction to Research Methods.* Oxford: Berg.

Nasi, R., A. Taber, and N. Van Vliet. 2011. "Empty Forests, Empty Stomachs? Bushmeat and Livelihoods in the Congo and Amazon Basins." *International Forestry Review* 13 (3): 355–68. doi:10.1505/146554811798293872.

Ngenwi, A.A., J.M. Mafeni, K.A. Etchu, and F.T. Oben. 2010. "Characteristics of Snail Farmers and Constraints to Increased Production in West and Central Africa." *African Journal of Environmental Science and Technology* 4 (5): 274–8.

Ngoumou, Tite. 2010. "Urban Food Provisioning in Cameroon: Regional Banana Plantain Network Linking Yaoundé and the Villages of Koumou and Oban." In

Donald C. Wood, ed., *Economic Action in Theory and Practice: Anthropological Investigations (Research in Economic Anthropology*, Volume 30). Bingley, UK: Emerald, 187–207. doi:10.1108/S0190-1281(2010)0000030011.

Niger-Thomas, Margaret. 2001. "Women and the Arts of Smuggling." *African Studies Review* 44 (2): 43–70. doi:10.2307/525574.

Pinstrup-Andersen, Per, ed. 2010. *The African Food System and its Interaction with Human Health and Nutrition*. Ithaca, NY: Cornell University Press.

Rao, Pavithra. 2014. "Food Crisis in Cameroon." *Africa Renewal* 28 (1): 3.

Robben, Antonius C.G.M., and Jeffrey A. Sluka, eds. 2007. *Ethnographic Fieldwork: An Anthropological Reader*. Oxford: Blackwell.

Roitman, Janet L. 1990. "The Politics of Informal Markets in Sub-Saharan Africa." *Journal of Modern African Studies* 28 (4): 671–96. doi:10.1017/S0022278X 00054781.

Roitman, Janet L. 2005. *Fiscal Disobedience: An Anthropology of Economic Regulation in Central Africa*. Princeton, NJ: Princeton University Press.

Ruiz Pérez, Manuel, Ousseynou Ndoye, Antoine Eyebe, and Danielle Lema Ngono. 2002. "A Gender Analysis of Forest Product Markets in Cameroon." *Africa Today* 49 (3): 97–126.

Seligmann, Linda J., ed. 2001. *Women Traders in Cross-Cultural Perspective: Mediating Identities, Marketing Wares*. Stanford, CA: Stanford University Press.

Sharma, Sangita, Jean Claude Mbanya, Kennedy Cruickshank, Janet Cade, Agatha K.N. Tanya, Xia Cao, . . . Matthew R.K.M. Wong. 2007. "Nutritional Composition of Commonly Consumed Composite Dishes from the Central Province of Cameroon." *International Journal of Food Sciences and Nutrition* 58 (6): 475–85. doi:10.1080/09637480701288454.

Sneyd, Lauren Q. 2013. "Wild Food, Prices, Diets and Development: Sustainability and Food Security in Urban Cameroon." *Sustainability* 5 (11): 4728–59. doi: 10.3390/su5114728.

Sneyd, Lauren Q. 2015. "Zoning In: The Contributions of *Buyam-Sellams* to Constructing Cameroon's Wild Food Zone." *Geoforum* 59: 73–68.

Steyn, Nelia P., and Zandile J. Mchiza. 2014. "Obesity and the Nutrition Transition in Sub-Saharan Africa." *Annals of the New York Academy of Sciences* 1311 (1): 88–101. doi:10.1111/nyas.12433.

Sunderlin, William D., Sona Dewi, Atie Puntodewo, Daniel Müller, Arild Angelsen, and Michael Epprecht. 2008. "Why Forests are Important for Global Poverty Alleviation: A Spatial Explanation." *Ecology and Society* 13 (2): 24.

Tacoli, Cecilia, Budoor Bukhari, and Susannah Fisher. 2013. *Urban Poverty, Food Security and Climate Change*. Human Settlements Working Paper No. 37. London: International Institute for Environment and Development.

Tchoundjeu, Z., E.K. Asaah, P. Anegbeh, A. Degrande, P. Mbile, C. Facheux, . . . A.J. Simons. 2006. "Putting Participatory Domestication into Practice in West and Central Africa." *Forests, Trees and Livelihoods* 16 (1): 53–69. doi:10.1080/147280 28.2006.9752545.

van Dijk, Han, Neree Awana Onguene, and Thomas W. Kuyper. 2003. "Knowledge and Utilization of Edible Mushrooms by Local Populations of the Rain Forests of South Cameroon." *Ambio: Royal Swedish Academy of Sciences* 32 (1): 19–23.

Vinceti, Barbara, Céline Termote, Amy Ickowitz, Bronwen Powell, Katja Kehlenbeck, and Danny Hunter. 2013. "The Contribution of Forests and Trees to Sustainable Diets." *Sustainability* 5 (11): 4797–4824. doi:10.3390/su5114797.

Waring, Marilyn. 1988. *If Women Counted: A New Feminist Economics*. New York: Harper and Row.

Watts, Michael J. 1983. *Silent Violence: Food, Famine and Peasantry in Northern Nigeria*. Berkeley: University of California Press.

Wiersum, K.F., V.J. Ingram, and M.A.F. Ros-Tonen. 2014. "Governing Access to Resources and Markets in Non-Timber Forest Product Chains." *Forests, Trees and Livelihoods* 23 (1–2): 6–18. doi:10.1080/14728028.2013.868676.

Wolf, Eric. 1982. *Europe and the People Without History*. Berkeley: University of California Press.

7 Gender and innovation in Peru's native potato market chains

Silvia Sarapura Escobar,
Helen Hambly Odame, and
Graham Thiele

Introduction

Peasants or *campesinos*[1] living in the Central Andes of South America are the traditional custodians of a vast genetic pool of Andean crops and tubers. To date, an estimated 4,000 varieties of native potatoes have been identified. Traditional Andean farming systems depend intrinsically on women's emic (insider) knowledge to maintain such vast biodiversity (Tapia 1997; Brush 2004). Women have preserved the genetic biodiversity of the potato despite serious adversities such as constant climate stress and food scarcity (de Haan 2009). Such adaptation and resilience are the foundation of peasant communities in the Andes.

To promote native potato innovation and help smallholder producers respond to emerging markets, the Papa Andina ("Andean Potato") Regional Initiative (hereinafter referred to as Papa Andina) has sought to expand opportunities that add value to the production, processing, use, and biodiversity of native potatoes.[2] Papa Andina facilitates what is referred to as the Participatory Market Chain Approach (PMCA) to market analysis and knowledge mobilisation, as well as the organisation of special meetings and demonstrations and events with value chain actors known as Stakeholder Platforms (Bernet et al. 2006; Meinzen-Dick et al. 2009; Thiele et al. 2011).

This chapter presents the condensed results of an in-depth gender analysis of Papa Andina based on mixed methods research conducted in two regions of Central Peru (Sarapura 2013). The theoretical approach taken in the study is informed by a feminist standpoint that privileges the indigenous knowledge and perspectives of peasant producers while recognising the mutable power position of women in relation to men within their households, communities, markets, and the Peruvian state. The chapter highlights the gender implications of the existing traditional management of native potatoes, as well as the technological and institutional innovations facilitated by Papa Andina. Within a context of systemic gender inequality, including the subjugation of peasants' understanding of their environment (or Andean Cosmo Vision) and, in turn, peasant women's knowledge of native potatoes, the central research questions addressed in this chapter are: how has Papa

Andina empowered the female peasant producers of Central Peru, and why are these results important to the wider understanding of gender, household food security, biodiversity, and the rights of peasant women in Peru?

The native potato farming system

In Peru, the term "farmer" generally designates the historically wealthy, large landowning class of agricultural producers. In contrast, the term "peasant" or *campesino* (male)/*campesina* (female) is applied to resource-poor producers, many of whom are descended from the Quechua, an indigenous people of the Andes. Peasant producers have preserved the genetic biodiversity of the potato despite serious adversities such as constant climate stress and food scarcity (de Haan 2009). Specifically, climate variations in the region are intense and frequent, with adverse impact on the production of diverse crops within specific elevations, which in turn threatens household food security (Tapia and De la Torre 2000). Constant environmental adaptation and resilience are the foundation of all life in Andean peasant communities.

Aside from ecological challenges, society and economy are rapidly changing. In Peruvian society, peasant producers are economically disadvantaged. Because of the separation between ceremonial and customary laws within peasant communities and the country's statutory laws, peasant communities have been largely excluded from national development (Diez Hurtado 2010). Pedersen et al. (2010) have discussed the suffering and long-term health problems associated with adversities such as violence, poverty, and household food insecurity. Especially for rural women, there is unequal access to resources – an imbalance rooted in pervasive traditional sociocultural norms that entrench outdated gender roles, unequal gender relations, and unfair treatment within formal and informal institutional environments (Urrutia Ceruti 2007). Peasant women are the poorest, most illiterate, monolingual, and malnourished demographic group in Peru (Deere and Leon 2003; INEI 2007). Trivelli (2004) reports that female heads of peasant households have an average of 2.7 years of schooling, compared to 7.3 years among non-indigenous women, and they have little, if any, access to agricultural training and technology.

Despite these exclusionary practices, the growth of the Andean population and the increased affluence of Peruvian society at large have led to higher demand for greater quantities of local produce and improved food quality (Devaux, Andrade-Piedra et al. 2011). Potatoes are widely consumed and culturally valued in the Andes. This staple crop has significant nutritive value, with high levels of iron and zinc. Increasingly, native potatoes have earned distinction within Peru's culinary arts and achieved higher domestic and export market value, fostering market opportunities for small-scale producers who experience persistent and pervasive poverty.

Yet without access to markets, peasant producers, particularly rural women, cannot mobilise their emic knowledge to innovate the native potato value chain. Innovation will require developing resource-poor peasant producers' capacities to integrate themselves into established institutions that can support the commercialisation of the agricultural products they have been cultivating for generations (Barrientos 2001).

Papa Andina and the Participatory Market Chain Approach

Papa Andina is an agricultural innovation initiative that began in 1998 and involved responding to market niches to add value to native potatoes (Devaux, Horton et al. 2011). The initiative has worked with partners in Bolivia, Ecuador, and Peru, and evidence of its work can be found within international, regional, and domestic market chains for potato-based products (Ordinola et al. 2014). Market chain actors, both in and across the national systems within Papa Andina, are diverse: they include government or public, non-profit, and for-profit groups of stakeholders (Meinzen-Dick et al. 2011).

Papa Andina's response to the challenge of fostering innovation, knowledge sharing, and capacity development is explained in detail in a text by Devaux, Horton et al. (2011). Market chain assessment and investment focussed on two principal methods: the PMCA and Stakeholder Platforms. The integration of gender-responsive actions in these methods has been specifically discussed in recent years (Avilés et al. 2010; Cadima et al. 2011; Conlago et al. 2011; Sarapura 2012).

The PMCA fostered innovation through a three-step structured process that built interest, trust, and collaboration. Through female and male farmer-to-farmer field visits, demonstrations, group meetings, collaborative marketing, and other linkage activities, emphasis was placed on stimulating "pro-poor" innovation and creating new or more innovative institutions and organisations (Sarapura 2012). One example of such activity in Peru has been the promotion of the native potato within the culinary arts. With the participation of leading "novo-Andean" chefs from Lima's most recognised restaurants, ancestral practices of conservation and processing are featured in national culinary events. The culinary artists have endorsed peasant production and *in situ* selection and maintenance of biodiversity. Social networks facilitated by Papa Andina have also stimulated commercial innovation and introduced new supermarket native potato products (for example, a range of native potato snack foods) which, in turn, have stimulated knowledge exchange that feeds back into technical, social, and institutional innovation (for example, new research on little-known varieties, new packaging that recognises local and female producers, etc.).

Second, Papa Andina has fostered Stakeholder Platforms that provided impressive special events and/or permanent fora for improved relationship-building among market chain actors. Innovation fairs may, for example, showcase traditional ways of preserving biodiversity, ensuring household food security, or recognising women's knowledge of native potato varieties, processing techniques, and products derived from them. Stakeholder Platforms provide an opportunity for individuals and organisations to inter-act, identify their mutual interests, build trust, and participate in common initiatives.

In Central Peru, and relevant to the specific area of this study in the regions of Junín and Huancavelica, Papa Andina works collaboratively with Fomento de la Vida (FOVIDA) (in English, "Life Fund"), a registered non-profit organisation that facilitates social, economic, and technological development in Peruvian agriculture. FOVIDA provides highly specialised training and services for market chain development for potatoes and other tubers culti-vated in the highlands of Peru. FOVIDA has been part of the Cadenas Productivas Agricolas de Calidad (CAPAC – in English, "Agricultural Productivity and Quality Brands of Peru"), a permanent Stakeholder Platform for agricultural innovation processes. CAPAC enables peasant producers to interact with private-sector actors as fellow members (formal membership) and as partners (for example, with supermarkets). FOVIDA also engages private-sector actors as both members and partners for innovation (Thiele et al. 2009). Both FOVIDA, with its extensive experience in promoting "pro-poor" innovation and market chains, and CAPAC, the Stakeholder Platform, have been connecting peasant producers to new national and inter-national markets (Devaux et al. 2007). Native potatoes and other Andean crops, such as quinoa, are exported across the region and around the world.

With this context of Papa Andina's work in mind, the relevant theoretical framework for a feminist analysis of the agricultural innovation system of native potatoes is now presented. This discussion addresses peasant producer relations to the market and organisations and institutions at all levels, and proposes a way of understanding household food security as implicitly tied to the promotion of biodiversity and the realisation of gender equality at the individual peasant producer level.

Theoretical perspectives on agricultural innovation and gender

Different bodies of social science literature pertaining to Andean farming systems and sociocultural aspects of peasant production are relevant to this study. First, the study is situated within the historical, ethnographic literature on traditional agricultural production in the Andes and what is referred to as the Andean Cosmo Vision (Tapia Ponce et al. 2012). For Andean people, their ways of knowing themselves and the world around them are based on agrocentric principles in social organisation (Brush et al. 1994). Their philosophy considers the crucial relationship between peasant knowledge, or *saber campesino* (Haverkort et al. 2003), and the protection of native potato biodiversity in the high Andes (Brush 2004). The Quechua person walks with *kawsay mama* (the living mother, the living seed) along its multiple paths, through which diversity is cultivated as a spiritual practice of biocultural sustainability (Grillo Fernández 1998; Choque Copari 2001; Valladolid and Apffel-Marglin 2001). Viewed from the perspective of the West, this world order is a difference of paradigm, a cycle of life that is conversant with the vitality of all beings. In the Andes, the Earth is Pachamama, or Mother, who is the guardian of agro-ecological relations and revered by men and women alike (Ishizawa and Grillo Fernández 2002).

The second relevant body of literature for this study covers more than 50 years of gender, agriculture, and rural development studies. As reviewed by Sarapura (2013) among others (including Cornwall 2006), the analysis of gender in development processes was influenced by political economy scholars who identified distinct theoretical perspectives on women, and, subsequently, gender (which includes attention to the difference among women as well as between women and men) (McIlwaine and Datta 2003). The term *feminism* has been defined as "the awareness of women's oppression and exploitation in society, at work and within the family, and a conscious action by men and women to change this situation" (Pati 2006: 14). The plural *feminisms* exists to refer to how the concept arises from various bodies of theory and is established in historical contexts (Kabeer 1999; Razavi 1999). From ecofeminism and radical feminism to pro-market liberal feminism, anti-capitalist Marxist feminism, and "women of colour" feminism, the scholarship informs many different policy approaches and practice-based interventions (Jaggar and Rothenberg 1984).

Importantly, further elaborations of feminism also rest on cultural "realities and levels of consciousness, perception and action" (Pati 2006: 11). She continues that "the social roles and the modes women use to negotiate the world also differ among women in diverse environments and contexts (cultural, social, political, racial or ethnic, religious, etc.), and with diverse personal characteristics (age, education, and caste)" (Pati 2006: 14). For example, the Andean Cosmo Vision can be considered *feminocentric*, that is, female-focussed, but it may occur alongside a deeply cultural context of gender inequality. As readings of feminist research on peasant society and economy in Peru attest, including Urrutia Ceruti (2007) and Diez Hurtado (2010), the biological differences between men and women are translated into cultural beliefs, meanings, and activities that are deemed appropriate for each gender, and also inform their rights, resources, knowledge, and power (Ortner 1974; Tapia and De la Torre 2000).

The theoretical approach and concept of gender adopted in this study emphasises the many cultural underpinnings attached to the analysis of socially constructed power relations within the native potato agricultural innovation system. The approach taken here also appreciates the contribution of socialists and post-colonial feminists, who as systems thinkers recognise that there is a direct link between social structure and the oppression of women. Productive resources may give men power and control over women whereas the opposite thinking is that women's productive responsibilities may not empower them in relation to men. Socialist feminists reject the idea that biology predetermines a person's social role in either the public or private spheres.

Rural women may be actively excluded from sources of power – including their productive assets (land, labour, capital) and access to knowledge and technologies – by men and masculine hegemonic practices, as well as by institutions, including local organisations (Hambly Odame 2001; Kabeer 2005; Chant and Sweetman 2012).

The directions peasant women's and men's lives are taking, and their roles and relations throughout the wider system, often result in inequalities. As played out in the life cycles of women and men in Peru, gender can be understood as intersecting power-based relations in the form of access to resources, leadership, and use of power, and limits to participation in places such as markets, the household, and the community. Consequently, socialist and post-colonial feminists target systemic change – specifically, how gender roles and relations to resources of power are being transformed within society.

Finally, the chapter examines a third body of literature that pertains to agricultural innovation systems as relevant to improved household food security. Based on extensive research dating back to the 1960s, agricultural innovation, for the purpose of the study, is understood as not simply diffusing new technologies but encompassing a dynamic, innovating system that constantly negotiates technologies and institutions with unconventional forms of "organising by reorganising" markets, labour, land tenure, and distribution of benefits (Leeuwis 2004; Röling 2009; Klerkx et al. 2010). "Agricultural innovation is not an intrinsically good and value-free process. It is normatively laden and driven by different worldviews and visions", state Klerkx et al. (2012: 451). This is because multiple stakeholders come in and out of market chains and influence the outcomes.

Networks and partnerships are instrumental within innovation processes (Ekboir and Rajalahti 2012). At the same time, the interactions of stakeholders in the agricultural innovation system must often deal with "dialectical divides" and anticipate regular renegotiation (Pant and Hambly Odame 2009). From a gender perspective, agricultural innovation offers opportunities to renegotiate and transform institutions and effect behavioural change among men and women, both in terms of technical innovation and in relation to new social norms and relations that emerge as market, value, and knowledge chains are challenged (KIT et al. 2012; Sarapura 2012). Key gender outcomes may also include evidence of new-found leadership and capacity to influence policymaking processes. Hypothetically, development occurs when institutions are transformed formally to support interaction and to ensure that women and excluded groups are fully engaged in policymaking processes (World Bank 2012).

With these theoretical contributions in mind, the chapter examines how Papa Andina has presented an opportunity for negotiating gender transformation within an innovation system at the *macro* level (an enabling environment and cultural meanings), *meso* level (organisations and institutions), and *micro* level (households as well as individuals within households). It also highlights key implications for a new understanding of household food security in the Central Andes.

Methodology

Examining Papa Andina's PMCA and Stakeholder Platforms from a feminist perspective involved conducting a context-specific analysis of the traditional production and commercialisation of native potatoes, and evaluating the recent experiences of peasant producers (particularly women) in the promotion of innovative native potato market chains. Two groups were nominally identified within the population: (1) the intervention group, COGEPAN, a local consortium of four associations of peasant producers participating in the native potato market chain facilitated by Papa Andina; and (2) a control group of non-COGEPAN peasant communities which traditionally cultivate native potatoes. The COGEPAN participants were from the Junín and Huancavelica regions in Central Peru; the second group was from the Junín region, which is part of the Alto and *Bajo Tulumayo* watershed of Peru. The communities are located in the Central Andes of Peru at an altitude that varies from 3,500 to 4,500 metres above sea level. Both areas are considered "hot spots of biodiversity" (de Haan 2009).

As the research was conducted from a feminist standpoint, a compatible and specialised methodology was required. Feminist research typically emphasises understanding the context of the research and privileging women's voices while enabling critical reflection on emergent data (Reinharz 1992). Therefore, a three-phase sequential explanatory design was used to obtain background and contextual data, organised so as to couple collecting sex-disaggregated data (using a survey) with iterative participatory and discussion-based activities that continuously readjusted the research to sharpen its focus on women.[3]

In the first stage of data collection, descriptive explanations about native potato production and market chains were obtained from 42 peasant producers (referred to as COGEPAN respondents) involved in the innovative market chains. Women and men shared their views and stories through a video reporting tool. This technique was complemented with focus group sessions, semi-structured interviews, and participant observation. Using a combination of video storytelling, discussions, and interviews, women and men documented and discussed their farming practices and knowledge of native potatoes, the importance of this crop in their lives, and their worldviews as Andean people.[4] This stage was crucial to "back and forth" unscripted interactions between male and female peasant producers. In total, six people (four women and two men) were trained in the use of the video camera and in interview processing (transcription, translation, and data cleaning). Participants worked together and helped each other accomplish these tasks as part of the exploratory process, as opposed to having the researchers compile data independent of interaction with and validation from the participants.

The second stage of data collection took place with a sub-set of the 42 COGEPAN participants from stage one. This was a reflective/analytical stage that made use of specific qualitative research tools (force field analysis, timelines, and the social network analysis). The techniques used were from the Social Analysis Systems Approach (SAS²), an International Development Research Centre (IDRC)-supported toolkit developed by Chevalier and Buckles (2008). These tools were adjusted and modified to the fieldwork context.

During this stage of data collection, the study paid attention to gendered cultural constructs (beliefs, meanings, activities) among male and female participants about the native potato farming system. The process emphasised interaction among and between respondents, and, specifically, expressions of how they felt about their lives, their activities, roles, and relations, and their relation to other levels (at macro, meso, and micro levels) of the society, economy, and polity in which they were all involved. This stage of data generation emphasised the description of peasants' understandings of life and their ways of living and practices based on their emic knowledge and experiences.

In the third stage, a larger representative sample of 220 respondents (36 COGEPAN participants randomly selected from stages one and two of the research process, plus 184 non-COGEPAN participants randomly selected from three communities in the region) was used to obtain general findings about native potato production. This method generated quantitative data to triangulate and complement information collected in the earlier qualitative research stages. The survey generated additional contextual and demographic information that identified gender roles and relations in the production of native potatoes, and, specifically, the resources women and men in both groups (COGEPAN and non-COGEPAN) accessed and controlled. Qualitative data were analysed using thematic grouping of the data with open and selective coding. The demographic and socioeconomic data from the survey were analysed using SPSS statistics software v.19.

Results

This section presents the key findings of the study, beginning with the results of the feminocentric Andean Cosmo Vision and an explanation of how this cultural worldview influences women's and men's traditional and contemporary agricultural practices. It then presents the changing experiences of peasant producers involved in Papa Andina and how these transfer to socially constructed power relations within agriculture and household food security. It concludes with an overview of the outcomes of Papa Andina for peasant producers, particularly women's capacity to negotiate within native potato value chains and transform system-level innovation, including key networks and partnerships.

Reproducing the Andean Cosmo Vision of the native potato farming system

According to participants' discourse, in the Andean Cosmo Vision the individual is embedded into the system: humans, cosmos, and land are one, and no one can function independently or separately. Respect for the land and the concept that the land is part of a whole comprising humans, water, land, and the universe was cited by peasant women and men as fundamental to the preservation of the biodiversity of native potatoes and maintenance of household food security. The feminocentric perspective of the native potato farming system is evident in the emphasis placed on women's taking care of and nurturing native potatoes, in a way reciprocating what native potatoes do for peasant producers (male and female). Noteworthy is that all respondents personified potatoes as having families (ancestors, children, and other relatives). As well, potatoes are "gendered", with particular cultivar groups differing in shape and colour being labelled as "male" or "female", a phenomenon found widely in the Andes. This shows how Andean peoples use genetic differences between the potatoes they grow and eat as a symbolic language to signal cultural difference between women and men. A sense of cohesion and reciprocity is closely related to the nurturing of potatoes. As one respondent explained,

> We have to visit the fields and talk to the plants. Plants listen and you would see when they are in the time to produce flowers. They have different colours and they look happy when we talk to them.
>
> (Female respondent, Chuquitambo community)

Respect for Pachamama (Mother Earth) is essential. In the Andean view, women are not necessarily closer to Pachamama than men, a reductionist radical feminist argument that would otherwise risk romanticising the feminocentric natural world. Rather, Andean Cosmo Vision gives demands and gives power, and acknowledges nature's power over humans when she is not respected or treated well.

> Pachamama does not want fertilisers and pesticides. She becomes angry and stops producing the potatoes. In the last years, she is very upset because we do not treat her as we used to . . . The soil looks different now, it is pale and dry. The soil is tired.
>
> (Male respondent, Chicche community)

In the discussions of Pachamama, comments about peasant producers' constant adaptation to climate change – a reflection of the integral relationship between the natural world and human existence – were particularly frequent. The strain of changing climates is lower on household food security than on market production. The Andean Cosmo Vision requires peasant producers to feed themselves and their families first and foremost; to sacrifice human well-being is to jeopardise the nurturing of Pachamama. To respond to climate change and ensure household food security, including the preservation of native potato varieties, peasant producers, male and female, both within the Papa Andina project area and outside, have maintained a vast knowledge of native potato production, and observe a cycle of seasonal agricultural rituals and celebrations.

The study found that all farming activities are carried out using agricultural and festive calendars that allow farmers to cultivate the native potatoes in phases so they can manage production for the whole year (Figure 7.1). These activities arise from traditional beliefs and cultural practices. "Grassroots indicators", namely, the movements of the moon, sun and stars, determine the start of the planting season, control of pests, and harvest time (Hambly Odame and Onweng Angura 1996).

Women depend on various plants and animals to control diseases and pests. For example, they use a repellent extracted from *Minthostachys mollis* (*muña*), a medicinal herb, to repel the potato tuber moth (*Phthorimaea operculella*) from potatoes in storage.

Most of the activities involving seed selection and varietal identification depend on women's emic knowledge. Women usually carry out the activities collectively, through dyadic communication, often interspersed with singing. The videos clearly showed that as the women work together, every decision made in evaluating and characterising native potatoes is implicitly both individual and collective knowledge sharing.

Men also participate in the activities, but women usually have the final say with regard to the preservation and maintenance of the native potatoes.

Roles and relations within agriculture and household food security

The tasks identified in the seasonal calendar were found to be implicitly linked to the gender roles associated with native potatoes, the conservation of biodiversity, and the achievement of food security within peasant households and communities. Nearly all male respondents admitted that women, as custodians of the seed of native potatoes, knew best how to adapt the potatoes to different climatic conditions and protect the crops against natural and anthropomorphic disasters. Overall, women were responsible for the vast majority of productive and reproductive roles associated with native potato production, while men dominated the post-harvest market chain.

Women reported, however, a strong sense of the power obtained from their gender roles, particularly those associated with safeguarding the viability of the native potatoes under their cultural beliefs of respect, support, and reciprocal relationships with men and all family members, the community, and nature. The diversity of native potatoes is not only a source of food variety for Andean people, but an indicator of the astonishing range of

	Jan.	Feb.	March	April	May	June	July	Aug.	Sept.	Oct.	Nov.	Dec.
Climatic conditions	Rainy, humid days. Mix of sunny and cloudy periods	Rainy, humid days. Mix of sunny and cloudy periods	Rainy, humid days. Mix of sunny and cloudy periods	Sunny and dry days	Sunny and dry days	Sunny and dry days	Sunny and dry days	Sunny and dry days	Sunny and dry days	Rainy, humid days. Mix of sunny and cloudy periods	Rainy, humid days. Mix of sunny and cloudy periods	Rainy, humid days. Mix of sunny and cloudy periods
Climatic phenomena	Risk of hail	Risk of frost									Risk of frost	Risk of hail
Incidence of diseases	Phytophthora infestans, Paco luma	Phytophthora infestans, Paco luma	Phytophthora infestans, Paco luma			Fusarium spp., Globodera spp.	Fusarium spp., Globodera spp.	Windy days				Phytophthora infestans, Paco luma
Incidence of insects	Premnotrypes spp., Frankliniella spp.	Phtorimaea operculella				Premnotrypes spp.	Premnotrypes spp.				Frankliniella spp.	Premnotrypes spp.
Indicators	Presence of plants and animals	Red sky, hot and dry days	Cloudy, hot, rainy, humid days	Presence of plants and animals	Hot, dry days	Hot, dry days	Hot, dry days	Presence of plants and animals	Presence of plants and animals	Presence of plants and animals	Many luminous stars visible at night	Cloudy, hot, rainy, humid days
Festivities	Pascua de Reyes	La Candelaria			Fiesta de las Cruces	San Juan/ Summer Solstice	Fiesta de Santiago				Day of the Dead Santa Cecilia	
Agricultural activities												
Communal land distribution							1, 2	1, 2				

Activity													
Preparation of land	2	2											
First application of fertiliser									2	2	2	2	
Planting season										Start of secondary planting season (*siembra chica*)		Start of primary planting season (*siembra grande*)	
Second application of fertiliser				1, 2	1, 2				1, 2	1, 2		1, 2	
First hilling				1, 2	1, 2				1, 2	1, 2		1, 2	
Marking mother plants				1	1						1		
Second hilling						1, 2	1, 2				1, 2	1, 2	
Stem removal					1, 2	1, 2					1, 2	1, 2	
Harvest						1, 2	1, 2	1, 2					
Post-harvest activities													
Seed/tuber selection						1	1		1				
Processing								1	1	1			
Transporting the tubers to the field								1, 2	1, 2	1, 2			
Peeling the tubers by trampling								1	1	1			

Figure 7.1 Seasonal agricultural and festive calendar of native potato

(*Continued*)

Figure 7.1 (Continued)

	Jan.	Feb.	March	April	May	June	July	Aug.	Sept.	Oct.	Nov.	Dec.
Transporting and placing the tubers in the pond						2	2	2				
Drying the *chuño* (freeze-dried potatoes)						1, 2	1, 2	1, 2				
Transferring *chuño* to storage						2	2	2				
Adding value to *chuño* for commercialisation						1	1	1	1			
Commercialisation of fresh tubers of native potatoes						1	1	1	1			
Bartering						1, 2	1, 2	1, 2	1, 2			

KEY
1 = Reported by female respondents
2 = Reported by male respondents

peasant innovation within diverse microclimates and ecological zones. As one non-COGEPAN respondent explained,

> Communal work and life lead us to respect the Pachamama and take care of it so we can cultivate our *papitas*. We have to respect the land and nature and appreciate what it gives us. In return, we have to maintain it free of pesticides, fertilisers, and other dangers. The land has to renew itself in order to produce well.
>
> (Female respondent, Chuquitambo community)

Coding of the qualitative data obtained from the video storytelling, force field analysis, and network analysis found that the Andean Cosmo Vision exists in conjunction with peasant producers' awareness of modern innovation and markets, particularly the increasing demand for native potatoes across Peru and internationally. The number of peasant producers engaged in market chains outside of Papa Andina is, however, only a small fraction of the population that cultivates native potatoes. This was confirmed by comparing qualitative data with the results of the quantitative survey, which identified that 83.6 percent of households (all non-COGEPAN) have not yet been part of any market chain of native potatoes. Of this number, three-quarters of the market chain peasant producers are men. It is noted that once producers became involved in formal market chains like the Papa Andina, women producers were more motivated to join market chain initiatives, and their participation was reported to exceed the men's. Table 7.1 summarises further findings from this study on the benefits of women's involvement in native potato market chains.

To some extent, Papa Andina has made some progress with respect to enabling female peasant producers' access to key resources such as land and capital. The findings in this area are not conclusive, because there were no baseline data to conduct a full *ex ante* analysis of resource access among COGEPAN farmers prior to their involvement in Papa Andina. Statements from respondents did suggest that the financial gains realised by producers (by adding value to the native potatoes and introducing them to new markets) have supported peasant women's access to and control over the land. Compared to non-COGEPAN peasant farmers, all COGEPAN respondents indicated that their access to the land in order to cultivate the native potatoes had improved. Married women participating in COGEPAN and who did not previously have direct access to community land are buying land under their names (11.1 percent of women). In addition, 30.6 percent of women indicated that they had access to land through other means, such as renting and sharecropping.

Finally, through their involvement in the native potato market chains, peasant women and men have started to have access to credit and financial services. Female respondents involved in COGEPAN (19.4 percent) indicated that they had access to credit, and 13.9 percent of men in the same

Table 7.1 Gender roles and benefits in native potato market chains

Acquired benefit	Indicator
Creating opportunities for economically disadvantaged female and male producers	The market chain of native potatoes supports and promotes the participation of marginalised producers, and has reduced poverty. Through this process, female and male producers are able to move from income insecurity and poverty to economic self-sufficiency and ownership.
Developing and strengthening relational skills	Women can now move freely beyond/outside their communities and informal markets. They are able to attend fairs and agri-food events, exchange plant genetic material, and interact with different people at the community, regional, national and international level.
	Now, female producers form part of a more diverse and heterogeneous group where they position themselves among the other actors in the market chain.
	Women and men have the opportunity to interact with male and female representatives of public and private sector organisations, NGOs, and other stakeholders.
Building capacities and leadership	Women are practising new skills and meeting new challenges, including participating directly in meetings where they can learn about and discuss prices and contracts.
	In spite of limited education, women are overcoming disadvantages in relation to men. They take advantage of meetings and workshops to speak out, and feel confident when speaking in public.
	Women and men have the opportunity to participate in external internships where they meet new people and encounter contexts and realities different from their communities. For example, COGEPAN's women had an internship position in Cajamarca where they learned new agricultural practices and acquired new varieties of native potatoes.
	For the first time, women are learning to perform financial activities. Most payments are made by cheque, and women have learned to open a bank account and make financial transactions.
Undertaking old and new responsibilities with innovative ideas	Women as producers: maintaining, selecting, producing, cultivating, processing, adding value, and storing the biodiversity of native potatoes.
	Women as entrepreneurs: hiring people to work in the fields (reciprocal assistance, access to money).
	Women as marketers: commercialising native potatoes as wholesalers, retailers, or intermediaries (formally and informally) in the market chain and at local fairs and regional informal markets.

Acquired benefit	Indicator
	Women diversify their activities on and off the farm: they cultivate the land, commercialise their products in informal markets, process the products, and raise animals in the house (guinea pigs, sheep, cows, and pigs). Women have learned that formal markets offer more security and better prices. Most of the women attend fairs and rent a spot where they can sell their products directly to consumers or wholesalers. Women usually attend all local fairs during the week. Female producers sell potatoes in established locations where they become familiar with clients. They also have to pay a fee to the municipality for use of the space.
Making use of information and communication technologies	Women as communicators: women have become familiar with cell phones, which they use to help commercialise native potatoes by taking advantage of the information FOVIDA provides through voice mail and text messages to the leaders.

group reported having access to financial institutions. Female and male respondents confirmed that as a result of their inclusion in the Papa Andina initiative and the commercialisation of native potatoes with the support of FOVIDA and other stakeholders from the private sector, women have had the opportunity to open bank accounts and obtain a bank card. In contrast, not a single non-COGEPAN respondent indicated that he or she had access to credit and financial services. It was also noted that in both groups (COGEPAN and non-COGEPAN), there are apparent limitations and constraints on women with respect to using or trusting banks, because they prefer to keep their money with them at home rather than entrust it to banks or micro-finance institutions.

Capacity to negotiate and transform system-level innovation

The study identified key interventions by Papa Andina that enabled female peasant producers to become successfully involved in market chains, and benefit from their involvement. For a start, women's access to applied and scientific knowledge was found to improve their production, and added value to their marketing of native potatoes. Female peasant producers gained new knowledge about techniques for the production of native potatoes. They also learned, by networking with scientists and extension workers (including market agents), how to classify the different varieties for different market segments according to colour of skin and flesh, shape of tuber, and the vegetative cycle of the plant. Findings identified that female and male peasant producers easily integrated emic and modern knowledge (acquired through the training and technological support facilitated by Papa Andina) on how to produce improved and virus-free seeds. COGEPAN participants reported that Papa Andina's Stakeholder Platforms, particularly innovation fairs, were instrumental in making this possible. Post-harvest activities were enhanced and improved to prolong storage of the tubers; women in the discussion groups indicated that they were able to combine their own knowledge with the scientific ideas provided on how to preserve potato tubers for longer periods, thereby benefiting both household food security and the commercialisation of seed and potatoes. This statement also positions their knowledge as complementary or equal to scientific advice.

The research results confirmed that women continue to be in charge of selecting and preserving the native potatoes. With the support of the Papa Andina initiative, women and men have enhanced their knowledge and been able to add value to fresh tubers for consumption, industry, and export purposes. Similarly, women involved in COGEPAN have also been able to marry their technical abilities with new social enterprise skills. COGEPAN respondents indicated that they knew how to deal with national and international formal markets, and that they had become familiar with transactions, contracts, and adding value; presenting, handling, and packing the products; and differentiating formal and informal markets, and the potential benefits of dealing with international markets. Female and male producers recognised that agricultural and technological practices go hand in hand with leadership skills. Female respondents reported increased self-confidence through having developed the capacity to network and create partnerships to share knowledge and commercialise their products. Coding indicated that the vast majority of COGEPAN respondents directly stated that knowledge and individual confidence gave them power to transform their lives and those of their dependants.

The introduction of technological innovations was intended to increase the leadership potential of female peasant farmers and can call attention to gender norms that limit women within their social, economic, and political surroundings. Figure 7.2 illustrates the life journey of a typical female peasant producer who has become a leader within her community and the native potato market chain. She has challenged changes in the market chain by overcoming her own perceived stigma of being a Peruvian peasant woman who is illiterate, poor, and food and income insecure. Positioned now as a mentor in her community and showing self-confidence and self-worth, she has been able to challenge patriarchal structures and penetrate formerly male-dominated groups. The institutional settings and the new enabling environment allow women leaders to develop their skills and participate in innovative activities (such as innovation fairs and internships) that can strengthen partnerships and alliances for knowledge and biodiversity exchange, and influence policymaking.

Findings from key interviews indicate that with the support of organisations like FOVIDA and CAPAC, peasant producers (male and female) experienced and negotiated a rapid scaling up of production, from local to national and international markets. Additional technologies and

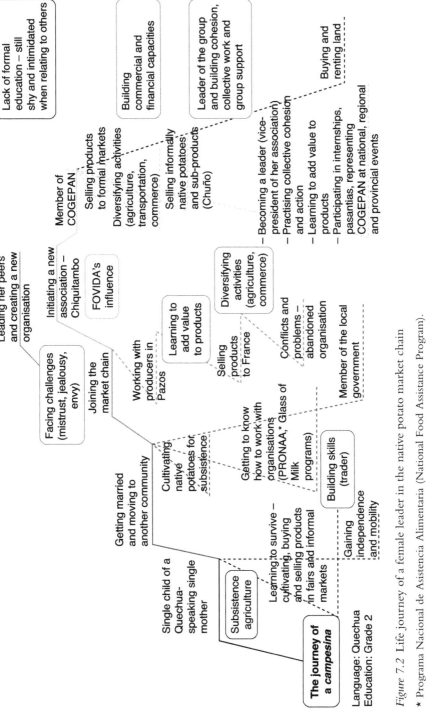

Figure 7.2 Life journey of a female leader in the native potato market chain

★ Programa Nacional de Asistencia Alimentaria (National Food Assistance Program).

networking practices played a role in this scaled-up participation in market chains. For example, the use of cell phones and the internet were reported to have successfully enhanced women's control over such fundamental strategic considerations as information about current market prices, and decisions about the transport of native potatoes to primary markets (regional and national).

Discussion

Among peasant producers of native potatoes, both within and outside Papa Andina, there is an awareness of peasants' oppression and exploitation by society. Among Papa Andina participants, through their collaborative activities, there is a "conscious action by men and women to change this situation", which indicates gender transformative experiences as defined by Pati (2006: 14). The present study found that COGEPAN producers, as compared to non-COGEPAN participants, were empowered with respect to translating their roles in the native potato farming system and market chains into access to resources and benefits.

Furthermore, results of this study confirmed the importance of a wider cultural and contextual understanding of gender relations (Bailey 2000). In particular, household food security is intrinsically linked to biodiversity. The promulgation of the Andean Cosmo Vision through male and female acceptance of its feminocentric meanings supports peasant women's knowledge of native potatoes and the production of the single most important staple food crop of the Central Andes. Gender roles (as illustrated by the seasonal calendar) and the gender relation indicated by men's deferral to women's knowledge of seed reproduction, varietal identification, and selection support household food security.

At the same time, among non-COGEPAN households in particular, gender roles confirmed neglect of the resource rights of peasant women. Land and capital are specifically difficult to access and/or control, and become points for negotiation only through organisational involvement (i.e., FOVIDA and COGEPAN) and strategic interventions such as Papa Andina. This case confirms that "equality is not mechanically perpetuated. It is negotiated, disputed and ultimately changed through the conscious actions of individuals" (Bourque and Warren 1981: 48).

Deserving of further investigation is the existence of a parallel dimension within the agricultural innovation system that is based on traditional, cultural feminocentric meanings (the Andean Cosmo Vision) as well as male hegemonic practices that sustain discrimination against women. Of concern is that within the modern, technical, and institutional complex there is evidence of systemic gender inequality, including the subjugation of individual female peasant producers who lie outside the PMCA and Stakeholder Platforms and away from the capacity development opportunities of agencies such as FOVIDA. This finding is particularly relevant when one considers the wider development discourse that tends to claim that traditional cultures are blamed for gender inequality (Ortner 1974; Cornwall 1997).

In the case of Papa Andina, at the macro and meso level, transformations have not yet occurred, particularly for non-COGEPAN female producers of native potatoes. The results of this study would seem to indicate that market chains have not addressed women's legal and social networking strategies, a macro level change essential to overcoming systemic discrimination against women (KIT et al. 2012). In general, while the agricultural innovation system in Peru is changing in important ways to support the integration of knowledge systems (local and traditional as well as modern), the wider complex of agricultural policies, national government, and public institutions in Peru is less than supportive of women's and men's traditional agricultural knowledge, micro level forms of community organisation, and the validity of customary law in managing biodiversity. Rural women's knowledge and Andean ways of adapting and innovating are part and parcel of the population's capacity to maintain the biodiversity of native potatoes. Producers have preserved the potatoes' genetic biodiversity and coped with such major challenges as climate change, globalisation, and food scarcity. More research and stakeholder collaboration are needed at the macro and meso levels to overcome this lack of gender transformation in Peru's agricultural innovation system.

Overall, the case of Papa Andina presents an important contribution to the literature on gender and agricultural innovation, particularly with respect to household food security through market involvement. The initiative has supported the empowerment of peasant women in Central Peru in many ways. Individually and collectively, female respondents in the COGEPAN group not only gained control over land, but were empowered to go further and combine their emic knowledge with new ideas in order to make choices and decisions about what needs to be produced on that land. Women's roles and organisational involvement in native potato management and production have allowed them to become community leaders with the authority to negotiate individually and collectively with diverse groups of actors in order to commercialise their potatoes. Peasant women are actively changing male hegemonic norms and class rules long entrenched in Peruvian society.

This study confirms similar trends found in Bolivia and Ecuador (Avilés et al. 2010; Cadima et al. 2011; Conlago et al. 2011). Across the Andean region, gender empowerment is intrinsic to female peasant producers' safeguarding of native potato production – first and foremost for their own households, thereby demonstrating their respect for Pachamama – while maintaining the native potato farming system that will support and expand market chains.

Again, the work that remains to be done is at the macro and meso level of enabling institutions (domestic and export markets), and challenging chains and regulatory structures that are resistant to gender equality, particularly with regard to access to technologies, land, and capital.

Conclusion

The study confirmed that as a result of the technological innovations introduced by Papa Andina, peasant producers, including women, gained access to and became familiar with new technologies available to them in the PMCA and Stakeholder Platforms. These technologies include access to crucial information (such as market access and product standards) and inputs (such as seed, transport, packaging, etc.) that enhance producers' innovative capacities in production, post-production, and commercialisation.

The new knowledge has not subjugated the Andean Cosmo Vision. Women's knowledge of biodiversity plays a significant role in integrating vast traditional knowledge with contemporary improvements to the native potato farming system. Participants in COGEPAN in Central Peru have benefited from the market chain of native potatoes, and female producers have been enabled to negotiate changes in market chains by interacting with a range of stakeholders, engaging in training, and exploring unprecedented income-generating opportunities.

Changes at the macro and meso levels are still needed to enable peasant producers to strengthen their feminocentric Andean Cosmo Vision, reinforce their rights to land, and adapt to climate changes. From a feminist standpoint, the market chain approach and the worldview of peasant producers are not necessarily at odds with one another. Nevertheless, the persistence of the power relations implicit in the technological dimensions of innovation suggest that the institutional transformations that will ensure gender equality are not yet apparent in the case of Papa Andina. The empowerment of women in COGEPAN has not come easily; it is the result of intentional efforts to challenge inequities at the micro level. Further action at the macro level is recommended, notably by challenging social exclusion in Central Peru and across the Andes with the continued involvement of meso-level organisations such as FOVIDA, to secure learning and other resources for peasant producers. As well, positioning women as guardians of biodiversity knowledge and not simply recipients of agricultural information has been essential to overcoming discrimination. Women's protection of their household food security needs, first and foremost, defends their rights within their households and communities, as well as the agricultural innovation system. Female peasant producers of native potatoes involved in Papa Andina have individually demonstrated, especially as leaders, that transformation is possible.

Notes

1 Peasant or *campesino* is not only a social class; the term also encompasses race, social status, income, and other aspects (de la Cadena 2000). Most of the population under similar conditions define themselves as indigenous people (Contreras 2000). Later in this text, the analysis will problematise the sociocultural stigma of the female peasant as *campesina*.

2 *Papa* is the Quechua word for potato, a loan word from the Spanish *patata*. Respondents often used the diminutive *papita* in reference to the nurturing potato/human relationship.
3 Creswell (2009: 5) refers to this type of approach as "two forms of data that are separate but connected".
4 Video summary in English: www.youtube.com/watch?v=upbxpUQ8gt8.

References

Avilés, Denis Lucy, Ivonne Antezana, Magaly Salazar, Fausto Yumisaca, and Cristina Fonseca. 2010. *Fortalecimiento del Enfoque de Género y Empoderamiento en el Enfoque Participativo en Cadenas Productivas (EPCP), Plataformas de Concertación y Evaluación Horizontal: Guía de Pautas*. Lima, Peru: International Potato Center.

Bailey, Barbara, ed. 2000. *Gender Issues in Caribbean Education: A Module for Teacher Education*. Georgetown, Guyana: Caribbean Community Secretariat in association with the Centre for Gender and Development Studies, Regional Coordinating Unit, University of the West Indies, Mona.

Barrientos, Stephanie. 2001. "Gender, Flexibility and Global Value Chains." *IDS Bulletin* 32 (3): 83–93. doi:10.1111/j.1759-5436.2001.mp32003009.x.

Bernet, Thomas, Graham Thiele, and Thomas Zschocke, eds. 2006. *Participatory Market Chain Approach (PMCA): User Guide*. Lima, Peru: International Potato Center, Papa Andina.

Bourque, Susan, and Barbara Warren. 1981. *Women of the Andes: Patriarchy and Social Change in Two Peruvian Towns*. Ann Arbor: University of Michigan Press.

Brush, Stephen B. 2004. *Farmers' Bounty: Locating Crop Diversity in the Contemporary World*. New Haven, CT: Yale University Press.

Brush, Stephen B., Rick Kesseli, Ramiro Ortega, Pedro Cisneros, Karl Zimmerer, and Carlos Quiros. 1994. "Potato Diversity in the Andean Center of Crop Domestication." *Conservation Biology* 9 (5): 1189–98. doi:10.1046/j.1523-1739.1995.9051176.x-i1.

Cadima, Ximena, Franz Terrazas, Magaly Salazar, Rayne Calderón, Ivonne Antezana, Víctor Iriarte, . . . Nathalia Ferrufino. 2011. "Preserving Biodiversity of Andean Roots and Tubers: Working with Women." In André Devaux, Miguel Ordinola, and Douglas Horton, eds, *Innovation for Development: The Papa Andina Experience*. Lima, Peru: International Potato Center.

Chant, Sylvia, and Caroline Sweetman. 2012. "Fixing Women or Fixing the World? 'Smart Economics', Efficiency Approaches, and Gender Equality in Development." *Gender & Development* 20 (3): 517–29. doi:10.1080/13552074.2012.731812.

Chevalier, Jacques M., and Daniel J. Buckles. 2008. *SAS²: A Guide to Collaborative Inquiry and Social Engagement*. New Delhi, India: SAGE Publications and Ottawa, Canada: International Development Research Centre (IDRC).

Choque Copari, Elizabeth. 2001. *El marani, autoridad que armoniza la crianza de las chacras*. Puno, Peru: Proyecto Andino de Tecnologías Campesinas (PRATEC).

Conlago, Maria, Fabián Montesdeoca, Magdalena Mayorga, Fausto Yumisaca, Ivonne Antezana, and Jorge L. Andrade-Piedra, 2011. *Gender Relationships in Production and Commercialization of Potato Seed with Small-Scale Farmers in the Central Andes of Ecuador*. Paper presented at the 15th Triennial International Symposium of the International Society for Tropical Root Crops (ISTRC). Lima, Peru, 2–7 November 2009.

Contreras, Antonio P. 2000. "Rethinking Participation and Empowerment in the Uplands." In Peter Utting, ed., *Forest Policy and Politics in the Philippines: The Dynamics of Participatory Conservation*. Manila: Ateneo de Manila University Press, 144–70.

Cornwall, Andrea. 1997. "Men, Masculinity and 'Gender in Development'." *Gender & Development* 5 (2): 8–13. doi:10.1080/741922358.

Cornwall, Andrea. 2006. "Historical Perspectives on Participation in Development." *Journal of Comparative and Commonwealth Politics* 44 (1): 62–83. doi:10.1080/14662040600624460.

Creswell, John W. 2009. *Research Design: Qualitative, Quantitative, and Mixed Methods Approaches* (3rd ed.). London: SAGE Publications.

Deere, Carmen Diana, and Magdalena Leon. 2003. "The Gender Asset Gap: Land in Latin America." *World Development* 31 (6): 925–47.

de Haan, Stef. 2009. "Potato Diversity at Height: Multiple Dimensions of Farmer-Driven *In-Situ* Conservation in the Andes." PhD thesis. Wageningen, Netherlands: Wageningen University.

de la Cadena, Marisol. 2000. *Indigenous Mestizos: The Politics of Race and Culture in Cuzco, Peru, 1919–1991*. Durham, NC, and London: Duke University Press.

Devaux, André, Jorge Andrade-Piedra, Douglas Horton, Miguel Ordinola, Graham Thiele, Alice Thomann, and Claudio Velasco. 2011. "Brokering Innovation for Sustainable Development: The Papa Andina Case." In André Devaux, Miguel Ordinola, and Douglas Horton, eds, *Innovation for Development: The Papa Andina Experience*. Lima, Peru: International Potato Center, 76–110.

Devaux, André, Douglas Horton, Claudio Velasco, Graham Thiele, Gastón López, Thomas Bernet, Iván Reinoso, and Miguel Ordinola. 2011. "Collective Action for Market Chain Innovation in the Andes." In André Devaux, Miguel Ordinola, and Douglas Horton, eds, *Innovation for Development: The Papa Andina Experience*. Lima, Peru: International Potato Center, 59–75.

Devaux, André, Claudio Velasco, Gastón López, Thomas Bernet, Miguel Ordinola, . . . Douglas Horton. 2007. *Collective Action for Innovation and Small Farmer Market Access: The Papa Andina Experience*. CAPRi Working Paper No. 68. Washington, DC: CGIAR Systemwide Program on Collective Action and Property Rights (CAPRi) c/o International Food Policy Research Institute (IFPRI). doi:10.2499/CAPRiWP68.

Diez Hurtado, Alejandro. 2010. *Derechos formales y derechos reales: Acceso de mujeres campesinas a tierras de comunidades en el marco del proceso de formalización de la propiedad en comunidades de Huancavelica* [informe de investigación]. Lima, Peru: Centro de Investigaciones Sociológicas, Económicas, Políticas y Antropológicas and International Land Coalition.

Ekboir, Javier M., and Riikka Rajalahti. 2012. "Coordination and Collective Action for Agricultural Innovation." In Riikka Rajalahti, ed., *Agricultural Innovation Systems: An Investment Sourcebook*. Washington, DC: World Bank, 15–106. doi:10.1596/9780821386842_CH01.

Grillo Fernández, Eduardo. 1998. "Development or Cultural Affirmation in the Andes?" In Frédérique Apffel-Marglin, ed., *The Spirit of Regeneration: Andean Culture Confronting Western Notions of Development*. London: Zed Books, 124–45.

Hambly Odame, Helen. 2001. *The Rise and Fall of Women's Groups: Agricultural Development and Local Institutions*. ISS Seminar Series paper, 9 February. The Hague: Institute of Social Studies (ISS).

Hambly Odame, Helen, and Tobias Onweng Angura, eds. 1996. *Grassroots Indicators for Desertification: Experience and Perspectives from Eastern and Southern Africa*. Ottawa, Canada: International Development Research Centre (IDRC).

Haverkort, Bertus, Katrien van't Hooft, and Wim Hiemstra, eds. 2003. *Ancient Roots, New Shoots: Endogenous Development in Practice*. Leusden/London: ETC/Compas and Zed Books.

INEI (Instituto Nacional de Estadística e Informática). 2007. *Perú: Perfil de la Pobreza según departamentos, 2004–2006*. Lima, Peru: Dirección Técnica de Demografía e Indicadores Sociales del INEI.

Ishizawa, Jorge, and Eduardo Grillo Fernández. 2002. "Loving the World As It Is: Western Abstraction and Andean Nurturance." *Revision* 24 (4): 21–6.

Jaggar, Alison M., and Paula S. Rothenberg, eds. 1984. *Feminist Frameworks*. New York: McGraw-Hill.

Kabeer, Naila. 1999. "Resources, Agency and Achievements: Reflections on the Measurement of Women's Empowerment." *Development and Change* 30 (3): 435–64. doi:10.1111/1467-7660.00125.

Kabeer, Naila. 2005. "Gender Equality and Women's Empowerment: A Critical Analysis of the Third Millennium Development Goal." *Gender & Development* 13 (1): 13–24. doi:10.1080/13552070512331332273.

KIT (Royal Tropical Institute), Agri-ProFocus, and IIRR (International Institute of Rural Reconstruction). 2012. *Challenging Chains to Change: Gender Equity in Agricultural Value Chain Development*. Amsterdam: KIT Publishers, Royal Tropical Institute.

Klerkx, Laurens, Noelle Aarts, and Cees Leeuwis. 2010. "Adaptive Management in Agricultural Innovation Systems: The Interaction between Innovation Networks and their Environment." *Agricultural Systems* 103 (6): 390–400.

Klerkx, Laurens, Barbara van Mierlo, and Cees Leeuwis. 2012. "Evolution of Systems Approaches to Agricultural Innovation: Concepts, Analysis and Interventions." In Ika Darnhofer, David Gibbon, and Benoît Dedieu, eds, *Farming Systems Research into the 21st Century: The New Dynamic*. Dordrecht: Springer, 457–83. doi:10.1007/978-94-007-4503-2_20.

Leeuwis, Cees. 2004. *Communication for Rural Innovation: Rethinking Agricultural Extension*. Oxford: Blackwell Science.

McIlwaine, Cathy, and Kavita Datta. 2003. "From Feminising to Engendering Development." *Gender, Place and Culture* 10 (4): 369–82. doi:10.1080/09663690 32000155564.

Meinzen-Dick, Ruth S., André Devaux, and Ivonne Antezana. 2009. "Underground Assets: Potato Biodiversity to Improve the Livelihoods of the Poor." *International Journal of Agricultural Sustainability* 7 (4): 235–48. doi:10.3763/ijas.2009.0380.

Meinzen-Dick, Ruth S., André Devaux, and Ivonne Antezana. 2011. "Underground Assets: Potato Biodiversity to Improve the Livelihoods of the Poor." In André Devaux, Miguel Ordinola, and Douglas Horton, eds, *Innovation for Development: The Papa Andina Experience*. Lima, Peru: International Potato Center, 40–58.

Ordinola, Miguel, André Devaux, Thomas Bernet, Kurt Manrique, Gastón López, Cristina Fonseca, and Douglas Horton. 2014. *The PMCA and Potato Market Chain Innovation in Peru*. Papa Andina Innovation Brief 3. Lima, Peru: International Potato Center.

Ortner, Sherry B. 1974. "Is Female to Male as Nature Is to Culture?" *Feminist Studies* 1 (2): 5–31. doi:10.2307/3177638.

Pant, Laxmi, and Helen Hambly Odame. 2009. "Innovation Systems in Renewable Natural Resource Management and Sustainable Agriculture: A Literature Review." *African Journal of Science, Technology, Innovation and Development* 1 (1): 103–35.

Pati, Anuradha. 2006. *Development Paradigms, Feminist Perspectives and Commons: A Theoretical Intersection.* Paper presented at the 11th Biennial Conference of the International Association for the Study of Common Property (IASCP), Bali, Indonesia, 19–23 June.

Pedersen, Duncan, Hanna Kienzler, and Jeffrey Gamarra. 2010. "*Llaki* and *Ñakary*: Idioms of Distress and Suffering among the Highland Quechua in the Peruvian Andes." *Culture, Medicine, and Psychiatry* 34 (2): 279–300. doi:10.1007/s11013-010-9173-z.

Razavi, Shahra. 1999. "Gendered Poverty and Well-Being: Introduction." *Development and Change* 30 (3): 409–33. doi:10.1111/1467-7660.00124.

Reinharz, Shulamit. 1992. *Feminist Methods in Social Research.* New York: Oxford University Press.

Röling, Neils. 2009. "Conceptual and Methodological Development in Innovation." In Pascal C. Sanginga, Ann Waters-Bayer, Susan Kaaria, Jemimah Njuki, and Chesha Wettasinha, eds, *Innovation Africa: Enriching Farmers' Livelihoods.* New York and Abingdon: Earthscan, 9–34.

Sarapura, Silvia. 2012. "Gender Analysis for the Assessment of Innovation Processes: The Case of Papa Andina in Peru." In Riikka Rajalahti, ed., *Agricultural Innovation Systems: An Investment Sourcebook.* Washington, DC: World Bank, 211–30.

Sarapura, Silvia. 2013. *Gender and Agricultural Innovation in Peasant Production of Native Potatoes in the Central Andes of Peru.* PhD dissertation. Guelph, Canada: University of Guelph.

Tapia, Mario E. 1997. *Cultivos Andinos sub explotados y su aporte a la alimentacion.* Lima, Peru: Food and Agriculture Organization of the United Nations (FAO).

Tapia, Mario E., and Ana De la Torre. 2000. *La mujer campesina y las semillas andinas: Género y el manejo de los recursos genéticos* (2nd ed.). Lima, Peru: FAO and Instituto Internacional para los Recursos Fitogenéticos (IPGRI).

Tapia Ponce, Nelson, Domingo Torrico Vallejos, Miguel Rodrigo Chirveches Seborga, and Angélica Machaca. 2012. *Indicadores del tiempo y la predicción climatic: Estrategias agroecológicas campesinas para la adaptación al cambio climático en la puna Cochabambina.* Bolivia: Fundación PIEB, AGRUCO, Embajada de Dinamarca.

Thiele, Graham, André Devaux, Hernán Pico, Fabián Montesdeoca, Manuel Pumisacho, . . . Kurt Manrique. 2009. *Multi-Stakeholder Platforms for Innovation and Coordination in Market Chains: Evidence from the Andes.* Paper presented at the 15th Triennial Symposium of the International Society for Tropical Root Crops (ISTRC), Lima, Peru, 2–6 November.

Thiele, Graham, André Devaux, Iván Reinoso, Hernán Pico, Fabián Montesdeoca, Manuel Pumisacho, . . . and Douglas Horton. 2011. "Multi-Stakeholder Platforms for Linking Small Farmers to Value Chains: Evidence from the Andes." *International Journal of Agricultural Sustainability* 9 (3): 423–33. doi:10.1080/14735903.2011.589206.

Trivelli, Carolina. 2004. "Women, Poverty and Survival of the Household: Peru." In Peter H. Smith, Jennifer Troutner, and Christine Hünefeldt, eds, *Promises of Empowerment. Women in Asia and Latin America.* Lanham, MD: Rowman & Littlefield, 248–74.

Urrutia Ceruti, Jaime. 2007. "Los estudios sobre comunidades y la perspectiva de género." In Pedro Castillo, Alejandro Diez, Zulema Burneo, Jaime Urrutia, and Pablo del Valle, eds., *¿Qué sabemos de las comunidades campesinas?* Lima, Peru: Centro Peruano de Estudios Sociales and Grupo Allpa, 259–90.

Valladolid, Julio, and Frédérique Apffel-Marglin. 2001. "Andean Cosmovision and the Nurturing of Biodiversity." In John A. Grim, ed., *Indigenous Traditions and Ecology: The Interbeing of Cosmology and Community*. Cambridge, MA: Harvard University Press, 639–70.

World Bank. 2012. *Agricultural Innovation Systems: An Investment Sourcebook*. Report No. 67207, Agriculture and Rural Development Series. Washington, DC: World Bank. doi:10.1596/978-0-8213-8684-2.

Part IV

Approaches to transforming gender relations

8 From gender analysis to transforming gender norms

Using empowerment pathways to enhance gender equity and food security in Tanzania[1]

Alessandra Galiè and Paula Kantor

Introduction

For some decades now, there have been compelling arguments for, and good evidence of, the contributions towards alleviating poverty and food insecurity that can be achieved by addressing gender disparities in access to agricultural inputs, markets, resources, and advice. Numerous projects and programs have made efforts to integrate gender into agricultural research and development practice to reduce these gaps. However, these efforts have been insufficient on their own to bring about desired changes in ingrained patterns of inequality, because providing rural households with access to resources and technologies does not automatically translate into women's control over them or their benefits, or into social acceptance of new roles and opportunities for women and men. The limited progress in reducing and reversing many gender inequities, and the persistence of poverty and food insecurity after decades of research and program intervention, highlight the need to assess the challenges and opportunities associated with integrating gender transformative approaches (GTAs) – approaches that address both the fundamental causes and consequences of gender inequality – into agricultural development programs.

CGIAR's Research Program on Livestock and Fish (Livestock and Fish CRP) focusses on meat, milk, and fish value chains worldwide in order to contribute to gender-equal global food security and livelihood enhancement. Gender is one of the program's six research themes (with animal health, animal genetics, feeds and forages, targeting sustainable interventions, and value chain development). Even so, most Livestock and Fish value chain projects struggle to develop clear pathways that lead from gender analysis to changes in the underlying social institutions that constrain the achievement of agricultural development goals. In most cases, the focus is on addressing individual-level gender imbalances (e.g., in access to and control of assets) within the existing social context. Limited space is provided to appreciate aspirations for self-determination and development beyond current gender roles, and to address gender-based power imbalances across value chain actors.

One of these Livestock and Fish CRP projects is "Integrating Dairy Goat and Root Crop Production for Increasing Food, Nutrition, and Income Security of Smallholder Farmers in Tanzania" (referred to as the Crop and Goat Project, or CGP). Funded by Canada's International Development Research Centre (IDRC), the three-and-a-half-year CGP, which ended in August 2014, involved the University of Alberta in Canada, Sokoine University of Agriculture in Tanzania, and the International Livestock Research Institute (ILRI) in Kenya. It targeted 112 households, 19 of which were female-headed, in four villages in Morogoro and Dodoma regions. The project aimed to improve the household income, food security, and well-being of poor and female-headed households in agropastoral communities in Tanzania through the introduction of a community-based crossbreeding program for dairy goats, and improved participatory farm trials for cassava and sweet potato varieties (Figure 8.1).

This chapter analyses the CGP's gender strategy and how it affected gender equity and food security in participating households. The aim is to identify the inter-linkages between gender analysis, empowerment, and GTAs, and present a participatory empowerment pathway as a possible approach for operationalising GTAs. The key question this chapter addresses is whether the project's approach to gender integration is sufficient to achieve movement towards the "transformative outcome" of more equitable gender relations. The main research question therefore is: How did the CGP affect gender relations in the households selected, from the perspectives of the

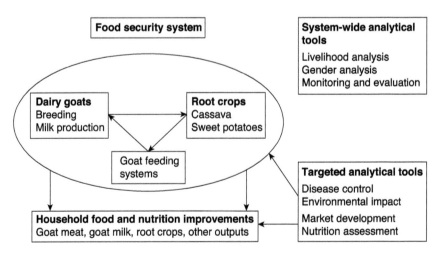

Figure 8.1 Project impact pathway

participating livestock keepers and agriculturalists? The responses to this question raised subsequent questions that are addressed in the discussion session, including: How can gender analysis better contribute to the design of GTAs that include the framing of bottom-up approaches to fostering empowerment? Is a non-participatory approach to empowerment intrinsically disempowering? How can purposeful plans for transformative approaches to technology design and delivery foster questioning of the status quo?

Evidence from the field and a review of project documents shed light on the conceptual complexities involved in designing GTAs and the challenges involved in implementing them in the field, and are used to discuss what gender strategies may better address the fundamental causes and consequences of gender inequality.

After providing an overview of the theory and literature on empowerment and GTAs, the chapter introduces the research methodology and provides an overview of the CGP's gender strategy. Next, the findings from the assessment of gender-related outcomes are presented and their implications are discussed in terms of progress towards empowerment and equity, changing gender roles, and the role of technology as a catalyst for change. The chapter concludes with a methodology to operationalise participatory empowerment pathways and transformative approaches.

Theoretical perspective

Empowerment

Empowerment of rural women is regarded as a means to enhance gender equity in agricultural development, and is often considered as a development activity in its own right (Cornwall and Anyidoho 2010). It is seen as a means to enable rural women to participate in development as equal partners alongside scientists, and to enhance the effectiveness of Agricultural Research for Development (AR4D) interventions (Song and Vernooy 2010). Empowerment is also considered essential for farmers to safeguard their own livelihood interests (Almekinders and Hardon 2006). Yet, empowerment is an elusive concept that generates debate over who has the power to decide "what empowerment means" and "whose empowerment counts" (Charrad 2007; Galiè 2013). Limited efforts have been made to appreciate local conceptualisations of empowerment and the process by which it might unfold. Kabeer (1999) highlights the gap between the understanding of empowerment as a process, and more instrumentalist approaches that entail the quantification of empowerment.

For instance, in agriculture, the Women's Empowerment in Agriculture Index (WEAI) methodology (Alkire et al. 2013) provides a tool to assess quantitatively the empowerment of women farmers. While this is important to bring as much attention to the issue of empowerment as to other measurable outcomes (income, for example), the tool does not provide space for local concepts of empowerment. Instead, it assesses gradients of empowerment based on set, universal dimensions used by external evaluators to classify men and women as "empowered" or "disempowered". Friis–Hansen and Duveskog (2012) argue that agricultural development programs should focus more on the "processes of empowerment", as opposed to the technical solutions that characterise most programs, in order to create an appropriate mix of technological and social advancement for a development process that is sustainable. Attempts at appreciating the local understandings and processes of empowerment in agriculture-related contexts are the focus of this chapter.

Sen (1990: 44) conceptualises empowerment as "replacing the domination of circumstances and chance by the domination of individuals over change and circumstances". Kabeer (1999: 437) defines empowerment as "the expansion of people's ability to make strategic life choices in a context where this ability was previously denied to them". The literature on empowerment emphasises "agency" and "voice" as key in transforming unequal power relations, as well as the contextual specificity of empowerment pathways (Kabeer 2010). Giddens (1976) speaks of the transformative capacity of power, that is, the capacity or agency of each human being to act as well as to participate effectively in shaping the social limits that define what is possible. Kabeer's expanded conceptualisation of women's empowerment reflects Giddens' focus on shaping social limits, in that she adds a dimension on agency in relation to the structures creating and perpetuating gender inequality. In this expanded conceptualisation, empowerment involves changes in women's sense of self-worth and social identity; their willingness and ability to question their subordinate status; their capacity to renegotiate their relationships with others; and their ability to participate on equal terms with men in reshaping society in ways that contribute to a more equitable distribution of power and possibilities (Rowlands 1997; Kabeer 2008, 2010, 2012).

In all of these conceptualisations, empowerment has a significant personal component whereby people develop a sense of themselves and their entitlements, and their capacities to act and make claims. Thus, empowerment is not something that can be bestowed; it is something individuals must work to achieve for themselves (Rowlands 1997; Tsikata and Darkwah 2014). Therefore, the question of who has the power to define what empowerment is and how to achieve it becomes central. The participatory approach to conceptualising empowerment and defining a pathway to achieve it described in this chapter recognises that challenging and changing unequal gender relations rest on local ownership of the change process, and that this ownership needs to extend not only to women but also to the range of actors involved in or affected by the empowerment process. In a value chain context, this means inclusion of actors along the whole chain, as well as those with a role in creating and maintaining unequal gender relations in the related spheres of the family and state.

Gender transformative approaches (GTAs)

Gender integration in agricultural research and practice tends to sit closer to the accommodative than to the transformative end of a continuum of gender-responsive approaches, all of which invest in understanding the social and gender context within which projects operate, but then vary in how they engage with that understanding. Gender accommodative approaches recognise and respond to the specific needs and realities of men and women, based on their existing roles and responsibilities. They tend to be influenced by understandings of gender as a characteristic of individuals and not of society (Peterson 2005; Okali 2011a, 2011b, 2012). This understanding leads to analysis that focusses on women and men and comparisons of their situations, instead of on the complexities of gendered power relations, and to action that targets women for training, technologies, or credit within existing social and economic structures without questioning the barriers put up by that context, or seeing these barriers as objects for action (Cornwall and Edwards 2010). Accommodative approaches make a contribution through raising awareness of gender-based disparities and through improving the availability of resources to women. They are easier to implement, since they are less challenging to the status quo.

However, they may only partially address the problem of gender inequality, since they do not act on the underlying causes of the disparities – the systems, norms, and attitudes making gender inequality an acceptable part of everyday life (Peterson 2005; Okali 2011a, 2011b, 2012). Therefore, these approaches *by themselves* offer little assurance that women will be able to take advantage of or benefit from the availability of new agricultural opportunities or technologies, because society's understandings of what is acceptable for women and men to do, own, and control may continue to impose barriers. For example, accommodative approaches would not address the customary beliefs and gender norms that reduce women's access to livestock and fisheries resources and decision-making power, and that relegate women to low-value segments of a value chain.

GTAs are a means of integrating gender into development that seek to act on the social context and create an enabling environment for gender equality and women's empowerment. They accomplish this by supporting women and men to critically examine gender norms and inequalities, to act to strengthen norms that support equality, and to challenge and change the underlying social structures, policies, and norms that perpetuate gender inequalities (Razavi 2009; Chant and Sweetman 2012; Kabeer 2012; Okali 2012). Creating this enabling environment means looking beyond women to the other actors and institutions that frame women's and men's "horizons of possibility" through complex sets of relationships that cross scales and institutional locations (Cornwall and Edwards 2010). For example, family members, particularly spouses, can facilitate or constrain the expansion of women's agricultural opportunities, depending on their willingness to share domestic work and free women's time for new value chain activities, while community opinion leaders and local service providers, including agricultural extension agents, can hold fast to norms and attitudes that limit women's access to market opportunities, information, and technologies. Private-sector value chain actors may be blind to women as economic agents, consequently bypassing their needs and interests in product or technology design and dissemination.

GTAs therefore start from an understanding that gender is a social construct, embedded in how societies define women's and men's roles and relations and distribute resources (Risman 2004). So, gender infuses all aspects of women's and men's daily lives, shaping what it is acceptable and appropriate for them to be and do. This means that gender affects how women and men perceive themselves and their capabilities; how women and men interact and relate in the home, community, and market within the framework of social expectations; and how opportunities are structured and resources are distributed within institutions like the market and the state. Core characteristics that distinguish GTAs from accommodative approaches to integrating gender into agricultural research and development interventions include (Kantor 2013):

- development of a deep understanding of people in their context and the way social inequalities affect different groups' choices and outcomes;
- engagement with both women and men, as both have a role and stake in gender transformative change;
- commitment to address unequal power relations and to challenge oppressive norms, behaviours, and structures;
- commitment to foster iterative cycles of critical reflection and action among all participants; and
- engagement with different actors across scales in response to how the power relations and norms underlying gender inequality and affecting the process of women's empowerment are distributed.

GTAs have been part of the conceptual framework of gender and development for decades (Young 1993; Kabeer 1994). A key challenge has been and continues to be operationalising them in practice. This is due in large part to their focus on engaging with power and seeking to act on, and not just within, the existing social context. Shifting entrenched attitudes, norms, and power relations is a long-term, political process; there is little knowledge of how to enable such systemic change in enduring ways, in general or through agricultural entry points. Many mainstream agricultural development agencies focus primarily on technical issues and consider these wider social factors as outside their purview. Hence, it can be challenging to obtain buy-in to take up and invest in agricultural research on GTAs; to build staff capacity to engage in such research; and to establish "unusual" (for agricultural research and development organisations) partnerships – with, for example, community theatre groups or policy advocacy groups – that enable implementation of GTAs. Overcoming these institutional challenges is vital, because the pace and scale of change in livelihood and food security occurring through technology-centric approaches, without attention to social equality, have not been great. More equitable and enduring improvements in the livelihoods of the poor and marginalised in the agricultural sector can be achieved by engaging with social change processes as well as resolving technical agricultural problems.

Both gender accommodative and transformative approaches can add value to this process of jointly fostering social and technological change, with the mix of approaches at different points in the change process determined by contextual conditions. In some places there may be scope for quicker movement to actions that foster critical dialogue on gender along with technical interventions, while in other places, even in the same country, this shift may take longer, in which case accommodative approaches that improve women's practical situation will provide early entry points for engagement with women and gender. The key is infusing a country, program, or project strategy with long-term transformative aims, and then identifying steps along the pathway to that goal that mix accommodative and transformative approaches in ways that foster locally owned change without causing backlash (Kabeer 1994).

There is no "silver bullet", simple checklist, or known set of intervention packages to guide this process, making identifying change mechanisms that work together for different groups under different contextual conditions a key research area for GTAs in agriculture. The balance of the chapter contributes to learning about what works in practice, and, based on that learning, identifies a promising way forward to operationalise GTAs through a locally owned empowerment pathway approach.

Methodology

The research was designed as a small-N impact evaluation. A small-N approach (Mahoney and Goertz 2006) was used because it is more appropriate for in-depth causal analysis of change in the respondent households as affected by the CGP, and for appreciation of processes of change related to complex concepts such as empowerment. Flyvbjerg (2006) argues that the largest amount of information about a given problem is more likely obtained through the strategic selection of a few instances and their in-depth analysis than by a random sample. The outputs of such small-N research can provide proof of concept evidence, help to identify issues, and generate questions that can be examined in large-N studies and extrapolated to similar settings and interpolated into similar activity elsewhere (such as a scale-out of the CGP in Tanzania or similar dairy goat interventions in East Africa), as hypotheses that need further testing and analysis.

The respondents and their villages

The CGP targeted crop-growing, goat-owning, and non-goat-owning farmers in the regions of Morogoro and Dodoma in Tanzania.

The Morogoro region is located in the eastern part of mainland Tanzania. Mvomero, in the northeast of the region, was chosen as the target district, and Wami Luhindo and Kunke villages were selected to implement project activities (Figure 8.2). The 2012 Tanzania population census reported 312,109 inhabitants in Mvomero. There are about 142,155 farmers (of whom 49.8 percent are women) in the district, and 2,534 pastoralists. Average annual income per capita in 2007–8 was approximately 337,000 Tanzanian shillings (TZS), or roughly US$213. Eighty percent of the adult population relies on agriculture and livestock keeping for their livelihood (Table 8.1).

The Dodoma region is located in central Tanzania. Here, Kongwa (population 309,973 according to the 2012 census) was selected as the target

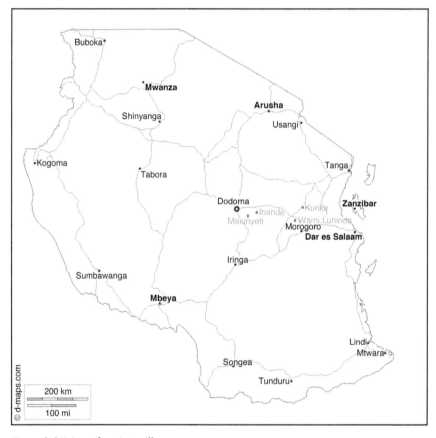

Figure 8.2 Map of project villages

Source: Authors, based on maps from http://d-maps.com/.

Table 8.1 Description of selected communities in Tanzania

District	Community	Agricultural potential	Production system	Market access	Major enterprise		Food crops	Livestock
					Cash crops			
Mvomero	1. Wami Luhindo 2. Kunke	Good and fertile land available for agriculture and livestock keeping	Rainfed subsistence farming Mixed crop-livestock Agropastoralism	Domestic markets available but unreliable for agricultural products	Cotton, coffee, sesame, sunflower, sugarcane, bananas, and vegetables		Maize, rice, millet, cassava, pulses, and arrowroot	Cattle, indigenous and dairy goats, sheep, and chickens
Kongwa	1. Masinyeti 2. Ihanda	Good and fertile land available for agriculture and livestock keeping	Rainfed subsistence farming Mixed crop-livestock Agropastoralism	Domestic markets available but unreliable for agricultural products	Groundnuts, sesame, sunflower, castor oil seeds, and cashew nuts		Maize, rice, millet, cassava, legumes, and sweet potatoes	Cattle, indigenous and dairy goats, sheep, chickens, and donkeys

Source: Saghir et al. (2012).

district, and project activities were implemented in Masinyeti and Ihanda villages (Figure 8.2). Eighty-five percent of households rely on farming, and 4.7 percent on livestock keeping (Table 8.1). Kongwa is reported to have significantly lower per capita incomes than Mvomero.

The four villages in the project were selected based on their levels of food insecurity, potential for increased production, low dairy goat population, and the absence of other development projects in the area. The latter arguably contributes to a stronger attribution to the project of the changes reported in this paper. One hundred and twelve households (19 of them female-headed), represented by 49 women and 69 men (six households were represented by both a man and a woman), were involved in the project, and received dairy goats and planting material of cassava and sweet potatoes. Dairy goats were received by 107 farmers (69 men and 38 women). Table 8.2 shows the households' characteristics. The households were selected based on a list provided by the village council in response to priority criteria: vicinity to roads, female-headed, most poor, and HIV/AIDS (Parkins and Lekule 2012).

Table 8.2 Characteristics of households participating in the CGP

	Kongwa		Mvomero	
	Project village		*Project village*	
	MHH[a]	*FHH[b]*	*MHH[a]*	*FHH[b]*
	(n = 173)	*(n = 59)*	*(n = 197)*	*(n = 32)*
Average household income (TZS)	638,000	253,000	277,000	765,000
Average age of household head (years)	43 (173)	44 (59)	44 (197)	51 (32)
Average age of spouse (years)	34 (172)	53 (5)	36 (194)	44.3 (6)
Households producing cassava (%)	32.3 (167)	23.2 (56)	29.1 (182)	32.4 (31)
Households producing sweet potato (%)	7.2 (167)	9.6 (52)	36.9 (179)	30.0 (30)
Households rearing goats (%)	21.1 (171)	19.3 (57)	16.6 (187)	9.7 (31)
Households rearing goats and producing cassava (%)	11.7 (171)	14.0 (57)	4.3 (187)	3.2 (31)
Households rearing goats and producing sweet potato (%)	2.9 (171)	3.5 (57)	4.8 (187)	6.5 (31)
Education				
No formal and illiterate (%)	34.1	44.1	19.3	43.8
No formal and literate (%)	16.2	17.0	6.1	0.0

	Kongwa		Mvomero	
	Project village		Project village	
	MHH[a] (n = 173)	*FHH*[b] (n = 59)	*MHH*[a] (n = 197)	*FHH*[b] (n = 32)
Primary school not completed (%)	10.4	8.5	9.1	15.6
Completed primary level or higher (%)	39.3	30.4	65.5	40.6
Total area per village (hectares) under:				
Cassava	6.87 (13)	0.53 (2)	5.26 (10)	1.01 (2)
Sweet potato	2.75 (7)	0.72 (2)	0.4 (1)	—
Average plot size per village (hectares) under:				
Cassava	0.53 (13)	0.24 (2)	0.53 (10)	0.53 (3)
Sweet potato	0.4 (7)	0.36 (2)	0.4 (1)	—
Average production per unit area per household (kg/ha):				
Cassava	1,714 (10)	97.1 (1)	837.6 (8)	118.6 (2)
Sweet potato	753.4 (5)	86.5 (2)	185.3 (1)	—

Source: Household Baseline Survey (2011) conducted by the project.

Note: Numbers in parentheses indicate number of respondents in each category.
a MHH: Male-headed households.
b FHH: Female-headed households.

Data collection

The study used in-depth, semi-structured interviews undertaken in two phases (August 2013 and January 2014) with 44 women and 40 men, ranging in age from 16 to 75. In August 2013, a total of 27 women and 23 men were interviewed as part of a Knowledge, Attitude, and Practices (KAP) study. These included 5 women and 1 man in Ihanda, 4 women and 8 men in Kunke, 13 women and 8 men in Masinyeti, and 5 women and 6 men in Wami Luhindo. The KAP study aimed to assess the gender-based perceptions of dairy goat/root crop farmers about dairy goat management, gender-based division of labour and decision-making in dairy goat management, food security, and overall project benefits. Some of the gender-related questions leading the discussion were: "Did the introduction of goats and crops affect the way your household organises its work?"; "Did the household decision-making change?"; "From which project outputs have you benefitted and how has it improved your life?"; and "How did the project affect your household food security?"

In January 2014, 17 women and 17 men representing different households (five women and six men from Masinyeti, six women and seven men from Ihanda, and six women and four men from Kunke) participated in semi-structured interviews that explored changes in gender relations and roles and in food security vis-à-vis the project intervention. The questions that led the discussion included: "How are the dairy goats managed in the household?"; "What changed after the introduction of the dairy goats in your household management?"; "How did the dairy goats change relations with house-hold or community members?"; "Did the dairy goats affect your food security?"; "What project activities or approaches most affected the changes above?"; and "Is ownership of the goats important for decision-making?"

The farmers participating in both sets of semi-structured interviews were selected by two extension officers (male and female) at the village level, based on their availability and willingness to take part in the discussions. Generally, only farmers whose goats had kidded and had milk available were interested in sharing their experiences with the project. Three male and five female respondents (one man from Wami Luhindo, two men from Kunke, two women from Ihanda, and three women from Masinyeti) had had no goat kids and no milk, and participated in the discussion mostly to ask for solutions to the lack of fertility of their goats or complain about the expenses incurred in maintaining the goats and seeing no benefits. The findings reported in this chapter refer mostly to respondents whose goats had milk. The semi-structured and KAP interviews were mostly organised by gender, with the support and presence of one facilitator and one young female translator from Sokoine University of Agriculture.

Data analysis

All interviews were written down, digitally transcribed, and verified by one female assistant and the respondents during follow-up visits. The software package QRS Nvivo 10 (International PTY 1999–2013) was used to organise, code, and disaggregate the textual material for qualitative analysis. The findings from both interview sets are reported in this chapter under the headings *Food security*, *Division of labour*, *Decision-making*, and *Independence* as these topics were recurrently mentioned by the respondents as areas in which major changes in gender relations had occurred.

The gender strategy of the CGP and its implementation

The CGP gender strategy (Njuki and Saghir 2012) was developed by ILRI to integrate gender concerns into program design and implementation as well as monitoring and evaluation, as an element essential to the success of the project and as a means to support gender equity and empowerment.

To support gender integration, the strategy commits to conduct gender analysis throughout the project to identify gender-based constraints and opportunities related to decision-making, roles, and ownership of and control over resources in relation to crop and goat production and marketing. Standard indicators and those identified by community members are utilised to monitor and evaluate changes in these realms over time.

The strategy also aims to ensure proportional representation of women in key project activities, as well as women's participation in the crossbreeding program, in the participatory development of locally adapted sweet potato and cassava varieties, and in the development of feeding packages for the dairy goats. Gender-specific activities include gender transformative training and awareness raising for staff and communities, with training for the latter targeting women, girls, men, and boys, and addressing issues raised by the project communities themselves; providing women with co-ownership of goats and access to seed; and facilitating women's participation in technical training opportunities. To reach the most resource-poor women and female heads of households in particular, the strategy stresses the need to support group dynamics and leverage collective action through the formation of women's groups.

Figure 8.3 is a representation of the project's approach to integrating gender into the various project stages. The expected gender-related outcomes are (1) increased ability of women to independently participate in various stages of the value chains, and (2) more equitable social relationships between men and women involved in the goat and root crop value chains. The strategy mentions transformative and empowerment outcomes; however, it does not define the concepts, or identify a pathway that leads from gender analysis to gender-aware program design and changes in empowerment and gender norms.

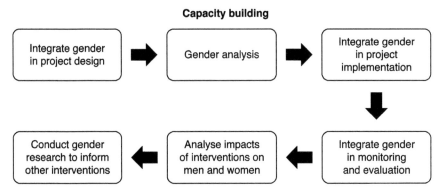

Figure 8.3 Approach for integrating gender in the Crop and Goat Project (CGP), Tanzania

Source: Njuki and Saghir (2012).

The gender activities implemented by the project fall into four main categories (Brandes et al. 2014): (1) capacity development and group creation, (2) resource allocation and co-ownership, (3) field studies, and (4) monitoring and evaluation.

Capacity development and group creation

Capacity development on gender integration was carried out for project staff, project partners, and community members. Training sessions were held at two levels: general gender awareness and analysis, which covered such topics as introduction to gender, GTAs, gender-sensitive facilitation skills, and gender analysis; and gender-specific training tailored to the specific functions and roles of different team members and partners, on such topics as gender and nutrition, marketing, leadership, and conflict management. A gender study to identify existing and potential women's groups was conducted in all four project villages in June/July 2012, and highlighted three types of groups: crop production, Village and Community Banks (VICOBAs)/Savings and Credit Cooperatives (SACCOs), and self-help social groups.

Resource allocation and co-ownership

Farmer participatory trials were set up with 115 farmers (56 of them women) to evaluate the acceptability and agronomic potential of improved cassava and sweet potato varieties. The CGP supported joint ownership of goats by adult men and women in the households, and discussed with them the advantages of sharing goat management roles and responsibilities.

Field studies

One gender-disaggregated baseline and one endline study were completed, in 2013 and 2014 respectively. An inventory of female-headed households and their specific needs and opportunities in keeping and marketing goats and crops was undertaken in 2012 (Mosha-Kilave and Lyimo-Macha 2013). Two sets of interviews were undertaken in 2012 and 2013 by ILRI to assess the changes in knowledge, attitudes, and practices related to dairy goats, cassava and sweet potatoes, and gender relations brought about by the project intervention. A study was carried out in 2013 (Meena et al. 2013) to assess child nutritional status and gender relations among the beneficiaries of dairy goat and root crop improvement projects in Mvomero and Kongwa districts.

Monitoring and evaluation

A monitoring and evaluation framework was developed and presented at the project's inception workshop in May 2011. This framework included tools for data collection and tracking key results/progress of the project. Two training sessions were conducted with project implementers, extension workers, and research technicians on gender-disaggregated data collection and analysis, and feedback to farmers.

Findings

Food security

Both the KAP and semi-structured interviews revealed strong gender norms related to food security and decision-making. In the four villages, men and women alike believed that men were in charge of ensuring food security at home. Men were generally considered the owners of the livestock, although chickens were mostly owned by women, and the project's goats and cow (provided by Heifer International, a non-governmental organisation working to eradicate poverty and hunger through sustainable community development) were mostly co-owned by women and men (see Galiè et al. 2015, for an exploration of the meaning of ownership in these communities). Men were also considered the main household decision-makers.

The men interviewed from Ihanda shared a common opinion about the women from the village of Masinyeti (a couple of kilometres away), who belonged to a different tribe: the men would not marry them because these women were too strong, had too much decision power and independence – as a matter of fact, they were often divorced from their husbands, they pointed out – and ate too much. As a male respondent from Ihanda stated:

> They eat up to three meals a day and are not full! This jeopardises the household food security!
>
> (Interview, 17 January 2014)

However, further discussions revealed that in practice, women were heavily involved in food production and provision, and shared decision-making roles (see below) in ways that often seemed to contradict the normative roles reported above.

The varieties of sweet potatoes and cassava distributed by the CGP did not contribute much to food security, as the farmers involved in the project accessed the project's planting material only in the first year of the project (2012) and because of problems in the institutional arrangements for distribution. Dairy goats contributed to household food security as follows: both female and male respondents whose goats produced milk believed that their household food security had increased because they had reliable access to milk they could consume in the household, sell to buy other food, or exchange for other food. Many farmers, both women and men, also used goat manure in their fields to produce better vegetable crops that they ate or sold to buy other food; they also sold the manure to buy food. They also appreciated the money they saved by not having to buy milk. However, the contribution of milk to household food security seemed more important for poorer households, particularly female-headed households (both poorer and less poor ones), and for women in male-headed households. One possible explanation of this is that female-headed households had fewer income-generating options, and women generally appreciated the availability of milk for children and their control over it.

For example, in Kunke, where both the male and female farmers owned only the CGP dairy goats – i.e., did not own any livestock before the project – even the small amount of milk produced (approximately one litre a day) was considered very important by both men and women, probably because of their limited income-generating options. A woman head of household from Kunke stated that now that she owned a goat, instead of borrowing money she earned money through the sale of goat milk and manure. She also used the milk to feed her family and to exchange for neighbours' vegetables. The male farmers explained that the value of the dairy goats was confirmed by the fact that five dairy goats had been stolen in the village since the beginning of the project. In Ihanda, male-headed households owned more livestock than female-headed households. Women considered the availability of milk in their courtyard important, both for their control over it and for the ability to feed their children whenever needed. All respondents mentioned the health benefits related to milk consumption that they observed in themselves and their children. However, all respondents, male and female, believed that larger quantities of milk produced by their goats would have had a significantly higher impact on food security, and asked that the project provide more dairy goats, and in some cases, cows.

Division of labour

The KAP and the semi-structured interviews conducted in the project villages showed that the introduction of dairy goats had changed the division of labour. Dairy goats are kept in sheds in the farm courtyard with the zero grazing system, where grass is mechanically mown and brought to the livestock. Generally, the men (and sometimes boys) take the household livestock into the savannah for grazing during the day, so the dairy goats are managed mostly by the women, with help from the children, who look for fodder after school. Women are generally in charge of milking the goats, selling the milk, and using the milk for household nutrition. Other tasks, such as cleaning the sheds and fetching fodder, are shared among women, men, boys, and girls. In Wami Luhindo, women are in charge of looking after sick animals, while in the other three villages this is a men's task. In two households, however, all the tasks related to goats were said to be shared between women and men, depending on the availability of other job options.

Eighteen women respondents whose goats had kidded and were producing milk, particularly the female heads of household, mentioned that the additional work with the goats was a positive new task, because the benefits of accessing milk were more important than the extra work. While the increased burden on women's workload is often considered a potential negative outcome of the introduction of new technologies, particularly when dissemination processes are gender-blind, this case shows that the women welcomed the increased workload, as it was paralleled by their increased control of milk and its distribution in the household.

Generally, when asked how the introduction of dairy goats had changed the household labour, the men asserted that the overall household workload had increased, and acknowledged the extra burden on women (and to some extent on children) only when explicitly asked about changes in intra-household labour allocation with a gender focus. Gender analysis was important, therefore, to reveal how a newly introduced technology impacted the workload of men, women, and children differently.

Gender analysis also helped reveal more complex intra-household arrangements than declared in initial answers. When asked about the impact of the project on farm management, most women and men stated that they consulted with family members on all goat-related tasks and decisions. Some qualified their statements by adding that the project made them aware of the importance of working together. For instance, the eight male respondents from Wami Luhindo indicated that because of the project they now realised the importance of joint planning for the households. The 13 female respondents from Masinyeti indicated that the project had helped them understand their position and improve it with regard to ownership, labour, and decision-making. Only through more in-depth discussions – with a focus on women's and men's daily tasks – was a clear gender-based division of labour, in some cases characterised by flexible arrangements, revealed.

This discrepancy between the collaboration patterns reported and the more nuanced collaborative arrangements undertaken in practice raises the issue of whether the project participants adopted the project's *language* of "gender equity" shared during the gender trainings and project activities, rather than adopting gender-equal *attitudes and behaviours*. In other words, was the project's gender equity language effective in creating new spaces to conceive and engage in roles across gender barriers or even in questioning gender norms, or did it simply standardise the language of project participants and censor the mentioning of "unequal behaviours" because participants understood that the project viewed these as "wrong"?

Decision-making

Decision-making about revenues rests primarily with the men, according to most male respondents and 18 women respondents (five from Wami Luhindo and 13 from Masinyeti). Two men and 13 women from Masinyeti added that the project's gender training helped their family members recognise their own and other members' contribution to the farm work, and that as a consequence, both the work and decision-making were shared more equally. The men interviewed in Masinyeti reported that while participating in the project, they started to share information with their womenfolk so that the latter could take care of the goats when the men were away. This was not needed with local breeds that are grazed by men and boys only. In the words of a middle-aged woman from Masinyeti:

> Before the project, men wanted to take decisions alone, while now they understood they need to consult with us women – and they do.
> (Interview, Masinyeti, 17 January 2014)

Seven women in Kongwa and 13 from Masinyeti maintained that because of limited quantities, they had not yet sold the milk or crops, but thought that at the moment of sale their menfolk would take over the management of the revenues. Ten women and ten men (six women and two men from Ihanda, and four women and eight men from Kunke) felt their contribution to household decision-making had increased.

The findings indicate that the training was perceived as helping to increase sharing of decision-making, but were insufficient to achieve gender-equitable patterns. Moreover, when asked to specify why the work and decision-making relative to the dairy goats were (according to many) shared more equally than in the past, both the female and male respondents reported that the main reason was the co-ownership of the goats. Most men stated that they had no issue with women's ownership of livestock; however, they seemed uncomfortable about handing over decision-making power to women. Both women and men respondents stated that co-ownership of the goats was the only way to ensure that men and women felt equally responsible for the management of the goats. Ownership by one family member only would likely disengage the other member from any work associated with the goats and their produce.

The mentioned changes in decision-making, information exchange, and work-sharing behaviours, apparently motivated by changes in awareness of each other's roles or of the benefits of collaboration and co-ownership, show the potential for change in gender norms. The statements of the respondent women from Kongwa, however, and the fact that the men did not recognise a change in decision-making, show only partial acceptance of gender equity: that is, gender equity in decision-making and willingness to publicly report shared decision-making have not changed much.

This raises the issue of whether the project's gender equity approach, transmitted to the participants through training and other project activities, provided a sufficient opening towards new gender norms and behaviour patterns. Would an explicit focus on the mutual benefits of gender equity in decision-making lead to more equitable sharing of decision-making in practice, and a willingness to admit to this sharing behaviour? Alternatively, this evidence can reveal that the gender equity approach provided a space for change only as long as symbols of masculinity or men's power – in such areas as decision-making – were not undermined. In other words, does the limited increase in decision-making, independence, and ability to own indicate a positive space of opening for gender transformation, resistance to gender change, or both, as gender transformative change will not be linear? In any event, the findings show the importance of gender analysis in assessing how gender relations shape household livelihood activities and strategies, in order for projects to respond adequately.

Some respondents associated gender equity in decision-making to age. Five women from Wami Luhindo indicated that among older couples, men always make the final decision; similarly, seven women and two men from Ihanda thought that older generations have the idea that men have the decision-making role. When asked whether the concern voiced by a female participant at the beginning of the project – namely, that men would not accept women's owning livestock and might turn violent if the women did own goats through the project – was realised, most women maintained that no such episodes had occurred. Some mentioned that such male behaviours might occur among older couples, because younger generations aspire to a more modern lifestyle that includes more equal gender relations. This evidence provides an interesting entry point for a better understanding of intergenerational change and how it can be leveraged to enhance more gender-equal norms among youth.

Independence

Female and male respondents whose goats had kidded and who had milk available noted that the dairy goats increased their independence, because they could sell milk (one litre a day or less) and use the revenues to buy small necessities (such as school notebooks, salt, charcoal, cooking oil, etc.) and/ or drink the milk in the house. Previously, they needed to borrow money from family members or shopkeepers to purchase milk and other basic products. This increased independence for family members or partners seemed particularly valued by the women, as illustrated by a woman from Masinyeti:

> I am not selling the goat milk, because I use it to feed my family. Previously I had to borrow milk from neighbours or borrow money to buy milk. Now I do not need to; I have milk. This makes me feel more independent from the relatives I needed to rely on.
>
> (Interview, Masinyeti, 17 January 2014)

A second woman from Masinyeti added:

> We are happy now that we have the goats. Previously, women in this village were sleeping and depending on the men; now women are waking up!
>
> (Interview, Masinyeti, 17 January 2014)

A woman from the Ihanda village said:

> Before, I was borrowing money from my partner, but now I get the money from the sale of milk and I also have more power to decide how to use the revenues.
>
> (Interview, Ihanda, 17 January 2014)

The male respondents from Masinyeti reported that the income generated through the sale of goat milk had increased both their wives' and their own independence: wives did not need to ask their husbands for money to buy food, and the men could spend their money more freely. Other men might have shared the women's feelings about increased independence, but seemed less willing to talk about it, perhaps because admitting that they had previously relied on credit could call into question their general ability to provide for the family. The implications of men's increased access to milk on their independence and food security vis-à-vis their role as food providers merits further research.

These findings show that access to milk and its revenues can provide an opening to shift traditional gender norms that cast men as primary food providers towards a joint responsibility model that is a closer match to existing practices. They also show that, as indicated by the quotes above, the agency and self-awareness of women was enhanced by access to milk and its associated income. At the same time, the findings raise the question of whether the increased independence of women is a strategic move towards their economic empowerment, or rather imposes on them a further burden and responsibility as food providers while also disenfranchising men. A participatory development of an empowerment pathway might reveal whether or not the respondents perceive these changes to be in line with their ultimate self-development goals.

Discussion

Ownership of resources, decision-making power, and independence are often considered key elements of empowerment. So are improved sense of self-worth, willingness and ability to question one's subordinate status, and capacity to negotiate relationships. These outcomes are expressed in some of the women's statements above. The CGP was therefore able to positively improve some of the key domains of empowerment. These changes, however, were limited in scope and possibly restricted to the less destabilising components in the gender power structures (not, for instance, decision-making or public recognition of women's role as food providers). They might in time lead to deeper, more enduring changes in these structures, if, this chapter argues, a clear pathway to these outcomes were formulated to guide action.

The findings also show that training on gender equity and gender equity-enhancing activities was successful in supporting these positive changes. The findings also raise concern, however, about the extent and depth of these changes, which in some cases seemed more about "adopting the equity language" than actually changing perceptions of women and men's appropriate roles and spaces. The project's use of gender analysis in design, implementation, and evaluation was helpful in understanding the complexity of household gender relations and labour organisation and how they shape household strategies and power dynamics, and in appreciating the differential impact of the project on household members. Yet, the limited extent of the impacts, and their potentially short-term nature, raises the question, "How can gender analysis better contribute to design of GTAs that include the framing of bottom-up approaches to fostering empowerment?"

If empowerment is first of all an individual process of change in self-perception of worth and identity, involving increased capability to identify constraints and ways to act upon them, then the project's impact on local understandings of gender equity – defined by most farmers as undertaking all dairy-related chores together – seems to speak of "sameness" rather than enabling expanded choices and opportunities for women and men based on their diverse needs, opportunities, and preferences. This in turn raises the question of whether the project needed to increase its emphasis on these aspects of gender equity in its conceptualisation, or whether these outcomes resulted from the lack of an "operationalisation pathway" that could more systematically guide the implementation of activities to enhance empowerment and changes in gender norms.

This study found measuring the CGP's progress on empowerment difficult because of the lack of a firm definition of empowerment in the project, and the absence of indicators to assess related changes. Identifying indicators of change along the pathway, across scales and actors, could help track progress towards gender transformative and empowerment goals. However, this chapter recommends that projects include, from the outset, an approach to understand and engage with local conceptualisations of empowerment, and identify appropriate indicators through this process, rather than apply a prescribed definition of the concept and set of indicators. Such a participatory approach can help assess pragmatically whether identified changes in women's independence and their role as food providers represent strategic progress towards empowerment and gender equity in absolute terms, or whether such progress is relative to a personal understanding of these concepts. Engaging with local and participatory conceptualisations of empowerment also helps address ethical concerns about empowerment.

Gender researchers investigating gender equity and empowerment as means to address unequal power relations cannot limit their scope of analysis to the relations between women and men within households and communities without also questioning the power relations between respondents and researchers. Adopting an external definition of empowerment and using pre-identified indicators runs the risk of imposing a new hierarchy of gender norms. In other words, who decides what are desirable gender relations, and is a non-participatory approach to empowerment intrinsically disempowering? It is in its approach to these fundamental questions that this chapter differs substantially from the epistemology of the WEAI methodology. The next section proposes an approach for a participatory conceptualisation of empowerment as a means of operationalising GTAs and fostering enduring change in gender relations from the bottom up.

The findings show that the project provided a space for gender roles or their public recognition to change (e.g., roles as food providers or decision-makers). They also show the potential for change in intergenerational gaps: younger respondents identified gender inequity in decision-making as belonging to the past. However, some of the changes that took place at the individual level were mentioned in parallel to normative statements depicting men as food providers, and women decision-makers as not worth marrying. This raises the question, "What is the potential for larger-scale impact of approaches to individual empowerment on gender relations when project participants return to daily routines that are infused with patriarchal gender norms?" The next section suggests an approach to extend individual empowerment and changes in gender norms to a wider societal level, and to youth in particular.

Finally, the findings show the key role of new technologies (such as new varieties) and resources (such as dairy goats) in providing opportunities for the abovementioned changes in social and gender relations to take place. Because the goats had to be kept in the household yard, a space frequented mostly by women and children, new goat-related labour and management arrangements had to be defined that also provided a space to change wider gender roles in the household. This highlights how the impact of new technologies, far from being purely technical, inevitably affects social relations. However, the goats that had not produced milk and the crops that were not successfully cultivated did not seem to provide transformative opportunities, but only a change in the distribution of labour. This raises several questions:

1   Do appropriate and effective technologies on their own provide opportunities for social change, or does the way technologies are distributed also affect social outcomes?
2   What technologies does AR4D need to focus on (specifically, technologies that directly address the most marginal groups or women – such as dairy goats that need to be kept in the courtyard and are therefore likely to

involve women – or target households as a whole), given the desirability of mixing technological and social advancements for a sustainable development process (Friis-Hansen and Duveskog 2012)?

3   How can purposeful plans for transformative approaches to technology design and delivery encourage questioning of the status quo?

A methodology to operationalise GTA: empowerment pathways

The participatory approach to conceptualising empowerment, defining empowerment pathways, and identifying related indicators is based on the idea that challenging unequal gender relations rests on local ownership of the change process, a process that needs to involve women as well as the actors engaged in or affected by the empowerment process. In a value chain context, this means inclusion of actors along the whole chain, as well as those with a role in creating and maintaining unequal gender relations in the related spheres of the family and state. The participatory empowerment pathway approach proposed by this chapter aims to achieve ownership across this range of stakeholders through applying critical participatory action research (PAR) to engage the actors in defining empowerment; identifying the opportunities and threats associated with progressing towards individual empowerment goals; diagnosing how both technical (e.g., lack of credit) and social (e.g., limited physical mobility) constraints affect value chain functioning and outcomes; identifying ways to overcome both sources of constraints; defining key indicators to monitor progress towards set goals; learning from the outcomes of the actions; and applying this learning to future actions. This process aims to foster questioning of the assumptions and practices underlying gender inequality, as part of a process of challenging gender-based power imbalances and developing people's aspirations for self-determination beyond existing gender roles. Participatory monitoring of progress in the selected indicators towards the identified goals will help adjust project activities, and provide insights on the unfolding of empowerment processes from the perspectives of different actors involved (see Box 8.1).

The adoption of such a participatory approach that engages in in-depth and time-consuming discussions with value chain actors is likely to be feasible with a small number (small-N) of respondents only. The resulting findings can provide an understanding of what factors the respondents consider important for their self-determination, and what they consider to affect their empowerment; shed light on the complexity and possible unfolding of empowerment processes; provide novel understandings of empowerment and its local dimensions; and help refine locally relevant methodologies to assess and appreciate processes of empowerment. These understandings can inform new strategies for participatory empowerment pathways in broadly similar contexts. Moreover, the findings can engage respondents in processes of self-exploration and questioning of gender roles that are arguably the first step towards empowerment. Finally, small-N research helps establish causal

---

Box 8.1   The experience of participatory empowerment pathways in Syria

Participatory empowerment pathways were undertaken in the context of a participatory plant breeding program in Syria to assess the impact of participating in the program on the empowerment of newly involved women farmers. The research started by engaging 12 women respondents from four villages in defining their vision of self-determination and related goals by asking the question, "What would allow you to make your life what you wish it to be like?" Based on the resulting visions and on intensive dialogue to assess the constraints women faced in achieving their self-determination goals, four indicators of empowerment were identified: recognition of women as farmers; access to and control of productive resources, particularly seed and information; access to opportunities; and intra-household decision-making. Participatory exercises, participant observation, semi-structured interviews, and individual and group discussions, performed repeatedly in three stages over four years (2007–10), were used to monitor and assess ongoing changes in identified indicators of empowerment that focussed on change as a process (rather than an outcome) (Galiè 2013, 2014).

---

links – between, for example, project interventions and changes in the participants' households – by exploring what processes result in a specific outcome in a particular context (Donmoyer 2012; Bennett and Elman 2006). In the case of this study, the approach would have helped elicit how the CGP intervention contributed to changes in the process of empowerment and provide recommendations for the CGP scale-out phase.

The process of articulating empowerment pathways is expected to enhance individuals' capabilities to define their needs, voice them, and act to satisfy them; it is part of the empowerment process itself. However, enhanced individual capabilities can be undermined when interactions take place in social contexts with rigid gender norms. For example, the risk of punitive sanctions, such as ostracism or marginalisation by communities of individuals who transgress gender norms (Galiè 2013), needs to be mitigated through efforts to shift norms at the community level. Therefore, GTAs that seek to foster a more enabling social environment are needed to provide the context in which individual empowerment processes can be realised and sustained. Part of the empowerment process may involve women working individually and collectively to foster gender transformative change, as part of engaging with existing structures of constraint that limit individual choices and outcomes. So the two processes are intertwined.

Groups are one means of building on individual empowerment pathways to effect wider social change. When organised and mobilised with social as well as instrumental ends (e.g., technology or credit delivery), they can be an important source of solidarity or power, through which women and men can act on existing structures of constraint. They provide a "critical mass" that enables actions that individuals may not take alone.

Multi-stakeholder dialogue processes that seek to identify the consequences of gender-based constraints for different value chain actors, and to relate them to incentives for gender transformative change across these actors, are another way forward. These dialogues and change processes can be informed and/or sparked by media projects for social change. Such projects can catalyse questioning of gender norms at the community level, and drive movement towards less strict normative frameworks that can create new spaces for the adoption of more gender-equitable behaviours.

Being clear about what these actors, particularly those from the market and state, stand to gain from the change process is key to motivating their engagement. For example, for private-sector value chain actors, revenues and reputation may be important incentives. Part of the role of gender analysis in the design of gender transformative programs is to develop an understanding of different actors' incentives to participate in the change process.

Conclusion

This chapter analysed the impact of the CGP on household gender relations, as reported by the participating livestock keepers and agriculturalists and in the framework of food security. It scrutinised changes effected by the introduction of dairy goats on the division of labour, decision-making, and independence. The findings showed that the introduction of the goats increased the workload of women and children, had positive impacts on the independence and perceived food security of both women and men, and increased women's decision-making authority. However, these changes were limited in depth and scope, and did not seem to question or challenge normative perceptions of gender-based roles. While highlighting the importance of gender analysis in project implementation and learning, the authors discussed some of the challenges involved in enhancing empowerment and operationalising transformative approaches.

The balance of the chapter presented a framework that responds to some if not all of the identified challenges around operationalising GTAs. It made a case for a participatory and transformative approach to gender analysis and integration rooted in empowerment, that builds empowerment pathways from the ground up while simultaneously working to influence the social environment in which movement along those pathways can be realised. This new methodology contributes to the discussion on how to practically move GTAs into practice in the agricultural sector. What is needed now is applied research to document lessons on how to implement the empowerment pathway approach in different contexts, and on how the resulting process of gender transformative change unfolds.

Note

References

Alkire, Sabina, Ruth Meinzen-Dick, Amber Peterman, Agnes Quisumbing, Greg Seymour, and Ana Vaz. 2013. "The Women's Empowerment in Agriculture Index." *World Development* 52: 71–91. doi:10.1016/j.worlddev.2013.06.007.

Almekinders, Conny, and Jaap Hardon, eds. 2006. *Bringing Farmers Back into Breeding: Experiences with Participatory Plant Breeding.* Wageningen, The Netherlands: Agromisa Foundation.

Bennett, Andrew, and Colin Elman. 2006. "Qualitative Research: Recent Developments in Case Study Methods." *Annual Review of Political Science* 9 (1): 455–76. doi:10.1146/annurev.polisci.8.082103.104918.

Brandes, Raymond, Petra Saghir, Alessandra Galiè, and Violet Barasa. 2014. *ILRI's Experience with the Crop and Goat Project in Tanzania from a Gender Perspective.* ILRI Discussion Paper 30. Nairobi, Kenya: International Livestock Research Institute (ILRI).

Chant, Sylvia, and Caroline Sweetman. 2012. "Fixing Women or Fixing the World? 'Smart Economics', Efficiency Approaches, and Gender Equality in Development." *Gender & Development* 20 (3): 517–29. doi:10.1080/13552074.2012.731812.

Charrad, Mounira M. 2007. "Contexts, Concepts and Contentions: Gender Legislation as Politics in the Middle East." *Hawwa* 5 (1): 55–72. doi:10.1163/156920807781787635.

Cornwall, Andrea, and Nana Akua Anyidoho. 2010. "Introduction: Women's Empowerment: Contentions and Contestations." *Development* 53 (2): 144–9. doi:10.1057/dev.2010.34.

Cornwall, Andrea, and Jenny Edwards. 2010. "Introduction: Negotiating Empowerment." *IDS Bulletin* 42 (2): 1–9. doi:10.1111/j.1759-5436.2010.00117.x

Donmoyer, Robert. 2012. "Attributing Causality in Qualitative Research: Viable Option or Inappropriate Aspiration? An Introduction to a Collection of Papers." *Qualitative Inquiry* 18 (8): 651–4. doi:10.1177/1077800412455012.

Flyvbjerg, Bent. 2006. "Five Misunderstandings about Case-Study Research." *Qualitative Inquiry* 12 (2): 219–45. doi:10.1177/1077800405284363.

Friis-Hansen, Esbern, and Deborah Duveskog. 2012. "The Empowerment Route to Well-Being: An Analysis of Farmer Field Schools in East Africa." *World Development* 40 (2): 414–27. doi:10.1016/j.worlddev.2011.05.005.

Galiè, Alessandra. 2013. "Empowering Women Farmers: The Case of Participatory Plant Breeding in Ten Syrian Households." *Frontiers: A Journal of Women Studies* 34 (1): 58–92. doi:10.5250/fronjwomestud.34.1.0058.

Galiè, Alessandra. 2014. "Syrian Women Farmers: Seeking Gender Balance in Participatory Plant Breeding." In Sharon Brisolara, Denise Seigart, and Saumitra SenGupta, eds, *Feminist Evaluation and Research: Theory and Practice.* New York: Guilford, 284–310.

Galiè, Alessandra, Annet Mulema, Maria A. Mora Benard, Sheila N. Onzere, and Kathleen E. Colverson. 2015. "Exploring Gender Perceptions of Resource

Ownership and their Implications for Food Security among Rural Livestock Owners in Tanzania, Ethiopia, and Nicaragua." *Agriculture & Food Security* 4 (1): 1.

Giddens, Anthony. 1976. *New Rules of Sociological Method: A Positive Critique of Interpretative Sociologies.* London: Routledge.

Kabeer, Naila. 1994. *Reversed Realities.* London: Verso.

Kabeer, Naila. 1999. "Resources, Agency, Achievements: Reflections on the Measurement of Women's Empowerment." *Development and Change,* 30 (3): 435–64. doi:10.1111/1467-7660.00125.

Kabeer, Naila. 2008. *Paid Work, Women's Empowerment and Gender Justice: Critical Pathways of Social Change.* Pathways Working Paper 3. Sussex: Pathways of Women's Empowerment, Institute of Development Studies (IDS).

Kabeer, Naila. 2010. "Women's Empowerment, Development Interventions and the Management of Information Flows." *IDS Bulletin* 41 (6): 105–13. doi:10.1111/j.1759-5436.2010.00188.x.

Kabeer, Naila. 2012. *Women's Economic Empowerment and Inclusive Growth: Labour Markets and Enterprise Development.* SIG Working Paper 2012/1. London: Department for International Development (DFID) and Ottawa: International Development Research Centre (IDRC).

Kantor, Paula. 2013. *Transforming Gender Relations: Key to Positive Development Outcomes in Aquatic Agricultural Systems.* Brief AAS-2013–12. Penang, Malaysia: CGIAR Research Program on Aquatic Agricultural Systems.

Mahoney, James, and Gary Goertz. 2006. "A Tale of Two Cultures: Contrasting Quantitative and Qualitative Research." *Political Analysis* 14 (3): 227–49. doi:10.1093/pan/mpj017.

Meena, Pamela, Joyce Lyimo-Macha, and Cornelio N.M. Nyaruhucha. 2013. *Nutritional Status of Under Five Years Old Children in Selected Villages of Mvomero and Kongwa Districts, Tanzania.* Morogoro, Tanzania: Sokoine University of Agriculture.

Mosha-Kilave, Devotha, and Joyce Lyimo-Macha. 2013. "Gender Relations in Root Crops Production and Dairy Goats Farming in Kongwa and Mvomero Districts, Tanzania." Manuscript submitted to the *Journal of Continuing Education and Extension.*

Njuki, Jemimah, and Petra Saghir. 2012. *Gender Strategy of the Integrated Crop and Goats Project, Tanzania.* Nairobi, Kenya: International Livestock Research Institute (ILRI).

Okali, Christine. 2011a. *Searching for New Pathways towards Achieving Gender Equity: Beyond Boserup and Women's Role in Economic Development.* ESA Working Paper No. 11–09. Rome: Food and Agriculture Organization of the United Nations (FAO).

Okali, Christine. 2011b. *Achieving Transformative Change for Rural Women's Empowerment.* Expert paper prepared for the Expert Group Meeting "Enabling Rural Women's Economic Empowerment: Institutions, Opportunities and Participation" (Accra, Ghana, 20–23 September). UN Women in cooperation with Food and Agriculture Organization of the United Nations (FAO), International Fund for Agricultural Development (IFAD), and World Food Programme (WFP).

Okali, Christine. 2012. *Gender Analysis: Engaging with Rural Development and Agricultural Policy Processes.* FAC Working Paper 26. Brighton, UK: Future Agricultures Consortium (FAC).

Parkins, John, and Fausting Lekule. 2012. *Annual Progress Report to IDRC – Tanzania, March 2011–September 2012* [project report]. Ottawa, Canada: International Development Research Centre (IDRC).

Peterson, V. Spike. 2005. "How (the Meaning of) Gender Matters in Political Economy." *New Political Economy* 10 (4): 499–521. doi:10.1080/13563460500344468.

Razavi, Shahra. 2009. "Engendering the Political Economy of Agrarian Change." *Journal of Peasant Studies* 36 (1): 197–226. doi:10.1080/03066150902820412.

Risman, Barbara J. 2004. "Gender as a Social Structure: Theory Wrestling with Activism." *Gender & Society* 18 (4): 429–50. doi:10.1177/0891243204265349.

Rowlands, Jo. 1997. *Questioning Empowerment: Working with Women in Honduras.* Oxford: Oxfam.

Saghir, Petra, Jemimah Njuki, Elizabeth Waithanji, Juliet Kariuki, and Anna Sikira. 2012. *Integrating Improved Goat Breeds with New Varieties of Sweetpotatoes and Cassava in the Agro-Pastoral Systems of Tanzania: A Gendered Analysis.* ILRI Discussion Paper 21. Nairobi, Kenya: International Livestock Research Institute (ILRI).

Sen, Amartya K. 1990. "Development as Capability Expansion." In Keith B. Griffin and John B. Knight, eds, *Human Development and the International Development Strategy for the 1990s.* London: Macmillan, 41–58.

Song, Yiching, and Ronnie Vernooy. 2010. "Seeds of Empowerment: Action Research in the Context of the Feminization of Agriculture in Southwest China." *Gender Technology and Development* 14 (1): 25–44. doi:10.1177/097185241001400 102.

Tsikata, Dzodzi, and Akosua Darkwah. 2014. "Researching Empowerment: On Methodological Innovations, Pitfalls and Challenges." *Women's Studies International Forum* 45: 81–9.

Young, Kate. 1993. *Planning Development with Women: Making a World of Difference.* London: Macmillan.

9 Gender transformative approaches with socially and environmentally vulnerable groups

Indigenous fishers of the Bolivian Amazon

Alison E. Macnaughton, Tiffanie K. Rainville, Claudia I. Coca Méndez, Elaine M. Ward, John M. Wojciechowski, and Joachim Carolsfeld

Introduction

Small-scale fisheries are a critical source of subsistence and livelihoods for many vulnerable people in the world (see, e.g., Charles 2011). These fisheries remain understudied, with research to date showing significant data gaps (e.g., data disaggregated by sex, age group, ethnicity, etc.), making subsequent gender and diversity analyses difficult. Past regional and global level studies regarding gender and fisheries have focussed on the high rates of female participation in pre- and post-harvest activities, and a variety of associated issues (lack of professional identity, lower pay, unsafe working conditions, health risks, exploitation, etc.). However, few studies present information for both males and females regarding aspects such as decision-making and distribution of returns among the production, pre-harvest, and post-harvest spheres, that would support more complete comparative analysis of the relations and differences between actors (Weeratunge et al. 2010). Additionally, the broader historic, sociocultural, and ecological context should be considered in order to understand and address current situations of inequality, especially with respect to gender. In fisheries, this is a critical and often overlooked element, as highlighted by a variety of authors (WorldFish Center 2010; FAO 2012; Williams et al. 2012). These are essential elements to developing pathways for improved livelihoods, social equality, and environmental resilience in small-scale fisheries.

This chapter presents a case study of a gender transformative approach (GTA) developed and implemented to investigate and address social and gender inequality in rural Indigenous fishing communities in Bolivia through the *Peces para la vida* (PPV) project ("Fish for Life").[1] PPV examined how to optimise fisheries' contributions to food security and livelihoods in the northern Bolivian Amazon, with special attention to the roles of women and Indigenous families within fisheries value chains.[2]

Fish are a cornerstone of food security for thousands of rural families, who make use of high fish diversity for subsistence and small-scale commercial activities within the context of mixed agrarian or extractive livelihoods. Despite remarkable biodiversity, poverty and food insecurity are significant in this region, and the interplay between historical, cultural, and environmental stressors is significant. Indigenous families engaged in subsistence and commercial fishing are among the most vulnerable and marginalised groups in this region. Regionally, female participation in this already under-recognised sector is typically underrepresented and undervalued (Ríos Pool 2014). This chapter describes the implementation of a transformative approach that helped to improve the researchers' understandings of gender inequality in the area, and contributed to the improved well-being of female and male fishers.

Following some initial baseline data collection on fisheries, food security, climate vulnerabilities, and community histories, the authors developed and implemented an integrated participatory value chain analysis and development strategy (Wojciechowski and Coca Méndez 2014), based on action research, from Thiollent (1996) and others, structured as knowledge dialogue sessions – *diálogo de saberes* (Balbin 1986). The strategy included workshops, community meetings, and hands-on activities carried out with a pilot group of three Indigenous communities to address project objectives for improved food security, livelihoods, and gender equality. Women and men were engaged together, to identify social and technical bottlenecks in the fisheries value chains, and to plan and implement improvements.

Overall, the diverse inequalities experienced by rural Indigenous fishers in the study region, including historical, social, and ethnocultural aspects, are best described by considering intersectionality (Cho et al. 2013) as an approach to gender analysis. The historic and environmental stressors and continuing uncertainty regarding the material situation of the communities present significant barriers to improvements to well-being and social equality. In this context, with the value chain strategy as an overarching research and intervention framework, the most significant gender equality contributions are considered to be the small, incremental shifts towards a more holistic and integrated understanding of local needs. This coincides with Kantor's (2013) recommended rigorous social analysis and practice to build an appropriate enabling framework for social transformation and outcomes.

The *diálogo de saberes* interventions improved transparency and awareness about the distribution of activities, responsibilities, and benefits among different actors in the regional fisheries value chain. They provided a fresh space for dialogue regarding local food security strategies and behaviours (including sharing reproductive roles) and their links to livelihoods, and seasonal variation and vulnerabilities. The process supported capacity development for leadership and positive social capital within local groups, and contributed to empowerment of females and males. Finally, it provided unique opportunities to test the application of novel, locally informed, and low-cost technology to improve returns to fishing (improved gear, better handling, and more informed price negotiations) and food security (better knowledge and practices for nutrition and dietary diversity using locally available ingredients, and improved hygiene).

Integrating empowerment and intersectionality in transformative approaches

Over 20 years ago, Moser (1993) proposed that the oppression of women is not limited to subordination relative to men, but can also be more broadly associated with the oppressive exploitation of different societies at a variety of levels that is typical of colonial invasions. Today's Latin American societies, in particular, often reflect this history. Despite a somewhat limited focus on labour force participation (women and men in productive and reproductive roles), Moser's ideas have a very significant contribution to play. Notably, Moser states that "power" in an empowerment approach should be less specifically associated with increasing women's domination or control over people or resources (and associated loss of control by men), and instead more strongly rooted in improving the capacity for self-determination, "self-reliance and internal strength" (1993: 74). Similarly, Kabeer (1999) defined women's empowerment as the acquisition, by people who had previously been denied, of an ability to make strategic life choices, involving interrelated and inseparable dimensions of resources, agency, and the achievement of well-being. Since that time, the conceptualisation and measurement of empowerment in gender research and development interventions have continued to advance and become more nuanced.[3] However, in practice case study research demonstrating methods and pathways for change that supports the empowerment of women or socially marginalised groups continues to be limited, and fisheries is no exception.

Marginalisation in small-scale fisheries often combines a variety of environmental vulnerabilities and ethnocultural, generational, gender, and class influences, or intersectionality (Cho et al. 2013). Intersectionality theory has emerged as an attempt for gender analysis to move beyond a limited examination of labour participation inequalities, stemming from a traditional feminist perspective and conceptualised as "patriarchy" or the "monolithic oppression of females" (Patil 2013). It incorporates examining the broader social and environmental context of vulnerability, poverty, inequality, participation, empowerment, and well-being affecting all people in a given context, and situating male and female relations within this.

Specific to fisheries and gender, Weeratunge et al. (2010) point to integrative and holistic approaches, such as livelihoods and well-being approaches, in order to advance from the limited focus on demonstrating that "women *do* fish" and associated inequalities in labour force participation.

The authors progress to achieving a broader understanding of the social and environmental contexts affecting both men and women, and their experiences in fishing and related activities. They suggest reframing gender analysis in fisheries to examine a range of factors affecting opportunities, participation, and returns, including markets and migration, capabilities and well-being, networks and identities, and governance and rights. Kantor (2013) also argues that the gender gap in agriculture and aquatic resources is still wide, with programs focussing on improving female participation and access to new technology, thus treating only symptoms of inequality, and failing to recognise or adequately address underlying social constraints. She calls instead for "a more political and transformative approach to integrating gender" (Kantor 2013: 2) and an investment in rigorous social analysis.

The present case study represents an effort to do so, with a focus first on understanding the sociohistorical, environmental, and other dynamics that contribute to differential participation and returns within the fisheries value chain, and on moving forward with an agenda of transformation in livelihoods and well-being of rural Indigenous communities. The authors worked with women and men of different ages and ethnic groups, examining identities, perceptions of vulnerabilities and capacities, livelihoods, and associated social interactions in the fisheries value chain. In the analysis and ensuing interventions, the historical power dynamics associated with extractive industries in the region, and the vulnerability associated with the ongoing and increasingly frequent environmental stressors (mostly flooding) emerged as important contextual elements. In addition, it became clear that gender-based domestic violence was pervasive, contributing to disempowerment along with the traditional *habilito* system[4] and lack of transparency in the fisheries value chain.

The study's practical focus was to improve the situation of women (and men) who are disempowered by a lack of transparency, and the historic *habilito* relationship. Overall, it was found that Kantor's (2013) GTA (Figure 9.1) represents the analysis and intervention strategy very well, where a multi-dimensional social analysis and associated participatory multi-scale planning were applied. An example is given of how a GTA applied in practice allowed the authors to understand the complex context, and how accompanying technical interventions helped develop an enabling framework towards lasting, positive change in social relations and livelihoods (Figure 9.2).

Methodology

Study region and pilot communities

The northern Bolivian Amazon is a sparsely populated lowland rainforest and savannah region, covered by extensive floodplain areas, meandering rivers, and oxbow lakes, subject to seasonal (and occasional extreme) flooding. Historically, it was one of the world's principal regions for rubber extraction,

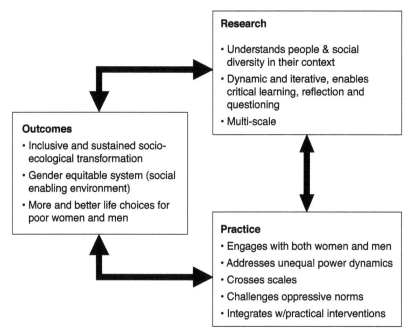

Figure 9.1 Framework of gender transformative approach

Source: Kantor (2013).

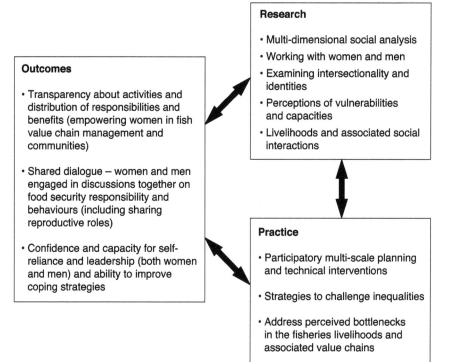

Figure 9.2 *Peces para la vida* integrated gender lens – a gender transformative approach

with enormous tracts of privately controlled lands and an extensive system of forced labour and indentured servitude among Indigenous and other groups recruited to rubber-tapping *haciendas* (estates) in the 19th and early 20th centuries (Garland and Silva-Santiesteban 2004). Since the 1950s, as the rubber industry in the region began to decline, wild harvesting of *castaña* (Brazil nut, *Bertholletia excelsa*) grew in importance, following a similar pattern of concentration of access and exploitation of labour (Cardona 2012). While *castaña* continues to be the main economic driver for the region,[5] land reforms in the 1990s broke up these large holdings with a system of *Tierras Comunitarias de Origen* (TCOs) (Original Indigenous Territories) created in the early 2000s. TCOs provide significant communal tenure and resource access rights to dispersed Indigenous communities. TCO communities in the Amazon region pursue mixed livelihoods, including small-scale agriculture and *castaña* extraction (Alcides Vadillo and Miranda 2012) and more recently, commercial fishing, including significant fisheries for the introduced *paiche* fish (Van Damme et al. 2011; Argote Soliz et al. 2014; Macnaughton et al. 2015).[6]

El Sur ("The South") is a group of three small Tacana Indigenous communities (Flor de Octubre, Lago El Carmen, and 27 de Mayo) located about three hours from the regional urban centre Riberalta, near the Beni River and several recently formed floodplain lakes, in the Municipality of Riberalta, Vaca Diez Province, Department of Beni. They are among the 34 Indigenous communities (including Tacana, Ese Eja, and Cavineño groups)[7] in the TCO known as *Territorio Indígena Multiétnico* II (TCO TIM II) (Multiethnic Indigenous Territory) and are located in the southern portion of this reserve. They were selected as pilot study communities because of their participation in commercial fisheries (based primarily on native species) and local interest in project interventions (supported by the TCO TIM II government and two regional Indigenous organisations, *Central Indígena de la Región Norte Amazónica de Bolivia* (CIRABO) (Indigenous Centre of the Northern Amazon Region of Bolivia) and *Central Indígena de los Pueblos Originarios Amazónicos de Pando* (CIPOAP) (Indigenous Centre of the Original Amazon Peoples of Pando)). While a small portion of the information presented in this chapter refers more broadly to female and Indigenous participation in fisheries in the TCO TIM II and Riberalta (results from the household survey and from the regional workshop *Mujeres y Peces*, or "Women and Fish"), most of the information presented is specific to the research and interventions implemented with females and males in the *El Sur* communities.

Baseline surveys, interviews, and focus groups

The intervention strategy was informed by a significant amount of baseline information collected in the first two years of the project, with gender and diversity data, comprising a household survey of food security ($N = 811$), carried out for high-water and low-water seasons for four urban strata in

Riberalta and 15 rural communities with varying livelihoods and degrees of access to the fish resources (Baker-French 2013); a regional workshop to map fisheries value chain dynamics and bottlenecks from different local actors perspectives (Coca Méndez et al. 2012); and a regional forum, *Mujeres y Peces* carried out in April 2013, including focus group and individual activities regarding fisheries livelihoods and female participation (Soto et al. 2013). Detailed information on female and male participation in reproductive and productive roles related to fishing livelihoods was also collected between 2011 and 2012 in semi-structured interviews, focus groups, and workshops (Ríos Pool 2014).

Integrated participatory value chain analysis strategy with diálogo de saberes

Within an overall social intervention strategy based on integrated participatory value chain analysis (Wojciechowski and Coca Méndez 2014), the study implemented a series of community workshop dialogues, including methods from *diálogo de saberes*. This technique shares many characteristics with experiential and practice-based approaches to transformative learning (O'Sullivan et al. 2003). It is closely aligned with emancipatory popular education and social learning models associated with the work of Paulo Freire (2000) and Michel Thiollent (1996) in Latin America, and others (e.g., Friedmann 1987) in community planning literature. In the PPV project, this strategy was adapted and applied to the specific needs of two different groups: rural Indigenous fishing families (the main focus of this chapter), and women in fishing-related livelihoods in an urban environment (wives of fishers generally, not *comerciantes* or fish-sellers).

In working with the *El Sur* families, the methodology focussed on:

- learning with local people about their development priorities through trust-building and integrated entry points (see also Moser 1993) that promote opportunities for inclusive participation in areas otherwise assumed to be "for men" or "for women";
- creating spaces for leadership development and empowerment through the coproduction of knowledge and valuing of contributions of women, men, and families, including special initiatives to identify the strategic contributions and needs of women in the fisheries and aquaculture value chains; and
- applying locally adapted training and learning-by-doing capacity building to address bottlenecks (fisheries management, hygiene and processing, participation of women, social organisation) and ultimately to improve food security.

This was implemented through four types of interaction and reflection: *para adentro*, or "to the inside" (collective consciousness and group identity construction with fishers at the community level); *para afuera*, or "to the outside" (consolidating identities and testing approaches in engagements and negotiations with other actors in the value chain); *para arriba*, or "upward" (intersection of technical-local and new knowledge); and *para abajo*, or "downward" (practical knowledge application), including working together in hands-on projects within the community, generation of appropriate solutions for locally identified priorities, and a focus on engaging families (females and males of different age groups).

Results

The chapter presents a broad characterisation of fisheries livelihoods, food security, and gender and social inequality issues in the region within the perspective of the fisheries value chain, and the contributing uncertainties and risks. Following this, a summary is presented of the integrated participatory value chain analysis interventions using *diálogo de saberes* and associated results in the *El Sur* communities.

Food security and fisheries participation

The overall results of a household survey for the region ($N = 811$), presented in Baker-French (2013), indicate early childhood malnutrition in the study region. A high overall percentage of rural households (including the study communities and seven others, all with similar rates) reported moderate to severe food insecurity for both seasons (66.7 percent of households for low-water, 60.9 percent for high-water). There is an association in both seasons between higher levels of food insecurity and the following factors: female-headed households, Indigenous households, households that participate in hunting and gathering activities, and households that own fishing gear (participating in subsistence or commercial fisheries or both). Childhood stunting, lack of appropriate knowledge and practices regarding infant and young child feeding, and high rates of infection (diarrhoea) coupled with low access to water supply and low incidence of adequate water treatment were also evident in the survey results for rural communities (Baker-French 2013).

Fish consumption levels are relatively high in the study communities, based on over 57 native species (Argote Soliz et al. 2014). Focus group results corroborated this, and also indicated mixed livelihood strategies and a high seasonal variation in dietary diversity (including a number of highly nutritive forest products harvested seasonally) not adequately represented in the survey results (Rainville et al. 2014). The research revealed that fishing contributes to stabilising rural food security and resilience, with most respondents indicating that fisheries activity is carried out daily or several times a week, and involves both men and women. Twenty-nine of the 41 families living in the study communities confirmed regular participation in commercial fishing, and almost all (37, or 90 percent) participated in subsistence fishing. Twenty-nine men and four women fishers were recorded in a survey that included 72 commercial fish landings for the study communities (Argote Soliz et al. 2014). Compared to other livelihood activities (such as harvesting *castaña*), where earnings are commonly invested in larger purchases such as motorcycles or housing, "fishing is what people do to make sure there is food to eat" (R. Salas Peredo, personal comment).

Social inequality in the regional value chain

Within the fisheries for native species and the introduced *paiche* fish (Carvajal-Vallejos and Zeballos Fernández 2011; Carvajal-Vallejos et al. 2011, 2013), women participate in a variety of different actor groups in the value chain, from the most vulnerable, economically and socially marginalised wives of rural Indigenous fishers to the most economically and politically powerful *mayoristas*, these are medium- to large-scale fish buyers and exporters and boat owners (Coca Méndez et al. 2012). They are also active in fishing for subsistence and commerce (mostly native species, rarely *paiche*), making fishing gear, as processors, as *minoristas* (small-scale vendors in the local markets), as restaurant owners, or as small entrepreneurs who make and sell fish-based food products (Soto et al. 2013).

Among all of these rural and urban actors, physical and sexual violence was common – a serious and daily issue for interviewees. Of a group of 12 female participants in an urban value-added processing group supported by the project, ten reported having suffered physical or sexual violence during their lifetime (Ríos Pool 2014). This fact is confirmed by the following three short quotes, reprinted with permission (Ríos Pool 2014).

> I don't sleep, this work is very hard . . . as a woman, I have to look after my children, and I raise them by myself; also, I have my boat. I have to look after that, because men always want to deceive me, but now I know well, I have my people . . .
>
> (Interview, urban female *mayorista*, April 2013)

> Women are treated poorly by everyone. My dad hit me, my brother hit me, my husband hit me . . . my daughter's husband beats her . . . when will it change?
>
> (Interview, urban female *minorista* (widowed), Riberalta, April 2013)

> My mother left me and my three brothers, because my father beat her often, my father went crazy. We used to go to the forest, and we'd stay there until he fell asleep. When I was 14 years old, a man arrived, old, and my father delivered me to him, I had to go with that old man. He

brought me to his house, and there I had to be his woman; he beat me, he did everything to me. After a time I had my little son, then my little daughter, and then another son, but I couldn't stand how he beat me and treated me poorly. One day, I left my house and without thinking I started walking and walking, and I didn't want to return to my house *[crying]*. I just feel sorry for my children, they are grown now, and afterwards I sought them and asked for forgiveness.

(Interview, Tacana female, Riberalta, April 2013)

El Sur *communities*

The three communities that became *El Sur* were established in the late 1950s at the site of historic floodplain fishing and hunting grounds, once a satellite port of one of the larger rubber *haciendas* in the region. The first residents were from two Indigenous families searching for land after exiting the regional militia and rubber-tapping activity farther north. Several of the older female members had lived in Riberalta or other urban centres before moving to the communities upon marriage.

Subsequently, the communities self-declared as having Tacana heritage during a regional Indigenous survey carried out in the 1990s, leading up to the formation of the TCO TIM II. The Tacana group in particular has suffered centuries of exploitation and cultural assimilation (Fischermann 2010). Linked to Bolivia's colonial history, there is significant marginalisation of the Indigenous groups. Until the time of the land reforms in the 1990s, with an associated incentive for "re-tribalisation", there was very little advantage perceived for people to self-identify as Tacana (Bathurst 2005). In *El Sur*, families have a very detailed knowledge of the history of the community and its inception, as well as the land reform process and titling of the TCO in the early 2000s. However, they express limited knowledge of ancestors, and very few Tacana language speakers are present in the communities – evidence of a possible cultural break or suppression of traditional culture during repeated migration, and historic trauma from the colonial and rubber-tapping era. Some cite that their parents or grandparents previously lived in other parts of the Pando Department (while working in resource extraction), or came from Tumupasa, a missionary settlement near the Andean foothills, which became a centre of Tacana people in the 17th century. One of the community elders spoke of the recently revived Tacana Indigenous identity:

In 1996 there was a commission from CIRABO, a regional-level organisation, and they did an Indigenous Census . . . We affiliated with the indigenous sector because we legally belong to the Tacana ethnicity. We were very clear, why would we deny our origin? Sincerely, we told them that we belong to the Tacana ethnicity. To which they said: "Tell us at least one word in your language". I told him "uchi", which

means "dog" as we say in Spanish. From there came the demand for
territory, where we demanded for ourselves the title for our territory as
the indigenous sector of TCO TIM II.

(Male Indigenous Elder interviewee and Community President,
Lago El Carmen, July 2013)

The *El Sur* communities are relatively unique in the TCO for their lack
of access to *castaña* (generally December to March in the rainy season) and
high vulnerability to seasonal flooding, which has increased in frequency in
recent years (Martínez et al. 2013). This makes them highly dependent on
fisheries for income and subsistence. Agriculture was the main livelihood
activity until 2005, when severe flooding destroyed most homes and crops,
leaving families with no reserve capital to purchase new seeds. Commercial
fishing emerged at this time, as many strove to save money to restart their
agricultural activities. The vulnerability to flooding continues to intensify in
the region: in February 2014, a major flood forced the communities and
nearly 2,000 other residents of the area to migrate to other communities or
the nearby city, with many families living in temporary camps, depending
for several months entirely on flood relief assistance for food, and losing most
of their possessions.[8]

El Sur communities are now among a small group in the region that
practise commercial fishing year round (Argote Soliz et al. 2014), obtaining
better prices and filling demand while other communities are not fishing
(usually because of *castaña* harvesting). They now occupy an important
role in the regional value chain for native species fisheries, contributing an
estimated 30 percent of the total catch sold in the main regional fish market
in Riberalta (Coca Méndez et al. 2012). However, despite high market
demand and apparent abundance of the fishery resource, the returns on
fisheries production to fishers from these communities are marginal at best.
The main limitations, described in Wojciechowski and Coca Méndez (2014),
include high fixed and variable costs, transportation bottlenecks, lack of
agency among fishers, and low prices paid by middlemen (female and male),
who exercise control over fishers through *habilito*.

Interview results show that in the *habilito* system, "money is not seen".
Instead, goods and fish are traded and exchanged, usually resulting in
lower benefits to the fisher due to inconsistent or absent control over
prices. Families are always in a situation of selling the fish to pay off a
previous advance on supplies, and most end up "borrowing" after delivering
fish in order to get the supplies and basic foodstuffs they require for the
next period, thus augmenting their debt (Ríos Pool 2014) and continuing
the cycle.

Men from *El Sur* communities carry their fish in 80–100-litre *thermos*
(Styrofoam boxes with ice) to a regional port location, from where it is
shipped via public transportation paid for by the fishers. When the *thermo*
arrives in the urban centre, it is delivered to the middleman/woman, who

examines the contents and determines the amount owing to the fishers. The fishers are rarely present at this stage to verify fish species, quantity, quality, and total amounts owed to them. Advances on supplies (generally ice and household staples) are delivered to the port location by the same transport truck, where the male heads of households collect them. Women, who are generally responsible for preparing meals for the family, depend on supplies or money received through the male head of household for any food purchases to supplement what can be grown or harvested locally. Men are in turn dependent on a payment or advance determined by the middleman with very little or no negotiation. This generates insecurity and high pressure on women, who must guarantee the subsistence and food security of their family despite having limited economic means and almost no direct access to markets. This situation is not exclusive to fisheries activity in the region; it is also present in other extractive industries.

In addition, generally, the contribution of women in work or product is less valued and receives less remuneration. For example, men are paid 30 percent more than women and children for the collection of *castaña* (Nina and Von Vacano 2009). Prices paid to women for fish were not clear; it was not possible to record any women fishers being paid directly, and all fish was sold through the male head of household's *thermo* deliveries.

Diálogo de saberes

Para adentro

During the regional *Mujeres y Peces* gender workshop, personal history interviews, focus group activities, and participatory theatre using role-play of gendered historic and current roles in fishing all demonstrated that fish and fisheries are inextricably woven into the lives of females and males in the rural Indigenous communities, often from a very young age. Interviews in *El Sur* study communities indicated that women participated frequently in many land-based tasks, such as net-making, fish processing, and commercialisation and fishing for subsistence, while many also accompanied partners or family members on commercial fishing trips. Most women demonstrated knowledge of fishing technology and frequent (daily or weekly) participation in and enjoyment of the activity.

> When I was a little girl, we liked to go to the lake with my father. We used to jump into the water up to here, we needed to catch the fish like this, with our hands, the ones called bucheres. And sometimes my father would make funnels of tacuara, that worked and we would catch them with that, with my father we would carry loads of bucheres, lots of fish and then we would go home to eat.
>
> (Interview, Tacana female, Flor de Octubre, April 2013)

All female interviewees expressed some practical knowledge of fishing gear and techniques, most indicating that they learned to fish with a family member, often their father, mother, or husband. Almost all reported engaging in frequent subsistence fishing, and a significant number were visibly involved in the commercial fisheries value chain. Despite this, most described their role as simply "helping" or "supporting" their partner (husband or other male family member) and did not recognise their contributions as "fishing" or actual "work", with a few exceptions, including this story from a female commercial fisherwoman:

> Me, when I didn't have my smallest baby, I didn't return to the house until eleven or twelve at night. I took my [other] baby with me to set nets . . . From five in the evening to eleven at night we would go fishing and all of that. I have always liked it, I like this and that's it, no more! Of course, now, I work with my own *thermos*; I have been working independently for a while now. And now I'm not going out with my husband, because all of the boys go with him from when they are small, and now he is taking my brother-in-law. That's why I don't go to keep him company anymore. My baby I always left with my brother-in-law, because he holds me back, and I go because I have always liked to do this. I love this! I like fishing, yes . . . getting out is what I love! Because there, in the house, it is frustrating and boring.
>
> (Interview, Tacana female, 27 de Mayo, Beni, June 2013)

Despite the central role that fisheries play in regional food security for most households, men and women rarely self-identified as fishers; men were more likely to self-identify as farmers, or prefer farming as a livelihood activity. The *Mujeres y Peces* regional dialogue workshop allowed for greater transparency between actors of the fisheries value chain, and both a valuation and appreciation for the role women play, thereby contributing to awareness about current activities and the distribution of responsibilities and benefits among different actors.

Para adentro *and* para arriba

Community training included two principal activities: cooking and dialogue workshops named "Healthy and Diverse Cooking with Fish", and training on participatory *estudios de viabilidad economico* (EVE) (economic feasibility analysis) of fisheries operations. Combining these two activities created new spaces for dialogue and local level cooperation involving men and women together. Topics of the cooking workshop included early child feeding practices, nutrition and diet diversity, and water treatment and sanitation, but went beyond these to include reflections on food security responsibility and behaviours (including sharing reproductive roles).

Both the cooking and EVE workshops were held in the community, generally afternoon and evening sessions on the same day, and appealed to men and women; 95 percent of community members from all three communities participated in all activities. Men and women cooked and learned about hygiene, discussed resource management, learned to calculate fixed and variable monthly costs of fishing and to monitor production, and discussed economic feasibility, organisation, and price negotiation. These spaces also fostered discussions on how to improve returns on fishing, and empowered fishing families to make some of their livelihood decisions based on co-created economic information.

In the EVE workshops, fixed and variable costs of fishing were found to exceed income for these communities, and many fishers reported lack of transparency, low prices, and other issues regarding sale of fish to middlemen (Coca Méndez et al. 2012). Overall, the value chain bottlenecks can be summarised as low levels of social capital, the magnitude of passive demand (ranging from inadequate housing and electricity to poor health and education services), and low levels of transparency and inter-institutional dialogue (Wojciechowski and Coca Méndez 2014).

The participatory cooking was an opportunity to co-create and introduce new dishes and more diverse ways of cooking fish while incorporating key locally available vitamins A and C and iron-rich foods (increasing diet diversity). Sharing food was central to bringing people together during these multiple-day interventions, as it allowed for informal information-sharing and trust-building. Results showed positive perceptions of fish consumption and new food combinations. The intervention successfully supported context-appropriate and locally relevant advances on practical issues, and provided opportunities for reflection and negotiation on strategic needs. The intervention team of males and females collaborated with municipal health officials and relevant actors to create shared spaces for improved networks, community access to information, and lobbying to address their rights to clean water, health care, and other basic services.

There was an active investment to remove barriers to female participation: workshops were held locally, organised around regular daily routines, or included preparing meals together; child care was provided, and transportation and meals for whole families were provided during regional workshops. In some cases, if women or men were unable to participate together in the workshop and practice sessions, there were visits to individual families, and interviews and focus groups were conducted in parallel to the workshops ($N = 20$).

The collaborative nature of the workshops lent itself to greater participation by both sexes, and increased recognition of women as valuable players in the fisheries value chain, as well as key protagonists for the food security of their families. Both male and female participants in the training events in rural communities expressed higher confidence in their own knowledge and ability to effect change, as well as increased trust in the facilitators and the change process, demonstrated by increased participation and vocalisation at subsequent regional value chain negotiation meetings.

Para abajo

Hands-on project intervention activities occurred in tandem with other community training, and included boat building, net mending, building live boxes (floating boxes for storage of live fish), and creating community and school gardens. In total, 26 community gardens and three school gardens were created, along with three boats and four live boxes. Participation in these recurring workshops is an indicator of their uptake success, with 95–97 percent of community members partaking (including men, women, youth, elders, and children, up from slightly fewer than 50 percent, primarily women and children, during initial project workshops and focus group activities). These activities were opportunities to solve problems collaboratively, test and validate new ideas, and build positive self-esteem.

During two separate monitoring entries, a multi-disciplinary team interviewed project participants to assess the positive impacts of the community training and hands-on project intervention. Results showed that the mutual trust built by including men in traditional "female" workshops (e.g., nutrition and cooking), and inviting women to participate in more "male" activities – such as building live boxes and assessing the economic value chain feasibility of fisheries operations – broke down traditional gender lines and allowed individuals to recognise previously undervalued skills. Men appreciated and valued female knowledge and contributions on topics related to fisheries, management, and technology, as well as their more advanced skills in mathematics and writing. In a variety of examples, men were observed asking or encouraging their wives to provide details of fish catch composition or volumes, other technical knowledge specific to the fishery, and historical knowledge relevant to the community (previously assumed to be a male-dominated domain of knowledge). Women especially reported appreciating these training and hands-on formats, as they allowed for co-learning in a less formal and thus less threatening environment. During the household nutrition discussions, spaces were created for men to demonstrate their knowledge about family meals and child feeding, and men were surprisingly engaged and interested in topics traditionally seen as "for women". Overall, a variety of opportunities were successfully created for local leaders to emerge and shine in their new roles.

Discussion

Frameworks, matrices and tools are merely a means to an end – in this case, rigorous gender analysis in research toward gender equality in small-scale fisheries and aquaculture. They cannot be applied mechanically but need to be used with flexibility and creativity, adapted to the needs of local sociocultural and linguistic contexts, and the overall research questions and the project implementation goals. Care needs to be exercised in translation. Vital skills such as listening, building rapport, discussing and learning from respondents are necessary.

(WorldFish Center 2014)

Linking fishing and food insecurity

A common element of many Amazonian communities is the role of fisheries as a fallback or "insurance" strategy, contributing to livelihoods and food security as a supplementary activity, or when other options do not work out (Coomes et al. 2010). In the case of Bolivia's northern Amazon, commercial fisheries are expanding and changing rapidly as development, climate variability, road access, lack of regulation, and introduced species impact the region. Indigenous fishers make use of a diversity of species for subsistence and commercial purposes.

Worrisome levels of food insecurity were identified in the household survey, particularly for rural communities, with fishing and hunting appearing among the main determinants of insecurity in the statistical analysis (Baker-French 2013). However, these factors are likely part of the multifaceted characterisation of marginalised Indigenous groups that also includes low education. Further interviews and focus groups suggested that this marginalisation is due to some extent to the historical social discrepancies and displacement of Indigenous groups from the rubber era and similar colonial processes. In addition, high rural diversity, not well characterised by the higher-level survey, drives specific, localised strategies in the face of seasonal stressors (floods, drought).

Fishing and hunting, in the current context, contribute to stabilising rural food security and resilience to climatic and social change. They appear to be cultural survival strategies rather than preferred livelihoods, and possibly not yet contributing as much as they could to well-being in the region. Women and men are both involved in many aspects of fishing, as indicated by the evaluation of relative roles by women of the communities, with some separation of roles, but no obvious great attitudinal exclusion of women from the work. In comparison, rubber era livelihoods were much more male dominated, with associated greater marginalisation of and violence towards females[9] – likely contributing factors to ongoing high levels of domestic violence and other negative aspects of gender relationships in community life.

The communities suffer from a combination of generational trauma of exploitation, high levels of vulnerability, limited livelihood activities, high rates of infection and illness (often related to water quality and hygiene), frequent displacement, loss of income and assets by flooding, and high rates of food insecurity. New access rights to territory and natural resources, resulting from land tenure reforms under the INRA Law of 1996, ironically, may also be a factor in maintaining poverty and vulnerability, as this creates incentive for communities to stay on marginal land (where they hold communal title) despite substantial risk from flooding or other threats.

The low self-identification as "fishers" that emerged in the interviews is sometimes suggested in the global literature to be related to women's supportive roles, or their focus on pre- and post-harvest activities. However, in the project region, this lack of fishing identity is not limited to women, but includes most of the men in the *El Sur* communities as well, despite fisheries' representing their most significant source of income in recent years. Historically, communities or camps in the rubber *hacienda* system were expected to do their duty, working the land, and many were prohibited from participating in any additional economic activities beyond rubber-tapping, such as fishing (Cardona 2012). The Tacana Indigenous people are thought to have been traditionally an agricultural group, with strong knowledge of soils, planting, and related skills (Fischermann 2010), and it would seem that this identity remains ingrained. Fishing was considered a subsistence activity to feed the family, and has only recently emerged as a commercial, income-generating activity. Interestingly, this may be significantly different for Tacana groups in other parts of the Bolivian Amazon with a longer history of settlement and continuous participation in fishing (CIPTA/WCS 2010).

Social aspects clearly demonstrate the triple jeopardy of "female/ Indigenous/poor", shown through augmented vulnerabilities in terms of lesser control of family finance and strong dependence on (generally male) partners, gender-based violence, and few formal leadership roles. Exploitive social systems inherited from the rubber-harvesting era, such as the *habilito*, help to keep vulnerable families in a state of poverty. Most possess little ability to accumulate assets, and poor access to banking and credit. The influence of this chronic stress on gender inequities is equivocal. Data from the present research suggest that a need for cooperation is recognised culturally, enhancing gender equality in certain areas of life, rather than exacerbating inequality and marginalisation; even so, however, inequality and marginalisation continue to be significant challenges.

The intervention strategy was based on recognition of the complex context in which the Indigenous communities live, and how they participate in the fisheries value chain. The activities were developed based on an iterative, participatory process of male and female facilitators working in different settings (workshops, training, interviews, focus groups, public forums, home visits) with different groupings of local people. This allowed them to unpack perceptions and develop shared understandings of gender, difference, and inequality while identifying and addressing the practical and strategic needs of marginalised groups in the fisheries value chain (both horizontally, within actor groups, and vertically, between groups).

According to Moser's (1993) empowerment approach, the triple burden of reproductive, productive, and community management roles must be recognised and explored. Participatory processes serve to promote bottom-up, grassroots organisations that can raise this consciousness, challenging these forms of oppression (Moser 1993). Participatory research and planning are viewed not as neutral or objective, technical processes, but as iterative, political and technical practices involving conflict, debate, or negotiation and transformative processes. Initiatives to address practical needs thus become a platform for reflection, critical thinking, and consolidation of debate around relationships of exclusion and inequality. This strategy supported capacity development for leadership and empowerment, and provided a useful addition of practical implementation methods for a GTA in aquatic agricultural systems.

The process of exploring perceptions and understandings of exclusion **together** through the *diálogo de saberes* method is emancipatory, because it increases awareness and is based on principles of developing trust and mutual respect. It does not inherently change people's material position, but is part of the process of self-recognition essential to the project of intentional change. Through increased transparency, demystification of the numbers, and collaboration on solving practical problems, opportunities emerge for improved self-esteem and recognition and articulation of strategic needs within the group, as well as key opportunities to engage with different levels (horizontal and vertical linkages respectively – see Wojciechowski and Coca Méndez 2014). The debate necessarily involves women *and* men, and people in different positions on the spectrum of social inclusion.

The result in the PPV project was participatively achieved through economic evaluation of the fisheries value chain, identifying key new realisations. For example, it became clear that *minoristas* (including women) make their greatest profit from low-cost fish, on which marginalised fishers (also including women) concentrate their efforts but lose money because of the cost of nets, ice, and time. This improved transparency allowed for a multi-stakeholder discussion on pricing and focussing development efforts. Surprisingly, the strong family networks of mutual support seen at the community level did not necessarily continue once families bridged the fishing–fish selling step. It is felt that this illustrates clearly the strength of the cultural hierarchical norms that keep vulnerable fishers poor, but this inequality is not drawn along gender lines.

The authors tried to avoid certain key assumptions or biases, notably the assumptions that (1) the most significant or pressing issue of inequality in the different social groups was the gendered relationships between men and women specifically, and (2) social inequalities between the different groups are most strongly associated with income or control over access to resources, as there may be other significant factors at play. Thus, the research examined not only the position and relationships of women, but also the intersectionality of social relationships of class and ethnicity; this was done within the context of a practical discussion of the fisheries value chain and the regional economy.

The interventions were not targeted specifically to improving the situation of women, but rather to improving conditions overall for rural Indigenous families engaged in fish-based livelihoods. This involved a mix of internal and external ideas, with community members generally not interested in discussing perceived esoteric development goals that challenge a status quo that may not be optimal, but is predictable, and accepted. Cooking together, including training sessions on preparing diverse, healthy meals with locally sourced ingredients, proved to be an excellent entry point and practical environment in which a social context for positive change could be developed. Men, women, and children participated in the cooking workshops, which also provided opportunities to learn about hygiene, dietary diversity, and planning for the fisheries sector, including demystifying numbers and understanding complexities of the fisheries value chain in a supportive hands-on context that also allowed leaders to take a step forward.

Conclusion

Through the combined processes of empirical research and analysis, ongoing dialogue with the communities, and targeted, participatory interventions, the study explored situations of inequality and exploitation experienced in the relationships of females and males in various situations, as well as in the relationships between different social groups in Bolivia's Northern Amazon fisheries value chain. It was found that strategy to understand and address gender inequality is necessarily adaptive. It must evolve according to the specific realities, practical and strategic needs, livelihoods, and overall well-being of families in each situation.

The historic, social, and environmental vulnerability context is an immediate and driving element that needs to be considered when situating gender and social inequality perspectives. It can also be useful in informing the development of GTAs that are appropriate, inclusive, and feasible. In this case study, the intersectionality of these varied contexts, the impact of the *habilito* system, the high levels of environmental vulnerability, and the low availability of livelihood options combined to create significant social exclusion. This affects the communities very directly, and more pervasively than gender inequalities (for example, those reported in the regional statistics), especially considering local perceptions and attitudes (defeated by vulnerability). In this context, empowerment of women and of the community are very necessary and can possibly be addressed together in some aspects.

Integrated participatory value chain analysis can offer novel pathways to empowerment through the operationalisation of a GTA. In this case study, *diálogo de saberes* (knowledge dialogue) created new space to indirectly address key aspects of gender equity, through working on practical problems together. The practical activities implemented in the project often did not challenge gender roles explicitly, but instead took an issue that affected both males and females (awareness of economic costs of production and decision-making ability), and found a new pathway to enable transparency, improved knowledge, and power for both males and females. The *diálogo de saberes* model is useful in this context for supporting the fisher communities in creating a collective identity, negotiating with other actors, and reflecting about conceptual approaches. It was enriched with hands-on activities to meet practical needs that are locally identified, and was successful in engaging males and females in integrated training modules that would traditionally be identified as exclusively men's or women's domains.

Notes

1 *Peces para la vida* was a 3-year research project (2011–14) supported by the Canadian International Food Security Research Fund through the International Development Research Centre (IDRC) and with the financial support of the Government of Canada. See project website at www.pecesvida.org.
2 See KIT et al. (2012). See also Dey de Pryck (2013) and De Silva (2011).
3 See, for example, CIDA (2010).
4 *Habilito* is an exploitive credit relationship with roots in historic resource exploitation activities, most significantly rubber-tapping (Garland and Silva-Santiesteban 2004).
5 Notably, this region of Bolivia is now the world's leading producer of Brazil nuts (Coslovsky 2014). For Indigenous communities with access to this resource (harvested between December and March), it often provides the most significant source of income for the whole year.
6 An introduced species, known locally as *paiche* (*Arapaima gigas*), now makes up 80 percent of the commercial fisheries catch for the region (Coca Méndez et al. 2012). Participation in *paiche* fishing is mostly male (Argote Soliz et al. 2014), and is limited by access to specific fishing gear types, fisher skill, and location of the fish. Generally, *paiche* reside in lagoons that are nominally controlled by Indigenous communities according to rights associated with the TCOs, providing new opportunities and fisheries conflicts (Salas Peredo et al. 2013).
7 The Tacana people, while native to the Bolivian Amazon, are thought to have historic roots in the region farther south, closer to the Andean foothills. They have a long history of contact with colonisation, exploitation, and associated migration, including the impact of Incas, Franciscan and Jesuit missionaries, quinoa, rubber, Brazil nut, gold, and hardwood extraction. Consequently, they suffer from significant cultural assimilation and a lack of connection with their traditional language, etc. (Fischermann 2010). The Ese Eja people are a traditionally semi-nomadic group native to this region of Bolivia and parts of Peru. They are thought to have more successfully resisted contact and cultural assimilation, maintaining more of their traditional culture and language to this day, compared to many other groups in the region. See Herrera Sarmiento (2014), which describes the Ese Eja from the region.
8 Official reports of the February 2014 floods, which affected the entire Amazon region, representing two-thirds of the country, indicated only 60 deaths, with 60,000 families directly affected. Data on the numbers specific to the northern Amazon are not available. Overall, 16 million hectares were flooded, and approximately 200,000 head of cattle are estimated to have been lost (see Vásquez 2014).
9 There was significant abuse of women during the rubber-tapping boom that extended from the end of the 19th century to the late 1950s and continued on a smaller scale until the 1980s. For one thing, when women participated in productive activities, they received lower pay than men for the same amount of work or production. They also suffered from exclusion because their presence in rubber-tapping camps was negatively viewed as a "distraction" to the men, or simply opposed because of women's perceived lack of "useful ability" (Vallvé

Vallori 2012). Women who accompanied their husbands to these camps were paid only to smoke (cure) the rubber. Because of the scarcity of women in the *barracas* (rubber extraction settlements), many, especially Indigenous women, were viewed as goods and brought in as prostitutes.

References

All website URLs accessed on 7 April 2016.

Alcides Vadillo, P., and Carmen E. Miranda. 2012. *Análisis de derecho internacional, legislación nacional, fallos, e instituciones al interrelacionarse con territorios y áreas de conservación de los pueblos indígenas y comunidades locales*. Report No. 7, Bolivia. Bangalore: Natural Justice, and Pune and Delhi: Kalpavriksh.

Argote Soliz, Adalid, Paul A. Van Damme, Alison E. Macnaughton, and Fernando A. Carvajal-Vallejos. 2014. "Pesca indígena en la Amazonía boliviana: Un caso de estudio en la Tierra Comunitaria de Origen Multiétnico II (Pando y Beni)." In Ministerio de Relaciones del Exterior and Ministerio de Medio Ambiente y Agua, eds, *Línea de base sobre ecosistemas y recursos acuáticos*. Cochabamba, Bolivia: Editorial INIA, 167–75.

Baker-French, Sophia. 2013. "Food Security and Nutritional Status in Fishing Communities in Bolivia's Northern Amazon: Results of a Household Survey." Master's thesis. Vancouver, Canada: University of British Columbia.

Balbin, Jesús. 1986. *Diálogo de saberes: una búsqueda*. Bogotá: Lenguaje popular.

Bathurst, Laura Ann. 2005. "Reconfiguring Identities: Tacana Retribalization in Bolivia's Amazonia." PhD thesis. University of California, Berkeley.

Cardona, Walter Cano. 2012. *Formal Institutions, Local Arrangements and Conflicts in Northern Bolivian Communities after Forest Governance Reforms*. PROMAB Scientific Series 14. Riberalta, Bolivia: Programa Manejo de Bosques de la Amazonia Boliviana (PROMAB).

Carvajal-Vallejos, Fernando M., and A.J. Zeballos Fernández. 2011. "Diversidad y distribución de los peces de la Amazonía boliviana." In Paul A. Van Damme, Fernando M. Carvajal-Vallejos, and Jorge Molina Carpio, eds, *Los peces y delfines de la Amazonía boliviana: habitats, potencialidades y amenazas*. Cochabamba, Bolivia: Editorial INIA, 101–47.

Carvajal-Vallejos, Fernando M., Paul A. Van Damme, L. Córdova, and Claudia I. Coca Méndez. 2011. "La introducción de *Arapaima gigas* (paiche) en la Amazonía boliviana." In Paul A. Van Damme, Fernando M. Carvajal-Vallejos, and Jorge Molina Carpio, eds., *Los peces y delfines de la Amazonía boliviana: habitats, potencialidades y amenazas*. Cochabamba, Bolivia: Editorial INIA, 367–95.

Carvajal-Vallejos, Fernando M., Alison E. Macnaughton, Claudia I. Coca Méndez, Selín Trujillo Bravo, Joachim Carolsfeld, and Paul A. Van Damme. 2013. "The Introduction of *Arapaima gigas* in the Bolivian Amazon: Impacts on Fisheries, Emerging Value Chains and Perspectives for Community-Based Management." In Ellen Sílvia Amaral Figueiredo, ed., *Biologia, conservação e manejo de pirarucus na Pan-Amazônia*. Tefé, Brazil: Instituto de Desenvolvimento Sustentável Mamirauá (IDSM), 131–50.

Charles, Anthony T. 2011. "Small-Scale Fisheries: On Rights, Trade and Subsidies." *Maritime Studies* 10 (2): 85–94.

Cho, Sumi, Kimberlé Williams Crenshaw, and Leslie McCall. 2013. "Toward a Field of Intersectionality Studies: Theory, Applications, and Praxis." *Signs* 38 (4): 785–810.

CIDA (Canadian International Development Agency). 2010. *Gender Equality Policy and Tools: CIDA's Policy on Gender Equality* (revised version of *CIDA's Policy on Gender Equality*, 1999). www.acdi-cida.gc.ca/INET/IMAGES.NSF/vLUImages/Policy/$file/Policy-on-Gender-Equality-EN.pdf.

CIPTA/WCS (Consejo Indigena del Pueblo Takana/Wildlife Conservation Society). 2010. *La pesca en el territorio Takana.* La Paz: CIPTA/WCS.

Coca Méndez, Claudia I., Gabriela Rico López, Fernando M. Carvajal-Vallejos, Roxana Salas Peredo, John M. Wojciechowski, and Paul A. Van Damme. 2012. *La Cadena de valor del pescado en el norte amazónico de Bolivia: Contribución de especies nativas y de una especie introducida (el paiche* – Arapaima gigas*) (Fisheries Value Chain in Bolivia's Northern Amazon: Contributions of Native Species and an Introduced Species [paiche* – Arapaima gigas*]).* La Paz: Programa de Investigación Estratégica en Bolivia (PIEB). http://hdl.handle.net/10625/53643.

Coomes, Oliver T., Yoshiko Takasaki, Christian Abizaid, and Brandford L. Barham. 2010. "Floodplain Fisheries as Natural Insurance for the Rural Poor in Tropical Forest Environments: Evidence from Amazonia." *Fisheries Management and Ecology* 17 (6): 513–21. doi:10.1111/j.1365-2400.2010.00750.x.

Coslovsky, Salo V. 2014. "Economic Development without Pre-Requisites: How Bolivian Producers Met Strict Food Safety Standards and Dominated the Global Brazil-Nut Market." *World Development* 54 (Feb.): 32–45. doi:10.1016/j.world dev.2013.07.012.

De Silva, D.A.M. 2011. *Faces of Women in Global Fisheries Value Chains: Female Involvement, Impact and Importance in the Fisheries of Developed and Developing Countries.* Norwegian Agency for Development Cooperation (NORAD)/Food and Agriculture Organization of the United Nations (FAO) Value Chain Project. Rome: FAO. www.fao.org/fileadmin/user_upload/fisheries/docs/The_role_of_Women_in_the_fishery_value_chain_Dr__De_Silva.doc.

Dey de Pryck, Jennie. 2013. *Good Practice Policies to Eliminate Gender Inequalities in Fish Value Chains.* Rome: Food and Agriculture Organization of the United Nations (FAO). www.fao.org/docrep/019/i3553e/i3553e.pdf.

FAO (Food and Agriculture Organization of the United Nations). 2012. *Report of the FAO Workshop on Future Directions for Gender in Aquaculture and Fisheries Action, Research and Development.* Shanghai, China, 23–24 April 2011. FAO Fisheries and Aquaculture Report No. 998. Rome: FAO, 1–28. www.fao.org/docrep/015/i2762e/i2762e00.pdf.

Fischermann, B. 2010. "Pueblos indígenas y nacionales originarios en Bolivia tierras bajas: pueblos Esse-Ejja y Tacana." In Mariano Flores Choque, ed., *Atlas de territorios indígenas y originarios en Bolivia.* La Paz: Ministerio de Desarrollo Rural y Tierras and Viceministerio de Tierras, 31–4.

Freire, Paulo. 2000. *Pedagogy of the Oppressed* (30th anniversary edition). New York and London: Continuum. (1st ed. 1970, New York: Herder & Herder, from Portuguese manuscript written in 1968.)

Friedmann, John. 1987. *Planning in the Public Domain: From Knowledge to Action.* Princeton, NJ: Princeton University Press.

Garland, Eduardo Bedoya, and Alvaro Bedoya Silva-Santiesteban. 2004. *Enganche y Servidumbre por Deudas en Bolivia.* Working Paper 41. Geneva: International Labour Organization.

Herrera Sarmiento, Enrique. 2014. *Los Ese Ejja y la pesca: adaptación y continuidad de una actividad productiva en un pueblo indígena de la Amazonía peruano-boliviana (Ese Ejja and Fishing: Adaptation and Continuity of a Productive Activity among an Indigenous People of the Peruvian and Bolivian Amazon).* Cochabamba, Bolivia: Editorial INIA. http://hdl.handle.net/10625/53646.

Kabeer, Naila. 1999. "Resources, Agency, Achievements. Reflections on the Measurement of Women's Empowerment." *Development and Change* 30 (3): 435–64. doi:10.1111/1467-7660.00125.

Kantor, Paula. 2013. *Transforming Gender Relations: A Key to Lasting Positive Agricultural Development Outcomes.* Brief AAS-2013-12, CGIAR Research Program on Aquatic Agricultural Systems. Penang, Malaysia: CGIAR.

KIT (Royal Tropical Institute), Agri-ProFocus, and IIRR (International Institute of Rural Reconstruction). 2012. *Challenging Chains to Change: Gender Equity in Agricultural Value Chain Development.* Amsterdam: KIT Publishers, Royal Tropical Institute. www.cordaid.org/media/publications/Challenging_chains_to_change. pdf.

Macnaughton, Alison E., Fernando M. Carvajal-Vallejos, Adalid Argote Soliz, Tiffanie K. Rainville, Joachim Carolsfeld, and Paul A. Van Damme. 2015. "'Paiche Reigns!' Species Introduction and Indigenous Fisheries in the Bolivian Amazon." *Maritime Studies* 14 (June): 11. doi:10.1186/s40152-015-0030-0.

Martínez, N., A. Soto, and T. Rainville. 2013. "Análisis de vulnerabilidad y estrategias de adaptación espontánea a la variabilidad climática, cambio climático y cambios sociopolíticos de 5 comunidades de la TCO TIM II." Technical Report. *Peces para la vida – Food Security, Fisheries and Aquaculture in the Bolivian Amazon,* IDRC Project #106524. Cochabamba, Bolivia and Victoria, Canada: Asociación Agua Sustentable, Asociación Faunagua and World Fisheries Trust.

Moser, Caroline O.N. 1993. *Gender, Planning and Development: Theory, Practice and Training.* London and New York: Routledge.

Nina, O., and P. Von Vacano. 2009. "La Dinámica del sector de la castaña y su impacto sobre el mercado laboral y la pobreza en el norte amazonico de Bolivia." In *Dialogo Nacional de Politicas de Apoyo a la Castaña: Un impulso al desarrollo de la castaña en el Amazonas Bolivia,* La Paz, 14 November 2008. La Paz, Bolivia: Grupo Integral SRL.

O'Sullivan, Edmund, Amish Morrell, and Mary Ann O'Connor. 2003. "Introduction." In Edmund O'Sullivan, Amish Morrell, and Mary Ann O'Connor, eds, *Expanding the Boundaries of Transformative Learning: Essays on Theory and Praxis.* New York: Palgrave Macmillan.

Patil, Vrushali. 2013. "From Patriarchy to Intersectionality: A Transnational Feminist Assessment of How Far We've Really Come." *Signs* 38 (4) (Summer): 847–67. www.jstor.org/stable/10.1086/669610.

Rainville, T., C. Coca, V. Cuevas, and A. Macnaughton. 2014. "Línea base e intervenciones Seguridad Alimentaria en la Zona Sur." Technical Report. *Peces para la vida – Food Security, Fisheries and Aquaculture in the Bolivian Amazon,* IDRC Project #106524. Cochabamba, Bolivia and Victoria, Canada: Asociación Agua Sustentable, Asociación Faunagua and World Fisheries Trust.

Ríos Pool, Fabiola. 2014. "Mujeres en la cadena de valor del pescado del norte amazónico de Bolivia" (Women in the Fisheries Value Chain in Bolivia's Northern Amazon). Technical Report. *Peces para la vida – Food Security, Fisheries and Aquaculture in the Bolivian Amazon,* IDRC Project #106524. Cochabamba, Bolivia and Victoria, Canada: Asociación Agua Sustentable, Asociación Faunagua and World Fisheries Trust.

Salas Peredo, Roxana, Alison E. Macnaughton, Paul A. Van Damme, and Joachim Carolsfeld. 2013. "La Amazonía boliviana en tiempos de cambio: oportunidades y desafíos para la pesca artesanal y la acuicultura." In Luis Collado, Edgardo Castro, and Max Hidalgo, eds., *Hacia el manejo de las pesquerías en la cuenca amazónica: Perspectivas transfronterizas*. Lima: Instituto del Bien Común, 135–44.

Soto, A., Alison E. Macnaughton, A. Suarez, F. Ríos Pool, N. Martínez, V. Carranza, and Tiffanie K. Rainville. 2013. "Mujeres y peces en el norte amazónico de Bolivia, Riberalta, April 2–3, 2013." Workshop Report. *Peces para la vida – Food Security, Fisheries and Aquaculture in the Bolivian Amazon*, IDRC Project #106524. Cochabamba, Bolivia and Victoria, Canada: Asociación Agua Sustentable, Asociación Faunagua and World Fisheries Trust.

Thiollent, Michel. 1996. *Metodologia de Pesquisa Ação* (7th ed). São Paulo: Cortez.

Vallvé Vallori, Frederic. 2012. "La barraca Gomera Boliviana: Etnicidad mano de obra y aculturación (1880–1920)." *Boletín Americanista* 65: 65–83.

Van Damme, Paul A., Fernando M. Carvajal-Vallejos, A. Rua, L. Córdova, and P. Becerra. 2011. "Pesca comercial en la cuenca amazónica boliviana." In Paul A. Van Damme, Fernando M. Carvajal-Vallejos, and Jorge Molina Carpio, eds., *Los peces y delfines de la Amazonía boliviana: Hábitats, potencialidades y amenazas*. Cochabamba, Bolivia: Editorial INIA, 247–91.

Vásquez, Katiuska. 2014. "Bolivia soporta segundo embate por inundaciones." *Los Tiempos* (Cochabamba, Bolivia), 2 March. www.lostiempos.com/diario/actualidad/local/20140302/bolivia-soporta-segundo-embate-por-inundaciones_246694_538057.html.

Weeratunge, Nireka, Katherine A. Snyder, and Poh Sze Choo. 2010. "Gleaner, Fisher, Trader, Processor: Understanding Gendered Employment in Fisheries and Aquaculture." *Fish and Fisheries* 11 (4): 405–20. doi:10.1111/j.1467-2979.2010.00368.x.

Williams, Meryl J., Marilyn Porter, Poh Sze Choo, Kyoko Kusakabe, Veikila Vuki, Nikita Gopal, and Melba Bondad-Reantaso. 2012. "Guest Editorial: Gender in Aquaculture and Fisheries – Moving the Agenda Forward." *Asian Fisheries Science* 25 (S): 1–13.

Wojciechowski, M.J., and C.I. Coca Méndez. 2014. "Value Chain Optimization within an SSF 'Economic-Welfare' Hybrid Model: An Analysis of Interventions in the Indigenous Small Scale Fisheries Value Chain in Bolivia's Northern Amazon Region of Riberalta." Technical Report. *Peces para la vida – Fisheries, Food Security and Aquaculture in the Bolivian Amazon*, IDRC Project #106524. Cochabamba, Bolivia and Victoria, Canada: Asociación Agua Sustentable, Asociación Faunagua and World Fisheries Trust.

WorldFish Center. 2010. *Gender and Fisheries: Do Women Support, Complement, or Subsidize Men's Small-Scale Fishing Activities?* Issues Brief 2108. Penang, Malaysia: WorldFish. www.worldfishcenter.org/resource_centre/WF_2711.pdf.

WorldFish Center. 2014. *A Matrix and Tools for Gender Analysis in Fisheries and Aquaculture*. Penang, Malaysia: WorldFish.

10 "Doing *jenda* deliberatively" in a participatory agriculture–nutrition project in Malawi

*Rachel Bezner Kerr, Esther Lupafya,
Lizzie Shumba, Laifolo Dakishoni,
Rodgers Msachi, Anita Chitaya,
Paul Nkhonjera, Mwapi Mkandawire,
Tinkani Gondwe, and Esther Maona*

Introduction

While it is widely accepted that gender issues need to be incorporated into policies and programs that address food security, putting this into practice is another question. Many health and nutrition development programs tend to focus on women of childbearing age, particularly mothers, with limited attention to the roles of men or older women in child care and feeding (Aubel 2012). In doing so, these programs avoid addressing issues of control of resources, decision-making, or the division of labour, in effect treating these dynamics as structural issues that cannot be changed. Over the past 30 years, there has been considerable effort to take gender issues into account in agricultural research and activities. Participatory approaches in agricultural research are also recognised as having validity, and are supported by many donors; however, the depth, engagement, and impact of participatory methods in practice is highly variable, with some institutions using the methods as an instrumental approach to involving people in a perfunctory way (Cornwall 2008). In her discussion of participatory methods as praxis, Cornwall argues that they can be viewed as a "terrain of contestation" that involves different actors with different intentions and interests, which "shape and reshape the boundaries of action" (2008: 276). Although outsiders may bring in participatory methods, who participates and how they participate will influence the outcome, in terms of both equity issues and outcomes such as food security. At times, the discourse and application of participation is used to reinforce structures of power and control, and the language of consensus and deliberation may silence the contrasting views of women and other groups (Cornwall and Goetz 2005).

Intersectional feminist praxis includes several approaches to foster equity, as outlined by Naples (2011): strategies for inclusion, methods of empowerment, countering power imbalances, organising across differences, and reflexivity. Hassim (2009) cautions that issues of tolerance, trust, and solidarity are crucial for ensuring a vibrant political culture. Deliberative democracy can be fostered through different participatory spaces that encourage those who may have limited political clout to have discussions, share ideas, resolve conflicts, or raise concerns (Hassim 2009). Such participatory spaces may be opportunities for more marginalised groups to negotiate, contest, and overcome inequalities (Hassim 2009). What do these strategies mean in practice, in a context of high levels of seasonal food insecurity and gender inequality? Can various methods of fostering "deliberative democracy" enable communities to address deeper structural inequalities across gender, class, and ethnicity that worsen conditions of food insecurity? What are the factors that make this kind of dialogue work?

Description of project

This chapter draws on a long-term research and development project based in northern Malawi, called the Soils, Food, and Healthy Communities (SFHC) project. Malawi is a small landlocked country in south-eastern Africa, where the majority of people are smallholder farmers who grow maize as their staple crop, alongside groundnuts, beans, sweet potatoes, and various cash crops, particularly tobacco. In the late 1990s, structural adjustment policies imposed by the Malawian government led to the removal of fertiliser subsidies, a decline in credit availability, the closure of rural depots, and the reduction of agricultural extension. Food insecurity rose, as did rates of child malnutrition. In 1997, the first and second author conducted 55 in-depth interviews with families of children who were severely malnourished. We learned that smallholder farmers had little knowledge of alternatives to commercial fertilisers and low ability to purchase fertiliser, and, as a consequence, were dealing with depleted soils, declining maize yields, and limited food options. There were often crucial gender dimensions to the farmers' situation, with high levels of alcohol use by men alongside high levels of domestic violence: 44 percent of women reported physical violence from spouses (Bezner Kerr 2005a).

As a follow-up to the study, the hospital and the first author explored alternatives to fertiliser, and learned that a considerable amount of on-farm research had been conducted on different organic options for these smallholder farmers (see, e.g., Snapp et al. 1998). Farmers can intercrop edible grain or perennial legumes (e.g., pigeon pea, peanut, and soybean). The legumes fix nitrogen from the atmosphere, such that when the leaves and roots are incorporated directly into the soil they add nitrogen, other nutrients, and organic matter. Farmers harvest the edible grain, and then grow another crop (e.g., maize) in the improved soil the following year. Although there is evidence for improvement in soil fertility, the link to improved food security or nutrition was not well established, and much of the research had been in the form of structured on-farm trials with a fair amount of scientific control.

We decided to implement a pilot project to test these organic options under "real life" conditions, and, in 2000, a small group of hospital staff and researchers presented the project concept to local village headmen, who approved the idea. Seven villages in the surrounding area were then approached, based on criteria including high levels of food insecurity and child malnutrition, active farmer leadership, and limited previous donor assistance, and asked to consider experimenting with these organic methods (Bezner Kerr and Chirwa 2004). A farmer research team (FRT) was formed, initially made up of 18 men and 12 women from the seven villages, comprising a range of ages, marital status, and food security conditions. The FRT went on a field trip to learn about the different legume options, then developed their own on-farm experiments, and taught other villagers who wanted to try these options. The first year, 183 farmers decided to test the legumes (Bezner Kerr and Chirwa 2004).

The story of what followed has been written up in several other publications (Bezner Kerr and Chirwa 2004; Msachi et al. 2009; Satzinger et al. 2009; Bezner Kerr et al. 2012, among others). While initially only a few farmers tried different legume options to improve soil fertility, over a few years interest in these options increased, and eventually thousands of farmers were testing the legume combinations (Bezner Kerr, Berti et al. 2007). Through a combination of quantitative and qualitative research and participatory workshops, we identified conflicts between older and younger women regarding early child care feeding practices that had negative impacts on child growth (Bezner Kerr, Snapp et al. 2007). We developed discussion groups to address these issues, with special attention to being sensitive to cultural concepts and practices and power imbalances between hospital staff and researchers, as well as intergenerational and gender differences (Bezner Kerr et al. 2008). Researchers working with the project documented improvements in nutrition (Bezner Kerr et al. 2010) and reduced reliance on fertiliser (Msachi et al. 2009), and recorded other environmental benefits such as increased soil cover (Snapp et al. 2010).

The research used participatory methods, including farmer-to-farmer teaching, farmer experimentation, and leadership. Farmers began to articulate an alternative vision for their communities, which they contrasted to the dominant model of agriculture that relied on purchased fertilisers and seeds (Msachi et al. 2009; Bezner Kerr 2010). They formed a farmer association, built a community seed legume bank, managed all seed collection and distribution, and took over more and more of the project management, eventually making up the majority of the project staff. At the time of writing, the project had recently been expanded to work with thousands of farmers in northern and central Malawi using this farmer-to-farmer teaching approach.

Research methods

The overall design was a longitudinal mixed methods case study of an integrated agriculture–nutrition project. In-depth interviews, structured

Table 10.1 Research methods, sample size, and topics covered, 2000–12

Year	Method	Sample size	Topics covered
2000	In-depth interviews	30 households	Farming practices, food security, nutrition.
2001	Baseline survey	235 households	Farming practices, household decision-making, child care.
2006	Workshop	11 people	Gender and other social inequalities.
2009	In-depth interviews	33 households	Farming practices, child care, gender relations, food security.
2009	Workshop	60 people	Successes and challenges of project, including gender relations.
2012	In-depth interviews	50 households	Food security, farming practices, gender relations, child care.

surveys, participatory workshops, and informal observations were all used (Table 10.1).

At the beginning of the project, in-depth interviews were conducted with the 30 members of the FRT. A baseline survey was also carried out (in 2001) of 235 households in 14 villages, which included questions on household decision-making related to crops. The data were entered into SPSS and basic descriptive and bivariate analysis was carried out. In 2006, the research team decided to examine whether project interventions were having any effect on gender and other social inequalities in households and communities. A three-day workshop was held with four farmer leaders (two men and two women) and seven staff, during which key gender and other social relations were identified.

In March 2009, 33 in-depth interviews were conducted with participating households, purposively selected for maximum variation of gender, age, level of food security, region of Ekwendeni, health status, and participation in SFHC. The interviews took place in the participants' homes, and the questions were designed to assess changes in dietary diversity, child feeding practices, gender relations, and community dynamics. The results were also compared to earlier research conducted by the SFHC team. The authors also observed and documented various farmer educational activities and the FRT monthly meetings, and their findings were shared with the FRT and SFHC staff for feedback and discussion.

A three-day participatory workshop was held in May 2009 to discuss the project results and to assess the way forward with 60 project participants from a diverse range of groups. The workshop used small group activities to assess the effects of the project and potential activities for the future – for example, a discussion of challenges and successes, and dramas about challenges based on different activities in the project. In addition, research results from the last three years were shared and discussed.

Findings

In this section, we report on several key gender issues that have been identified through this research: household decision-making about crop use, women's leadership, household labour, and, finally, control of and access to household resources. We describe the approaches taken to address these issues, the challenges experienced in the attempt to increase food security through participatory processes while being attentive to gender, and other social inequalities. A key theme throughout our work has been the importance of linking key family priorities, such as improved food security, to gender issues.

Household decision-making about crop use

The initial survey results showed that among married couples, most decisions about what to do with the crop were made by either the husband or the husband's parents (Figure 10.1); wives made approximately one-quarter of all crop decisions. The crops for which the husband most often made the decision were, in order of highest to lowest: tobacco (79 percent), cassava (68 percent), hybrid maize (65 percent), and finger millet (58 percent), all of which are often cash crops. The crops for which the wife most often made the decision were, in order of highest to lowest: pumpkins (40 percent), cowpeas (33 percent), Bambara groundnuts (32 percent), pigeon pea (31 percent), and common bean and groundnuts (30 percent). Very few households reported shared decision-making for any crops, but parents figured significantly as decision-makers: for example, 31 percent of households said that it was the parents who had decided to grow pigeon pea, while parents made the decision to grow finger millet in 24 percent of households (Figure 10.1).

Initially, legume production increased; however, the higher yields did not translate into household food security, because men were controlling crop use and sales (Bezner Kerr 2008). These issues came to light at a participatory workshop, held in 2003, to which we explicitly invited a mix of people of different ages, food security levels, community roles, and gender. This approach is in keeping with deliberative democracy approaches designed to involve a diversity of views, increasing both options and the legitimacy of the process (Ryfe 2005). At this workshop, the initial project findings were presented in different ways, including dramas, talks, and posters. The workshop presentations generated a very vibrant group discussion, including a wide-ranging dialogue on the perceived causes of child malnutrition, which helped reveal some of the current child feeding practices that had

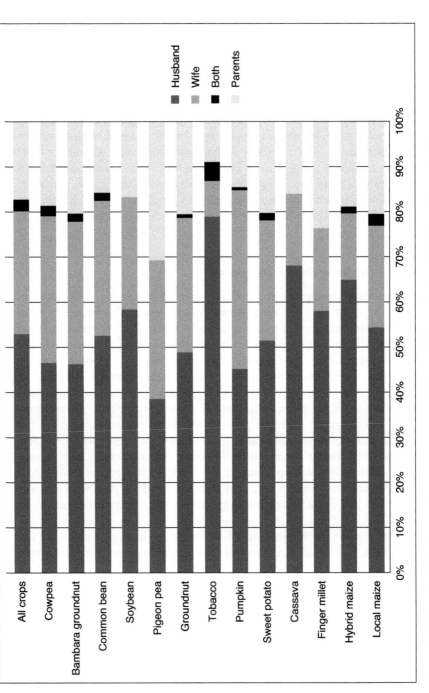

Figure 10.1 Household decision-maker on crop use. *n* = 231 married households and 1,886 total crop decisions

negative effects (Bezner Kerr, Berti et al. 2007; Bezner Kerr et al. 2008). It emerged that paternal grandmothers, who held a relatively powerful position within the extended family, felt threatened by the emphasis on men's taking on more child care and feeding practices, seeing the problem instead as laziness on the part of their daughters-in-law. Many older women considered child malnutrition to be caused by the violation of sociocultural norms rather than by feeding practices such as exclusive breastfeeding, but kept their views to themselves because of hospital teachings (Bezner Kerr et al. 2008).

At this same workshop, based on our rich discussion, we decided to focus on four key nutrition themes in the coming years to address some of these sensitive conflicts within households and extended families: exclusive breast-feeding, frequent feeding of young children, dietary diversity, and what we referred to as "family cooperation". Initially, a nutrition research team was set up to make house visits to families who had severely malnourished children, to advise them on healthy child feeding practices, and to raise some concerns about gender inequalities and competing views on causes of child malnutrition. The team was made up of men and women of different ages, but over time most of the men dropped out, and, despite the intensity of the visits, their impact was negligible (Patel et al. 2014).

We then developed "agriculture and nutrition discussion groups" to raise this type of issue in a safe space, in line with the deliberative democracy approach (Satzinger et al. 2009). One important component was to integrate agriculture and nutrition in the same discussion, in order to draw men into the conversation. We did this in part to overcome the men's lack of interest in participating in a "nutrition team", which they viewed as women's work.

The discussion groups were set up so that there was opportunity for men and women to meet separately, and to meet based on age, in order to create "safe spaces" where difficult issues could be raised and discussed openly. Small groups divided by age and gender (i.e., older men, younger men, older women, and younger women) then met and discussed themes decided on by the community facilitators, who were trained in participatory methods (Satzinger et al. 2009). The themes were seasonally based, and included both an agricultural and a nutritional component. For example, during the growing season there might be a discussion of good weeding methods and of healthy snacks to provide young children during times of food scarcity.

The discussions were organised as conversations rather than "lessons", with open-ended questions posed to the group to generate discussion. After an hour of small group discussion, the groups converged and shared the main ideas raised in each group. In this way, sensitive issues could be discussed and facilitated in the broader group without risking personal attacks or revealing names. These discussion groups were welcomed by the farmers as a unique experience in horizontal learning: they noted during in-depth interviews that they rarely had opportunity to share ideas and problem-solve about these issues in this way (Satzinger et al. 2009). They also noted that they had not previously had a forum where men and women sat down to discuss agriculture and nutrition together. While the men initially attended because of the agricultural topics, they found themselves drawn into discussions about nutritional issues, including exclusive breastfeeding or healthy child feeding practices – an experience that was in and of itself quite revolutionary for them.

Women's leadership roles in the FRT

The initial formation of the FRT was open: while the team had to include both women and men, gender equity was not required. The first seven villages selected 11 women and 18 men to make up the FRT, some of whom came from highly food insecure households (Bezner Kerr 2005b). However, in later formations in new villages, only men were voted to be members of the FRT. After analysis of the rising unequal ratios of men versus women, we decided that new FRTs had to have equal numbers of men and women, despite this approach being less "participatory".

Once the FRT was formed, a second challenge was women's active leadership. As a participatory project, and using deliberative democracy principles, the project encouraged all participants to speak during meetings, but according to local norms, women (particularly younger women) tended to be quiet. Women's participation had to be actively fostered by calling on them during meetings, by having small group discussions as part of meetings, and through one-on-one discussions.

Another issue arose as meetings and training were extended to villages that were farther away and required overnight stays. Men whose wives were FRT members expressed concern about infidelity, and at times even refused to allow their wives to participate in training. "Spousal meetings" with husbands and wives were held to discuss the role of the FRT and the project goals, and to provide assurance that people were not having affairs when travelling to other villages. This approach worked for most couples, although some active women leaders withdrew because of spousal jealousy and mistrust.

The FRT meetings also exposed the unequal division of labour at the village demonstration plots, with some people putting in hours of agricultural labour only to have the crop harvest seized by more powerful team members or village leaders. Again, there was a conflict between participatory methods, which tended to benefit the more vocal, powerful male members of the FRT, and a focus on gender equality. Multiple small group meetings with FRT members were held to resolve these issues and establish rules about village plot management.

Household labour

Various community activities, such as village "recipe days" and "crop residue incorporation days", were initiated by the FRT. Recipe days involve coming together in a village, cooking different healthy recipes, teaching one another how the food is prepared, and then eating together. They are often very festive events, and their popularity has increased over time, as has men's active involvement (Patel et al. 2014).

Crop residue incorporation days are explicit efforts for men to take on the task of incorporating legume residue soon after harvest. In this exercise, the FRT gathers in a village and invites farmers to participate in burying crop residue to improve soil fertility, demonstrating the activity on a local field, often the one belonging to the village headman.

Both activities were also intended subtly to increase men's involvement in such tasks as child care and feeding, and crop residue incorporation. While the recipe days appear to have influenced the role of men in child care and feeding (Chilanga 2013; Patel et al. 2014), it would seem that the crop residue incorporation days have not had a strong influence on the gender division of labour around this task. Field observations suggest that women are still primarily responsible for burying legume residue.

Evidence of change

Field observations, alongside the in-depth interviews conducted in 2009 and repeated in 2012 with different participants, showed strong evidence of change in gender relations between men and women. Much of the change is related to men taking on more household tasks, such as feeding young children and doing laundry. Of the 50 people interviewed in 2012, 23 described changes in the division of household labour since the previous round of interviews. As one woman stated when asked if there had been a change in her household:

> Every work that was considered as women's now can also be done by men. When I am busy or sick, my husband helps with child care and feeding. The work is done by both of us. Our voice [of women] is also accepted in the families.
>
> (Interview, Ekwendeni region, October 2012)

Another important area of change is shared decision-making, which has increased, according to many respondents. The project's educational activities stressed the need for couples to discuss what crops to grow, how to grow them, and what to do with the harvest. While there are still areas that are considered strictly men's or women's decision-making prerogative, people report a significant change in shared decision-making with regard to farming and food. As one woman reported:

> At first my husband was saying soya beans and groundnuts are under the care of women, but now he goes with me to plant, look after, and harvest both the soya and groundnuts. In short I can say we do all the activities in our family together . . . We all make decisions together and

we even remind each other what to do. We all discuss everything we do in our family. At first he [my husband] was making all decisions.

(Interview, Ekwendeni region, May 2009)

One participant described the following changes in his home:

We work very well with my wife and we agree in all our activities like farming, cooking and we always share ideas as a family. At first when my wife was asking me to give her a good stick [for starting a fire for the meal] I was refusing and saying I can never give you that, I am a man. I was even refusing to cook even when she was sick. Now we work together and we are good friends. Now we stay together very well because we understand each other. I and my wife, we make decisions together about our crops – if we want to sell or eat, or even when to harvest. This is so because we now know our needs and problems.

(Interview, Ekwendeni region, May 2009)

Some respondents indicated more wide-ranging decision-making, including family planning:

Our family relations have changed because we agree in many things which we do, and again because we have enough resources at the house. I and my husband budget together, even we agreed to stop having children.

(Interview, Ekwendeni region, May 2009)

In the description of shared decision-making, people emphasised not only making decisions together, but also doing more together in general. The act of farming and cooking together for their children, and making decisions jointly has brought couples closer together.

Before I joined SFHC I was the one making all the decisions, but now we do things together and plan and implement together. We harvest, plant, and do everything together. We all cook and care for the children together as a family.

(Interview, Ekwendeni region, May 2009)

Family relations are very good because we have all the needs . . . I have a good relationship with my family and community because we all have food and our discussions are always toward good crops and enough food. When my wife is away I cook and look after the children. When she comes back she eats the food which I left for her, while at first I was refusing all the domestic jobs like carrying firewood, water and cooking food. I was saying, "These are not my jobs, it's for you women". I thought my job was building and farming and having children. I look after children, bathe them and even feed them. I take my children to the hospital if sick, even my wife. Before I was making decisions alone. I was even just buying things for her, even clothes without asking her. She did not make any choices for anything, but now we discuss and do things together. I and my wife discuss what to plant in the garden and how much.

(Interview, Ekwendeni region, May 2009)

A common theme that arose in the interviews was the connection between agriculture, food, and improved household relations. People made connections between working together more in the field, having more food and a greater variety of food available, and experiencing less conflict. Some of the participants described quite profound changes within their homes. As one woman stated:

My husband and I used to quarrel. Now we have enough food, we don't quarrel. He used to leave me when there was nothing, go drinking with his friends. Now there is peace in our home. These legumes which we grow, we help each other. When we find money, we share together. Now these two years I have seen a great change. We don't quarrel. He has stopped drinking beer . . . He used to beat me after drinking. He has truly changed. People can tell you . . . We work together and help our children together. Sometimes if he is busy, we will come together and work together. We sit down and say, "how about if we sell a bit of this, a bit of that".

(Interview, Ekwendeni region, May 2009)

Complementing the many comments made during interviews are the long-term observations of two of the authors, who are both farmers from the villages and who are now working as community promoters with the project. Based on these observations, there are significant differences in gender relations in the communities. The two greatest areas of change are in the division of labour and in decision-making. Men have been observed going to collect water, going to the maize mill, helping with cooking, and caring for young children. Discussions in the villages reflect much more shared decision-making, and recognition of the importance of more equitable gender relations within the home. Fewer men drink heavily during the harvest period. In the past, there was much more conflict at home, which often surfaced during the late harvest period. Women would secretly sell crops or hide them from their husbands, to avoid having the crops used to buy alcohol. When the husband discovered the crops had been sold, he would shout and often beat his wife. These occurrences are much less common. There is still considerable gender inequality, and some households have not changed, despite these efforts, but the changes observed in the villages are significant.

One of the authors reported this example of a profound change. One of the participating farmers in his village, Mr Moyo,[1] did not do any domestic tasks, left most of the agricultural work to his wife, and was known to beat her regularly. Attendance at various project discussions and activities seemed to have a little impact on this situation, and so the farmer leader visited Mr Moyo and encouraged him to be more equitable. He also invited Mr Moyo over to his house numerous times, and then while Mr Moyo was visiting, prepared a meal, gathered firewood, or did other domestic tasks, as well as consulted with his wife, in the hopes that his example might have an influence. Over time, Mr Moyo began to slowly change his ways, and now actively helps with different household activities as well as contributing more to agricultural labour. This is an example of how participatory, dialogue-based, iterative methods can generate transformative change.

Gender and other forms of social inequality, however, occur at many different levels, and we observed several inequities at the community level. A common problem, for example, was village leaders who took advantage of improved land by letting their livestock forage in pigeon pea fields, or by seizing land that had been improved with legumes. The land was often taken from "tenants" – farmers, usually from southern Malawi, who were share-cropping tobacco, or widows who had been allowed to farm land after their husband's death (usufruct rights). Both groups have insecure land access in this part of Malawi, where most land is managed under customary tenure practices and inherited through a patrilineal system (Takane 2008). The village headman acts as the trustee of this land, with the right to allocate land within the area. Although sons inherit land, widows have temporary rights to the land after their husband dies, and can remain on the land until their sons are of age to farm (Takane 2008). Widows may also return to their natal village to request land from their kin, but, because of increasing land short-ages in Malawi, this often leads to land conflicts. In some situations, the husband's kin may seize land that is being farmed by a widow, even if this contravenes customary law (Takane 2008).

Several examples of these land seizures and livestock invasions emerged through field visits, observations, interviews, and focus group discussions. In the case of livestock, particular villages where this was a consistent problem were identified, and "livestock discussion meetings" were organised to try to convince the village leader to change his ways. During these meetings, a gift of pigeon pea was presented to the village headman with an explanation about how pigeon pea is a valuable resource, since it both improves soil and provides food for families and livestock. The village headman was implored to protect the pigeon pea from foraging livestock, for the long-term sustenance of the community. Some village leaders were very amenable to this request, and took steps to protect pigeon pea fields; others were disinclined to take action, not seeing the benefits for themselves, and later visits to these communities confirmed that livestock continued to graze on the pigeon pea fields. Some farmers abandoned pigeon pea because of this ongoing problem.

To date, the project has not tackled the issue of widows losing access to their husbands' land, in part because the problem seems intractable, and also because some staff and farmers see these practices as acceptable under cultural norms.

Discussion

The findings demonstrate that linking agriculture and food through multiple educational activities in the village, and using a dialogue-based approach rather than a simple set of lessons, can be effective at changing some unequal gender relations at the household and community level. The educational approach was based on both theories of feminist praxis and deliberative democracy (Table 10.2). Respondents indicated that doing educational activities *in the village* was important. As one community promoter commented, "The hospital does not go into the villages, but people were called to come to the hospital and learn on the flip chart. But here we go into the villages, teaching each other, so people hear more."

A second important component that draws from both feminist praxis and deliberative democracy is ensuring that everyone is involved in the discussion for change. As noted above, parents of both spouses are often involved in crop decisions, as well as child care and feeding practices. In keeping with a feminist intersectional praxis, the authors were attentive to different forms

Table 10.2 Educational approach and key theoretical concepts

Key aspects of educational approach	Description	Relevant theoretical concepts
Who	Involve everyone – older men and women, younger men and women – from the community, including village leaders	Inclusive, methods for empowerment
What	Integrated agriculture, food, and nutrition, which brings everyone "to the table"	Organising across differences Multi-sited gender inequality
When	Educational activities done multiple times, not just once	Iterative
Where	Training done in the villages, using practical examples (e.g., making recipes together)	Safe spaces for dialogue in deliberative democracy
How	Dialogue, problem-solving approach – pose questions, and solicit answers and ideas from the community	Deliberate dialogue Reflexive
	Small groups based on age, position, and gender, to allow discussion of sensitive issues	Countering power imbalances

of inequality, including age, status in the community, ethnicity, and kinship, and integrated different types of participatory methods that might address these inequalities (Bezner Kerr et al. 2008; Satzinger et al. 2009). An invitation was extended to elderly people, men and women from severely food insecure households, village leaders, midwives and traditional healers, and women of childbearing age to discuss how to improve the nutrition of young children in the community. Bringing in a diversity of views is in keeping with deliberative democratic approaches: it increases the legitimacy of the process and destabilises social norms, thereby increasing the likelihood of transformational change (Ryfe 2005). This approach is also in line with recent critiques of the autonomy paradigm in the reproductive health sector (Mumtaz and Salway 2009). Similar to findings in Pakistan on women's reproductive health and gender relations, the ethical principles of togetherness and cooperation were found to be important in Malawian communities, and kinship relations, including virilocal residence, to shape gender relations in crucial ways. By taking into account multi-sited gender relations and inequality, and not assuming that women's autonomy or independence is a good measure of improved gender equality, the research is moving beyond this autonomy paradigm.

Simply including everyone, however, was not enough to ensure that inequality was addressed. The project tried to create "safe spaces" where people could express sensitive or difficult topics, and to allow time for facilitated discussion of these issues. A key aspect that differed from conventional workshops, and was in keeping with a deliberative approach, was not delivering standardised messages or ideas, but instead fostering a dialogue in which problems were discussed, different views sought, and solutions generated collectively by the group. This approach, however, sometimes led to limited change. It was in the political interest of the more powerful members of communities to say that concerns of equity were being addressed, and having public discussions was often an ineffective way to explore more politically sensitive concerns. Domestic violence, for example, or seizure of people's improved land were not directly raised in these discussion groups. Various strategic and focused activities (e.g., livestock discussion meetings) were used to try to shift the power dynamics, to the benefit of more marginalised groups, but because of the participatory approach – discussing topics that arose spontaneously within the group, rather than deliberately introducing difficult issues – these more challenging topics were not addressed.

Paradoxically, the fact that the issue of gender inequality was not tackled directly may have been positive: in later interviews, men talked scornfully about "*jenda* [gender] activists" from non-governmental organisations that came into their communities and told them what to do (Chilanga 2013). The approach of the present study, which began with a focus on food security and nutrition, was viewed more favourably: men admitted that they began to trust the program, and thus were more inclined to listen when discussions of *jenda* came up (Chilanga 2013). The more indirect route, however, may mean that some women felt silenced or unable to speak about these more difficult issues.

The ideas were reinforced through educational activities carried out many times, in different formats, including hands-on demonstrations (e.g., recipes, farming practices). The iterative approach – i.e., visiting people multiple times to discuss the issues – allowed people to reflect and try out some of the ideas and then discuss their experiences and challenges. This repetition of ideas through multiple forms also worked to contest norms and beliefs previously held about gender. As one of the authors, himself an FRT member, stated, "At first I had intensive training from the project about gender, but I thought that if I tried these things, I might change into a woman, and my wife might also change. Over time I saw this wasn't the case, so I decided to follow these things."

Ambiguity, tensions, and complications are undeniably associated with the term *jenda*, as experienced during this project in Malawi. The participatory approach at times generated grand and unrealistic visions of what could be achieved in a short time. There was a tendency among staff to assume that a few meetings or discussions about gender would lead to extensive change in households. People sometimes applied the notion of *jenda* in very simplistic ways: for example, upon seeing a man carrying a bucket on his head, one woman shouted, "We are doing *jenda!*" Visible changes in a few tasks (such as carrying water or looking after young children) did not necessarily mean that more profound and difficult issues (such as domestic violence or control over finances) had changed. The interviews uncovered ongoing domestic violence, alcohol use, and minimal changes in division of labour and control of resources.

While the concept of gender and the use of participatory methods were often applied in very simplistic ways, the process revealed deep fissures within communities and households. Much of the tension lay between generations. Older women complained about "*jenda* activists" who were trying to destroy their culture. As other researchers have found (Cornwall and Goetz 2005; Hassim 2009), there were real tensions between a participatory approach and addressing unequal power dynamics within communities and households. The concerns of other marginalised groups, such as tenants and widows, were not always addressed through attention to gender. The power dynamics depended on context and scale: older women were often powerful in local communities but not in the hospital or broader society; younger women might have higher workloads with burying crop residue, but this investment of time and effort might be worthwhile if they benefited from reduced fertiliser application.

Nonetheless, multiple research activities (e.g., interviews, observations, focus group discussions) suggest that there are significant changes underway in communities where these combined approaches were applied. Linking farmer-led experimentation on organic methods, which built up farmer capacity and food security, to various educational activities around both nutrition and gender issues was effective, at least in relation to shared decision-making and division of labour. Men and women both reflected on the value of working together and having public and private discussions about household issues.

More deep-rooted and difficult issues such as domestic violence, and structurally embedded aspects such as ownership of land, were less open to change with these approaches. While there was some limited evidence of reduced domestic violence, the interventions did not have any measurable impact on laws or practices related to women's ownership of land. This may be due in part to an overemphasis on household relations, and lack of adequate attention to the multi-sited gender inequalities at work in communities, at the national and international level (Mumtaz and Salway 2009).

In terms of land seizures, the problem was in some ways more intractable, and the participatory methods utilised were inadequate for resolving the issue. Land distribution is highly unequal both for gender and wealth in Malawi, in large part because of colonial and postcolonial policies that benefited an elite group of landholders (Chinsinga 2011). The majority of smallholder farmers (approximately 2 million) cultivate on average 1 hectare of land, while 30,000 estates farm between 10 and 500 hectares (Kanyongolo 2005). Land policies have tended to duplicate a colonial land system that differentiated between smallholders on customary land and estates on private land. Women's loss of land due to widowhood is common in southern Africa, with one study in neighbouring Zambia (with a similar inheritance system) estimating that women farmed on average 35 percent less land, one to three years after the death of their husband (Chapoto et al. 2007). Recent studies in Malawi have documented increased land disputes in general, alongside a flexible interpretation of customary law, as smallholder farming families seek land by whatever means possible to eke out a livelihood (Takane 2008; Peters 2002; Peters and Kambewa 2007).

As a participatory project, we strove to respect local norms and leadership, but, in also aiming to change unequal relationships, we found ourselves in a contradictory position, given the disproportionate power that village headmen currently wield in land allocation in Malawi (Chinsinga and Chasukwa 2012). Addressing issues of land use and distribution would require a more explicit attempt to change land tenure systems, which in the current political context would be very difficult. A new land policy was drafted in 2002, but it has yet to be approved and is a highly politically charged issue, with elite politicians reluctant to adopt a land reform policy that would reduce their ready access to land (Peters and Kambewa 2007; IRIN 2010; Chinsinga 2011).

Conclusion

There are many contradictions embedded in the combination of participatory methods and attention to gender. We took a transformational approach that draws on concepts of "safe spaces" in deliberative democracy as well as a feminist praxis, emphasising the need for inclusion, dialogue, and iterative methods that allow for reflexivity and address power imbalances. These methods facilitated the development of multiple educational tools and methods – deployed in numerous places and involving various combinations of people – to counter gender inequality.

Despite the challenges of combining participatory approaches and attention to gender, the research indicated potential in the opening up of different spaces that foster dialogue and encourage deeper "deliberative" approaches to resolving conflicts, including those related to gender. Long-term research and work in these communities strongly suggests that there has been considerable movement towards a more equitable distribution of work among men and women, and that women are more involved in decision-making, particularly with regard to agriculture and food. We conclude that that creating "democratic" spaces that allow for creative problem-solving, organising practical and festive activities at the community level, ensuring that a diverse group of people is involved in the discussions, and providing multiple opportunities to voice different perspectives are all important ways to effect change in *jenda* relations.

Acknowledgements

The research and development activities reported in this chapter were carried out with financial support from the Social Sciences and Humanities Research Council of Canada, the International Development Research Centre, Canada, the Canadian Foodgrains Bank, and Presbyterian World Service and Development. Ideas inspired from Dr. Raj Patel along with the active contribution of farmers who are part of the Soils, Food, and Healthy Communities organization (www.soilsandfood.org) are also gratefully acknowledged.

Note

1 Pseudonyms are used to protect identity.

References

All website URLs accessed on 7 April 2016.

Aubel, Judi. 2012. "The Role and Influence of Grandmothers on Child Nutrition: Culturally Designated Advisors and Caregivers." *Maternal and Child Nutrition* 8 (1): 19–35. doi:10.1111/j.1740-8709.2011.00333.x.

Bezner Kerr, Rachel. 2005a. "Food Security, Entitlements and Gender Relations in Northern Malawi." *Journal of Southern African Studies* 31 (1): 53–74.

Bezner Kerr, Rachel. 2005b. "Informal Labor and Social Relations in Northern Malawi: The Theoretical Challenges and Implications of Ganyu Labor." *Rural Sociology* 70 (2): 167–87.

Bezner Kerr, Rachel. 2008. "Gender and Agrarian Inequality at the Local Scale." In Sieglinde S. Snapp and Barry Pound, eds, *Agricultural Systems: Agroecology and Rural Innovation.* San Diego, CA: Elsevier Press, 279–306.

Bezner Kerr, Rachel. 2010. "The Land Is Changing: Contested Agricultural Narratives in Northern Malawi." In Philip McMichael, ed., *Contesting Development: Critical Struggles for Social Change.* New York and London: Routledge, 98–115.

Bezner Kerr, Rachel, and Marko Chirwa. 2004. "Soils, Food and Healthy Communities: Participatory Research Approaches in Northern Malawi." *Ecohealth* 1 (Supplement 2): 109–19.

Bezner Kerr, Rachel, Peter R. Berti, and Marko Chirwa. 2007. "Breastfeeding and Mixed Feeding Practices in Malawi: Timing, Reasons, Decision Makers, and Child Health Consequences." *Food and Nutrition Bulletin* 28 (1): 90–9.

Bezner Kerr, Rachel, Peter R. Berti, and Lizzie Shumba. 2010. "Effects of a Participatory Agriculture and Nutrition Project on Child Growth in Northern Malawi." *Public Health Nutrition* 14 (8): 1466–72. doi:10.1017/S1368980010002545.

Bezner Kerr, Rachel, Laifolo Dakishoni, Lizzie Shumba, Rodgers Msachi, and Marko Chirwa. 2008. "'We Grandmothers Know Plenty': Breastfeeding, Complementary Feeding and the Multifaceted Role of Grandmothers in Malawi." *Social Science and Medicine* 66 (5): 1095–105. doi:10.1016/j.socscimed.2007.11.019.

Bezner Kerr, Rachel, Sieglinde S. Snapp, Marko Chirwa, Lizzie Shumba, and Rodgers Msachi. 2007. "Participatory Research on Legume Diversification with Malawian Smallholder Farmers for Improved Human Nutrition and Soil Fertility." *Experimental Agriculture* 43 (4): 437–53. doi:10.1017/S0014479707005339.

Bezner Kerr, Rachel, Rodgers Msachi, Laifolo Dakishoni, Lizzie Shumba, Zachariah Nkhonya, Peter R. Berti, . . . and Sheila Pachanya. 2012. "Growing Healthy Communities: Farmer Participatory Research to Improve Child Nutrition, Food Security, and Soils in Ekwendeni, Malawi." In Dominique F. Charron, ed., *Ecohealth Research in Practice: Innovative Applications of an Ecosystem Approach to Health.* Ottawa/New York: International Development and Research Centre (IDRC)/Springer.

Chapoto, Antony, T.S. Jayne, and Nicole Mason. 2011. "Widows' Land Security in the Era of HIV/AIDS: Panel Survey Evidence from Zambia." *Economic Development and Cultural Change* 59 (3): 511–47.

Chilanga, Emmanuel. 2013. *Assessing the Impact of Nutrition Education on Gender Roles and Child Care in Northern Malawi.* Master's thesis. Western University, London, Canada.

Chinsinga, Blessings. 2011. "Seeds and Subsidies: The Political Economy of Input Subsidies in Malawi." *IDS Bulletin* 42 (4): 59–68. doi:10.1111/j.1759-5436.2011.00236.x.

Chinsinga, Blessings, and Michael Chasukwa. 2012. "Youth, Agriculture and Land Grabs in Malawi." *IDS Bulletin* 43 (6): 67–77. doi:10.1111/j.1759-5436.2012.00380.x.

Cornwall, Andrea. 2008. "Unpacking 'Participation': Models, Meanings and Practices." *Community Development Journal* 43 (3): 269–83. doi:10.1093/cdj/bsn010.

Cornwall, Andrea, and Anne Marie Goetz. 2005. "Democratizing Democracy: Feminist Perspectives." *Democratization* 12 (5): 783–800. doi:10.1080/13510340500322181.

Hassim, Shireen. 2009. "After Apartheid: Consensus, Contention, and Gender in South Africa's Public Sphere." *International Journal of Politics, Culture, and Society* 22 (4): 453–64.

IRIN (Integrated Regional Information Networks). 2010. "Malawi: Without Land Reform, Small Farmers become 'Trespassers'" (online). www.irinnews.org/ report/95363/malawi-without-land-reform-small-farmers-become-trespassers.

Kanyongolo, Fidelis E. 2005. "Land Occupations in Malawi: Challenging the Neoliberal Legal Order." In Sam Moyo and Paris Yeros, eds, *Reclaiming the Land: The Resurgence of Rural Movements in Africa, Asia, and Latin America.* London: Zed Books, 118–41.

Msachi, Rodgers, Laifolo Dakishoni, and Rachel Bezner Kerr. 2009. "Soils, Food and Healthy Communities: Working towards Food Sovereignty in Malawi." *Journal of Peasant Studies* 36 (3): 700–6.

Mumtaz, Zubia, and Sarah Salway. 2009. "Understanding Gendered Influences on Women's Reproductive Health in Pakistan: Moving Beyond the Autonomy Paradigm." *Social Science and Medicine* 68 (7): 1349–56. doi:10.1016/j.socscimed. 2009.01.025.

Naples, Nancy A. 2011. "Sustaining Democracy: Localization, Globalization, and Feminist Praxis." *Sociological Forum* 28 (4): 657–81. doi:10.1111/socf.12054.

Patel, Raj, Rachel Bezner Kerr, Lizzie Shumba, and Laifolo Dakishoni. 2014. "Cook, Eat, Man, Woman: Understanding the New Alliance for Food Security and Nutrition, Nutritionism, and its Alternatives from Malawi." *Journal of Peasant Studies* 42 (1): 21–44. doi:10.1080/03066150.2014.971767.

Peters, Pauline E. 2002. "Bewitching Land: The Role of Land Disputes in Converting Kin to Strangers and in Class Formation in Malawi." *Journal of Southern African Studies* 28 (1): 155–78.

Peters, Pauline E., and Daimon Kambewa. 2007. "Whose Security? Deepening Social Conflict Over 'Customary' Land in the Shadow of Land Tenure Reform in Malawi." *Journal of Modern African Studies* 45 (3): 447–72. doi:10.1017/ S0022278X07002704.

Ryfe, David M. 2005. "Does Deliberative Democracy Work?" *Annual Review of Political Science* 8: 49–71. doi:10.1146/annurev.polisci.8.032904.154633.

Satzinger, Franziska, Rachel Bezner Kerr, and Lizzie Shumba. 2009. "Farmers Integrate Nutrition, Social Issues and Agriculture through Knowledge Exchange in Northern Malawi." *Ecology of Food and Nutrition* 48 (5): 369–82.

Snapp, Sieglinde S., P.L. Mafongoya, and Stephen R. Waddington. 1998. "Organic Matter Technologies for Integrated Nutrient Management in Smallholder Cropping Systems of Southern Africa." *Agriculture, Ecosystems & Environment* 71 (1–3): 185–200. doi:10.1016/S0167-8809(98)00140-6.

Snapp, Sieglinde S., Malcolm J. Blackie, Robert A. Gilbert, Rachel Bezner Kerr, and George Y. Kanyama-Phiri. 2010. "Biodiversity Can Support a Greener Revolution in Africa." *Proceedings of the National Academy of Sciences* 107 (48): 20840–5. doi:10.1073/pnas.1007199107.

Takane, Tsutomu. 2008. "Customary Land Tenure, Inheritance Rules, and Smallholder Farmers in Malawi." *Journal of Southern African Studies* 34 (2): 269–91. doi:10.1080/03057070802037969.

11 Gendered technology adoption and household food security in semi-arid Eastern Kenya

Esther Njuguna, Leigh Brownhill,
Esther Kihoro, Lutta Muhammad,
and Gordon M. Hickey

Introduction

Hunger and malnutrition are scientific and moral problems that lie at the root of most other global development challenges, since malnutrition effectively blocks development and achievement across generations (Kavishe 1995). In Kenya, agriculture is the cornerstone of the economy. It employs millions, feeds more, and has a multiplier effect in that farming supplies raw materials to, and supports, many other industries. Small-scale farming (on plots averaging 0.2–0.3 hectares) dominates food production in Kenya, pointing to the importance of directing research and development efforts towards smallholder and subsistence farming systems (Hickey et al. 2012).

Because most agricultural production takes place at the household level, gender relations are central to understanding both how the farming system works and the extent to which initiatives to build resilience in the farming system (e.g., in relation to project research activities) support equity and improve food and nutrition security. Men and women in various types of households may make separate and autonomous decisions, as well as joint decisions, on important matters such as adoption of new agricultural technologies and practices. These decisions have implications for who provides the labour and who reaps what rewards of that adoption. For example, it has been shown that when women control income, they generally allocate a higher percentage to food, health, clothing, and education for their children than men do (FAO n.d.). As a result, a better understanding of the gendered division of household labour is an essential component of enabling household food provisioning and the marketing of agricultural products through agricultural innovation systems capable of supporting resilience.

One premise on which this study was grounded is that food insecurity is closely related to inequitable household power relations, within which women lack sufficient access to, control over, and use and ownership of livelihood resources (Meinzen-Dick et al. 2011), including the elusive assets of time and mobility. As a result, better understanding of where

such inequities lie may help identify ways in which research can better contribute to overcoming barriers to resilient household food and nutrition
security.

Literature review/theoretical perspective

Many authors have observed and measured gendered differences in the
adoption of agricultural innovations and technologies (Sanginga et al. 1999;
Doss and Morris 2001; Tiruneh et al. 2001; Kinkingninhoun-Mêdagbé et al.
2010). Constraints to innovation adoption among women include risk
aversion, insecure access to as well as land and other natural resources,
labour, credit, research, and extension; poor or poorly implemented policies;
and insufficient knowledge sharing and joint action among key actors
(Quisumbing 1996; Ogunlana 2004; Eidt et al. 2012). Differences in culturally and socially constructed food customs, economic interactions, and
mobility also impact women's capacity to adopt. Historical and geographical
differences further add to the overall complexity of research on adoption of
agricultural innovations to address food insecurity.

In addressing the specific dilemma of women's *not adopting* agricultural
innovations at the same rates as men, our analysis considered both on-farm
household decision-making and the scientific research methods employed
by agricultural researchers. This study sought to better understand the
adoption cycle from the household perspective, with an examination of *what*
is being "offered" for adoption; *how* it is introduced; and *what women
do adopt*, under what terms and conditions, and *with what results* for household food security. The findings have practical and conceptual implications,
suggesting mechanisms for supporting household and community resilience
by identifying ways in which barriers to women and men farmers' adoption
of resilience-building agricultural innovations can be lowered.

Since our study examined the dynamics of adoption in relation to the
achievement of improvements in food security, it was of central importance
that *what* was included for adoption in the study was capable of improving
food security outcomes and measures. While this may seem like an obvious
point, it is important to state it directly because a segment of the literature
on adoption of agricultural innovations does not explicitly assess the food
security outcomes of the technologies under consideration, but focuses
on return on investments, both at farm and stock market levels. Scholarly
discussion of adoption of agricultural innovations is strongly rooted in
econometric analyses of the diffusion of technologies arising through the
Green Revolution (Feder and Umali 1993). Much focus has subsequently
been placed on casting adoption as a determinant of economic growth, and
on understanding adoption decisions in terms of risk assessment, profitability,
and the spread or diffusion of "modern" technologies (Feder and Umali
1993; Teklewold et al. 2013; Fisher and Kandiwa 2014). Recognising that
economic growth alone is not a reliable indicator of household food security,

the scope of the study also considered other values and benefits accrued by farmers in the adoption cycle, chiefly nutritional, social, and ecological.

Gender analyses have clearly demonstrated that power is frequently unequally distributed among farm household members. This can be seen in inequities in control over resources, and in unequal division of labour and benefits (Alderman et al. 1995). The fact that women suffer higher rates of malnutrition and hunger than men – "twice as many women suffer from malnutrition as men, and girls are twice as likely to die from malnutrition as boys" (FAO n.d.) – further highlights the inadequacy of "increased farm product profitability" as a singular solution to hunger and malnutrition among all household members (see also Quisumbing 2003; Brownhill et al. 2016). In the Kenyan context, the promotion of cash cropping has at times diverted natural and financial resources from women's to men's control, sometimes leading to women's reluctance or even resistance to engage in adoption (Turner et al. 1997).

The dominant drive in development and research is towards the commercialisation of farming. This shifts the focus of many studies away from actual health outcomes and other non-priced benefits of innovation adoption, such as improved ecological well-being and social capital. Some studies do consider non-priced benefits, but separately – for instance, studies on the ecological benefits derived from adoption of particular production techniques (Terry and Khatri 2009). The present study extended such analyses to examine an integrated range of non-priced values (e.g., dietary diversity) associated with an integrated set of technologies and farm practices, in order to better understand what women and men consider and value when they make decisions about innovation adoption.

Scholarship on the centrality of women to agricultural development in general, and to the achievement of food security in particular, has spurred a turn in the adoption literature to include more attention to gendered patterns of adoption (Doss and Morris 2001). While female-headed households are widely understood to be more food insecure than male-headed households (Kassie et al. 2014), and while men tend to adopt new agricultural technologies more robustly than women (Doss and Morris 2001; Peterman et al. 2010), there remains some definitional confusion about how to distinguish male and female activities within farming households (Appleton 1996; Ragasa 2012). Doss's influential 2002 study on gendered cropping patterns in Ghana argues that "few crops can be defined as men's crops and none are clearly women's crops", a finding that flies in the face of common perceptions about the crops that women and men prefer, and from which they reap benefits. Doss addresses a key limitation of her study, which does not count women farmers who "farm for household consumption on plots held by men" or whose "individual plots may contain crops for which different individuals claim ownership rights" (2002: 1999). These categories of women comprise a significant proportion of female farmers, and their exclusion from analysis has important implications for understanding the gendered patterns of agricultural labour.

Doss et al. elaborated on the distinctions among households, in particular with regard to land ownership: "When only household-level data are collected, researchers do often compare the landownership patterns of male- and female-headed households. However, this approach may underestimate women's landownership by ignoring the land owned by women in male- headed households" (2013: 4). Such analyses provide a useful caution against generalisations concerning women's and men's rates of adoption and crop preferences. They also indicate a need for more in-depth consideration of the relations among women and men in the specific households under study. This was addressed by including categories of male-headed, female-headed, and male-headed–female-managed households in the data analysis, as well as considering overlapping entitlements, such as wives' power over gardens on land owned by their husbands.

This chapter acknowledges the negative impact of inequality, in particular in the way that, in silencing or sidelining women's knowledge and prefer- ences, inequality impoverishes dialogues and debates on local solutions to hunger and malnutrition. Drawing women back into the discussions of science, technology, development, and policy likewise enriches the debates. In particular, a gendered analysis offers insight into women's adoption prefer- ences, their capabilities to choose, and the sometimes hidden and undervalued benefits that they, and their children, derive from their subsistence-informed farming decisions. Our intent was to contribute to "unblocking" existing adoption pathways, in ways that complement and strengthen efforts to improve women's access to resources. Women's priorities and preferences (as well as men's) were used to inform next steps (e.g., in research directions and policy recommendations) to increase women's adoption of food and nutrition security-enhancing agricultural innovations. During the three-year study, the need also arose to clear new pathways (for adoption, information, enterprise) through the less-charted territories connecting women's farming preferences with priorities in science, development, policy, and the market.

The analytical lens used here focused on both "non-adopting women" and those who promote the innovations: the local and international researchers, development officials, funders, and policymakers. By including a focus on those promoting technologies and other innovations for farmer adoption, this analysis addressed the extent to which research, development, and policy have been sufficiently informed by women's preferences, interests, capacities, and expertise. In the process, the authors drew self-reflectively on their own experiences in a participatory research project, both to assess the outcomes of the research in terms of women's rates of adoption of innovations, and to contrast their methodology with others that are less fully guided by gender transformative and farmer-led approaches.

As important as the question of the food security merits of what is promoted for adoption are the questions of what methods of diffusion are employed, and with what potential benefits, for whom. These questions recognise the long history of agricultural and environmental interventions in

Kenya in general, and in the eastern counties in particular (Tiffen et al. 1994; Ifejike Speranza et al. 2008). Colonial initiatives in the 1930s and 1940s accomplished the terracing of thousands of miles of hillside in Machakos by enforcing compulsory labour among villagers in the vicinity, who were mainly women, as men were engaged in migrant labour (Tiffen et al. 1994). A good "innovation" was thus introduced in a top-down, punitive manner that engendered serious resistance.

At other points on the spectrum are soil conservation initiatives, and development efforts of all kinds, that are founded on participatory principles, differentiated by their varied goals, methodologies, and outcomes. Indeed, it was in a Kenya Agricultural Research Institute (KARI) partnership study of soil conservation efforts in Kenya that researchers developed the participatory learning and action research (PLAR) model to engage community knowledge, interests, and "ownership" of conservation practices (Defoer 2002; Eksvärd and Björklund 2010). The present study focused on both the *whats* of adoption (evaluating the food and nutrition security contributions of the innovations) and the *hows* (both in terms of research design and implementation, and in terms of farmers' day-to-day adoption activities), to assess food security outcomes in relation to the project's objectives and methodology.

The research sought to identify means by which both women and men farmers can empower themselves to adopt resilience-building agricultural innovations. The study was thus organised specifically to work with farmers to select the resilience-enhancing practices and technologies they want to evaluate as methods of addressing their own households' food and nutritional security needs. These local solutions and empowerment objectives are based on the scientific understanding that the social relations that support food and nutrition security are characterised by equity (Njuki and Sanginga 2013), diversity (Kumar 2002), and prioritisation of the reproduction of ecological conditions to allow for continued production (Shiva 2013) as well as inheritance by younger generations (Muriuki 1974).

Theoretical framing

In light of unsettled debates over men's and women's crops and land (Doss 2002; Doss et al. 2013), and over the importance of farm income to household food security strategies, an important conceptual starting point for this study was the recognition of the tensions and overlaps between subsistence and market-oriented farming systems.

Subsistence and smallholder farming systems are the starting places for the majority of Kenyan farmers. The project's participatory approach revealed that the semi-arid farming systems are surprisingly robust. This is true especially in light of the condition of the surrounding support systems, including extension, infrastructure, and markets, which require as much, or more, improvement and innovation as farming practices. More precisely, improvements to the farming system (through adoption of resilient technologies and practices) will perhaps succeed to the extent that extension and markets serve the development and maintenance of the nutrition and income value chains that this system might sustain.

The research was likewise guided by an eco-feminist perspective, which considers gendered and ecological intersections in examining food security concerns. This transformative gender approach, with its recognition of research "subjects" as active agents of innovation, finds methodological expression in Cooksey and others' insistence on two-way dialogue in research and development and, moreover, "webs of communication" among key actors (Vogel et al. 2007; Cooksey 2011). The results of the adoption survey were analysed in a step-wise tracing-out of who does all of the activities and makes the decisions in farm families' efforts to adopt farming innovations.

A few caveats must be added here. The crops being evaluated in the project were all high-value traditional crops, and while some had higher market demand and cash value than others, and some were more preferred as foodstuffs than others, all shared both income and nutritional benefits. None could be said to be only and purely a cash crop, and in fact, all of the crops evaluated by farmer groups in the project can be referred to as high-value traditional crops, such as sorghum, millet, green gram (mung beans), and cowpeas, which are typically women's preference and domain.

One effect of this choice of "typical subsistence" crops to be evaluated in the project is that the distinction between cash and food crops was not as strongly present as it would have been in a different setting. Mango and pawpaw (papaya) were included in the survey and analysis of findings; although they were not among the crops promoted for adoption in the project, they are important to the local farming systems in these semi-arid agro-ecological zones. They also provide a point of contrast to the high-value traditional crops that were more central to the project's overall goals. While sorghum and millet are valuable food crops, mango and pawpaw are typically market-oriented crops controlled by men, and the patterns of decision-making and division of labour and benefits are likewise strongly skewed in favour of men. These contextual factors are discussed further in the following sections.

Methodology

The project

The "Innovating for Resilient Farming Systems" food security research project, funded by the Canadian International Food Security Research Fund (CIFSRF) and implemented in Kenya by KARI and McGill University, facilitated farmer evaluation and adoption of a range of components of resilient farming systems in three semi-arid counties of Eastern Kenya: Tharaka-Nithi, Makueni, and Machakos. The research focused on an integrated assessment of social, economic, knowledge-based, institutional, and policy factors that impact farmers' ability to adopt socially and ecologically resilient farming system practices and technologies. These technologies drew on local resources, and included indigenous crop varieties and poultry breeds, as well as those varieties and practices developed by agricultural research institutes and government extension services. The general objective of the project was to contribute to improved food security among women and men in hunger-prone communities, by improving the conditions for sustained farmer adoption of resilience-enhancing farming practices.

Because of the context that it provides for the discussion of the survey that generated the data analysed in this chapter, a brief review of the methodology employed in the research project of which this particular gendered adoption study was a part is presented. The project's activities were undertaken in the lower midland (LM), lower humidity to semi-arid (LM4) and semi-arid (LM5) agro-ecological zones (AEZs), where 600–800 mm of annual rainfall is distributed in two peak seasons (March–May and October–November). Farmers in these AEZs typically combine subsistence food and livestock production under conditions of only moderate intensity of land use.

A combination of high-value traditional food crops (early-maturing or drought-tolerant varieties) and integrated practices including soil fertility, water harvesting, and livestock and pest management practices, were evaluated by and with smallholder farmers using an adaptation of the "mother and baby" trial design (Snapp 2002), termed primary participatory agricultural technology evaluations (PPATEs). In the PPATEs (equivalent to "mother" trials), farmers in selected groups grew, evaluated, and compared two or three varieties of eight different resilience-enhancing crop types. Members of the PPATE groups shared their knowledge with members of other farmer groups (secondary participatory agricultural technology evaluations (SPATEs), equivalent to "baby" trials) through a mentoring relationship, whereby secondary group members picked a subset of technologies that they found most attractive from the PPATE group evaluation set. The project engaged the participation of a total of 54 PPATE groups and 216 SPATE groups representing over 5,000 farmers.

As a result of this focus on farmer learning in the adoption process, adoption was reconceptualised as part of a cycle of farmer innovation, involving a triple-A cycle – analysis–action–assessment – through which farmers made daily and seasonal decisions (Kavishe 1995).

While taking direction from this change-oriented model, the three steps of the triple-A cycle were also modified to more fully represent the seasonal activities of farming. The three steps identified were *adoption*, *adjustment*, and *adaptation*. These steps completed the model's representation of the cycle of farm-level decision-making and activities concerning changes in farming practices.

The basic premise is that *adoption* requires some *adjustment* of the farmers' practices and work patterns. The success of these adjustments leads to *adaptation* of the farming system to be more resilient in the face of the climatic and socioeconomic conditions that farmers face. In iterative fashion, these adaptations feed back into further decisions and actions on adoption (of the same, new, or additional innovations), with subsequent further adjustment of farming practices, leading to deeper or more resilient adaptive capacity. Within the process of adjusting farming practices to meet the needs of the adopted innovation, it was noted that it is largely women's agricultural labour and related resources that undergo "adjustment".

The project's view of adoption as a seasonal cycle complemented its analysis of the household-level links on the agricultural value chains that bring crops from field to plate. These chains may take products to local or regional markets, and then to consumers' kitchens and tables; or they may channel food from the farmer's field, to their granary, and to their table directly, constituting an on-farm nutritional value chain. In either case, the people who inhabit or activate each link in a crop's value chain are identified, and the many overlaps among the several value chains that farmers pursue are examined. Thus a complex matrix of value chains, which represent both priced and non-priced values, forms the households' integrated farming system and wider livelihood system.

We attempted to nuance the analysis by teasing out the gender relations at different points in the adoption cycle and in the larger diversity of value chains, and from there assessing ways forward for gender equity in household food and nutrition security. It is important to recognise that market value chains are developed within a context of the enterprises' many other benefits, including direct household food consumption, and concomitant non-priced benefits of health, nutrition, ecological well-being, and the potential for youth employment generation. In this study, concepts of *local* value chains, and of *nutritional* value chains, expressed the intention to maintain a focus on these wider benefits of adoption not only for women, but for their communities and ecologies in general.

The gender survey

After five seasons of evaluation in the PPATE groups and three seasons in the SPATE groups, the gender research stream conducted a survey to assess the impacts of, and gender dynamics at play within, the adoption decision process. Households were sampled from the PPATE and SPATE groups in the three counties, while a set of randomly selected non-project households were also included in the sample for comparison. A total of 405 households were sampled. Tables 11.1 and 11.2 summarise the sample, by farmer group membership type and by head of household (male-headed, male-headed–female-managed, and female-headed).

The survey incorporated questions on adoption, resilience, labour, asset ownership, nutrition, and management of indigenous chickens (a project innovation). This chapter reports mainly on the results concerning adoption.

Table 11.1 Households differentiated by the way they participated in the KARI/
McGill University Food Security Research Project

Farmer group membership type	Machakos	Makueni	Tharaka-Nithi	Total
PPATE	59	73	55	187
SPATE	51	65	20	136
Non-project farmer	23	36	23	82
Total	133	174	98	405

Table 11.2 Number of households surveyed in each county, by type

	Machakos	Makueni	Tharaka-Nithi	Total
Male-headed and -managed	92	111	77	280
Male-headed–female-managed	14	34	9	57
Female-headed and -managed	25	29	12	66
Child/orphan	2	0	0	2
Total sample surveyed				405

The main disaggregating factor was the set of "who" questions: who benefits from various income streams; who participates in various tasks; who owns assets in the household; and who makes decisions over those assets. To assess the impacts of the project interventions, the questions were based on two time frames: before (2011) and after (2014) project implementation.

Results

Survey respondents

Among the respondents to the gender survey, 280 of the households were headed and managed by men; 57 were male-headed but female-managed, since the men lived away from home for a substantial number of months per year, leaving the women as *de facto* heads of household; and 66 households were *de jure* female-headed. Two households, in Machakos, were orphan-headed; because there were so few, they were not included in the statistical analysis.

Seed access by the respondents

The gender survey sought to understand the adoption cycle from its inception: where farmers get seeds (source, indicating the different trading centres), who is responsible for obtaining seed for the family, and how far from their homesteads the household members have to travel to obtain seed. The number of sources was highest for the male-headed and -managed households, who reported 16 options in Machakos, whereas the female-headed households (both *de facto* and *de jure*) indicated that they had only 4 to 7 options.

In terms of the distances covered in sourcing the appropriate seeds, Machakos farmers presented an interesting example. Across the sample, women reported having a smaller radius of mobility, measured in terms of how far they travelled to source seed. But in the Machakos sample, where the female-headed households reported covering an average of 4.9 km to source seed, and male-headed households covered 13 km on average, the members of male-headed–female-managed households covered an average of 20.2 km. This may be explained by the fact that the men from these households work in distant towns where they may be able to access seed and remit it to their families.

All farm household types in the sample reported an increase in the amounts of drought-tolerant or early-maturing seeds that they were planting after participating in the project (Table 11.3). The biggest gains were seen in the amount of green gram seed that farmers bought. Green gram is a crop that has a high demand among traders for retail sale to consumers in urban areas of Kenya, and occasionally as an export commodity to Asian countries. Farmers in the three counties were growing green gram as a cash crop more than they were using it for household consumption.

Adoption of, and labour provision in, different crops

The next objective was to find out who initiates the choice of crops to plant in a season, and who provides the labour for ploughing, planting, weeding, harvesting, and marketing farm produce.

The results generally showed that men are the main decision-makers when it comes to choice of enterprises and marketing of the produce in the survey sample. This became especially prominent in the permanent and market-oriented crops like mango and papaya. Even in female-headed households, where one might expect the women to make most decisions, it seemed there were male relatives who were influential in the decision to plant mango and pawpaw. Although there was a degree of collaboration in labour provision between men and women, women in all the household types provided considerably more labour than men in planting, weeding, and harvesting. However, there was a clear difference among the women who participated in the project as members of PPATEs: the PPATE women participated more in the marketing stage compared to SPATE members and non-project members. Women in the male-headed households appeared to have much less decision-making power and participation in labour provision in the different production steps when compared to women in *de facto* and *de jure* female-headed households.

Table 11.3 Amount (in kg) of drought-tolerant, early-maturing seeds planted by different types of farm households before and after participating in the project

	Male-headed and -managed				Male-headed–female-managed				Female-headed and -managed			
	Before		After		Before		After		Before		After	
	N	Mean	N	Mean	N	Mean	N	Mean	N	Mean	N	Mean
Maize	250	12.05	245	13.91	49	15.67	50	8.9	62	13.17	61	9.39
Sorghum	139	2.99	132	3.5	29	3.05	26	2.73	32	3.38	30	2.73
Millet	72	3.66	70	3.79	10	3.95	11	4.86	17	3.27	13	3.62
Green gram	220	5.08	217	6.33	42	5.8	46	8.45	58	4.43	58	4.86
Cowpeas	220	4.41	221	5.48	45	4.93	49	4.97	59	4.63	58	4.29
Pigeon peas	199	3.85	206	4.26	36	4.48	39	4.68	54	3.27	52	3.31
Dolichos	46	2.11	65	3.1	21	2.98	26	2.56	16	1.3	17	2.07
Beans	183	9.12	165	11.54	29	8.38	26	7.19	46	8.47	41	8.59

Participation in farmer groups

Farmer groups have been identified as an important avenue for agricultural knowledge dissemination within communities. The respondent households were therefore asked if both men and women belonged to farmer groups. Up to 50 percent of women in the PPATE and SPATE categories were members of farmer groups, some participating in up to six different groups. In contrast, fewer than 20 percent of men and women in the non-project farmers' category were members of a farmer group. Farmers in this category miss out on a number of opportunities to learn about innovations in the agricultural sector, and to give and receive mutual support for farming and related activities. These missed opportunities are reflected in household food security status.

In all categories in the household sample, women participated in groups more than men. This likely emphasises the social capital that women often build, maintain, use, and rely upon to strengthen their capacities to engage in labour as well as to compensate, to some degree, for lack of access to key assets through sharing of labour and resources.

Food security improvement

The ultimate goal of the project was to improve the participants' food security status. A proxy for food security in the study was the number of months per year of sufficiency in the provisioning of food for all members of the household. Respondents were asked to compare the period before and after the project. Among the PPATE farmers, the number of households reporting a shortage of food decreased for all months after the project. Among the SPATE farmers, the number of households without enough food decreased slightly in the period after the project. Among the non-project farmers, there were several months (May, June, September, and November) when more people did not have enough food (see Figure 11.1).

Discussion

By disaggregating gendered patterns of engagement along the range of activities that follow initial "adoption decisions", the research showed that the men in the survey sample contributed to decision-making more than to labour in the adoption cycle, and, moreover, that men's share of decision-making power over allocation or use of income was greater than both their labour contribution and their participation in initiating the adoption of the chosen technology. These findings support previous research suggesting that men benefit far more from crop income, and therefore from women's labour, than do the women themselves (Sorenson 1996; Turner et al. 1997).

Income is not the only measure of value in the agricultural product value chains, nor in farmers' adoption decisions. Feeding the family directly from

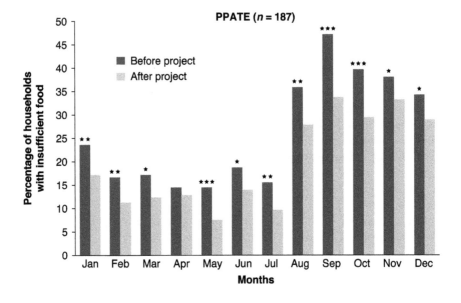

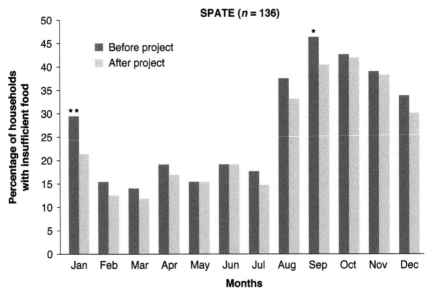

Figure 11.1 Percentage of households with insufficient food before and after the KARI/McGill project

Key: ★★★ P < 0.01; ★★ P < 0.05; ★ P < 0.10 (McNemar Test; one-tailed test).

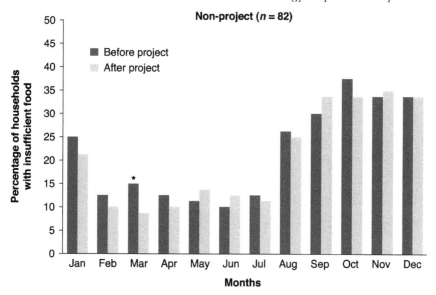

Figure 11.1 (Continued)

the farm is the prime example of a non-priced benefit that is of immense value in any adoption calculations farmers may make. Moreover, a review of the non-priced benefits of given agricultural innovations reveals a set of "in-kind" contributions to household food security, which in the end may be more important to, and more within the control of, women than the narrowly defined value of a cash income. The study turned to the dynamics of these priced and non-priced benefits to explore gendered adoption decisions, and some of the food security outcomes of those decisions.

The anticipated finding was that women preferred one type or set of crop(s) and that men preferred others, and that the food security impacts and outcomes would also differ between genders. What was found instead was a more nuanced gendered pattern in the adoption decision-making process (see Figure 11.2). Depending on household type, and on type of farmer group membership, women in the sample displayed considerable power in introducing both traditional "food" crops and "cash" crops, in terms of both sole decision-making and joint decision-making with spouses or other adult male relatives. At the same time, when it came to the implementation of "adoption" (jointly derived on-farm innovation decisions), inequalities re-entered the gendered division of labour in the production, sale, and share of consumption of particular crops (e.g., cowpea, green gram).

Joint decision-making did not, in the sample surveyed, lead to an equal division of agricultural labour. In adjustment of on-farm activities to accommodate the adopted innovations, women took on the bulk of these changes.

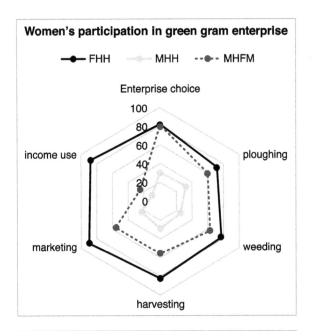

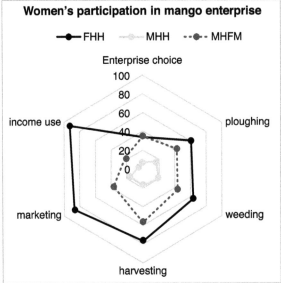

Figure 11.2 Analysis of women's participation in the various steps in selected
enterprises categorised by whether the household is male-headed,
male-headed–female-managed, or female-headed

Key: FHH: female-headed household; MHH: male-headed household; MHFM:
male-headed–female-managed household.

In terms of other values gained and reinforced in the process, socio-cultural, ecological, and nutritional benefits were shared generally across the households of those associated with the project's evaluations, with those most closely aligned with project farmer groups reaping greater gains than their counterparts less centrally involved in the project. The adaptations made included a greater diversity of income and food sources, inputs into natural resource management, and greater household food sufficiency.

The research findings identified a gendered complexity of on-farm adoption processes, and suggested measures capable of assessing complex innovation decisions and activities over time. Researchers' assessments would benefit from taking into account not only the moment of decision, but the entire adoption cycle through which the decision to adopt leads to adjustments of the farming system. To the degree that *what* is adopted and *how* it is implemented contribute to resilience, the cycle results in socioecological adaptations in response to shocks and uncertainties.

The adoption cycle and the subsequent development of local value chains are constituted by a complexity of highly gendered decisions, resource allocations, and livelihood activities. With this understanding, the questions of non-adoption and dis-adoption are also illuminated because the balance of women's decision-making may be more tightly tied to the whole adoption cycle than has previously been credited. In other words, women's decision-making on adoption is firmly grounded in their experience of various crops' successes and failures, and their balancing of resources, time, and labour to contribute to their households' daily subsistence (Ashraf et al. 2009). The existence of both market and nutritional value chains may make an important difference to women, whose access to market income is limited, but whose control over food in the granary is nearly complete.

Given women's historically low rates of agricultural innovation adoption, debate continues over how best to increase women's participation in, and share of the benefits from, particular scientific knowledge production processes. The project addressed this question by focusing on a range of crops and farming practices that women had ranked as highly preferred. As a result, two goals were achieved: gains in a range of measures of household food and nutrition security, and the reversal of women's non-adoption trend – *when something they had chosen and prioritised* was the subject of study.

In conjunction with adoption of women's preferred crops and farm management practices, group work offers a socially networked pathway towards improving household food security. Examination of the adoption cycle inquired into group membership to confirm what others have also found, namely, that group membership accelerates adoption (Abebaw and Haile 2013; Ramirez 2013; Kassie et al. 2014). There is much less attention in the literature, however, to how adoption, supported by group membership, in turn further contributes to maintaining and building social networks as a non-priced benefit that is especially valuable to women. During the project period, social networks were reported to have strengthened through a number of avenues, including training in dietary diversity and the formation of marketing opportunity groups to aggregate and negotiate produce prices with marketers. These positive steps are in line with what other scholars have noted: that "in order for development interventions to succeed, strategies must clearly rely on, and take cognizance of, local 'social capital' and the indigenous skills possessed by communities" (Nel et al. 2000: 26).

Farmers are agents of innovation and have experimented for generations to create most of the tremendous stock of seed varieties known to the world (Fowler and Mooney 1991; Kloppenburg 2004). Their agency is seen in their creativity, and also in their critiques, as farmers sometimes actively resist scientific interventions that "would seem like impositions or even as active attempts to 'convert' [farmers] to [the scientists'] way of thinking" (Cooksey 2011: 287). Resistance to adoption of agricultural innovations can point to a mismatch between the scientists' and farmers' views on what is a "successful", "proven", or "effective" technology, or between the scientists' and the farmers' expectations and resources. This mismatch is evocative of the inequities often found between women and men within households, and may contribute to the problem of low rates of farmer adoption of agricultural innovations.

The study of gendered adoption processes also brought to light a "missing link" in the local agricultural product value chain, that is, smallholder and subsistence farmers' links to local markets. This recognition points to a need to better support and develop Eastern Kenya's widely networked market system for locally preferred agricultural products to move the potential supply of, and demand for, healthy, nutritious, local grains, legumes, and produce. Among the households surveyed, what has been referred to as the *radius of women's mobility* appeared to impact women's adoption decisions, from sourcing of seed to their access to and control over market relations and transactions. Based on the research results, the scale and scope of trade most likely to empower women is the "walkable distance", suggesting that a multi-level strategy including trade that takes place within women's typical radius of mobility, with attention given to the sociocultural specificities of each local place, could be beneficial. The results also support the need for policies that not only promote local market development but also protect them from policies and programs that impede, weaken, or crowd out small-scale private-sector actors within these local markets.

Women's access to markets and income could also be increased by widening women's radius of mobility and expanding their resource ownership (e.g., land and vehicles). But these changes are not easily articulated in policies or implemented in programs, given the extent to which they require changes in intimate day-to-day livelihood activities and relations between husbands and wives, youth and elders, in culturally diverse households and communities. These kinds of changes bring development researchers into the realm of deeper social, cultural, and legal transformations that are perhaps more legitimately the purview of the Kenyan citizens and state. Research by

Kenyans and by international scientists can inform debates on such changes, and provide recommendations for policy and programming; but, for the time being, external agencies' efforts are better directed at strengthening existing institutions, such as women's and farmer groups, and market and extension networks.

And, while this participatory research project initiated some progress in terms of engaging farmers in processes of prioritising and evaluating the innovations under study, the research team could have gone much further in the direction of having its studies guided by women's expressed interests. Indeed, the analysis goes some way towards arguing that if Kenya's food security-related science and policy were more fully guided by women's preferences, then not only would adoption by women increase, but, more important, women's adoption of innovations that strengthen equitable, resilient, and food-secure farming systems could be expanded to a larger scale.

Conclusion and recommendations

The gendered dynamics of adoption identified in this research suggest that a longitudinal study of the further patterns involved both in adoption cycles (including innovation decisions at the "adjustment" stage) and the larger development of local agricultural product value chains (including market and nutritional chains) could help track changes in decision-making, food security measures, and overall farming system resilience (Andersson and D'Souza 2014). Such a study could provide insight into the extent to which the predominance of women's labour power in new enterprises feeds into renewed adoption and innovation decisions (decisions to continue with, localise, or drop an enterprise) season after season, and in turn how different patterns may result in women's greater or lesser power and benefits in ecological, nutritional, and income terms (Devereux and Longhurst 2010). These questions arise from, but lie beyond the scope of, the present study.

This chapter has examined the outcomes of a participatory research project in Eastern Kenya and assessed how gendered technology adoption practices impact the advancement of food and nutrition security goals. In focusing on the rationale behind women's adoption decisions, the researchers discovered a key driver of adoption in "non-priced values" (e.g., nutritional, ecological, institutional, educational), and located innovative measures of women's empowerment in group organisation and marketing in the geographic niches most soundly associated with the radius of mobility that women typically enjoy.

Where the geographic scope of market activity lies within a woman's typical radius of mobility, the benefits of that enterprise are less likely to be usurped by men, who have significant sway over the mobility of the female members of the household. Strengthening enterprises within the geographic settings most favourable to women's participation could also lay the groundwork for a densely networked development of post-harvest handling, processing, and onward transportation of products that could potentially fill an enormous need for youth self-employment in agricultural livelihood systems. The development of *local* agricultural value chains has greater potential to empower women financially than larger-scale or farther-flung market networks (Gurung 2011). Policies for *multi-level* development of food markets could then advance the empowerment of women and youth through income, healthy local food distribution, and youth employment. This further indicates the potential advances in household food security to be made by taking greater guidance from the direction of women's adoption decisions, as well as their rights, entitlements, resources, and knowledge, such that what is promoted for adoption is more closely tailored to meet women farmers' values, preferences, and mobility.

Non-priced values complement other drivers of adoption, including income generation; but the non-priced values are not wholly reducible to or replaceable by cash income. The nutritional, ecological, or cultural values provided by one crop may not be replaced by the money earned through growing another crop. Thus, non-priced values may either compete with or complement "priced" market values. The study findings suggest that the *diversity of benefits* beyond the income potentialities of the adopted technologies is one key to understanding gender dynamics in the farming system, as farmers test and evaluate resilience-enhancing innovations.

It has been noted that women are more likely to adopt enterprises with which they are familiar, to which they are accustomed, and which they already may be practising (and seeking to adopt new practices). But it has also long been noted that whether pursuing women's engagement in a traditionally male livelihood activity (such as goat rearing) or improvements in a typically female pursuit (such as cultivation of diverse varieties of bananas), when money begins to flow, men tend to become more interested in taking over the marketing aspect of the activity (Gurung 2011). The "non-priced values" that women and their households share, such as nutritious food, gifts, and compost, are concrete benefits from the adoption of particular enterprises which, it can be argued, partially explain women's adoption (and non-adoption) decisions.

Recommendations for policy and research include focusing on local agricultural value chains, multi-level market development, and recognition of the diversity of benefits and values, both priced and non-priced, that men and women bring to, and enjoy from, the implementation of their adoption choices. Proportionate emphasis can be given, in research, development, and policy priorities, to understanding and promoting the non-priced nutritional, ecological, and sociocultural outcomes of agricultural technology adoption initiatives. This would help to improve women's and children's health, nutrition, and food security, objectives that are foundational to the achievement of all other development goals.

Acknowledgements

The authors acknowledge Canada's International Development Research Centre (IDRC) and Department of Foreign Affairs, Trade and Development (DFATD), as well as the Government of Kenya, for their support of the partnership project "Innovating for Resilient Farming Systems in Semi-Arid Kenya". We further acknowledge McGill University and the Kenya Agricultural Research Institute (KARI) for hosting the project's management and research teams.

An earlier version of this chapter was presented at the International Food Security Dialogue 2014, "Enhancing Food Production, Gender Equity and Nutritional Security in a Changing World", presented by the Canadian International Food Security Research Fund (CIFSRF) with funding from IDRC/DFATD and hosted by the University of Alberta (Edmonton, Canada), 20 April–2 May.

References

All website URLs accessed on 7 April 2016.

Abebaw, Degnet, and Mekbib G. Haile. 2013. "The Impact of Cooperatives on Agricultural Technology Adoption: Empirical Evidence from Ethiopia." *Food Policy* 38: 82–91. doi:10.1016/j.foodpol.2012.10.003.

Alderman, Harold, John Hoddinott, Lawrence Haddad, and Christopher R. Udry. 1995. "Gender Differentials in Farm Productivity: Implications for Household Efficiency and Agricultural Policy." *Food Policy* 20 (5): 407–23.

Andersson, Jens A., and Shereen D'Souza. 2014. "From Adoption Claims to Understanding Farmers and Contexts: A Literature Review of Conservation Agriculture (CA) Adoption among Smallholder Farmers in Southern Africa." *Agriculture, Ecosystems and Environment* 187: 116–32. doi:10.1016/j.agee.2013.08.008.

Appleton, Simon. 1996. "Women-Headed Households and Household Welfare: An Empirical Deconstruction for Uganda." *World Development* 24 (12): 1811–27.

Ashraf, Nava, Xavier Giné, and Dean Karlan. 2009. "Finding Missing Markets (and a Disturbing Epilogue): Evidence from an Export Crop Adoption and Marketing Intervention in Kenya." *American Journal of Agricultural Economics* 91 (4): 973–90. doi:10.1111/j.1467-8276.2009.01319.x.

Brownhill, Leigh, Esther M. Njuguna, Kimberly L. Bothi, Lutta Muhammad, Bernard Pelletier, and Gordon M. Hickey, eds. 2016. *Food Security, Gender and Resilience: Improving Smallholder and Subsistence Farming.* London: Earthscan/Routledge.

Cooksey, Ray W. 2011. "Yours, Mine or Ours: What Counts as Innovation?" *Journal of Agricultural Education and Extension* 17 (3): 283–95. doi:10.1080/13892 24X.2011.559083.

Defoer, Toon. 2002. "Learning about Methodology Development for Integrated Soil Fertility Management." *Agricultural Systems* 73 (1): 57–81. doi:10.1016/ S0308-521X(01)00100-7.

Devereux, Stephen, and Richard Longhurst. 2010. "Incorporating Seasonality into Agricultural Project Design and Learning." *IDS Bulletin* 41 (6): 88–95. doi:10.1111/j.1759-5436.2010.00186.x.

Doss, Cheryl R. 2002. "Men's Crops? Women's Crops? The Gender Patterns of Cropping in Ghana." *World Development* 30 (11): 1987–2000. doi:10.1016/S0305-750X(02)00109-2.

Doss, Cheryl R., and Michael L. Morris. 2001. "How does Gender Affect the Adoption of Agricultural Innovations? The Case of Improved Maize Technology in Ghana." *Agricultural Economics* 25 (1): 27–39. doi:10.1016/S0169-5150(00)00096-7.

Doss, Cheryl R., Chiara Kovarik, Amber Peterman, Agnes R. Quisumbing, and Mara van den Bold. 2013. *Gender Inequalities in Ownership and Control of Land in Africa: Myth versus Reality.* Washington, DC: International Food Policy Research Institute (IFPRI).

Eidt, Colleen M., Gordon M. Hickey, and Mark A. Curtis. 2012. "Knowledge Integration and the Adoption of New Agricultural Technologies: Kenyan Perspectives." *Food Security* 4 (3): 355–67. doi:10.1007/s12571-012-0175-2.

Eksvärd, Karin, and Johanna Björklund. 2010. "Is PLAR (Participatory Learning and Action Research) a Sufficient Approach for the Purpose of Supporting Transitions for Sustainable Agriculture? A Case Study from Sweden." *Journal of Agricultural Extension and Rural Development* 2 (9): 179–90.

FAO (Food and Agriculture Organization of the United Nations). n.d. "Women Play a Decisive Role in Household Food Security, Dietary Diversity and Children's Health" (online). FAO Gender, www.fao.org/gender/gender-home/gender-programme/gender-food/en/.

Feder, Gershon, and Dina L. Umali. 1993. "The Adoption of Agricultural Innovations: A Review." *Technological Forecasting and Social Change* 43 (3–4): 215–39. doi:10.1016/0040-1625(93)90053-A.

Fisher, Monica, and Vongai Kandiwa. 2014. "Can Agricultural Input Subsidies Reduce the Gender Gap in Modern Maize Adoption? Evidence from Malawi." *Food Policy* 45: 101–11. doi:10.1016/j.foodpol.2014.01.007.

Fowler, Cary, and Pat Mooney. 1991. *The Threatened Gene: Food, Politics, and the Loss of Genetic Diversity.* Cambridge: Lutterworth Press.

Gurung, Barun. 2011. "Introduction: Engaging with the Challenges for Mainstreaming Gender in Agricultural Research and Development." In Barun Gurung, Elizabeth Ssendiwala, and Michael Waithaka, eds, *Influencing Change: Mainstreaming Gender Perspectives in Agricultural Research and Development in Eastern and Central Africa.* Cali, Colombia: International Center for Tropical Agriculture and Association for Strengthening Agricultural Research in Eastern and Central Africa, 1–9.

Hickey, Gordon M., Bernard Pelletier, Leigh Brownhill, Geoffrey M. Kamau, and Immaculate N. Maina. 2012. "Preface: Challenges and Opportunities for Enhancing Food Security in Kenya." *Food Security* 4 (3): 333–40. doi:10.1007/s12571-012-0203-2.

Ifejike Speranza, Chinwe, Boniface Kiteme, and Urs Wiesmann. 2008. "Droughts and Famines: The Underlying Factors and the Causal Links among Agro-Pastoral Households in Semi-Arid Makueni District, Kenya." *Global Environmental Change* 18 (1): 220–33.

Kassie, Menale, Simon Wagura Ndiritu, and Jesper Stage. 2014. "What Determines Gender Inequality in Household Food Security in Kenya? Application of Exogenous Switching Treatment Regression." *World Development* 56: 153–71. doi:10.1016/j.worlddev.2013.10.025.

Kavishe, Festo P. 1995. "Investing in Nutrition at the National Level: An African Perspective." *Proceedings of the Nutrition Society* 54 (2): 367–78. doi:10.1079/PNS19950006.

Kinkingninhoun-Mêdagbé, Florent M., Aliou Diagne, Franklin Simtowe, Afiavi Agboh-Noameshie, and Patrice Ygué Adegbola. 2010. "Gender Discrimination and its Impact on Income, Productivity and Technical Efficiency: Evidence from Benin." *Agriculture and Human Values* 27 (1): 57–69. doi:10.1007/s10460-008-9170-9.

Kloppenburg, Jack Ralph, Jr. 2004. *First the Seed: The Political Economy of Plant Biotechnology* (2nd edition). Madison: University of Wisconsin Press.

Kumar, Shashi. 2002. *Biodiversity and Food Security: Human Ecology for Globalization.* New Delhi: Atlantic Publishers & Distributors.

Meinzen-Dick, Ruth, Agnes R. Quisumbing, Julia Behrman, Patricia Biermayr-Jenzano, Vicki Wilde, Marco Noordeloos, . . . Nienke Beintema. 2011. *Engendering Agricultural Research, Development, and Extension.* IFPRI Research Monograph. Washington, DC: International Food Policy Research Institute (IFPRI).

Muriuki, Godfrey. 1974. *A History of the Kikuyu, 1500–1900.* London: Oxford University Press.

Nel, Etienne, Peter M. Illgner, K. Wilkins, and M.P. Robertson. 2000. "Rural Self-Reliance in Bondolfi, Zimbabwe: The Role of Bee-Keeping." *Geographical Journal* 166 (1): 26–34. doi:10.1111/j.1475-4959.2000.tb00004.x.

Njuki, Jemimah, and Pascal C. Sanginga, eds. 2013. *Women, Livestock Ownership and Markets: Bridging the Gender Gap in Eastern and Southern Africa.* London: Earthscan/Routledge and Ottawa, Canada: International Development Research Centre (IDRC).

Ogunlana, Elizabeth A. 2004. "The Technology Adoption Behavior of Women Farmers: The Case of Alley Farming in Nigeria." *Renewable Agriculture and Food Systems* 19 (1): 57–65. doi:10.1079/RAFS200366.

Peterman, Amber, Julia Behrman, and Agnes R. Quisumbing. 2010. *A Review of Empirical Evidence on Gender Differences in Nonland Agricultural Inputs, Technology, and Services in Developing Countries.* IFPRI Discussion Paper 00975. Washington, DC: International Food Policy Research Institute (IFPRI).

Quisumbing, Agnes R. 1996. "Male-Female Differences in Agricultural Productivity: Methodological Issues and Empirical Evidence." *World Development* 24 (10): 1579–95. doi:10.1016/0305-750X(96)00059-9.

Quisumbing, Agnes R. ed. 2003. *Household Decisions, Gender, and Development: A Synthesis of Recent Research.* Washington, DC: International Food Policy Research Institute (IFPRI).

Ragasa, Catherine. 2012. *Gender and Institutional Dimensions of Agricultural Technology Adoption: A Review of Literature and Synthesis of 35 Case Studies.* Paper presented at the International Association of Agricultural Economists Triennial Conference, Foz do Iguaçu, Brazil, 18–24 August.

Ramirez, Ana. 2013. "The Influence of Social Networks on Agricultural Technology Adoption." *Procedia: Social and Behavioral Sciences* 79: 101–16. doi:10.1016/j.sbspro.2013.05.059.

Sanginga, P.C., A.A. Adesina, V.M. Manyong, O. Otite, and K.E. Dashiell. 1999. *Social Impact of Soybean in Nigeria's Southern Guinea Savanna.* Ibadan, Nigeria: International Institute of Tropical Agriculture. http://impact.cgiar.org/pdf/142.pdf.

Shiva, Vandana. 2013. *Making Peace with the Earth*. London: Pluto Press.

Snapp, Sieglinde S. 2002. "Quantifying Farmer Evaluation of Technologies: The Mother and Baby Trial Design." In Mauricio R. Bellon and Jane Reeves, eds, *Quantitative Analysis of Data from Participatory Methods in Plant Breeding*. Mexico DF: International Maize and Wheat Improvement Center.

Sorensen, Pernille. 1996. "Commercialization of Food Crops in Busoga, Uganda, and the Renegotiation of Gender." *Gender and Society* 10 (5): 608–28. doi:10.117 7/089124396010005007.

Teklewold, Hailemariam, Menale Kassie, Bekele Shiferaw, and Gunnar Köhlin. 2013. "Cropping System Diversification, Conservation Tillage and Modern Seed Adoption in Ethiopia: Impacts on Household Income, Agrochemical Use and Demand for Labor." *Ecological Economics* 93: 85–93.

Terry, James P., and Kamal Khatri. 2009. "People, Pigs and Pollution – Experiences with Applying Participatory Learning and Action (PLA) Methodology to Identify Problems of Pig-Waste Management at the Village Level in Fiji." *Journal of Cleaner Production* 17 (16): 1393–1400.

Tiffen, Mary, Michael Mortimore, and Francis Gichuki. 1994. *More People, Less Erosion: Environmental Recovery in Kenya*. Nairobi: ODI and ACTS Press.

Tiruneh, A., T. Tesfaye, W. Mwangi, and H. Verkuijl. 2001. *Gender Differentials in Agricultural Production and Decision-Making among Smallholders in Ada, Lume, and Gimbichu Woredas of the Central Highlands of Ethiopia*. Mexico DF: International Maize and Wheat Improvement Center and Ethiopian Agricultural Research Organization.

Turner, Terisa E., Wahu M. Kaara, and Leigh Brownhill. 1997. "Social Reconstruction in Rural Africa: A Gendered Class Analysis of Women's Resistance to Cash Crop Production in Kenya." *Canadian Journal of Development Studies* 8 (2): 213–38. doi: 10.1080/02255189.1997.9669706.

Vogel, Coleen, Susanne C. Moser, Roger E. Kasperson, and Geoffrey D. Dabelko. 2007. "Linking Vulnerability, Adaptation, and Resilience Science to Practice: Pathways, Players, and Partnerships." *Global Environmental Change* 17 (3–4): 349–64. doi:10.1016/j.gloenvcha.2007.05.002.

Conclusion

Towards gender transformative agriculture and food systems: where next?

Jemimah Njuki, Amy Kaler, and John R. Parkins

Introduction

Gender inequality is a major cause of food insecurity, manifested in women farmers' low agricultural productivity, low access to technologies, and low market participation relative to men's, and women's lack of voice and agency in decision-making. This book makes the case that gender equality and the empowerment of women must be central to any efforts to improve agriculture productivity and food and nutrition security. However, the question of how to bring about a transformation of gender relations and structures, and significant empowerment for women, remains a big challenge not only for the agricultural sector but for other sectors as well.

In this concluding chapter, we glance back at the research and intervention approaches of past decades and offer some thoughts on how research and interventions can be more effective, emphasising both the documentation of gender disparities and the efforts to actively alter these disparities. We make the case that both gender-analytic research and gender transformative work are necessary to move towards equity and food security.

Addressing gender in agriculture and food systems

Decades of research have produced considerable evidence of "gender gaps" between women and men engaged in agriculture in terms of accessing resources, markets, and business services.[1] Ways of measuring gender equality and women's empowerment have also evolved over the last few years. For example, the Women's Empowerment in Agriculture Index (WEAI) measures the empowerment, agency, and inclusion of women in the agriculture sector. The WEAI is a composite measurement tool that indicates women's degree of control over critical parts of their lives in the household, community, and economy, and tracks progress in these areas over time. It allows the identification of women who are disempowered, and points to ways to increase their autonomy and decision-making in key domains.

Studies such as those in this volume show that the problems of food and nutrition insecurity, as well as low agricultural productivity, cannot be solved without addressing gender inequalities and the disempowerment of women.

It is clear *why* gender equity is crucial; however, it is less clear *how* it might be achieved.[2]

Gender mainstreaming in agriculture follows two broad strategic lines. The first strategy has been to identify gender gaps in health, control of assets, and decision-making, and attempt to close them in order to enhance household productivity, food security, and health outcomes. This body of evidence has focussed on measuring gaps between men and women, on the assumption that greater parity between men and women would improve outcomes at the individual, household, and community level. While useful, these efforts focussed primarily on reducing identified differences – the visible symptoms of gender inequality – and often overlooked the underlying factors that caused the differences in the first place (Chant 2012; Kantor 2013).

The second strategy has been to invest in women as a way to boost national economic performance. In this strategy, women's empowerment is a means to the greater good of increasing the productivity and economic success of countries as a whole. In the last few years, a common narrative has emerged: investing in women is described as "smart economics", that is, a rationalisation of "investing" in women and girls for more effective development outcomes (World Bank 1995; Chant and Sweetman 2012). Agriculture researchers and practitioners are often under pressure to justify interventions with gender equality aims on the basis of broader social and economic impact. This underlies the Women in Development (WID) approach, or what Moser (1989) calls the "efficiency approach" to women in development. Gender equality has been depicted as a tool of economic efficiency in that it enables women to direct their skills and energies to world economic development.

The chapters in this volume are situated mainly within the first strategy: identifying gender gaps and actively seeking ways to close them. In contrast to the narrowly economic rationales for gender-sensitive programming, the chapter authors share the conviction that gender equity is worthy in its own right, as well as a tool for boosting productivity. At the same time, the chapters illustrate the diversity of research approaches to gender-based agricultural programming.

The studies and findings described range from analytical research that documents gender differences in agricultural production to transformative research that seeks changes in gender and social relations. This variation is sometimes depicted as a gender continuum (see Figure C.1), with interventions that may exacerbate women's exploitation at one end, interventions that, while enhancing agricultural productivity, have a neutral impact on gender relations in the middle, and interventions that actively transform the relations between men and women at the other end (Interagency Gender Working Group 1997).

Like these interventions, gender-related research can also be conceptualised as a continuum, with research that describes and analyses but does not actively alter gender relations at one end, and research that is explicitly

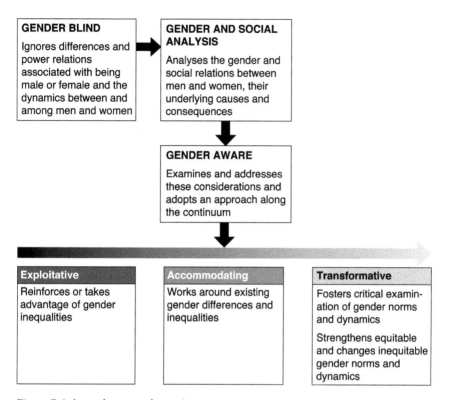

Figure C.1 A gender research continuum

transformative and emancipatory at the other. Neither approach in itself is sufficient: in order to move towards a more equitable gender order, we need precise data, analysis, and generative transformations

Advancing gender-analytic and transformative programs

Gender is now on the agenda of agricultural research and development agencies, so there has been some progress. However, those agencies' efforts have tended to focus on closing gaps between women and men in access to and control over resources, technologies, and markets, and on increasing the productivity of women smallholder farmers.

Yet gender inequality persists in the face of these technical approaches. Agriculture needs to be understood as a social as well as a technical practice. Without the crucial social dimension, research and development can lead to unintended consequences, ranging from the non-adoption of new technologies to exacerbation of existing inequalities.

The social dimension of agriculture means that it is imperative for donors, implementers, and researchers to create and sustain equitable social environments for new technologies and institutions. Agricultural research is not merely about tools and practices: it is also about creating the conditions under which women and marginalised people can participate in and benefit from agricultural development.

With a few exceptions, agriculture research organisations tend to treat social norms, such as gendered allocations of authority and labour, as though they were outside their purview; yet, without addressing these issues, the goals of agricultural productivity and food and nutrition security cannot be met. Social analysis that investigates men's and women's capabilities, opportunities, and interactions is not merely an add-on to agricultural interventions, it is the keystone. With this knowledge, implementers can move towards transformations in agriculture and food systems.

How can this gender transformation in agriculture and food systems be achieved?

Invest in rigorous analysis

Gender and gender analysis have become common themes in academia and in research and development organisations. With this emergence has come a proliferation of analytical methods aimed at understanding gender, most of them based on early gender analysis frameworks such as the Moser and Harvard frameworks. However, one weakness of these frameworks is their focus on the individual roles and resources of men and women, and their lack of attention to underlying causes of gender inequality (Locke and Okali 1999).

What these frameworks fail to address are the subtleties of the relations between men and women, the underlying values that define these relations, and the meanings attached to these roles and benefits. For instance, the idea of modesty may be very important to feminine identity, making it difficult for women farmers to assert their right to support from extension services or to take their products to public markets. Similarly, the concept of "household head" is often key to men's gendered self-esteem, with the result that turning control of labour and resources to female household members represents a challenge to local norms. Implementing a gender transformative approach to agriculture requires an analysis that not only identifies the differences between individual men and women, but also seeks to analyse the social, economic, and cultural context in which gender roles and benefits are situated. These social analyses challenge common practices in agricultural research because they engage the abstract aspects of meanings about gender relations. Women's empowerment and gender equality are long-term political projects, not quick-fix recommendations for action (Locke and Okali 1999).

Develop mechanisms to move from analysis to change

While most gender analyses address the *what* of gender relations, identifying *how* and *why* gender inequalities are formed and maintained is more elusive. There is no universal silver-bullet solution for inequality, so attention to social, historical, cultural, and economic contexts is essential.

One concrete way of moving from analysis to action is to identify what types of inequalities can be addressed through actions at the individual, interactional, or institutional level (Risman 2004) as shown in Figure C.2. Using the gender division of labour as an example, if unequal gender division of labour is caused by gendered identities, then the most effective action would engage the socialisation of boys and girls, men and women to reorient the norms, roles, and scripts associated with being male or female. If it is caused by interactional issues within households, then the most effective actions might be around power analysis, intra-household negotiation and bargaining, and relational expectations, especially between spouses. If the causes are institutional – for example, if women are not allowed access to markets – then an effective approach would be to address regulations, cultural structural norms, and organisational practices.

Invest in partnerships and capacity

Gender transformative research in development grapples with complex issues in diverse contexts. This means that researchers must experiment with context-specific approaches to merging social and technical interventions, in order to learn which works best, why, and how. It will require strategic decisions about working in association with stakeholders whose understanding and vision of the objectives may be very different from those of the research team; and flexibility in recognising opportunities for collaboration with a diverse range of partners.

Within research organisations, norms have shifted such that agricultural scientists are expected to conduct basic gender analysis and disaggregation, as well as deeper social analysis that requires a thorough understanding of sociological and anthropological approaches and methods and their application

Figure C.2 Ways of moving from analysis to action through types of inequality

Source: Adapted from Risman (2004).

in different contexts. Organisations will have to invest in these capacities. At the implementation level, the agriculture sector will need to engage not only women and girls, but also boys and men, to support the empowerment of women.

Evaluate agriculture programs from both a technical and gender transformative perspective

How can we evaluate interventions on their potential to transform gender? One way is by using a continuum to assess the extent to which interventions accommodate or transform gender norms, roles, and relationships (Muralidharan et al. 2014). In Muralidharan's typology, programs were categorised as "gender transformative" if they facilitated critical examination of gender norms, roles, and relationships; strengthened or created systems that support gender equity; and/or questioned and changed gender norms and dynamics. They were categorised as "gender-accommodating" if they recognised and worked around or adjusted for inequitable gender norms, roles, and relationships. The review looks at the processes through which gender interventions are implemented, as well as the outcomes.

Measuring changes in gender transformation in the agriculture and food sector requires a more sophisticated approach, beyond traditional evaluation and impact assessment methods. A combination of longitudinal studies that track both processes and outcomes, and process monitoring tools, as well as a rethinking of traditional participatory rural assessment approaches, will be required.

Conclusion

The existence of this volume testifies to the prominence of gender analysis in mainstream food security research. Gender inequity is recognised as a driver of hunger and insecurity, and we no longer have to justify or fight for the inclusion of gender concerns in debates over agricultural productivity and food security. However, our existing research methods and evaluation tools are not yet up to the task. Once gender disparities have been documented, the work of understanding how and why they came about is still before us. Both careful analysis and committed transformational work are essential to move towards a more equitable world.

Notes

1 Examples include early work related to gender differences in agriculture, such as Boserup's classic text (1970) documenting women's roles in African agriculture, and often-cited empirical work by Udry (1996), such as Saito et al. (1994) and Jones (1986), quantifying differences between women and men in agricultural inputs and in some cases estimating the productivity gains from their reversal. Recent additions to this literature include compilations such as the FAO's *The*

State of Food and Agriculture 2010–2011 (FAO 2011); the *Gender in Agriculture Sourcebook* (World Bank 2009); the World Bank report on *Gender Equality and the Empowerment of Women* (World Bank 2011); *Levelling the Field: Improving Opportunities for Women Farmers in Africa* (World Bank/ONE 2013); and *Voice and Agency* (Klugman et al. 2014).

2 In earlier decades, policies, research, and programs focussed on "farmers", "communities", or "households" without understanding the differences in experiences and outcomes these aggregations mask. However, both the persistence of gender differences in resources despite decades of development research and action, and conceptual developments regarding the social embeddedness of agriculture and gender, raise questions about the effectiveness of gender-responsive approaches.

References

All website URLs accessed on 7 April 2016.

Boserup, Ester. 1970. *Woman's Role in Economic Development*. London: George Allen & Unwin Ltd.

Chant, Sylvia. 2012. "The Disappearing of 'Smart Economics'? The *World Development Report 2012 on Gender Equality*: Some Concerns about the Preparatory Process and the Prospects for Paradigm Change." *Global Social Policy* 12 (2): 198–218. doi:10.1177/1468018112443674.

Chant, Sylvia, and Caroline Sweetman. 2012. "Fixing Women or Fixing the World? 'Smart Economics', Efficiency Approaches, and Gender Equality in Development." *Gender & Development* 20 (3): 517–29. doi:10.1080/13552074.2012.731812.

FAO (Food and Agriculture Organization of the United Nations). 2011. *The State of Food and Agriculture 2010–2011: Women in Agriculture: Closing the Gender Gap for Development*. Rome: FAO. www.fao.org/docrep/013/i2050e/i2050e.pdf.

Interagency Gender Working Group. 1997. *User's Guide for Gender Analysis and Gender Integration*. Washington, DC: Interagency Gender Working Group. www.igwg.org/igwg_media/Training/FG_IntegrGendr6StepsProgCycle.pdf

Jones, Christine W. 1986. "Intra-Household Bargaining in Response to the Introduction of New Crops: A Case Study from North Cameroon." In Joyce Lewinger Moock, ed., *Understanding Africa's Rural Households and Farming Systems*. Boulder, CO: Westview Press, 105–23.

Kantor, Paula. 2013. *Transforming Gender Relations: Key to Positive Development Outcomes in Aquatic Agricultural Systems*. CGIAR Research Program on Aquatic Agricultural Systems, Brief AAS–2013-12. Penang, Malaysia: WorldFish.

Klugman, Jeni, Lucia Hanmer, Sarah Twigg, Tazeen Hasan, Jennifer McCleary-Sills, and Julieth Santamaria. 2014. *Voice and Agency: Empowering Women and Girls for Shared Prosperity*. Washington, DC: World Bank. doi:10.1596/978-1-4648-0359-8. License: Creative Commons Attribution CC BY 3.0 IGO.

Locke, Catherine, and Christine Okali. 1999. "Analysing Changing Gender Relations: Methodological Challenges for Gender Planning." *Development in Practice* 9 (3): 274–86. www.jstor.org/stable/4029742.

Moser, Caroline O.N. 1989. "Gender Planning in the Third World: Meeting Practical and Strategic Gender Needs." *World Development* 17 (11): 1799–825. doi:10.1016/0305-750X(89)90201-5.

Muralidharan, Arundati, Jessica Fehringer, Sara Pappa, Elisabeth Rottach, Madhumita Das, and Mahua Mandal. 2014. *Transforming Gender Norms, Roles, and Power*

Dynamics for Better Health: Evidence from a Systematic Review of Gender-Integrated Health Programs in Low- and Middle-Income Countries. Washington, DC: Futures Group, Health Policy Project.

Risman, Barbara J. 2004. "Gender as a Social Structure: Theory Wrestling with Activism." *Gender & Society* 18 (4): 429–50. doi:10.1177/0891243204265349.

Saito, Katrine A., Hailu Mekonnen, and Daphne Spurling. 1994. *Raising Productivity of Women Farmers in Sub-Saharan Africa*. World Bank Discussion Paper 230. Washington, DC: World Bank. doi:10.1596/0-8213-2749-6.

Udry, Christopher R. 1996. "Gender, Agricultural Production, and the Theory of the Household." *Journal of Political Economy* 104 (6): 1010–46.

World Bank. 1995. *Enhancing Women's Participation in Economic Development*. Washington, DC: World Bank.

World Bank. 2009. *Gender in Agriculture Sourcebook*. Washington, DC: World Bank.

World Bank. 2011. *Gender Equality and the Empowerment of Women*. Washington, DC: World Bank.

World Bank and ONE. 2013. *Levelling the Field: Improving Opportunities for Women Farmers in Africa*. Washington, DC: World Bank and ONE.

Index

Numbers in *italic* indicate figures and tables

For Product Safety Concerns and Information please contact our EU
representative GPSR@taylorandfrancis.com
Taylor & Francis Verlag GmbH, Kaufingerstraße 24, 80331 München, Germany

www.ingramcontent.com/pod-product-compliance
Ingram Content Group UK Ltd.
Pitfield, Milton Keynes, MK11 3LW, UK
UKHW021017180425
457613UK00020B/967